T0197942

Get the eBook FREE!

(PDF, ePub, Kindle, and liveBook all included)

We believe that once you buy a book from us, you should be
able to read it in any format we have available. To get electronic
versions of this book at no additional cost to you, purchase and
then register this book at the Manning website.

Go to https://www.manning.com/freebook and follow the
instructions to complete your pBook registration.

That's it!
Thanks from Manning!

Relevant Search

With applications for
Solr and Elasticsearch

DOUG TURNBULL
JOHN BERRYMAN

MANNING

SHELTER ISLAND

For online information and ordering of this and other Manning books, please visit
www.manning.com. The publisher offers discounts on this book when ordered in quantity.
For more information, please contact

> Special Sales Department
> Manning Publications Co.
> 20 Baldwin Road
> PO Box 761
> Shelter Island, NY 11964
> Email: orders@manning.com

Manning Publications Co.
20 Baldwin Road
PO Box 761
Shelter Island, NY 11964

Development editor:	Marina Michaels
Technical development editor:	Aaron Colcord
Copy editor:	Sharon Wilkey
Proofreader:	Elizabeth Martin
Technical proofreader:	Valentin Crettaz
Typesetter:	Dennis Dalinnik
Cover designer:	Marija Tudor

ISBN: 9781617292774
Printed in the United States of America

brief contents

contents

foreword

Over the last decade, search has become ubiquitous—the keyword search box has evolved to become the de facto UI for exploring data and for navigating most websites and applications. At the same time, delivering a truly relevant search experience has been elusive, if not a critical blind spot for most organizations.

Powerful open source technologies have arisen to deliver fast, feature-rich search (Apache Lucene) in a distributed, highly scalable way with little-to-no coding required (Apache Solr and later Elasticsearch). This has provided the necessary infrastructure for almost any developer to build a "generally relevant" real-time search engine for the big data era. As more of the hard search infrastructure problems have been solved and their solutions commoditized, the competitive differentiators have moved away from providing fast, scalable search and more toward delivering the most relevant matches for a user's information need. In other words, delivering "generally relevant" results is no longer sufficient—Google and other top search engines have now trained users to expect search applications to almost read their minds. This book is about how to move more aggressively in that direction of understanding user intent.

Doug Turnbull and John Berryman are two highly experienced search and relevancy experts whom I've known for years, typically running into each other at search conferences where we've all presented. I fondly recall times spent with them discussing ideas to solve some of the world's hardest problems in search relevancy, recommendations, and personalization. No one is more excited than I to see their unique expertise codified in this book—one of the best and most engaging technical books I've ever read.

Relevancy tuning is a hard problem—it's usually misunderstood, and it's often not immediately obvious when something is wrong. It usually requires seeing many bad examples to identify problematic patterns, and it's often challenging to know what better results would look like without actually seeing them show up. Unfortunately, it's often not until well after a search system is deployed into production that organizations begin to realize the gap between out-of-the-box relevancy defaults and true domain-driven, personalized matching.

Not only that, but the skillsets needed to think about relevancy (domain expertise, feature engineering, machine learning, ontologies, user testing, natural language processing) are very different from those needed to build and maintain scalable infrastructure (distributed systems, data structures, performance and concurrency, hardware utilization, network calls and communication). The role of a relevance engineer is almost entirely lacking in many organizations, leaving so much potential untapped for building a search experience that truly delights users and significantly moves a company forward.

The spectrum of personalization between manually entered keyword searches and completely automated recommendations is also rich with opportunities to deliver relevant matches crafted for each specific user's needs. The authors do a great job of explaining some of the more nuanced ways that search features/signals can be modeled to take full advantage of this spectrum. With the techniques in this book, you will be well-equipped to take on the role of a relevance engineer and solve many of the most challenging problems inherent in creating a truly personalized, relevant search experience.

TREY GRAINGER
AUTHOR, *SOLR IN ACTION*
SENIOR VICE PRESIDENT OF ENGINEERING AT LUCIDWORKS

preface

John and I met while working together as consultants for OpenSource Connections (OSC) solving tough search problems for clients. Sometimes we triaged performance (make it go faster!). Other times we helped build out a search application. All of these projects had simple-to-measure success metrics. Did it go faster? Is the application complete?

Search relevance, though, doesn't play by these rules. And users, raised in the age of Google, won't tolerate "good enough" search. They want "damn smart" search. They want search to prioritize criteria they care about, not what the search engine often idiotically guesses relevant.

Like moths attracted to a flame, we both felt drawn to this hard problem. And just like said moths, we often found ourselves burned. Through these painful lessons, we persevered and grew, succeeding at tasks we initially considered too difficult.

During this time, we also found our voices on OSC's blog. We realized that little was being written about search relevance problems. We developed ideas such as test-driven relevancy. We documented our headaches, our problems, and our triumphs. Together we experimented with machine learning approaches, like latent semantic analysis. We dove into Lucene's guts and explored techniques for building custom search components to solve problems. We began exploring information retrieval research. As we learned more techniques to solve hard problems, we continued to write about them.

Still, blogs have their limits. John and I always hoped to express our ideas more systematically in book form. Luckily, we experienced one of those funny chains of events that often lead to opportunity knocking. I presented on Python concurrency at a local tech meet-up along with Andrew Montalenti. Since Andrew was giving this talk at PyCon, Manning called Andrew to discuss writing a book on Python concurrency. Andrew said he wasn't interested in writing a book, but perhaps his copresenter Doug would be.

It turns out I also wasn't interested in writing a Python concurrency book, but I did have an idea for another book. I approached John with the idea, and a couple of conversations later, we'd pulled together a pretty motivating book proposal—and the rest is history!

That momentous phone call with Manning occurred nearly two years ago. And what a roller-coaster ride it's been. As these things go, we bundled the book with other major life transitions. Both of us added babies to our families. I began a relevance consulting practice. John switched jobs, becoming Eventbrite's resident search expert. Still, we couldn't resist writing about this fascinating topic.

You'll find this book unlike others on tech topics. This book won't be an enumeration of one technology's features. It's more of a map through our years of pain, solving the hard problems that had no ready answers. In other words, we've walked through the search relevancy desert, stumbled upon the many oases, and learned how to avoid the sand people and the Stormtroopers.

We present to you this map through the desert, so you don't get quite as lost as we did. Now excuse us while we hunt for the nearest beach to take a nap on …

DOUG TURNBULL

acknowledgments

Weeks before we began *Relevant Search*, both of us welcomed new babies into our families. Our deepest thanks and love go to our spouses, Khara Turnbull and Kumiko Berryman. They suffered through many consecutive weekends of book writing—all while Khara finished her own book and Kumiko managed a cross-country move and a home sale. Time for a big vacation!

Relevant Search wouldn't be possible without OpenSource Connections founder Eric Pugh. As our "boss," he pushed us into the limelight to write, speak, and solve the big problems. As a leader, Eric makes your passion his passion. Without Eric taking the training wheels off (and sometimes insisting on a unicycle), we wouldn't have realized how capable we are as writers or problem solvers. Eric has taught us that everybody can be a thought leader, including us.

Thanks to TMDB for its data and support. We spent a lot of time trying to find good data sets. TMDB (http://themoviedb.org) not only provides a rich search data set, but also supported us and our early readers as we ferreted out bugs and issues, usually in our own code. Travis Bell, in particular, deserves our thanks for responding promptly to our issues and emails.

Writing books is a team sport, and we'd like to thank everyone at Manning on team *Relevant Search*: Marina Michaels, our development editor; Aaron Colcord, technical development editor; Valentin Crettaz, technical proofreader; Frank Pohlmann and Mike Stephens, acquisitions editors; and Candace Gillhoolley in marketing.

We would also like to thank the many reviewers who read early drafts of the book and provided helpful suggestions, including John Guthrie, Martin Beer, Arthur Zubarev,

Elman Krinker, Amit Lamba, Marc-Oliver Scheele, Ian Stirk, Joseph Wang, Stuart Woodward, Ursin Stauss, Russ Cam, Michael Fink, Gregor Zurowski, Dimitrios Kouzis-Loukas, Jeremy Gailor, and Keith Webster.

Additional thanks go to Andrew Montalenti, who connected us with Manning. Thanks to Shay Banon, creator of Elasticsearch for his support, and frankly, for just being a nice guy. Thanks to colleagues Trey Grainger, Matt Overstreet, Rena Morse, David Smiley, Grant Ingersoll, Yonik Seeley, Rene Kriegler, Peter Dixon-Moses, Charlie Hull, and Drew Farris for many great conversations about search and relevance through the years. And special thanks to Trey for contributing the foreword to our book.

Thanks to everyone in our families for your support. Especially to our children: Megume Berryman, Ian Turnbull, and Murray Turnbull. Thanks to our "work families" at OpenSource Connections and Eventbrite, for letting us invest significant mental and professional energy into this book.

about this book

Relevant Search teaches you to respond to users' searches with content that satisfies and sells. You'll learn to tightly control search results ranking based on your criteria instead of the mystical whims of the search engine. We outline an approach for deeply customizing Solr or Elasticsearch relevance ranking as well as methods to help you discover what *relevant* means for your application.

Who should read this book

Relevant Search is for Solr or Elasticsearch developers stuck wondering why the search engine doesn't "get" their users' searches. Readers with at least a basic familiarity of their search engine can use this book to take their skills to the next level. Although this book is technical, a great deal of its content frames relevance from an organizational and product-strategy point of view—for product managers, content strategists, marketing, or domain experts focused on search.

How this book is organized

We organize *Relevant Search* by progressing through a technical foundation, and building up to product strategy and cultural issues you'll face when defining and solving search relevance. The book ends with next steps: how to get started with personalized search, semantic search, and recommendations.

Chapter 1 starts by discussing the problem of relevance. It reflects on domains such as web search, e-commerce, and expert search. The chapter discusses the extent that academia supports our attempts at relevance. Finally, we outline our book's technical strategy for solving relevance.

Chapter 2 provides a quick review of Lucene's core data structures and algorithms, as they pertain to relevance. You'll see how Lucene-based search provides an incredible framework for finding relevant content.

Chapter 3 teaches you how to debug your relevance. When the data structures and algorithms introduced in chapter 2 don't work, you'll need to reach for your tool belt to understand where search broke down.

Chapter 4 shows you how to decompose content and searches into descriptive features by using the search engine's analysis process. This fundamental skill teaches you how to use analysis to make *anything* findable.

Chapter 5 begins the discussion of query strategies over multiple fields. In this chapter, we teach you how to construct queries that measure specific, search-time ranking factors important to your users.

Chapter 6 continues our discussion on query strategies. Here we focus on term-centric techniques, search strategies that support users' naïve understanding of relevance.

Chapter 7 demonstrates score-shaping techniques such as boosting and filtering. You'll often need to manipulate search by emphasizing recent content, profitable products, or nearby locations.

Chapter 8 shows you alternate paths to guide users to relevant content. Sometimes UI components such as browsable facets, autocomplete, and highlighting can be simpler ways to steer users in the right direction when relevance ranking doesn't succeed.

Chapter 9 builds a full, relevance-focused search application that will leave you Yowling with insights. Now that you're steeped in the skills of a relevance engineer, you'll see the full product development process from start to finish.

Chapter 10 steps a level higher from product strategy to focus on cultural and organizational factors. How does the search-focused organization determine what's relevant? You'll see that the organization must implement fast and accurate feedback loops to steer the relevance engineer's efforts.

Chapter 11 points you beyond the search engine. You'll get an introduction to how machine learning, personalization, and semantic search can work together to enhance the search engine's relevance ranking.

Appendix A walks you through the step-by-step process we went through to load the book's data into Elasticsearch through The Movie Database (TMDB) API.

Appendix B guides the Solr reader through the book by mapping between Elasticsearch and Solr relevance features.

About the code

This book contains many examples of source code, both in numbered listings and in line with normal text. In both cases, source code is formatted in a `fixed-width font like this` to separate it from ordinary text. Sometimes code is also **in bold** to highlight what has changed from previous steps in the chapter, such as when a new feature adds to an existing line of code.

In many cases, the original source code has been reformatted; we've added line breaks and reworked indentation to accommodate the available page space in the book. Additionally, comments in the source code have often been removed from the listings when the code is described in the text. Code annotations accompany many of the listings, highlighting important concepts.

Examples have been tested with Elasticsearch 2.0 and Python 2.7.

You can find code for chapters 3–9 on the Manning website (www.manning.com/books/relevant-search) and in our book's GitHub repository (http://github.com/o19s/relevant-search-book). Examples are written in iPython Notebook/Jupyter to allow easy experimentation. The README file details how to set up the code's prerequisites.

Author Online

The purchase of *Relevant Search* includes free access to a private forum run by Manning Publications where you can make comments about the book, ask technical questions, and receive help from the author and other users. To access and subscribe to the forum, point your browser to www.manning.com/books/relevant-search. This page provides information on how to get on the forum once you're registered, what kind of help is available, and the rules of conduct in the forum.

Manning's commitment to our readers is to provide a venue where a meaningful dialogue between individual readers and between readers and the authors can take place. It's not a commitment to any specific amount of participation on the part of the authors, whose contributions to the book's forum remains voluntary (and unpaid). We suggest you try asking them challenging questions, lest their interests stray!

The Author Online forum and the archives of previous discussions will be accessible from the publisher's website as long as the book is in print.

Other online resources

If you'd like to learn more, we recommend several high-quality resources:

- OpenSource Connection's blog (http://opensourceconnections.com/blog)
- John Berryman's personal blog (http://thoughtbox.solutions)
- Elastic's blog (www.elastic.co/blog)
- Lucidwork's blog (https://lucidworks.com/blog)
- Salmon Run, Sujit Pal's Solr blog (http://sujitpal.blogspot.com/)
- The Solr Start newsletter (www.solr-start.com)

On the more general topic of search and information retrieval, we recommend this canonical text:

- *Introduction to Information Retrieval* by Christopher Manning et al. (Cambridge University Press, 2008), http://nlp.stanford.edu/IR-book/.

For questions specific to Solr/Elasticsearch, we recommend the discussion forums for each technology:

- Elasticsearch: http://discuss.elastic.co
- Solr: http://lucene.apache.org/solr/resources.html

about the authors

 **Doug Turnbull** leads a search relevance consulting practice at OpenSource Connections, where he frequently speaks and blogs. Doug builds relevant, semantically enriched search experiences for clients across multiple domains using a variety of search and NLP technology.

 **John Berryman's** first career was as an aerospace engineer, but after several years in aerospace, he found that he most loved his job when programming or when working on a good math problem. Eventually, John cut out the aircraft and satellites and started working full-time with software development, infrastructure architecture, and search technology. These days, John works at Eventbrite, helping to build out event discovery, search, and recommendations using Elasticsearch.

about the cover illustration

The figure on the cover of *Relevant Search* is captioned "Homme de l'Isle de Pathmos," or a man from the island of Patmos in Greece. The illustration is taken from a collection of dress costumes from various countries by Jacques Grasset de Saint-Sauveur (1757–1810), titled *Costumes de Différents Pays,* published in France in 1797. Each illustration is finely drawn and colored by hand. The rich variety of Grasset de Saint-Sauveur's collection reminds us vividly of how culturally apart the world's towns and regions were just 200 years ago. Isolated from each other, people spoke different dialects and languages. In the streets or in the countryside, it was easy to identify where they lived and what their trade or station in life was just by their dress.

The way we dress has changed since then and the diversity by region, so rich at the time, has faded away. It is now hard to tell apart the inhabitants of different continents, let alone different towns, regions, or countries. Perhaps we have traded cultural diversity for a more varied personal life—certainly for a more varied and fast-paced technological life.

At a time when it is hard to tell one computer book from another, Manning celebrates the inventiveness and initiative of the computer business with book covers based on the rich diversity of regional life of two centuries ago, brought back to life by Grasset de Saint-Sauveur's pictures.

The search
relevance problem

This chapter covers

- The ubiquity of search (search is all around us!)
- The challenge of building a relevant search experience
- Examples of this challenge for prominent search domains
- The inability of out-of-the-box solutions to solve the problem
- This book's approach for building relevant search

Getting a search engine to behave can be maddening. Whether you're just getting started with Solr or Elasticsearch, or you have years of experience, you've likely struggled with low-quality search results. Out-of-the-box settings haven't met your needs, and you've fought to deliver even marginally relevant search results.

When it comes to relevance ranking, a search engine can seem like a mystical black box. It's tempting to ignore relevance problems—turning the focus away from search and toward other, less mystical parts of the application such as performance or the UI. Unfortunately, the work of search relevance ranking can't be avoided. Users increasingly need to work with large amounts of content in today's applications. Whether this means products, books, log messages, emails, vacation rentals, or medical articles—the search box is the first place your users go to explore and find answers. Without intuitive search to answer questions in human terms, they'll be hopelessly lost. Thus, despite the maddening, seemingly mystical nature of search, you have to find solutions.

Relevant Search demystifies relevance. What exactly is relevance? It's at the root of the search engine's value proposition. *Relevance* is the art of ranking content for a search based on how much that content satisfies the needs of the user and the business. The devil is completely in the details. Ranking search results for what content? (Tweets? Products? Beanie Babies?) For what sorts of users? (Doctors? Tech-savvy shoppers?) For what types of searches? (Written in Japanese? Full of grocery brands? Filled with legal jargon?) What do those users expect? (A shopping experience? A library card catalog?) And what does your employer hope to get out of this interaction? (Money? Page views? Goodwill?) Search has become such a ubiquitous part of our applications, creeping in inch by inch without much fanfare. Answering these questions (getting relevance right) means the difference between an engaging user experience and one that disappoints.

1.1   *Your goal: gaining the skills of a relevance engineer*

How will you get there? *Relevant Search* teaches you the skills of a relevance engineer. A *relevance engineer* transforms the search engine into a seemingly smart system that understands the needs of users and the business. To do this, you'll teach the search engine your content's important features: attributes such as a restaurant's location, the words in a book's text, or the color of a dress shirt. With the right features in place, you can measure what matters to your users when they search: How far is the restaurant from me? Is this book about the topic I need help with? Will this shirt match the pants I just bought? These search-time ranking factors that measure what users care about are called *signals*. The ever-present challenge, you'll see, is selecting features and implementing signals that map to the needs of your users and business.

But technical wizardry is only part of the job (as shown in figure 1.1). Understanding what to implement can be more important than how to do so. Ironically, the relevance engineer rarely knows what "relevant" means for a given application. Instead, others—usually nontechnical colleagues—understand the content, business, and users' goals. You'll learn to advocate for a *relevance-centered enterprise* that uses this broader business expertise as well as user behavioral data to reveal the experience that users need from search.

We refine these concepts later in the chapter (and throughout this book). But to help set the right foundation, the remainder of this chapter defines the relevance problem. Why is relevance so hard? What attempts have been made to solve it? Then we'll switch gears to outline this book's approach to solving relevance.

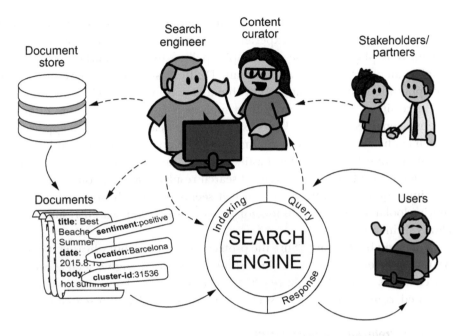

Figure 1.1 The relevance engineer works with the search engine and back-end technologies to express business-ranking logic. They collaborate on relevance closely with a cross-functional team and are informed heavily by user metrics.

1.2 Why is search relevance so hard?

Search relevance is such a hard problem in part because we take the act of *searching* for granted. Search applications take a user's search queries (the text typed into the search bar) and attempt to rank content by how likely it will satisfy.

This act occurs so frequently that it's barely noticed. Reflect on your own experiences. You probably woke up this morning, made your coffee, and started fiddling with your smartphone. You looked at the news, scanned Facebook, and checked your email. Before the coffee was even done brewing, you probably interacted with a dozen search applications without much thought. Did you send a message to a friend that you found in your phone's contact list? Search for a crucial email? Talk to Siri? Did you satisfy your curiosity with a Google search? Did you shop around for that dream 50-inch flat-screen TV on Amazon?

In a short time, you experienced the product of many thousands of hours of engineering effort. You engaged with the culmination of an even larger body of academic research that goes back a century in the field of information retrieval. Standing on the shoulders of giants, you sifted through millions of pieces of information—the entire human collection of information on the topic—and found the best reviewed and most popular TV in mere minutes.

Or maybe you didn't have such a great experience. It's just as likely that you found at least some of your search experiences frustrating. Maybe you couldn't find a contact on your phone because of a simple spelling mistake. Maybe the search engine didn't understand your idea of a dream TV. In frustration you gave up, uninstalling the application while thinking, "Why should a reasonable search be so difficult?"

In reality, a "simple" search that appears "reasonable" to users often requires extensive engineering work. Users expect a great deal out of search applications. Our search applications are asked, within the blink of an eye, to understand what information users want based on a few hastily entered search terms. To make it worse, users lack time to comb through dozens of search results. Users try your search a few fleeting times, quickly getting frustrated if it seems the search doesn't bring back what they're looking for. Your window for delivering relevant search results is small and always shrinking.

You might be thinking, "Sure the problem seems hard, but why isn't it easily solved?" Search has been around for a while; shouldn't a search engine such as Solr or Elasticsearch always return the right result? Or why not just send users to Google? Why won't a canned, commercial solution such as Amazon's A9 solve your search problems?

1.2.1 *What's a "relevant" search result?*

We're easily tricked into seeing search as a single problem. In reality, search applications differ greatly from one another. It's true that a typical search application lets the user enter text, filter through documents, and interact with a list of ranked results. But don't be fooled by superficial appearances. Each application has dramatically different relevance expectations. Let's look at some common classes of search applications to appreciate that your application likely has its own unique definition of relevance.

First, let's consider *web search*. As the web grew, early web search engines were easily tricked by unsavory sites. Shady site creators stuffed phrases into their pages to mislead the search engine. At best, early search engines returned any old match for a user query. At worst, they led users to spammy or malicious web pages.

Google realized that relevance for the web depended on trust, not just text. Users needed help sifting through the untrustworthy riffraff on the web. So Google developed its PageRank algorithm[1] to measure the trustworthiness of content. PageRank computes this trustworthiness score by determining how much the rest of the web links to a site. Using PageRank, Google brings back not only content that matches the user's search, but content that's seen as reliable and trustworthy by the rest of the web. This emphasis on returning trustworthy content continues today as Google plays a cat-and-mouse game with malicious websites that continually attempt to game the system.

---

[1] Read more at "The Anatomy of a Large-Scale Hypertextual Web Search Engine" by Sergey Brin and Lawrence Page at http://infolab.stanford.edu/~backrub/google.html.

Now let's contrast web search to *e-commerce*. A site such as Amazon, which has complete control over the content being searched, lacks the dire trustworthiness concern. Instead, what's relevant to e-commerce users is the same thing that matters to any kind of shopper: affordable, highly rated products that will satisfy them. But it's not just the shoppers that matter to a store. E-commerce sites have their own selfish interests. They must also return search results that generate profit, clear expiring inventory, and satisfy supplier relationships.

Search becomes the e-commerce site's salesperson. The same priorities that matter to the in-store sales experience must be programmed into the e-commerce search by the relevance engineer. The relevance engineer hopes to build a search that understands what shoppers want, so that they'll leave the store with satisfactory purchases. To e-commerce, relevant means not just leading users to satisfactory purchases, but also making a buck.

Still another kind of search, prominent in medicine, law, and research, digs deeper into text for its definition of relevance. This *expert search* depends on understanding jargon entered by specialists such as lawyers or doctors. These solutions must understand the subtle, domain-specific relationships—for instance, that "Heart Attack" is the same thing as "Myocardial Infarction". Or that acute "Myocardial Infarction" is a specific type of "Heart Attack".

Just as e-commerce search mirrors a shopper's interactions with a salesperson, expert search parallels a searcher's conversation with a research librarian. These librarians understand the lingo of specialized researchers. When asked a question, they guide specialists toward data and related research that specialists couldn't easily find on their own.

The basic definition of relevant to these search applications depends on solutions originally intended to organize information for libraries. For example, in medicine, the Medical Subject Headings (MeSH) taxonomy shown in figure 1.2 organizes medical concepts to help retrieve information on synonymous, more-specific, or less-specific subjects. To expert search, *relevant* means carefully linking subjects and topics between

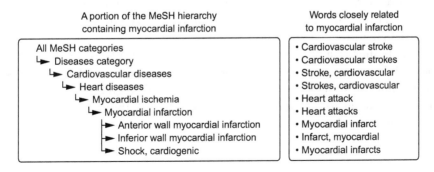

Figure 1.2 MeSH categorization of "Myocardial Infarction" (left) along with several MeSH topics closely related to "Myocardial Infarction"

search queries and content. A relevant result is something that delivers an "Aha!" moment to stuck researchers—a sudden insight they couldn't easily find on their own.

1.2.2   *Search: there's no silver bullet!*

The classes of search problems we've just discussed only scratch the surface in the amazing diversity of search. Is real-estate search a kind of e-commerce search? Certainly there's a resemblance (satisfying users with a satisfactory purchase), but many other factors come into play for a house buyer (good schools, neighborhood, number of bedrooms). What about a local restaurant search application? Or searching for groceries? Ordering food from a restaurant's menu? Searching volunteer opportunities? Or searching for someone to shovel the driveway after a snowstorm? What about intranet search? And what about your application? How do you define what's relevant?

Given this dramatic diversity of relevance requirements, it's surprising to find so many vendors eager to deliver a surefire, silver-bullet solution. Your definition of relevant is likely far more unique than you realize. Your users have expectations they may not even be aware of. Your content and business carry challenges you haven't appreciated yet.

Indeed, be grateful that Solr or Elasticsearch don't work well for your problem out of the box. You didn't choose a programming language because your product is just a module to import from its standard library. If that were true, there'd be nothing unique about your product! Rather, think of Solr or Elasticsearch as a search programming framework. An open source search engine lets you program *your* understanding of what's relevant into the search engine. We'll teach you just that: the art and science of delivering a relevance solution by using open source search technologies that satisfy users and meet business goals.

1.3   *Gaining insight from relevance research*

Okay, so you see that your application has its own definition of what's relevant. But why is there no universal, defined practice for delivering relevant search results to users? Search the web, and you'll find any number of one-off solutions that solved any author's problem particularly well. What you're not left with is a sense that search relevance has any holistic grounding or common engineering principles but is instead a bag of tricks that can't be generally applied.

In reality, there *is* a discipline behind relevance: the academic field of information retrieval. It has generally accepted practices to improve relevance broadly across many domains. But you've seen that what's relevant depends a great deal on your application. Given that, as we introduce information retrieval, think about how its general findings can be used to solve your narrower relevance problem.[2]

---

[2] For an introduction to the field of information retrieval, we highly recommend the classic text *Introduction to Information Retrieval* by Christopher D. Manning et al. (Cambridge University Press, 2008); see http://nlp.stanford .edu/IR-book/.

1.3.1   *Information retrieval*

Luckily, experts have been studying search for decades. The academic field of information retrieval focuses on the precise recall of information to satisfy a user's information need. What's an *information need?* Think of it as a *specification* of the ideal content that would satisfy the user's search. This specification goes beyond the search string itself. For example, consider a programming problem you're attempting to solve. You might be trying to figure out why the Java library function sort throws a NullPointer-Exception. The information need could be specified as follows:

> A solution as to why my particular use of the sort method causes a NullPointerException. (Though I won't admit it to myself, it'd be nice to have some code to copy-paste that solved my problem so I can go to lunch!)

To satisfy this information need, you're likely to formulate search queries to find solutions to your particular problem—for example, "sort method NullPointerException" or "<code snippet> NullPointerException." If you're fortunate, you'll find a result addressing a problem similar to your own. That information will solve your problem, and you'll move on.

In information retrieval, *relevance* is defined as the practice of returning search results that most satisfy the user's information needs. Further, classic information retrieval focuses on text ranking. Many findings in information retrieval try to measure how likely a given article is going to be relevant to a user's text search. You'll learn about several of these invaluable methods throughout this book—as many of these findings are implemented in open source search engines.

To discover better text-searching methods, information retrieval researchers benchmark different strategies by using test collections of articles. These test collections include Amazon reviews, Reuters news articles, Usenet posts, and other similar, article-length data sets. To help benchmark relevance solutions, these collections have been heavily annotated in an experimental search setting, grading which results are most relevant for a given query. For example, when searching for "Mitt Romney," news articles about his 2008 or 2012 presidential run would be considered highly relevant. Perhaps articles about Romney's early management consulting work would be considered moderately relevant. Articles that discuss his father, George Romney, likely would be graded much less relevant. These annotated lists of search results that are relevant with respect to a set of queries are known as *judgment lists* (see figure 1.3).

Using judgment lists, researchers aim to measure whether changes to text relevance calculations improve the overall relevance of the results across every test collection. To classic information retrieval, a solution that improves a dozen text-heavy test collections 1% overall is a success. Rather than focusing on one particular problem in depth, information retrieval focuses on solving search for a broad set of problems.

Searches to be evaluated

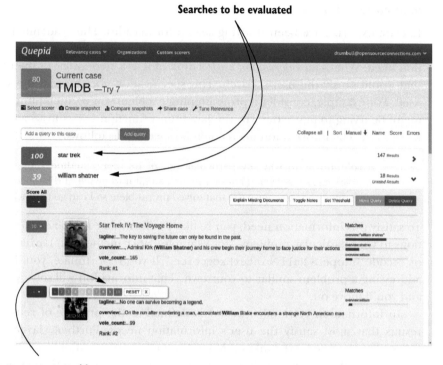

Content expert provides
judgment of relevance
of this result.

Figure 1.3   Example of making a relevance judgment for the query "Rambo" in Quepid, a
judgment list management application

1.3.2   *Can we use information retrieval to solve relevance?*

You've already seen there's no silver bullet. But information retrieval does seem to systematically create relevance solutions. So ask yourself: Do these insights apply to your application? Does your application care about solutions that offer incremental, general improvements to searching article-length text? Would it be better to solve the specific problems faced by your application, here and now?

To be more precise, classic information retrieval begs several questions when brought to bear on applied relevance problems. Let's reflect on these questions to see where information retrieval research can help and where it might stop being helpful.

- *Do we care only about information needs?* For many applications, satisfying users' information needs isn't the only goal. Search exists just as much to satisfy the business behind the search application. You saw this with e-commerce earlier. Although it's often said "the customer is always right," it's also true that businesses can't function without selling ads, making a profit, satisfying suppliers, and moving inventory. Many incentives exist in any search experience that puts business needs above the user's information needs. Just like the used-car sales-men trying to move an overpriced clunker off the lot, relevance engineers must work with these factors to keep their employer in business.

- *What besides text reflects information needs?* Classic information retrieval focuses on a generic, one-size-fits-all measure of text relevance. These factors may not mat-ter—at all—to your application. You need to focus with greater care on your specific problems. We discussed one example: how Google revolutionized web search by incorporating a numerical website trust measure (PageRank). Google uses PageRank to get around pure text-based measures easily gamed in its domain. Even text search doesn't always neatly fit into information retrieval's focus on article-length text. Good results for short text snippets such as tweets or titles require different thinking. You, not information retrieval researchers, must decide which factors matter to *your application*, and implement those. An approach that does poorly against the Reuters test set may be exactly what you need to satisfy your users.

- *What does the user experience imply about information needs?* Often the promises of the application itself influence what users consider relevant. We discussed expert search earlier. Consider two medical search applications. Both serve the same users (doctors). Both hold the same content (medical articles). But there's one important difference: one helps doctors serve sick patients at their bedsides, and the other allows doctors to explore their research interests casu-ally in their offices. These dramatically different expectations mean a different understanding of what's relevant for the same search queries. A search for "heart attack" at the patient's bedside must provide actionable, reliable solu-tions to a dire, life-and-death problem. The research application allows for more variety: doctors search for "heart attack" to explore interesting and new research findings less tied to solving specific problems.

  Often the hardest part of being a relevance engineer is understanding the rela-tionship between context and information needs. User searches arrive at your search engine with a great deal of baggage attached. This baggage comes in part as additional data, perhaps geolocation or user session. But other baggage is entirely implied in the promises made by the search application. Is the applica-tion built, sold, and marketed for sitting casually at one's desk and performing research? Or is it instead billed as almost an expert system, ready, willing, and able to solve any problem asked of it, including helping a doctor save a life?

Considering these questions, you can see that information retrieval builds a founda-tion for applying generally useful relevance measures to extremely broad classes of problems. Your job is to solve relevance for your application. As you'll see, much of this exists outside the realm of search technology and speaks to broader product strategy questions: Who are our users? What do they expect from this application? What implied and unspecified information needs will search need to address?

In fact, before we move on, let's refine our definition of *relevance* to what it takes to solve an applied relevance problem:

> *Relevance* is the practice of improving search results *for users* by satisfying *their information needs* in the context of a particular *user experience*, while balancing how ranking *impacts our business's needs.*

1.4   *How do you solve relevance?*

Informed now by information retrieval, let's focus on how to solve your relevance problems. Open source search engines recognize that what's relevant to your application depends on a broad range of factors. Many of these are application-specific (how far the user is from a restaurant, for instance). Others are broader, generic, text-ranking components from information retrieval.

Given the capabilities of open source search, how do you solve an applied relevance problem? What framework can we define that incorporates both the narrower, domain-specific factors alongside broader information-retrieval techniques?

To solve relevance, the relevance engineer:

1 Identifies salient *features* describing the content, the user, or the search query
2 Finds a way to tell the search engine about those features through extraction and enrichment
3 At search time, measures what's relevant to a user's search by crafting *signals*
4 Carefully balances the influence of multiple signals to rank results by manipulating the ranking function

This process is shown in figure 1.4.

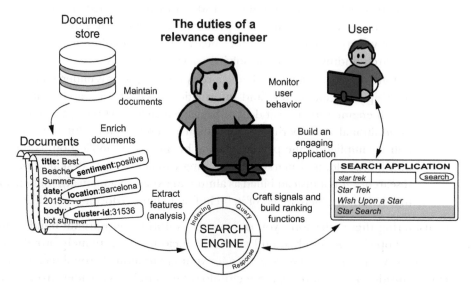

Figure 1.4   Relevance engineers select, enrich, or create important features from back-end systems and express ranking signals in terms of those features.

That sounds a bit abstract. What exactly do we mean? We discussed an example earlier: how Google susses out the feature of PageRank for websites (step 1). This feature is encoded in Google's search engine alongside each web page (thus achieving step 2). When you issue a search, Google measures many factors that you, with this search, consider relevant (step 3). For example, Google uses PageRank directly as a trustworthiness ranking signal. Other signals could include how frequently your search string is mentioned in a page's title/body or personalization factors using knowledge about your preferences. Google blends all of these signals (step 4) into a bigger ranking computation that orders search results in a way that it hopes you'll find satisfactory.

We discussed these ideas earlier in the chapter. But let's lay down some more-precise definitions. A *feature* is an attribute of the content or query. Features drive decisions. Much of the engineering work in search relevance is in *feature selection*—the act of discovering and generating features that give us the appropriate information when a user searches.

Those familiar with machine learning or classification may see something recognizable in these features. When performing classification, you identify new features of your data to make better classification decisions. Is a fruit a banana or an apple? If you know the color is yellow, there's a reasonable chance it's a banana. If you add data about the shape—round or long—then you can make an even more definitive decision. As you'll see, these features also help search solutions make definitive decisions about data.

Features describe, but what happens when users search? With *signals*, you program the search engine to rank by using your definition of what's relevant. Signals measure whether items are relevant for a given search (using features, of course!). For example, in our fruit search engine, the user might search for "yellow fruit." The search engine must evaluate whether a `Golden Delicious apple` might be relevant for this user. We know color matters to fruit shoppers, so one signal might measure how much this fruit's color corresponds to a color being searched for.

It's rare to have only one signal that measures relevance. More often, multiple signals combine to rank search results in the search engine's *ranking function*. For example, in addition to matching on color, perhaps the fruit shopper considers the freshness of produce. Or the user might recall preferred brands, using that as an additional signal. We'll teach you how to control the search engine's ranking function to rank results in a way that seems eerily "smart"—factoring in all the considerations (signals) that your users factor into their definitions of *relevant*.

Fear not—we know these ideas are abstract right now. As you get your hands dirty in future chapters, you'll begin to have the Aha! moment you need to grok what we mean. But to get the general idea, let's consider examples of features, and how they can be used as ranking-time search signals:

- *Sales data, user ratings*—Features used to signal popular results that users will probably be happier with.
- *Text with positional information*—Used to signal when phrases from the user's query match the content.

- *Text with synonyms*—Whether synonyms of query terms match the content.
- *Geolocation*—Whether something is near or far: Is the searcher close to the content? Is the sushi restaurant next to the user or in Manhattan?
- *Machine learning/classification features*—Is the search more easily classified into one type of content (a search for movies) and not easily classified into other types (a search for lawn equipment)?
- *Personalization/recommendation*—Has the user shown an affinity for any particular kind of content over others? Can you identify other users who are similar to the user making a search? Perhaps the historic preferences of the user issuing a search could be used as a signal to influence the search results.

As you work through future chapters, you'll see an approach that systematically improves search relevance based on selecting features and programming ranking signals. To form a foundation for this work, we'll first give you an overview of the search engine's internal mechanics and how to debug them in chapters 2 and 3. Chapters 4–7 get at the meaty problems of building features and signals. In chapter 8, we point out alternate strategies to guide users to relevant content when search by itself won't do.

Throughout this book, we use Elasticsearch as our example search engine. Elasticsearch is a modern search engine built upon Lucene, a commonly used Java search library. This book also applies to Solr, another search engine based on Lucene. Though our examples focus on Elasticsearch, these ideas are generally applicable. Solr readers in particular should follow along with appendix B, which helps map features between the two search engines.

1.5 *More than technology: curation, collaboration, and feedback*

Is a technical foundation enough to solve the search relevance problem? Armed with new skills from this book, you might be hungry to improve your employer's search. Targeting what you think are the biggest relevance problems, you deliver to your users what you consider to be an amazing search experience. You release your updates without much fuss; to the organization, that's yet another one of those heads-down, back-end tasks that engineers go off and just figure out. It's something akin to squeezing more performance out of the SQL database, right?

Unfortunately, shortly after the release, your boss is at your door. Things look pretty grim. Despite your best efforts, something is deeply amiss. Somehow, users aren't making purchases. They can't find the information they need. Instead, they're giving up and going to the competition. With revenue headed south, your boss grits her teeth. In desperation, she looks at you square in the face and pleads for you to "make it more relevant!" In other words, fix the bug, implement the feature—stay all weekend if you have to; just make it work!

"Make it more relevant"? Let's recall our definition of relevance. Perhaps if you meditate on this definition, you'll see how the organization in this story misses the mark:

> *Relevance* is the practice of improving search results *for users* by satisfying *their information needs* in the context of a particular *user experience*, while balancing how ranking *impacts our business's needs.*

When you think about this definition, you quickly see that *relevance engineers have no idea what relevant search should be!* To satisfy your users' information needs, you need to understand their goals, their domains, and the context of their searches. These could vary wildly, from a doctor helping a struggling patient to a grandparent shopping for baby shower presents. Satisfying these users means getting inside their heads. Understanding these users goes far beyond search technology, touching nearly every competence in the organization. This is especially true as you work to understand business needs such as politics, profit, business goals, and other internal factors.

Solving the search relevance problem requires shifting the organization's culture to emphasize cross-functional collaboration. How can the organization teach relevance engineers to understand the users' vernacular and what they expect from search? What happens when the application is built for doctors or lawyers? Who helps the engineer understand these users' domains? How does the organization teach a relevance engineer what makes the company the most money? Which suppliers should be kept happy? What content has "premium" access in search (and what's that even supposed to mean)?

Even seemingly mundane search applications can be fraught with these complications. Consider a restaurant search application. Your marketing colleagues worked hard to bring users "into the doors" of your application. Now the search, acting as the site's salesperson (or perhaps concierge?), needs to satisfy them and make them eager to come back for more.

Relevance engineers, though, aren't the sales department. When a user types "sushi" into the search bar, what restaurants does that user expect? Takeout? High-end restaurants? Nearby ones? Depends on the user? Others in the organization, *not* the relevance engineer, understand what goals users hope to achieve. The relevance engineer is working in isolation to define relevance ranking and might as well be painting a house blindfolded.

Further, this collaboration goes beyond simply educating the relevance engineer. *Curation*, the manipulation of content to be easily found by user searches, can matter just as much as teaching a relevance engineer. Recall the expert search examples earlier in this chapter. Here the expertise of the librarian can help you build better search by organizing content to make it easier to find. Often this organization requires a close meeting of the minds between those who understand the content deeply and the relevance engineers who grok how the search engine works.

Rooted in these forms of collaboration is the notion of feedback. An effective organization strives to bring relevance engineers accurate and quick feedback to inform and guide their efforts. You can visualize several important feedback loops as a series of increasingly focused circles, as shown in Figure 1.5. Starting on the outermost loop, the search developers operate within an organization, blissfully unaware of the impact of search relevance. As the organization evolves, it moves to inner, more mature forms of feedback: incorporating user behavioral data and expert feedback. Finally, the organization encodes its wisdom into relevance tests, enabling test-driven relevancy practice—the most mature organizational form.

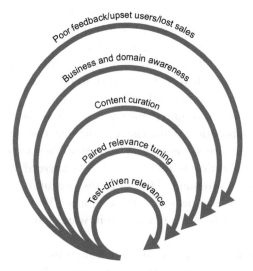

Figure 1.5 Forms of search-relevance feedback

This book primarily teaches you about the technical craft of relevance engineers. But reflecting on what you *should* be doing hopefully echoes in your mind as you learn these technical lessons. In many examples, we state unequivocally that a particular search result is what users want to see. We do this to teach you technical skills to manipulate the search to get those results. As you work through those examples, remember the examples in this section before applying lessons directly to your relevance problems. We'll dive deeper into organizational challenges in chapter 10.

1.6 *Summary*

- Relevance problems are pervasive. Even established domains such as web search, e-commerce, and expert search continue to struggle to improve the relevance of search results.
- Bringing users to relevant search results can turn into a multibillion-dollar business advantage; failing to do so can mean losing out to the competition.
- *Information retrieval* is the academic field of bringing users to content that satisfies their information needs, largely as specified in search queries.

- In practice, *relevance* is more than satisfying information needs as specified by searches. It also means satisfying business needs. Further, understanding a user's information needs often depends on implicit information, such as the application's context, purpose, marketing, and user experience.
- Relevance can be achieved by identifying the valuable *features* of your content, and using those features to compute relevance signals.
- Technologists can't do it alone. Based on business needs, the user audience, and the content domain, the relevance engineer often doesn't have the skills to evaluate what content is relevant for user searches.
- Feedback is vital. From the perspective of the relevance engineer, measuring the impact of relevance changes helps avoid delivering poor search to users.

Search—under the hood

2

This chapter covers

- Basic concepts required to understand search technologies
- Data structures that make search possible
- Internal mechanics for searching and retrieving documents
- Overview of data extraction, enrichment, analysis, and indexing

Search is a conversation between a user and a search engine. The user attempts to satisfy an information need by providing search with appropriate constraints describing relevant content. The search engine uses those constraints to collect matches, providing them to the user. If the user is satisfied with a match, that user will inspect individual items in further detail. Otherwise, the user will refine the search criteria and try again. Your work is to facilitate this conversation. You must ensure that search results are relevant and you must help users understand why results match, enabling them to refine their searches.

But creating relevant search requires more than you may initially anticipate. New search developers see search as a black box with just a few modes of interaction: you add content and allow users to query that content. In this chapter, we reveal the secrets under this dark mantel. And spoiler alert, there's no magic involved in search. Under the hood, a search engine's data structures perform rather dumb term-matching. Results are then ranked using simple heuristics. The search engine is mechanical: it has no understanding of the meaning of the terms, the intentions underlying a user's search, or the context of the application.

The science of relevance engineering is in coercing the mechanical search engine to fulfill relevance goals. By the end of this chapter, you'll begin to see how to do this. You'll see how to extract descriptive features from queries and content. You'll begin to understand how these features can be used to rank documents to bring back the most relevant content first. Aside from the *science* of relevance engineering, there's an *art* to understanding what constitutes a good, descriptive feature. There's skill in how factors should be weighted and balanced to meet the users' and business's relevance expectations. By the end of this book, you'll have a good grasp of these skills.

In this chapter, we first provide an overview of basic search concepts. Then we dive into deeper details of Lucene-based search, covering the data structures and processes involved in analyzing, indexing, and retrieving documents. In the next chapter, you'll see what to do when search breaks down. Together chapters 2 and 3 give you foundational tools for understanding the search engine. Subsequent chapters go further, applying search's data structures to implement real-world solutions.

2.1 Search 101

Your initial understanding of the search engine may be simple. With some basics under your belt, you might have roughly the mental model shown in figure 2.1. Content makes its way into the search engine, and users query and explore by interacting with a search application.

Before getting under the hood, into the arcane black box, let's quickly review the search engine's capabilities from an outsider's point of view. As you know, the central

Figure 2.1 A simple model of a search engine based on possible interactions

functions of a search engine are storing, finding, and retrieving content. Although these are all basic concepts, it's useful to review them in order to establish a shared set of definitions and fill in any technical gaps you may have.

2.1.1 What's a search document?

In search applications, the notion of a *document* is central, because documents are items being stored, searched, and returned. Documents are what search is all about! When you issue a query to a search engine, you're searching a collection of documents. These may be literal documents such as text files on a server. Or, more generally, documents may correspond to content such as:

- Products in a catalog
- Songs stored in an MP3 player
- People in a list of contacts
- Internal Word documents from your company's intranet
- Pages of a book
- Entire books in a library collection

A document contains a set of *fields*: the named attributes of the document. In this way, a document is similar to a row in an SQL table. Whereas an SQL table contains a set of named columns and their corresponding values, a document contains a set of fields with their values. Fields are typed, including the standard types you'd expect: string, integer, float, and Boolean.

String types are of particular interest for search. Strings are often *searched within*. Consider a newspaper article titled "Business Is Booming at the Beautiful Beach of Barcelona." You'd probably want a search for "barcelona beaches" to match the text in the title. Controlling exactly when text matches a search will occupy a great deal of your time as a relevance engineer. This may seem a bit fuzzy right now, but you'll learn more throughout this book, particularly in chapter 4.

Unlike an SQL table, every document can contain different fields. The fields in one document can be different from the fields in another. Let's say that you're building a search for items sold at a chain of convenience stores. Convenience stores carry a range of products. Although all products have some common fields (a `name` and a `price`, for instance), most types of products also require their own unique fields. Books in the convenience store require fields such as `author` and `page_count`. Food items likely need fields such as `calories` and `ingredients`.

2.1.2 Searching the content

With the notion of a document defined, we can talk about the main purpose of the search engine: searching for relevant content! Let's say your friend Sharon tells you about a great article about the beaches of Barcelona. She remembers it's in the Travel section of the *Relevant Times* newspaper from last summer. Eager to share that article with you, she navigates to the search page at RelevantTimes.com, shown in figure 2.2, and searches for an article that meets these criteria:

- Published in the months of June, July, or August (a date-range constraint)
- Ran in the Travel section (an exact match in a string field)
- Keywords barcelona and beach appear in the title and body fields (a text match in two text fields)

Relevant Times
Your News... *Yesterday!*

barcelona beaches	(search)	

June 1, 2015 ▽   Aug 31, 2015 ▽

no. results

☐ News 1
☐ Political 0
☒ Travel 12
☒ Economy 5
☐ Lifestyle 0
☐ Opinion 1

Business is Booming on the Beautiful Beaches of Barcelona
Ted Nisemono   *Economy*   *June 23, 2015*
... this summer season is projected to be the best on the books for **Barcelona's beach** resorts, a trend that is expected to continue ...

Best Beaches to Beat the Summer Heat
John Faux   *Travel*   *Aug 14, 2015*
... there are several **beach** destinations that you must visit ... or Waikiki which as placed just above **Barcelona** as a destination ...

Barcelona Festival Season is Upon Us
Cindy Falshung   *Travel*   *July 3, 2015*
... whether it's the giant's on the march or the 12 story tall human pyramids you'll find **Barcelona** an enchanting place to spend ...

Stinging Jelly Fish Plague Shoreline Industries
Phil Lazan   *Economy*   *June 3, 2015*
... the northside beach was worst hit, but will a little help from a ...

Figure 2.2   Typical search user interface and response page

Once supplied with these constraints, the search engine returns matching documents. But even more than this, the search engine *orders* documents, presenting the user with the most relevant matches first.

In Sharon's "barcelona beaches" search, the search engine's response will hopefully contain the article that she was looking for as the first result. How does the search engine know to rank this highly? Because the article is about the beaches of Barcelona, the article's title likely contains the phrase "Beaches of Barcelona". The terms "Barcelona" and "beach" probably also occur prominently in the article's text. The search engine considers these factors and ranks Sharon's target article more prominently than the competition: articles less relevant to the user's search but still related. Perhaps these articles are about beaches or Barcelona, but not the beaches of Barcelona per se, making only passing references to the search query.

You'll see more on exactly *how* the search engine makes these relevance calculations later. You'll also see how many factors, beyond text, and beyond even the user's priorities, can come into play in the relevance calculation. Remember from chapter 1, *relevance* is a measure of how well content satisfies the information needs of the user and *business*. So, for example, an e-commerce search with *good* relevance not only returns the appropriate documents, but also /ensures/might ensure that they're sorted so that paid promotional items are closer to the top.

2.1.3   *Exploring content through search*

Search engines go beyond returning documents based on relevance. Search is of little use unless it presents the relevant documents back to the user in a manner that encourages exploration. The UIs of search engines guide users to relevant content by using many common features you're probably familiar with.

Front and center, as illustrated in figure 2.2, the search engine provides users with a list of matching documents. Typically, the user won't see the entire document but a subset of fields deemed important to understanding the match. In the Barcelona beaches example, these fields would likely include the title of the article, the author, the section of the newspaper (in this case, Travel), date, and text from the article itself.

Instead of the field values, search engines often return summarized snippets that highlight the part that matches. These highlighted snippets (*highlights*, for short) convey exactly why a document is a match for the user's search. Often when reading through snippets, the user will discover ways of improving the original search. For instance, if *Barcelona Beach* happened to be the name of a local tapas restaurant, the user may be inclined to modify the search to filter out restaurants.

Search also encourages further exploration by describing the distribution of matching documents throughout the corpus. Sharon's original search for Barcelona beaches, for example, was constrained to articles only in the Travel section. But a good search implementation would indicate the number of articles matching "barcelona beaches" in all other sections of the newspaper. As illustrated in figure 2.2, this aggregate information is often presented in a sidebar as a set of filters also known as *facets*. Perhaps the article Sharon remembered reading is about the booming tourism of Barcelona beaches. It's in the Economy section of the newspaper. Given the data presented in the facets, she may choose to select that facet, filtering the search to include only information from that section.

2.1.4   *Getting content into the search engine*

The preceding section discusses how search enables content exploration, but how do you provide the search engine with the content to be searched? Data is first extracted from a location where content is stored. This might be a database, text files, web pages, or other source. This raw data is converted into the search fields and documents described previously. These documents may be further enriched by adding in new fields with external information helpful for matching or ranking.

After being handed to the search engine, the fields of a document undergo a process called *analysis*, shown in figure 2.3.

Analysis converts the field values (usually text) into elements called *tokens*. For text, tokens usually correspond to words, such as "best", "barcelona", "beach". You'll notice that these tokens look a bit different from the original words. In this case, one word (*the*) has been dropped, the tokens are lowercased, and the plural suffix of *beaches* has

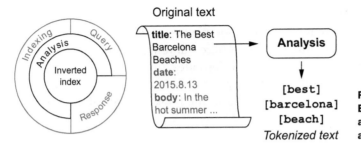

Figure 2.3 "Barcelona Beaches" article indexed and analyzed (only title-field analysis shown)

been removed. Why? A token extracted from our article and a token extracted from a future search query typically need to match *exactly* to be considered a match. Search often aids in matching by using language-specific heuristics to transform words to simpler forms. English text analysis removes capitalization (RUN -> run), suffixes (running -> run), and pluralization (runs -> run) and many other patterns. And although tokens are typically generated text, as you'll see in chapter 4, analysis can be applied and tokens generated for nontext values such as floating-point numbers and geographic locations.

In chapter 1, we mentioned the notion of features. In machine learning, features are descriptors for the items being classified. Features used to classify fruit may be things such as color, flavor, and shape. With full-text search, the tokens produced during analysis are the dominant features used to match a user's query with documents in the index. Don't worry if this seems vague right now; the greater portion of this book is dedicated to making these ideas clear.

After analysis is complete, the documents are *indexed*; the tokens from the analysis step are stored into search engine data structures for document retrieval. In addition, the original, untokenized text fields are stored so that they can be presented back to the user in search results. Storing numeric fields also allows numerical attributes to be used in ranking calculations.

2.2 Search engine data structures

Section 2.1 laid out the basic takeaways of any "intro to search" tutorial. Now the fun part. Let's begin to fill in the magical black box so you can understand how the brains within the search engine work. We'll start with the data structures, and then we'll show how the two processes, indexing and querying, interact with these data structures.

At its core, a search engine has a handful of highly optimized data structures that allow documents to be retrieved and scored. Understanding these structures and how they're used is requisite to understanding the search engine's inner workings. With an appreciation of the mechanics, you can use the search engine to build seemingly smart, relevant search experiences.

2.2.1 The inverted index

In the future when some relevancy issue plagues you, we hope that you'll return to this book for help. And when you do, where will you go? Most likely you'll flip straight to the back of this book and refer to the index (like the one shown in figure 2.4). There you can look up terms of interest: *analysis, tokenization, scoring,* and so forth. From there you'll be referred to pages in the book that talk about the things you're looking for.

A

acronyms 90–91
actionable information 186
ad hoc searches 148
add shingling 126
addCmd 45
additive boosting, with Boolean queries 176–178
  combining boost and base query 177–178
  function queries vs. 174–175
  optimizing boosts in isolation 176–177
  Solr 318
adjusted boosts 72
affinity 286
aggregate information 20
AND operator 32–33
anticipating
  user behavior 93
  user intent 76
api_key argument 304
assertion-based testing 273–274
asymmetric analysis 96, 100
asymmetric tokenization 101
autocomplete keyword 255

B

bag of words model 63, 65
base query, boosting 173
base signal 176
basic highlighter 225

Figure 2.4 The inverted index data structure used by search engines closely resembles the index that you can find in the back of a textbook.

At the core of a search engine is a data structure called the *inverted index,* analogous to the physical index at the back of this book. An inverted index is composed of two main pieces: a term dictionary and a postings list. The *term dictionary* is a sorted list of all terms that occur in a given field across a set of documents. For each term in the dictionary, there's a corresponding list of documents that contain that term. This list of documents is referred to as the *postings* for a particular term. To understand this more clearly, let's look at an example. Consider the set of documents shown in the following listing.

Listing 2.1 Documents

```
0. One shoe, two shoe, the red shoe, the blue shoe.
1. The blue dress shoe is the best shoe.
2. The best dress is the one red dress.
```

The term dictionary and postings list for this simple set of documents are presented in the following two listings, respectively.

```
Listing 2.2   Term dictionary

best  → 0
blue  → 1
dress → 2
is    → 3
one   → 4
red   → 5
shoe  → 6
the   → 7
two   → 8
```

```
Listing 2.3   Postings list

0 → [1,2]
1 → [0,1]
2 → [1,2]
3 → [1,2]
4 → [0,2]
5 → [0,2]
6 → [0,1]
7 → [0,1,2]
8 → [0]
```

Both the term dictionary and the postings list are mappings. The term dictionary maps terms to ordinal numbers that uniquely identify a term. Just like a book's index, this index is ordered lexicographically to make it easier to find terms. Once you have a term's ordinal, you use the ordinal's postings list to retrieve the documents that contain that term—just like the page numbers in a book's index.

Let's walk through an example to make that more concrete. Let's say you're looking for all documents containing the term "red." First you look up "red" in the term dictionary and find that it has a term identifier of 5. Next you go to the postings list and find the postings associated with term 5—in this case, the list refers to documents 0 and 2. Referring to the original documents in listing 2.1, you see that documents 0 and 2 do contain the word "red", whereas document 1 doesn't.

In this example it's worth noting that we've simplified things a bit. These documents contain a single field that contains the sentences themselves. But in practice, documents will likely contain several fields: title, description, address, price, and so forth. In this case, nothing really changes; there's still one inverted index, but the terms are sorted by field first and then sorted lexicographically within the fields.

2.2.2   *Other pieces of the inverted index*

The term dictionary and the postings list are the central pieces of the inverted index data structure, because they make it possible to quickly match documents against query terms. But in order for a search engine to provide relevant results and enable exploration, Lucene adds more data structures and metadata to the index.

Many of these components are optional. Disabling them can sometimes be an optimization. Other times, these data structures can be enabled to provide richer relevance or search features. Table 2.1 lists some of the most important pieces of information commonly associated with the inverted index. Throughout the book, we dig into these items in more detail and reveal how they can be used to tune search relevance.

Table 2.1   Important pieces of data associated with the inverted index

Name	Description
Doc frequency	A count of documents that contain a particular term, or the length of the postings associated with a particular term. In listing 2.3, the doc frequency for the term "shoe" is 2 because it occurs in documents 0 and 1. Doc frequency is useful in document scoring because it establishes a notion of *importance* for a particular term. For instance, the term "the" typically has a high document frequency, which indicates that it carries little discriminatory value when determining the relevancy of a document for a given search.
Term frequency	The number of times that a term occurs in a particular document. In listing 2.3, the term frequency for "shoe" in document 0 is 4, and the term frequency for "shoe" in document 1 is 2. Term frequency is useful in document scoring because it establishes a notion of how important a document is for a given term. So, loosely speaking, if someone searches for "shoe", document 0 can be considered twice as important as document 1 because "shoe" occurs twice as often in document 0.
Term positions	Word position is often important for search. Consider the semantic difference between a query for "dress AND shoes" and a query for "dress shoes." Term positions are a list of numbers indicating where a term occurs within a particular document. For instance, the term positions for "shoe" in document 0 from our example would be 1, 3, 6, 9. Term positions make it possible to find documents based on phrase matches so that a search for "dress shoes" will give users exactly what they're looking for.
Term offsets	One of the best ways to provide search users with feedback about *why* a particular document matches a query is to present them with highlighted snippets of the matching text. But reanalyzing the original text to extract highlights is often slow. The fastest way to highlight snippets is to keep track of the start and end character offsets of the terms when they're first analyzed during indexing. Then, at search "time" all that needs to be done is to insert the appropriate tags at the corresponding offsets.
Payloads	Each term in the index can be associated with arbitrary data. One common example is to tag a token with its part of speech and use this in relevance scoring. Another common example is to associate an externally generated score with a token (this mention of "Barcelona" ought to be scored as 100, this other "Barcelona" mention a 59).
Stored fields	Information stored in an inverted index is useful for searching, but this information is a rather scrambled version of the original document. Any fields are to be presented back to the user or must be saved separately in *stored fields*. These stored fields can take up a lot of disk space. For this reason, many search developers avoid storing data directly in the search engine, instead retrieving display fields from the source system.

Table 2.1 Important pieces of data associated with the inverted index

Name	Description
Doc values	It's common to incorporate auxiliary values into the relevance-scoring heuristic. For instance, an e-commerce search might boost catalog items that are on clearance or that have a high profit margin. It's also common to allow users to sort search results by a metric such as price or popularity. The doc values data structure allows for quick access to these auxiliary values and is useful when sorting, scoring, and grouping documents.

Now that you have a clearer understanding of the types of data structures that back search, it's time to see how information is placed into these data structures in the first place.

2.3 *Indexing content: extraction, enrichment, analysis, and indexing*

Section 2.1 provided basic information on how documents enter the index. In this section, we'll dig into this process. This sections helps you see how documents make their way into search's core data structures described in section 2.2.

When moving data into a data store, people talk about the process of extracting, transforming, and loading information, often referred to as *ETL*. Data is extracted from wherever it's warehoused, transformed into a format amenable to the destination data store, and then loaded into that data store. In this section, we use the ETL terminology to walk through how data makes its way into a search engine.

Because we know that we're dealing with a search engine, we can be more specific about the steps in search's ETL process. As illustrated in figure 2.5, these steps are extraction, enrichment, analysis, and indexing. Here, *extraction* is the process of retrieving the documents from their sources. The optional step of *enrichment* adds information to the documents useful for relevance. *Analysis*, as you saw earlier in this chapter, converts document text or data into tokens that enable matching. And finally, *indexing* is the process of placing data into those data structures.

We cover extraction and enrichment rather generically. Many times, the details of these steps depend entirely on how your source data is stored. Indexing concerns us only as it pertains to enabling/disabling features for enabling relevance. Analysis, however, has overriding importance to search relevance and is expounded on here. It's also discussed at several points throughout the book. Recall, analysis transforms raw text and data from the documents into tokens. These tokens represent the document's features. Engineering these to match features from a user's query is critical to satisfy the user's information need.

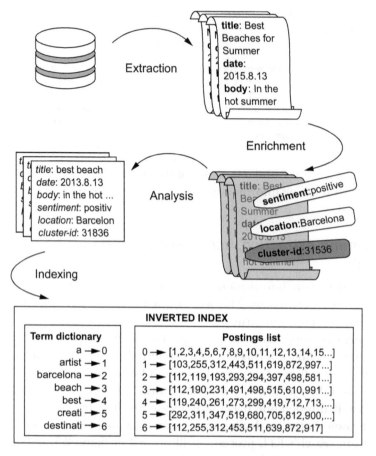

Figure 2.5   The full search ETL pipeline: extraction, enrichment, analysis, and indexing

2.3.1   *Extracting content into documents*

Crafting documents that can be easily retrieved can be just as important to relevance as manipulating the innards of the search engine. You'll see in particular later in this book that content curation (chapter 10) and careful field construction (chapters 4–7) often dictate whether a relevance solution is easy or hard. The basis for this work lies in controlling the extraction and enrichment process, which we outline in the following two sections.

Where do your search documents come from? Data has many possible sources. If you're fortunate, documents can be easily retrieved from a database or external data repository. In this case, extraction may be as simple as crafting a simple query to dump the necessary data. If you're less fortunate, you might have to *look for* your documents—for instance, by crawling web pages or filesystems. And if you're less fortunate still, you might find that your data is locked away behind files that require complex additional processing (such as MS Word documents, PDFs, or, worst of all, images of scanned text). But no matter the case, the end result of extraction is a set of documents to be sent to the search engine. Here, a document may be exactly like the document described in section 2.1.1, a collection of typed fields that contain various values. Or, for search engines such as Elasticsearch, these can be complex hierarchical documents represented as JSON.

The main takeaway is to own your extraction process. Extensive strategies, projects, plugins, and products exist for transforming data from a primary data source to a search engine. The permutations are so numerous that they'd fill dozens of books. We don't cover these options. But you should understand how your extraction process works so that you can control the structure of your documents. Simply living with the structure of data as plopped into the search engine from your source systems can limit your options. In this book's examples, we take control of this process by rolling our own code to extract documents from an external system and build search documents directly.

2.3.2 *Enriching documents to clean, augment, and merge data*

During the enrichment step, the documents from the extraction step are augmented with additional information. This can be an important step in building relevant search, because often the raw, extracted documents lack features that are sufficiently rich to be matched against the users' queries. Document enrichment comprises three main categories: cleaning data, augmenting existing data, and merging external data.

First, *cleaning*. If you want a top-notch search experience, it's usually well worth the time to parse through documents, look for silly mistakes such as misspellings and document duplications, and correct them. Otherwise, users might not find a document because it contains a misspelling of the query term. Or they may find 20 duplicates of the same document, which would have the effect of pushing other relevant documents off the end of the search results page.

Second, often the existing data can be post-processed to *augment* the features already there. For instance, machine-learning techniques can be used to classify or cluster documents. Or sentiment analysis can be used to determine whether the text in a document is more positive or negative in tone. The possibilities are endless. After this new metadata is attached to the documents, it can serve as a valuable feature for users to search upon.

Finally, new information can be merged into the documents from *external sources*. For instance, in e-commerce the products being sold often come from external vendors. Product data provided by the vendors can be sparse—for instance, missing important fields such as the product title. In this case, additional information can be joined into the documents. The existing product codes can be used to look up product titles, or missing descriptions can be written in by hand. The goal is to provide users with every opportunity possible to find the document they're looking for, and that means more search features and richer search features.

2.3.3   *Performing analysis*

Section 2.1 briefly described how the search engine transforms text into tokens. This step is foundational. Choosing how text (and other forms of data) is transformed into tokens dictates how the search engine performs matching. As a relevance engineer, you'll spend a great deal of time fine-tuning analysis to control exactly when matches occur. Let's dive deeper into this process.

After documents have been extracted from wherever they're warehoused, and after the optional step of document enrichment, documents are finally sent to the search engine, where they're analyzed. During analysis, the search engine processes the data in the documents and converts the data into tokens that can then be stored in the search engine's internal data structures.

As alluded to previously, *tokens* are symbols that represent the content of a field in a document. Often tokens correspond exactly to the words in a text field. Consider the text "The Brown's fiftieth wedding anniversary, at Café Olé". Depending on the configuration, analysis might split up this text into the tokens in the following listing.

> **Listing 2.4   Text tokenization example**

```
The, Brown's, fiftieth, wedding, anniversary, at, Café, Olé
```

But often the tokens aren't the literal words but a normalized and filtered version of the words. This same sentence could be tokenized as follows.

> **Listing 2.5   Text tokenization example with normalization and filtering**

```
brown, fiftieth, wedding, anniversary, cafe, ole
```

Here we've lowercased the words, stripped out accents over the letters, and removed common words.

Don't think that tokens always have to correspond to words; just about any data type can be tokenized. Geographic locations (for instance, the location of the White House, 38.8977° N, 77.0366° W) can be tokenized using geohashing. In this case, reasonable tokens might be as follows.

> **Listing 2.6   Geolocation tokenization using geohashing**

```
dqcjqcpee, dqcjqcpe, dqcjqcp, dqcjqc, dqcjq, dqcj, dqc, dq, d
```

These tokens correspond to the geohash representation of that location, with each token representing a gradually less precise representation of that location (more on this in chapter 4).

One of the main functions of a search engine is token matching. Token matching, after all, is how a search engine finds documents that match a user's query. On one side of the equation, text and other data from the documents are analyzed—that is, tokenized—and stored into the inverted index. And on the other side, queries are also analyzed and converted into tokens. Documents with tokens that match the query tokens are considered a match for the search.

The point that must be underscored is that you, the relevance engineer, control analysis. Changes in the way that data is converted into tokens dramatically impact search relevance. Let's demonstrate with the preceding example. If the phrase "The Brown's fiftieth wedding anniversary, at Café Olé" is tokenized as presented in listing 2.4 and a query, "fiftieth wedding anniversary," is issued to the search engine, then in this case the example document would be a match. The document tokens and the query tokens are identical. But, a query for "brown cafe ole" won't match, because the tokens in listing 2.4 contain capital letters, apostrophes, and accents, and the query tokens contain none of these.

> **NOTE** Search engines are *dumb*. If the query and document tokens aren't exactly—byte-for-byte—identical, the document isn't considered a match!

This is why analysis is so important. It's why you spend a great deal of time normalizing text so that query tokens will match documents even if the original document text isn't quite the same as the query text. For instance, looking at the alternative analysis in listing 2.5, when we normalize the example sentence to remove capitalization, apostrophes, and accents, then the same query for "brown cafe ole" is a perfect match to our example document on all three terms.

TOKENS AS SEARCH FEATURES

All of this ties in closely with our central focus on search features. Just as the color *red* and the shape *round* are features that might describe an apple, the *tokens* that come from the analysis process serve as the *features* that describe the document. Continuing with this analogy, if you were to look for an apple at a grocery store, you'd look for fruit that is both red and round. In the realm of search, it's much the same: a user looking for a document about the Brown's wedding anniversary would type this into a search engine, and the search engine would in turn analyze the query, extract the features (tokens), and then attempt to find the documents that have matching features. So throughout our discussion of search features, know that concretely we're often referring to tokens. We use the term *feature* to indicate that a token functions as a sort of descriptor for a document or a query.

As you can imagine, the analysis process affords the relevance engineer a great deal of expressive power in specifying how text and other values are converted into tokens. But, as they say, *with great power comes great responsibility*. Good, descriptive features can be useful in matching queries to documents, but irrelevant and even erroneous features can render a document un-findable! The only way to ensure that your analysis is generating good features is to become intimately familiar with analysis. So, let's look at the details!

COMPONENTS OF ANALYSIS

Analysis is composed of three steps: character filtering, tokenization, and token filtering. Let's walk through each step, following the previous example, and demonstrate end to end how we analyze the text "The Brown's fiftieth wedding anniversary, at Café Olé". In future chapters, we demonstrate how to control analysis, but for now let's just review the process and components.

During the first step, *character filtering*, the characters of text fields can be adjusted or filtered in various ways. A good example is `HTMLStripCharFilter`, which takes HTML as input and returns only the text contained within the HTML and not the HTML tags. In principle, you can do just about anything you want with a character filter, including using regular expressions or creating your own. During analysis, any number of character filters can be specified and will be executed in series in the order that they're specified. Figure 2.6 illustrates the process of character filtering.

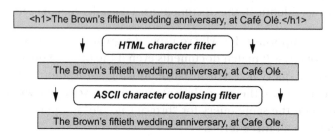

Figure 2.6 Analysis—character filtering

The next step is *tokenization*. As the name indicates, during this step raw text is converted into a stream of tokens. The most straightforward way to tokenize a text stream is to split it on whitespace, but this by itself is rarely the right thing to do. Why? Because you end up with tokens that contain punctuation. In our example, the word "anniversary" is followed by a comma, so the corresponding token when using whitespace tokenization would be `anniversary,`. This is clearly an example of a bad search feature, as it would prevent users from finding this document; no one will think to search for *anniversary* with the comma included. Instead, English and most European-language texts use the *standard tokenizer*, which splits on word whitespace and punctuation. Unlike the character filter, there can be only one tokenizer in any given analysis chain. Tokenization is demonstrated in figure 2.7.

The final step is *token filtering*. Here the stream of tokens can be adjusted, either by adding or removing the tokens or by changing them. In order to appropriately

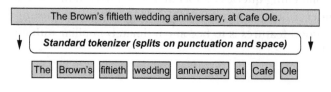

Figure 2.7 Analysis—tokenizing

normalize the tokens from our sample sentence, a typical choice would be to lower-case the tokens, remove common words such as the and at (these common words are called *stop words*), and remove the possessive after Brown. And like the character filter, several token filters can be applied in series during analysis in the order prescribed by the relevance engineer. Token filtering is shown in figure 2.8.

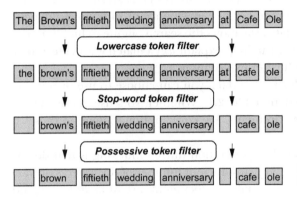

Figure 2.8 Analysis—token filtering

One final note before we move on to indexing. During analysis, it's common to store extra metadata with each token that the analysis process generates. The most common metadata are the term positions and term offsets, which are useful for phrase queries and highlighting, respectively. You can also create custom token filters that add arbitrary metadata to the tokens in values called *payloads*. But beware: all this data can consume a lot of storage. If you must tinker around with payloads, it's wise to be conservative. Please refer to table 2.1 for more details on these items. (We also bring these up again as needed later in this book.)

2.3.4 Indexing

After analysis is complete, *indexing* is the process by which the data is saved into the inverted index data structures described in section 2.2. Although the technical implementation of the indexing process is an engineering marvel in itself, the focus during indexing tends to be placed on computation performance and resource management rather than matters of relevance. But a few indexing decisions can influence relevance—namely, which pieces of data should be indexed and which data structures should be used.

Most importantly, you must decide which fields to index and/or store which fields to index and/or store, and which fields to both index and store. In a general sense, indexing refers to the process of storing data in the search engine. But both *indexing* and *storing* have a more specific meaning when placing field data into core data structures. Here *indexing* refers to the process of updating the inverted index with the extracted tokens to enable search on that field. A field is searchable only if it's indexed.

Storing refers to retaining the original, unaltered document content in the stored field's data structure (see table 2.1) so that it can be retrieved and presented to the user in search results. The search engine can present data back to the user only if it's stored. As an optimization, some engineers store as little information as possible, limiting storage to the bare essentials such as a unique identifier. To retrieve the full documents, these engineers pull the field's content from an external store. Others choose to store data in the search engine out of convenience or to remove a dependency on an external system. Storing data also allows the search engine to highlight matches. As we discussed, this highlighting can help explain *why* a match was made and enable the user to adjust the query for further exploration.

Besides storing and indexing the data, you can choose to use or not use many of the data structures covered in table 2.1. Whether you use these data structures depends on your search requirements. We cover optional usage of these data structures in later chapters.

One final relevance-related consideration during indexing is that documents are indexed in batches. After analyzing a sufficient number of documents or waiting a sufficiently long period of time, the analyzed documents are *committed* to the index. Only after a *commit* do documents become searchable. Because of this, you'll see a lag between sending a document to the search engine and retrieving it via search. Keep this in mind when doing relevance work. Luckily, on a development box you can always issue a manual commit. In production, both Solr and Elasticsearch allow you to tune, update, and commit settings to meet your requirements. We don't cover those in this book as they don't directly pertain to relevance.

2.4   *Document search and retrieval*

With the documents' tokens, values, and original content safely squirrelled away in the search engine's data structures, you're finally ready to search! In this section, we cover all the basic aspects of search, starting with the mechanics of document matching. We finish up with a discussion of how matching documents are scored, sorted, and returned to the user.

2.4.1   *Boolean search: AND/OR/NOT*

Section 2.2.1 described how to retrieve a set of documents that contains a single term: you look up the term in the term dictionary, grab the corresponding postings, and you're finished. The postings *is* the list of matching documents.

But what if you want to match multiple terms? That's what Boolean search is for. *Boolean search* combines the results of multiple queries to more tightly control results. For example: ("shoe" AND "blue"). Let's see how you can implement the typical Boolean operators (AND, OR, NOT) using the contents of the inverted index data structure.

First the AND operator. Referring to our earlier example from section 2.2.1, consider how you might use the term dictionary and the postings list to find documents matching both the term "shoe" *and* the term "blue". First you need to retrieve the postings for both "shoe" and "blue" and then find the documents that are present in both sets. Because the postings are sorted lists of numbers, the algorithm to find this intersection is pretty simple and is shown in Python in the following listing.

Listing 2.7   Boolean AND search

```
def AND(term1postings, term2postings):
    term1doc = term1postings.next()
    term2doc = term2postings.next()

    matches = []
    while term1doc != None and term2doc != None :
        if term1doc == term2doc:
            matches.append(term1doc)
            term1doc = term1postings.next()
            term2doc = term2postings.next()
        elif term1doc < term2doc:
            term1doc = term1postings.next()
        else:
            term2doc = term2postings.next()

    return matches
```

With two terms' postings, primes an iterator for each

Loops until one iterator is exhausted

If both iterators point at the same document, this is a match.

Otherwise, increments one of the iterators

All you're doing here is iterating through both postings simultaneously, by starting at the beginning document in both lists and iteratively incrementing whichever list points to the lowest-value document ID. Whenever the document IDs in both lists are the same, then that document ID is added to a working list of matches. The algorithm stops and returns the matches when the end of either list is reached.

Extending from AND to other Boolean operations is straightforward. For OR searches, rather than finding the intersection of the postings, you must return the union of all the documents in both lists. For the NOT operation, you take a list of matches and compute every document ID *between* the document IDs in the provided lists (as the postings lists are conveniently sorted, this computation turns out to be rather simple).

Boolean search can be easily extended to perform complex, compound Boolean queries and queries over several fields. You don't have to do anything special to get this functionality. In the case of the compound queries, notice that the input arguments and the output of the AND function of Listing 2.7 are all lists of document IDs, and the same thing is true for the OR and NOT operators. Because of this, Boolean functions can be composed together to make arbitrarily complex queries. Extending to multifield queries is also easy, because no matter which field the term resides in, the postings refer to the same documents using the same IDs, so postings from any fields and any term can be used together in the preceding algorithm.

2.4.2   *Boolean queries in Lucene-based search (MUST/MUST_NOT/SHOULD)*

Lucene has a query type named `BooleanQuery` that's used to achieve the behavior described previously. But the name is a bit misleading, and the behavior is not quite what you'd expect. You'd expect `BooleanQuery` to use the AND, OR, and NOT operators—but it doesn't! Instead, three clauses provide similar functionality, albeit with slightly different semantics: SHOULD, MUST, and MUST_NOT.

- A clause of type MUST has to have a match inside a document; otherwise, the document isn't considered a match.
- A clause of type SHOULD might or might not have a match in a given document, but documents that do have SHOULD clause matches are ranked higher than those that don't.
- Any document that contains a match for a MUST_NOT clause won't be considered a match for the search results even if it does match a MUST or a SHOULD clause.

A `BooleanQuery` can have any number of SHOULD, MUST, and MUST_NOT clauses. But if a query doesn't have a MUST clause, a document is considered a match only if one or more of the SHOULD clauses match.

Before we look at an example let's talk about the Lucene query syntax and how the `BooleanQuery` is represented. Elasticsearch and Solr use this syntax to provide query debug information, and we refer to this debug information throughout the book. In Lucene query syntax, the MUST and MUST_NOT queries are preceded by a prefix. The MUST clause is preceded by a +, and the MUST_NOT clause is preceded by a -. The SHOULD clause isn't prefixed. Consider a simple query and a set of documents:

Query:

```
black +cat -dog
```

Documents:

```
(a) my cat ran under the couch
(b) black cats are mysterious
(c) the dog scared the black cat
```

This query is looking for any documents that MUST contain `cat`, SHOULD contain `black`, and MUST_NOT contain `dog`. Therefore, both document (a) and (b) are matches because they contain the required term `cat`. Of these two documents, (b) will rank more highly than (a) because it contains the nonrequired term `black`. Even though document (c) contains both `black` and `cat`, it isn't considered a match because it contains the disallowed term `dog`.

Lucene clauses may be grouped together using parentheses. Here's a basic compound query:

```
+(cat dog) black
```

This MUST clause is a compound that contains cat and dog as SHOULD clauses. Either cat or dog must be present in the document for it to be a match. Because black is a SHOULD clause (because it has no prefix), a document matching black will be ranked higher in search results.

You might still be wondering why Lucene uses these strange clauses rather than the standard Boolean AND, OR, and NOT operators. The Lucene clauses have more "fuzzy" semantics that are appropriate for search, whereas the standard Boolean operators are used to imply strict set inclusion or exclusion. Consider again our first query example: black +cat -dog. How would you represent this simple query with AND, OR, and NOT? The answer is this rather convoluted Boolean query:

```
(cat OR (black AND cat)) AND NOT dog
```

As you can see, Lucene's more simple syntax has its advantages! It often helps users to be more concise. We'll revisit how Lucene ranks results given these queries in subsequent sections.

2.4.3 *Positional and phrase matching*

The relative positioning of words often carries important semantic value. For instance, a search for "dress shoes" should return men's leather shoes in the colors black or brown. If a search engine doesn't take term positions into account, then instead of dress shoes, we might find our search results filled with women's dresses and tennis shoes—certainly not what the user is expecting!

Because of this, Lucene has a *phrase query* that takes term positions into account. In Lucene query syntax, phrase queries are represented with quotations; for instance, "dress shoes". To find such a phrase, the search engine goes through two phases:

- Find all documents that match every phrase term (dress and shoes)
- Remove documents in which the terms aren't adjacent (remove "this *dress* looks good with your *shoes*" and keep "buy these handsome *dress shoes*")

The output of a phrase query is a list of document IDs; therefore, a phrase query is compatible with Lucene Boolean queries. Phrase queries depend on term positions (refer to table 2.1). Including positions with the inverted index is the default in both Elasticsearch and Solr.

Various settings, such as *phrase slop*, allow you to relax the strict phrase query positioning requirements. Further, it's worth noting that Lucene has a library of queries known as *span queries* that allow you to even more tightly control term ordering and positioning. We don't cover these advanced positional queries in this book. Nevertheless it's worth pointing them out should your search needs require this level of sophistication.

2.4.4   *Enabling exploration: filtering, facets, and aggregations*

When searching through tons of documents, it's often useful to filter the collection until you arrive at a more manageable working set of documents. If you're looking to purchase a Nikon digital camera on Amazon, you don't need to see products outside of electronics. Furthermore, you probably have a price range in mind. If you're an amateur photographer, you're probably not interested in the $6,000 Nikon D4S. Filtering in this manner is made possible by the search engine's capability to quickly match documents as presented in the previous sections. But there's an important distinction, in that Amazon-style filtering is typically done on low-cardinality fields (such as the department field) or on ranges of numerical or date fields (for instance, price field).

As discussed earlier, facets give users a top-down view of the search results. Facets, like those shown in figure 2.9, are usually presented as a list of filterable attributes alongside the number of results with each attribute. An interface that facilitates user exploration in this manner can help your users to quickly understand the collections and narrow down to the items most relevant to their needs. Thus facets serve as a sort of relevance feedback to users.

Lucene's data structures are amenable to complex, multilayered filtering, grouping, and aggregation, but facets expose only a small fraction of this power. Fortunately,

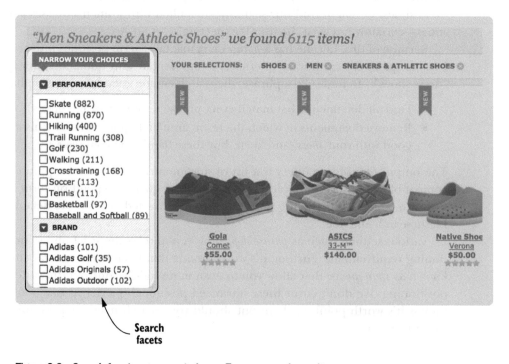

Figure 2.9   Search facets as presented on a Zappos search results page

Elasticsearch has *aggregations*, which allow users to perform powerful online analytical processing (OLAP) by filtering data according to certain field values, grouping on other fields' values, and finally aggregating data (sum, mean, count, min, max, and so forth) across other fields' values. Although aggregations typically require advanced users, they provide unprecedented power in search for slicing, dicing, and summarizing a set of documents.

2.4.5 Sorting, ranked results, and relevance

Like many other data stores, search engines allow documents to be retrieved with a specified sorting. The order can be based on the numerical value of a floating-point or integer field or on the lexicographical order of a string field. Additionally, sorting order can be specified by a function in which one or more field values can be used to calculate a numerical value by which documents should be sorted.

But in typical usage of search, sorting *isn't* specified. Instead, documents matching a search are returned in the order of most-to-least relevant. Throughout this chapter, we have made several references to the idea of *relevance* and how various search features can be used to improve it. Recall that in information retrieval, relevance measures how well search results satisfy a user's information need. In this book, we adopt a broader notion. In light of this, relevant search results must not only meet the user's information needs but also satisfy the business needs by, for instance, promoting high-margin products. The needs of the user and the business are sometimes at odds, and finding the appropriate balance can be challenging.

Let's make this abstract concept a bit more concrete. Relevance is specified by a *ranking function*. The ranking function takes in information from a query and from each matching document. And for each document, the ranking function computes a *score* representing how well the document matches the query. The ranking function can be complicated; chapters 5–7 teach you how to modify the ranking function. For now, let's consider a movie search example. For the sake of simplicity, our movie documents have three fields: title, description, (both text fields), and popularity (a numerical field). Our query is this: "back to the future."

Before any documents are ranked, we must first identify documents that match. This is done by analyzing the query in the same manner that documents are analyzed (see section 2.3.3), pulling out tokens, and finding matching documents roughly as described in section 2.4.1. Documents may also be filtered by some user-defined criteria as mentioned earlier.

With matching documents in hand, we then score them using the ranking function. As represented in figure 2.10, the ranking function takes on a hierarchical structure.

At its deepest layer, the ranking function calculates a score based on how often a particular query term occurs in a particular field (the *term frequency* in that field). This score is then multiplied by a factor based on how common the term is (its *doc frequency* in the collection) and how many terms the field contains. This multiplier is larger for

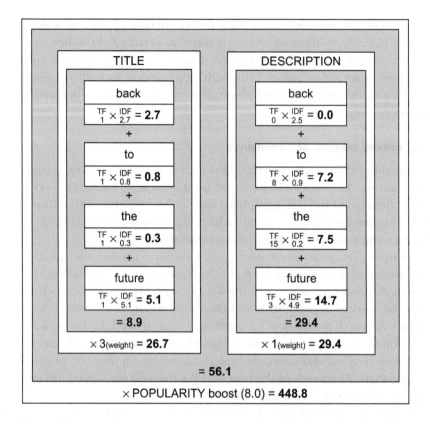

Figure 2.10 Example document-scoring function (simplified)

rare words and small fields. So for our "back to the future" example, any document that talks about the `future` in the description field will have a higher score by virtue of the number of times `future` is mentioned and also because of the relative rarity of the term `future` in the corpus. In contrast, documents containing the term `the` will get a small boost because `the` is such a common term.

At the next level up in the ranking function, term scores within a field are combined. Typically, the terms are part of a SHOULD clause in a Lucene `BooleanQuery`. All the terms don't have to be present for the document to match, but the more terms that are present, the higher the document will score. So in our example, a document that contains the terms `back` and `future` will be scored higher than a document containing only one of those terms. The intuitive scoring of the SHOULD clause is another reason that Lucene uses MUST, SHOULD, and MUST_NOT operators rather than the more standard AND, OR, NOT Boolean operators.

A query is typically structured so that several fields are searched at once. As a relevance engineer, you can apply numerical *boosts* to the fields to indicate how important you feel each field should be. For instance, you might index the title field twice: once with a standard analysis, and another time to incorporate common misspellings. In this case, a match on the non-misspelled fields should be weighted much more highly than the field with misspellings. The scores across all fields are then combined either by summing them or taking the value of the highest-scoring field.

Finally, the relevance engineer may choose to apply an additional multiplicative or additive boost based on the numerical value of a field or the numerical value of a function that itself uses values from one or more fields. This is where the "business logic" of search often comes into play. In our example movie search, it's probably advantageous to boost more-popular movies because they tend to sell better than older movies. Therefore, you can declare the final score to be the score across all fields (last paragraph) multiplied by whatever value is in the popularity field. Or, if this is too powerful of a boost, you can craft a function that more subtly boosts the final score by popularity (for instance, you can take the logarithm of the popularity field).

As a relevance engineer, you have the freedom to program the ranking function to accomplish any goal! Throughout this book, we reveal all the details you need to confidently shape the ranking function into whatever it needs to be to best suit your users' and business's needs. In chapter 3, we break this scoring down, linking Elasticsearch's debug output to the theoretical foundation for relevance scoring. Chapters 5–7 detail techniques for manipulating the ranking function to achieve relevance goals.

2.5   *Summary*

- Search engines allow you to index documents, enabling users to search and explore content through features such as highlights or facets.
- The inverted index is the mechanical heart of the search engine.
- Additional data structures and statistics support the inverted index in enabling users to match and explore content.
- The inverted index is dumb and respects only exact byte-for-byte term matches when searched.
- Analysis allows you to normalize tokens to common representations, to overcome the basic matching ability of the inverted index by using character filters, a tokenizer, and token filters.
- Analysis enables you to express important features of your search as tokens.
- Boolean search is a rather basic application of the inverted index data structure.
- Relevance results are controlled by a ranking function and based on numerous statistics such as term frequency and document frequency.
- You have the ultimate power to control matching through analysis (covered in chapter 4) and to control the ranking function (covered in chapters 5–7)!

Debugging your
first relevance problem

3

This chapter covers

- Basic extracting, indexing, and searching content in Elasticsearch
- Troubleshooting searches that don't return expected results
- Debugging the construction of the inverted index
- Troubleshooting relevance bugs
- Solving your first relevance issue

The previous chapter laid out a rather ideal blueprint for Lucene-based search. In this chapter, the search engine has broken down! You'll see what it takes to debug a real, live search engine. What tools are available to gain visibility into the behavior of search engine internals? Why do certain documents match the query, whereas other more relevant documents don't? Why do seemingly irrelevant documents outrank relevant ones?

This chapter introduces you to a beginner's problem. Although the solutions are straightforward, in order to solve them you'll need to master relevance debugging.

You'll use these techniques to solve every relevance problem you face. Just as in math, showing your work can be the most important step.

You'll begin to use our search engine, Elasticsearch, to search over a real data set. As you encounter the common beginner's problem, your focus will be on debugging two primary internal layers key to relevance: *matching* and *ranking*. Armed with renewed insights from the debugging capabilities of the search engine, you can begin to use the search engine to rank and match based on features that you know best describe your content.

Through this chapter, you'll experience a day in the life of the relevance engineer fighting fires (as shown in figure 3.1). You'll troubleshoot why queries and ranking don't match as your users expect, or why odd documents seem to be considered more relevant than others.

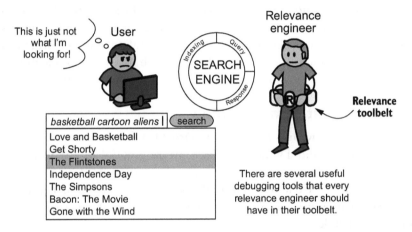

Figure 3.1 As a relevance engineer, you have several tools available for debugging relevance problems.

Before you start exploring what's possible, let's introduce the major building blocks: the search engine, the data set, and the programming environment you'll be using to work through relevance examples.

3.1 *Applications to Solr and Elasticsearch: examples in Elasticsearch*

The preceding chapter introduced the components of a Lucene-based search engine. Which one should we use for examples? Solr? Elasticsearch? Both?

In an effort to "go deep," we chose to develop our examples with just one search engine: Elasticsearch. Covering both search engines in equal depth would get you lost in the weeds as we endlessly compare identical but superficially different configuration details. This is rather uninteresting (shall we say, "irrelevant") information you can easily find with Google.

Luckily, despite superficial differences, Solr and Elasticsearch are very close in functionality. The information you'll learn in this book applies to either. Use this book as you'd use an algorithms book that happens to use C for its examples. We happen to use Elasticsearch. You can easily implement algorithms in any programming language. You can implement the relevance strategies here in either search engine.

If you're a Solr developer, fear not: our basic use of Elasticsearch APIs should feel familiar. We'll give you just enough of an explanation about what's happening with Elasticsearch that even a smidgen of familiarity with either search engine should help you feel at home. Further, in this chapter, as we lay the foundation for several basics, we sprinkle hints for the Solr reader. We also provide appendix B to help map features between the two search engines.

It's also important to note that this book isn't about Elasticsearch. We focus on features related to relevance, completely ignoring other features and concerns when using a search engine: analytics, ingesting your data, scaling, and performance. If you have absolutely no familiarity with Solr or Elasticsearch, there are excellent books and tutorials on both that we encourage you to read before diving into this book.

3.2   *Our most prominent data set: TMDB*

For much of this book, we use *The Movie Database* (TMDB) as our data set. TMDB is a popular online movie and TV-show database. We're grateful to TMDB for giving us permission to use its data set, and encourage you to support the project at http://themoviedb.org. We're excited about TMDB's data, as its content contains several attributes that many search applications must work with. When searching movies, these attributes include:

- Prose text (including overviews, synopsis, and user reviews)
- Shorter text (such as director and actor names, and titles)
- Numerical attributes (user ratings, movie revenue, number of awards)
- Movie release dates and other attributes important in search

In this book, you'll primarily use a prepackaged version of TMDB data. Packaged with the book's GitHub repository (http://github.com/o19s/relevant-search-book) is a file containing a snapshot of TMDB movies used at the time of writing this book. This file, tmdb.json, is a large JSON dictionary. Each entry is a movie with various properties such as title and overview. We recommend using this data, as the results will be consistent with the book's content. We welcome you, however, to use TMDB's data directly. We cover the steps you can take to index an up-to-date version of TMDB's data in appendix A. In this appendix, you'll see in particular how movies are extracted one by one from an external API and further enriched with cast and crew information.

3.3 *Examples programmed in Python*

When examples call for light coding, we use Python, a highly readable, imperative language that looks and feels like pseudocode. You don't need to know Python to follow along (just pretend we're writing pseudocode). We're not doing anything fancy with the language, so these examples should still be easy to follow. We also limit the dependencies (avoiding, for example, even Elasticsearch's excellent client libraries). Instead, it should be assumed that for every piece of Python code, the following imports are included. This code imports requests (an HTTP client library) and Python's JSON standard library:

```
import requests # requests HTTP library
import json # json parsing
```

Note also that we use Elasticsearch at localhost at its default port, 9200, throughout the examples for code readability. Change this as needed to point to your Elasticsearch instance as you work through the examples.

For detailed instructions on how to run the examples or to access the TMDB data, please refer to the book's GitHub repository (http://github.com/o19s/relevant-search-book). This repository contains the full set of examples and data for the book, along with detailed installation instructions in the README file should you need to install Python, Elasticsearch, or any of the required libraries.

3.4 *Your first search application*

To get started, you're going to index a few pieces of text about popular movies into Elasticsearch. In this chapter, we're pretty verbose about what we're doing, commenting carefully as we move forward. To avoid being verbose in future chapters, we wrap each component in a Python function. After you index TMDB data and issue your first search, you'll quickly hit a snag in your relevance that will force you to debug the seemingly mystical and odd behavior of the search engine.

To index movies, first you need to read them in! To access tmdb.json with the movie dictionary, you'll use a function called `extract`. In the following listing, you'll pull back each movie by parsing the JSON file into a Python dictionary.

Listing 3.1 Extract movies from tmdb.json

```
def extract():
    f = open('tmdb.json')
    if f:
        return json.loads(f.read());
```
Parses JSON file into Python dictionary; returns that dictionary

---

What does the returned dictionary look like? It's a mapping of TMDB movie IDs to the movies pulled back from TMDB. A movie has plenty of fields you'd expect to be in a movie. Let's look at an example. Here's a snippet of the movie *Aquamarine* as a Python dictionary.

Listing 3.2   Sample TMDB movie from tmdb.json

```
{
 ...
 "title": "Aquamarine",                                    ◄──────  Title of the
 "tagline": "A Fish-Out-Of-Water Comedy.",                          movie
 "release_date": "2006-03-03",                             ◄─┐
 "popularity": 0.340685029867431,                           │  The movie's
 "original_title": "Aquamarine",                            │  tagline
 "budget": 12000000,
 "cast": [                                    ◄─┐
  {                                             │  List of cast in
    "name": "Emma Roberts",                     │  the movie
    "character": "Claire",
    ...
  }
 ],
 "vote_average": 5.6,
 "runtime": 104
}
```

Now with some interesting data loaded, you'll index these documents into Elastic-search. Elasticsearch has several ways to index documents. You'll predominantly use the *bulk index API* that allows you to efficiently index multiple documents in one HTTP request. Don't worry too deeply about the ins and outs of the bulk index APIs; knowing the indexing APIs in any more depth than what's presented here isn't key for this book. What's crucial for relevance is having an ability to re-create the index with new analysis and index settings. Once it's re-created, you'll need to reprocess documents against the updated settings.

That being said, let's create a function, `reindex`, that you can refer to. The `reindex` function takes settings and the `movieDict` dictionary returned from `extract`, re-creates the Elasticsearch index, and indexes the data into Elasticsearch.

Listing 3.3   Indexing with Elasticsearch's bulk API—`reindex`

```
def reindex(analysisSettings={}, mappingSettings={}, movieDict={}):
    settings = {                                              ◄──  Settings for the index with
        "settings": {                                              provided custom analysis
            "number_of_shards": 1,                                 and field mappings
            "index": {
                    "analysis" : analysisSettings,        ◄──┐
            }}}                                              │  Elasticsearch's settings
                                                             │  for how fields should
    if mappingSettings:                                      │  be analyzed (covered in
        settings['mappings'] = mappingSettings    ◄──────────┘  future chapters)

    resp = requests.delete("http://localhost:9200/tmdb")   ◄─┐
    resp = requests.put("http://localhost:9200/tmdb",         │  Deletes/re-creates
                    data=json.dumps(settings))                ❷  TMDB index with
                                                                 new settings
```

Disables sharding to remove effects on global term statistics ❶

```
bulkMovies = ""
for id, movie in movieDict.iteritems():
    addCmd = {"index": {"_index": "tmdb",          ❸  Bulk-index each
                        "_type": "movie",               movie in the passed-
                        "_id": movie["id"]}}            in movieDict as is
    bulkMovies += json.dumps(addCmd) + "\n" + json.dumps(movie) + "\n"
resp = requests.post("http://localhost:9200/_bulk", data=bulkMovies)
```

In `reindex`, you first interact with Elasticsearch by re-creating a `tmdb` index for your data ❷ with passed-in settings. Creating an index is synonymous with creating a database in a relational database system. The index will contain your documents and other pieces of search configuration for `tmdb` content. You'll work with the `/tmdb` Elasticsearch HTTP endpoint when working with the `tmdb` index as a whole.

You may notice the shards setting passed in ❶. As you may recall from chapter 2, a term's document frequency is an important component of results ranking. Document frequency counts the number of times a term occurs across the entire index. In distributed search engines, where the index is physically subdivided into shards, document frequency is stored per shard. This can cause results ranking to appear to be broken for smaller test document sets. For larger document sets, the impacts of sharding usually average out. For the repeatability of our testing, we'll disable sharding.

Starting at ❸, you start to use the bulk index API. You begin to build up a string of bulk index commands to Elasticsearch. The `addCmd` here tells Elasticsearch that you're *indexing* the document. You tell Elasticsearch some metadata about each document, including where it should be stored (`_index: tmdb`), its type (`_type: movie`), and its unique ID (taken from TMDB's id). On the subsequent line, you append the document to be indexed. On the next line, you append the command and document to the `bulkMovies` string for indexing. You repeat this process for every movie in `movieDict`. Finally, after building the full bulk command, you `POST` the large `bulkMovies` string to Elasticsearch's `/_bulk` endpoint.

With all the pieces, you can finally index the movies. Combining `extract` and `reindex`, you can pull data into Elasticsearch in the following listing.

> **Listing 3.4 Pulling data from TMDB into Elasticsearch**

```
movieDict = extract()
reindex(movieDict=movieDict)
```

Congratulations! You've built your first ETL (extract, transform, load) pipeline. Here you've done the following:

- Extracted information from an external system
- Transformed the data into a form amenable to the search engine
- Indexed the data into Elasticsearch

Further, by telling Elasticsearch via the commands in `reindex` about a new index (`_index: tmdb`) and about a new type (`_type: movie`), you've created both an index (not an SQL database) and a type of document (not an SQL table). In the future, when you want to search or interact with the tmdb index, you'll reference tmdb/ movie/ or tmdb/ in the path of the Elasticsearch URL.

3.4.1 *Your first searches of the TMDB Elasticsearch index*

Now you can search! For this movie application, you need to figure out how to respond to user searches from your application's search bar. To do this, you'll use Elasticsearch's Query domain-specific language (DSL), or Query DSL.

The Query DSL tells Elasticsearch how to execute a search using a JSON format. Here you specify factors such as required clauses, clauses that shouldn't be included, boosts, field weights, scoring functions, and other factors that control matching and ranking. The Query DSL can be thought of as the search engine's SQL, a query language focused on ranked retrieval of flat, denormalized documents.

Being a fairly new relevance engineer, you'll start with a basic application of Elasticsearch's multi_match query. This is Elasticsearch's Swiss Army knife for constructing queries across multiple fields. Because most search problems involve searching multiple fields, it's where many start with a relevance solution. A common initial pass at a search relevance solution is to attempt to construct a multi_match query that lists the fields to be searched along with a few boosts (specified with the ^ symbol). *Boosting* is the act of adding or multiplying to a relevance score with a constant factor, query, or function. In this case, boosting is simple; you boost the title score by the constant 10 in an effort to tell the search engine about the relative importance of the field.

Let's implement a search function that lets you search with passed-in Query DSL queries. search is a fairly straightforward function that passes a query and prints the search results in order of relevance, as shown in the following listing.

Listing 3.5 The search function

```
def search(query):
    url = 'http://localhost:9200/tmdb/movie/_search'
    httpResp = requests.get(url, data=json.dumps(query))
    searchHits = json.loads(httpResp.text)['hits']
    print "Num\tRelevance Score\t\tMovie Title"
    for idx, hit in enumerate(searchHits['hits']):
        print "%s\t%s\t\t%s" %
(idx + 1, hit['_score'], hit['_source']['title'])
```

Runs the provided search using the Query DSL passed in query

Prints the search results

What do Query DSL queries look like that you pass to search? In listing 3.6, you construct a Query DSL search using multi_match. You attempt to tell Elasticsearch that a title field is 10 times more important than the overview field when ranking ❶. Through this chapter, you'll assess whether this attempt is working out.

HINT FOR SOLR READERS Instead of multi_match, Solr encourages you to start with the "dismax" family of query parsers. A starting query for the Solr user might be: http://localhost:8983/solr/tmdb/select?q=basketball with cartoon aliens&defType=edismax&qf=title^10 overview. Note that while this is the common starting point, this query works somewhat differently than Elasticsearch's multi_match query parser. See chapter 6 and appendix B for more details.

Here's your first "hello world" search using the Query DSL.

Listing 3.6 Your first search

```
usersSearch = 'basketball with cartoon aliens'
query = {
    "query": {
        "multi_match": {
            "query": usersSearch,
            "fields": ["title^10", "overview"],
        }
    }
}
search(query)
```

The user's search terms ←

① Boosts "title" to 10 times as important as "overview".

Output:

```
Num  Relevance Score      Movie Title
1    0.8424165            Aliens
2    0.5603433            The Basketball Diaries
3    0.52651036           Cowboys & Aliens
4    0.42120826           Aliens vs Predator: Requiem
5    0.42120826           Aliens in the Attic
6    0.42120826           Monsters vs Aliens
7    0.262869             Dances with Wolves
8    0.262869             Interview with the Vampire
9    0.262869             From Russia with Love
10   0.262869             Gone with the Wind
11   0.262869             Fire with Fire
```

Oh, no—these search results aren't good! You can infer from the query "basketball with cartoon aliens" that the user is likely searching for *Space Jam*—a movie about the *Looney Tunes* characters facing off against space aliens in a game of basketball with the help of Michael Jordan. It seems that the user doesn't know the name of the movie and is attempting to grope around for it with a descriptive query—a common use case. Unfortunately, most of the top movies listed seem to be about basketball or aliens, but not both. Other movies seem to be completely unrelated to basketball or aliens, and we're completely missing the mark. Where's *Space Jam*? If you request additional results from Elasticsearch, you finally see your result:

```
43   0.016977157          Space Jam
```

Why were seemingly irrelevant movies considered valuable by the search engine? How can you diagnose the problem and begin to seek solutions? Your day as a relevance engineer will be spent trying to diagnose the odd results returned by the search engine. You need to answer two main questions:

- Why did certain documents *match* query terms? Why did a movie such as *Fire with Fire* even match your query?
- Why did less relevant documents *rank* as highly as they did? Why is *The Basketball Diaries* ranked higher than our target *Space Jam*?

You'll want to be able to understand the problem fast. Time is ticking, and users aren't having a good search experience.

3.5   *Debugging query matching*

What could be happening in this failed search for "basketball with cartoon aliens"? The first, and most foundational, way to begin looking for answers is by debugging the query's term-*matching* behavior. In your work, you'll often find cases where a relevant document that should match doesn't. Conversely, you might be surprised when low-value or spurious terms match, adding an irrelevant document to the results. Even within the documents retrieved, matching or not matching a term might influence relevance ranking—unexpectedly causing poor results to be ranked highly because of spurious matches or ranked low because of unexpected misses. You need to be able to take apart this process with Elasticsearch's analysis and query validation debugging tools.

First, we'll remind you of what we mean by *matching*. Recall from chapter 2 that declaring a term a match in the inverted index is a strict, exact binary equivalence. Search engines don't have the intelligence to know that "Aliens" and "alien" refer to the same idea. Or that "extraterrestrial" refers to almost the same idea. English-speaking humans understand that these mentions should be counted as signifiers of the idea of *alien*; or, as we've discussed, an indicator of the feature of "alien-ness" present in the text. But to the unintelligent search engine, these two tokens exist as distinct UTF-8 binary strings. The two strings, 0x41,0x6c,0x69,0x65,0x6e,0x73 (Aliens) and 0x61,0x6c,0x69,0x65,0x6e (alien), aren't at all the same and don't match.

This exacting matching behavior points to two areas to take apart:

- *Query parsing*—How your Query DSL query translates into a matching strategy of specific terms to fields
- *Analysis*—The process of creating tokens from the query and document text

By understanding query parsing, you can see exactly how your Query DSL query uses Lucene's data structures to satisfy searches against different fields. Through analysis, you can massage, interrogate, pry, and prod text with hope that the text's true "alien-ness" can be boiled down to a single term. You can further identify meaningless terms, such as the that might match but represent no important feature, creating spurious matches on low-value terms.

Only after you understand how the underlying data structures are created and accessed can you hope to take control of the process. Let's walk through your search and see whether a matching problem is inadvertently including spurious matches such as *Fire with Fire*.

3.5.1 Examining the underlying query strategy

The first thing you'll do to inspect matching behavior is ask Elasticsearch to explain how the query was parsed. This will decompose your search query into an alternate description that more closely describes the underlying interaction with Lucene's data structures. To do this, you'll use Elasticsearch's query validation endpoint. This endpoint, shown in the next listing, takes as an argument a Query DSL query and returns a low-level explanation of the strategy used to satisfy the query.

> **HINT FOR SOLR READERS** Set the parameter debugQuery=true on your Solr query to get equivalent query parsing debug information. See your Solr response's parsedquery for what's equivalent to Elasticsearch's query validation endpoint output.

Listing 3.7 Explaining the behavior of your query

```
query = {
    "query": {
        "multi_match": {
            "query": usersSearch,
            "fields": ["title^10", "overview"]
        }
    }
}
httpResp = requests.get('http://localhost:9200' +          ← Issue validation
                        '/tmdb/movie/_validate/query?explain',    request to
                        data=json.dumps(query))                   validate API
print json.loads(httpResp.text)
```

Response:

```
{u'_shards': {u'failed': 0, u'successful': 1, u'total': 1},
 u'explanations': [
{u'explanation':
u'filtered(((((title:basketball title:with          ← How query is
  title:cartoon title:aliens)^10.0) |                  executed in
  (overview:basketball overview:with                   Lucene query
    overview:cartoon overview:aliens)))->cache(_type:movie)',   syntax
    u'index': u'tmdb',
    u'valid': True}],
 u'valid': True}
```

Here the returned explanation field (in bold) lists what you're interested in. Your query is translated into a more precise syntax that gives deeper information about how Lucene will work with your Elasticsearch query:

```
((title:basketball title:with title:cartoon title:aliens)^10.0) |
  (overview:basketball overview:with overview:cartoon overview:aliens)
```

3.5.2   *Taking apart query parsing*

The query validation endpoint has returned an alternative representation of your Query DSL query to help debug your matching issues. Let's examine this alternative syntax; we introduced the basics of this syntax in chapter 2. The query validation output is reminiscent of *Lucene query syntax*[1]—a low-level, precise way of specifying a search. Because of the additional precision, Lucene query syntax describes the requirements of a relevant document a bit more closely to how Lucene itself will perform the search using the inverted index.

As we discussed in chapter 2, Lucene queries are composed of the Boolean clauses MUST(+), SHOULD, and MUST_NOT(-). Each one specifies a field to search in the underlying document, and each takes the form `[+/-]<fieldName>:<query>`. To debug matching, the most important part of the clause is the component that specifies the match itself: `<fieldName>:<query>`. If you examine one of the preceding clauses, such as `title:basketball`, you can see that you're asking the `title` field to look for the specific term `basketball`. Each clause is a simple *term query*, a single term lookup in the inverted index. Besides the term query, the most prominent queries you'll encounter are *phrase queries*. We discussed these also in chapter 2. In Lucene query syntax, these are specified by using quotes, as in `title:"space jam"` to indicate that the terms should be adjacent.

In our example, as you move one layer out from each match, you can see Lucene's query strategy. Although you're currently focused on matching, this encompasses more than that. Above the innermost matches, you see four SHOULD clauses scored together (grouped with parentheses):

```
(title:basketball title:with title:cartoon title:aliens)
```

Boosted by a factor of 10 (as we've requested when searching), you have the following:

```
(title:basketball title:with title:cartoon title:aliens)^10
```

Compared to another query, with a maximum score taken (| symbol), you have this:

```
((title:basketball title:with title:cartoon title:aliens)^10.0) |
(overview:basketball overview:with overview:cartoon overview:aliens)
```

We present other pieces of this pseudo-Lucene query syntax as you move through the book.

It seems odd that a lot of surprising scoring mumbo-jumbo is already happening. You'll debug scoring in greater depth later in this chapter; for now what matters is using the term query information to answer why spurious matches such as *Dances with Wolves* or *Fire with Fire* are even considered matches.

---

[1]   In reality, the representation depends on each Lucene query's Java `toString` method, which attempts (but doesn't always accurately reflect) strict Lucene query syntax.

3.5.3   *Debugging analysis to solve matching issues*

Now that you know which terms are being searched for, the next step to debugging matching is to see how documents are decomposed into terms and placed in the index. After all, your searches will fail if the terms you're searching for don't exist in the index. We gave an example of this previously. Searches for the term Aliens won't match the term alien regardless of our intuition. Further, term searches might result in spurious matches that don't signify anything valuable. For example, matching on the in isolation is spurious for English. It signifies no important feature latent in the text to our user's English-language-trained minds.

Despite our intuitive notion of how a document should be decomposed into terms, the mechanics of analysis often surprise us. It's a process you'll need to debug often. You already know how these terms are extracted: through index-time analysis. *Analyzers* are the entities that define the analysis process. They contain the components discussed in chapter 2: character filters, a tokenizer, and token filters. In Elasticsearch, the analyzer used can be specified at many levels, including for the index (all of TMDB), a node (a running instance of Elasticsearch), a type (all movies), a field, or even at query time for a particular query. You have yet to specify an analyzer, so the default *standard* analyzer is used. You can use this knowledge along with Elasticsearch's useful *analyze* endpoint to view how text from your documents was transformed into the tokens that will form the inverted index.

Perhaps if you see how the analysis for the title *Fire with Fire* translates to the inverted index, you might see the terms that match your query. Then you might see why this seemingly random, irrelevant movie is included in the results.

> **HINT FOR SOLR READERS**   While there's a similar API in Solr, Solr comes with a tremendous admin UI that includes a debugging tool for analyzers. In the Admin UI select your core and "analyzers" to perform similar debugging.

Listing 3.8   Debugging analysis

```
resp = requests.get('http://localhost:9200/tmdb/_analyze' \
                '?analyzer=standard&format=yaml',
                data="Fire with Fire")
print resp.text
```

> **Requests analysis of the string "Fire with Fire" using the standard analyzer**

The result (in prettier YAML) is as follows:

```
tokens:
- token: "fire"
  start_offset: 0
  end_offset: 4
  type: "<ALPHANUM>"
```

> **An entry in the token stream, showing the extracted properties of a token.**

> **Start/end offsets indicate where the token exists in the source text.**

```
  position: 1
- token: "with"
  start_offset: 5
  end_offset: 9
  type: "<ALPHANUM>"
  position: 2
- token: "fire"
  start_offset: 10
  end_offset: 14
  type: "<ALPHANUM>"
  position: 3
```

Position indicates term ordering, distance, and adjacency.

This output shows you important properties of each token extracted from the snippet *Fire with Fire* by the standard analyzer. This list of tokens resulting from analysis is known as the *token stream*. In this token stream, you extract three tokens: fire, with, and fire. Notice how the text has been tokenized by whitespace and lowercased? Further notice how more attributes than just the token text are included. Notice the offset values, indicating the exact character position of each term in the source text, and position, indicating the position of the token in the stream.

After analysis, the token stream is indexed and placed into the inverted index. For debugging and illustration purposes, you can represent the inverted index in a simple data structure known as SimpleText[2]—an index storage format created by Mike McCandless purely for educational purposes. You'll use this layout to think through the structure of the inverted index.

Let's take a second to reflect on how the preceding token stream is translated to a SimpleText representation of an index, focused just on the term fire.

Listing 3.9 SimpleText index representation for the term fire

```
field title
  term fire
    doc 0
      freq 2
      position 1
      position 3
    doc 2
      ...
```

Indicates doc 0 contains the term "fire"

The search engine's goal when indexing is to consume the token stream into the inverted index, placing documents under their appropriate terms. After counting the number of occurrences of a particular token (in this case, two instances of fire), indexing adds entries to the postings list for the term fire. Under fire, you add your document, doc 0 ❶. You further store the number of occurrences of fire in doc 0 as freq and record where it occurred through each position entry. With all the tokens

---

[2] You can read more about SimpleText in Mike McCandless's blog post: http://blog.mikemccandless.com/2010/10/lucenes-simpletext-codec.html.

taken together, this document is added to the postings for two terms, `fire` and `with`, as shown in the following listing.

Listing 3.10 View of title index with *Fire with Fire* terms highlighted

```
field title
  term fire
    doc 0            ◁        "Fire with Fire" under
      freq 2                  "title:fire" posting
      position 1
      position 3
    doc 2
      ...
  term with                   "Fire with Fire" under
    doc 0            ◁        "title:with" posting
      freq 1
      position 2

  ...
```

As we've discussed, data structures other than the inverted index consume this token stream. Numerous features can be enabled in Lucene. For our purposes, you should consider data structures that consume this token stream to provide other forms of global-term statistics such as the document frequency. In this case, the document frequency of `fire` will increase by one, reflecting the new document.

It's important to note that you can deeply control this process. Typically, analysis is controlled on a field-by-field basis. You'll see how to define your own analyzers for your fields, using the components discussed in chapter 2: character filters, tokenizers, and token filters. But first, armed with what you know about the query and the terms in the index, you need to examine why a spurious result like *Fire with Fire* would even match in the first place.

3.5.4 *Comparing your query to the inverted index*

You're now prepared to compare your parsed query with the context of the inverted index. If you compare the parsed query

```
((title:basketball title:with title:cartoon title:aliens)^10.0) |
(overview:basketball overview:with overview:cartoon overview:aliens)
```

against the inverted index snippet from the token stream for *Fire with Fire, you* see exactly where the match occurs:

```
field title
  term fire
    doc 0
      freq 2
      position 1
      position 3
    doc 2
    ... (more docs)
```

```
term with
    doc 0.
        freq 1
        position 2
        ...
```

⊲———⌐ **"with" given equal
            prominence to "fire"
            in postings list**

The clause `title:with` pulls in doc 0, *Fire with Fire*, from the inverted index. Recalling how term matches work, you can start to understand the mechanics here. Our document is listed under `with` in the index. Therefore, it's included in the search results along with other matches for `with`. As we discussed in the previous chapter, this is an entirely mechanical process. Of course, to English speakers, a match on `with` isn't helpful and will leave them scratching their heads about why such a noisy word was considered important in matching.

Other spurious movies seem to fall into this category. Movies like *Dances with Wolves* or *From Russia with Love* get slurped up into the search results just as easily as documents that match more important terms like `basketball` or `aliens`. Without help, the search engine can't discriminate between meaningful, valid, and important English terms and those that are noise and low value.

3.5.5   *Fixing our matching by changing analyzers*

This matching problem luckily has a straightforward fix. We've teased Elasticsearch for not knowing much about English. In actuality, Elasticsearch has an analyzer that handles English text fairly well. It strings together character filters, a tokenizer, and token filters to normalize English to standard word forms. It can stem English terms to root forms (`running -> run`), and remove noise terms such as `the`, known as *stop words.* Lucky for us, `with` is one such stop word. Removing it from the index could solve our problem.

How do you do use this analyzer? Simple: you need to assign a different analyzer to the fields. Because modifications to index-time analysis alter the structure of the inverted index, you'll have to reindex your documents. To customize the analysis, you'll re-create your index and rerun the previous indexing code. The main difference is at ❶ in the following listing; you'll explicitly configure the field with the English analyzer before creating the index.

> **HINT FOR SOLR READER**   Solr's schema.xml specifies the configuration of Solr's fields. The analyzer used by a field is controlled by the analyzer associated with a field's `fieldType`. Out of the box, Solr's schema.xml defines a number of field types, including `text_en` which is appropriate for English text. Changing analyzers and field settings requires reindexing in Solr just as in Elasticsearch.

Listing 3.11   Reindexing with the English analyzer

```
mappingSettings = {
    "movie": {
        "properties": {
```

```
            "title": {
                "type": "string",
                "analyzer": "english"
            },
        "overview": {
                "type": "string",
                "analyzer": "english"
            }
        }
    }
}
movieDict = extract()
reindex(mappingSettings=mappingSettings, movieDict=movieDict)
```

① Modifies fields "title" and "overview" to use the English analyzer

Reindexes with new field mappings

Great! Did it work? Let's reanalyze *Fire with Fire* to see the results:

```
resp = requests.get('http://localhost:9200/tmdb/
    _analyze?field=title&format=yaml',
                data="Fire with Fire")
```

Response:

```
tokens:
- token: "fire"
  start_offset: 0
  end_offset: 4
  type: "<ALPHANUM>"
  position: 1
- token: "fire"
  start_offset: 10
  end_offset: 14
  type: "<ALPHANUM>"
  position: 3
```

"with" token no longer in the token stream

Position of second "fire" term unchanged

Notice the removal of with in this token stream. Particularly, notice the gap between positions 1 and 3. Elasticsearch is reflecting the removal of the token by this position gap to avoid spurious phrase matches. Rerunning the query validation also shows a removal of with from the query:

```
{u'_shards': {u'failed': 0, u'successful': 1, u'total': 1},
 u'explanations':
    [{u'explanation':
        u'filtered(((((title:basketbal  title:cartoon title:alien)^10.0) |
                    (overview:basketbal overview:cartoon overview:alien)))
                ->cache(_type:movie)',
    u'index': u'tmdb',
    u'valid': True}],
 u'valid': True}
```

The new query strategy. Note "basketball" is now stemmed to "basketbal" due to rules for stemming English.

And indeed, the matches become much closer to what you want. At least you're in the range of aliens. Further, because of more sophisticated analysis, stemming, and token normalization, you're picking up other matches of alien that were missing.

```
Num   Relevance Score      Movie Title
1     1.0643067            Alien
2     1.0643067            Aliens
3     1.0643067            Alien³
4     1.0254613            The Basketball Diaries
5     0.66519165           Cowboys & Aliens
6     0.66519165           Aliens in the Attic
7     0.66519165           Alien: Resurrection
8     0.53215337           Aliens vs Predator: Requiem
9     0.53215337           AVP: Alien vs. Predator
10    0.53215337           Monsters vs Aliens
11    0.08334568           Space Jam
```

Congratulations! By turning on the English analyzer, you've made a significant leap forward. Your target has moved up to #11. You've achieved a saner mapping of text that corresponds to the text's "alien-ness" feature through simple English-focused analysis. You've also eliminated text that shouldn't be thought of as corresponding to any feature of the text: stop words.

In future chapters, you'll explore more use cases that shape the representation of tokens even deeper than what you've done here. Because terms are analogues to textual features, the translation of text into tokens is often deeply customized per domain. For now, you need to switch gears to debug the next layer in the search equation: relevance ranking.

3.6   *Debugging ranking*

After resolving your matching issue, you're still left wondering why movies like *Alien, Aliens,* and *Basketball Diaries* rank above *Space Jam.* None of these movies have basketball-playing aliens. Our user is still left disappointed with the search. With results like these, the user is likely growing increasingly frustrated with the search application. You have to find a way to take apart the relevance ranking such that it more accurately aligns to your user's information needs. You need to ask Elasticsearch to explain itself. What you'll see is that debugging ranking means understanding the following:

- The calculation of individual match scores
- How these match scores factor into the document's overall relevance score

You saw in chapter 2 that underlying each of these factors is the idea of a *score.* The score is the number assigned by the search engine to a document matching a search. It indicates how relevant the document is to the search (higher score meaning more relevant). Relevance ranking, then, is typically a sort on this number. You'll see through debugging ranking that this score, although informed by a theoretical basis, is entirely in your hands to manipulate, to implement your notions of relevance. In fact, the majority of this book is about the best way to take mastery over this one number!

For matches, you must determine whether match scores accurately reflect your intuitive notion about the strength of the corresponding feature. We discussed that all mentions of `alien` or alien-related text (for example, `Aliens` or `extraterrestrial`) add weight to our notion of the "alien-ness" feature latent in the text. Do you feel that when you match on `alien`, the score for the term `alien` reflects your intuition of the true strength of the text's "alien-ness"? We'll decompose the math that goes into term scoring. Only then can you reflect on whether matches on `alien` or `basketball` really reflect your understanding of the true strength of a movie's true "alien-ness" or "basketball-ness."

You'll also see the mechanics of how other queries compose matches into larger score calculations by boosting, summing, and choosing between component scores. If term matches represent the strength of individual features in text, then these other operations relate the features to one another. Our example specifies a `multi_match` query with default settings, searching `title` with a boost of 10 and `overview` with no boost. How does this translate into a scoring formula? More important, how do you know whether the formula resulting from this query was the right thing to do?

To fix our *Space Jam* query, you'll need to get inside the search engine's head. You'll need to align the mechanical scoring process to reflect your business and user's notion of relevance—both in terms of how terms relate to features and how these feature strengths combine into a larger relevance score.

3.6.1 *Decomposing the relevance score with Lucene's explain feature*

Lucene's *explain* feature lets you decompose the calculation behind the relevance score. Before diving into the explain, let's revisit your initial pass at understanding the query for *Space Jam*. The query validation output helps reveal the scoring strategy that will be used:

```
((title:basketbal title:cartoon title:alien)^10.0) |
 (overview:basketbal overview:cartoon overview:alien)
```

In this query, you seek out `basketbal` (the stemmed form of `basketball`), `cartoon`, and `alien` terms in each field. The title score is boosted by 10. The search engine then chooses between the two fields, by taking the maximum of the field scores (the | symbol).

This is a starting point, but what you need to see isn't the strategy, but the after-action report. You need to see the scoring arithmetic for specific documents.

There are a couple of ways to ask for explain information, but because we often want to see this information in line with each search result, it's convenient to set `explain: true` when issuing the search query. This will return an `_explanation` entry in each search result returned. Let's reissue our search with an explain set so you can reflect on the scoring.

HINT FOR SOLR READER   The Solr parameter &debugQuery=true outputs the same scoring debug information as setting 'explain': True in Elasticsearch. Examine the "explain" section in your Solr's response.

Listing 3.12   Requesting a relevancy scoring explanation

```
query = {                                    Same search      Enables Elasticsearch's
                                             as before        explain feature
    "explain": True,
    "query": {
        "multi_match": {                              User's
            "query": usersSearch,                     query          Fetch _explanation
            "fields": ["title^10", "overview"]                       from first search
        }}}                                                                    result
httpResp = requests.get('http://localhost:9200/tmdb/movie/_search',
                        data=json.dumps(query))
jsonResp = json.loads(httpResp.text)
print "Explain for %s" % jsonResp['hits']['hits'][0]['_source']['title']
print json.dumps(jsonResp['hits']['hits'][0]['_explanation'], indent=True)
```

The full explain is lengthy, so we omit a great deal of the JSON output. It's here only to give a taste. We show the full explain in a more concise form farther down. Without further ado, here's a snippet of the JSON explain for *Alien*:

```
{
 "description": "max of:",
 "value": 1.0643067,
 "details": [
  {
   "description": "product of:",
   "value": 1.0643067,
   "details": [
    {
     "description": "sum of:",
     "value": 3.19292,
     "details": [
      {
       "description": "weight(title:alien in 223)
                       [PerFieldSimilarity], result of:",
       "value": 3.19292,
       "details": [
        {
         "description": "score(doc=223,freq=1.0 = termFreq=1.0\n),
                         product of:",
         "value": 3.19292,
         "details": [
          {
           "description": "queryWeight, product of:",
           "value": 0.4793294,
           "details": [
            {
             "description": "idf(docFreq=9, maxDocs=2875)",
             "value": 6.661223
```

```
        }
<omitted>
}
```

From now on, we'll summarize this explain format more concisely. We can simplify the preceding snippet by collapsing it for a shorter summary shown in the following listing. While this begins to take shape, it's still overwhelming. Don't focus on understanding this now; just scan it. We'll soon show a way to make sense of the madness.

Listing 3.13   Simplified explain for *Alien*

```
1.0646985, max of:
  1.0646985, product of:
    3.1940954, sum of:
      3.1940954, weight(title:alien in 223) [PerFieldSimilarity], result of:
        3.1940954, score(doc=223,freq=1.0 = termFreq=1.0
), product of:
          0.4793558, queryWeight, product of:
            6.6633077, idf(docFreq=9, maxDocs=2881)
            0.07193962, queryNorm
          6.6633077, fieldWeight in 223, product of:
            1.0, tf(freq=1.0), with freq of:
              1.0, termFreq=1.0
            6.6633077, idf(docFreq=9, maxDocs=2881)
            1.0, fieldNorm(doc=223)
    0.33333334, coord(1/3)
  0.053043984, product of:
    0.15913194, sum of:
      0.15913194, weight(overview:alien in 223)
              [PerFieldSimilarity], result of:
        0.15913194, score(doc=223,freq=1.0 = termFreq=1.0
), product of:
          0.033834733, queryWeight, product of:
            4.7032127, idf(docFreq=70, maxDocs=2881)
            0.0071939616, queryNorm
          4.7032127, fieldWeight in 223, product of:
            1.0, tf(freq=1.0), with freq of:
              1.0, termFreq=1.0
            4.7032127, idf(docFreq=70, maxDocs=2881)
            1.0, fieldNorm(doc=223)
    0.33333334, coord(1/3)
```

We'll compare this explanation for *Alien* to the explain for our target result *Space Jam*:

```
0.08334568, max of:
  0.08334568, product of:
    0.12501852, sum of:
      0.08526054, weight(overview:basketbal in 1289)
              [PerFieldSimilarity], result of:
        0.08526054, score(doc=1289,freq=1.0 = termFreq=1.0
), product of:
          0.049538642, queryWeight, product of:
            6.8843665, idf(docFreq=7, maxDocs=2875)
            0.0071958173, queryNorm
```

```
        1.7210916, fieldWeight in 1289, product of:
          1.0, tf(freq=1.0), with freq of:
            1.0, termFreq=1.0
          6.8843665, idf(docFreq=7, maxDocs=2875)
          0.25, fieldNorm(doc=1289)
      0.03975798, weight(overview:alien in 1289)
              [PerFieldSimilarity], result of:
        0.03975798, score(doc=1289,freq=1.0 = termFreq=1.0
), product of:
        0.03382846, queryWeight, product of:
          4.701128, idf(docFreq=70, maxDocs=2875)
          0.0071958173, queryNorm
        1.175282, fieldWeight in 1289, product of:
          1.0, tf(freq=1.0), with freq of:
            1.0, termFreq=1.0
          4.701128, idf(docFreq=70, maxDocs=2875)
          0.25, fieldNorm(doc=1289)
    0.6666667, coord(2/3)
```

At first blush, these explains appear terrifying. The first thing to realize is that the explain is simply a decomposition of the arithmetic behind the relevance score. Each number on the outside is explained by the details nested within. At the outermost explain, you have the document's relevance score. As you move deeper into the details, you can see how that score is calculated with increased granularity.

Eventually, you get to the layer listing the scores for specific matches (title:alien). Under this layer, you describe the components involved in the scoring of a specific match in a field. This match level is a bit of a dividing line in the explain. Inside, a match is scored by directly consulting Lucene's data structures for a term in a field. Outside, scores for matches are combined into a larger formula. You may wish to compare this output to what's presented in figure 2.10, near the end of chapter 2.

If you elide what's inside the explains for each match (looking only at what's "outside" matches), you have an even more concise explain for *Alien*:

```
1.0643067, max of:
  1.0643067, product of:
    3.19292, sum of:
      3.19292, weight(title:alien in 223) [PerFieldSimilarity]
    0.33333334, coord(1/3)
  0.066263296, product of:
    0.19878988, sum of:
      0.19878988, weight(overview:alien in 223) [PerFieldSimilarity
```

What you're left with is a set of operations on the matches themselves. Internally, these operations reflect queries that wrap other queries. These wrapping queries are known as *compound queries*. Compound queries allow us to express how different features represented by the underlying term-match scores relate to each other mathematically. They reflect the query strategy you've already seen:

```
((title:basketbal title:cartoon title:aliens)^10.0) |
 (overview:basketbal overview:cartoon overview:aliens)
```

After combining the matches, they in turn can be combined at arbitrary depth by other compound queries to create even more-complex query scoring and matching. A great deal of relevance engineering is learning how a Query DSL query maps to a set of compound queries.

If you pull back the veil and examine inside a match, you see a different sort of calculation happening. The scoring begins to look more cryptic, filled with deeper search-engine jargon. At this point, you're seeing a more fundamental reflection of the information retrieval intelligence built into the search engine. At this level, you begin to see information about match statistics for a field. These matches are the basic building blocks of the scoring calculation—hopefully, accurately reflecting the strength of a particular latent feature in the text.

```
0.03975798, weight(overview:alien in 1289) [PerFieldSimilarity], result of:
  0.03975798, score(doc=1289,freq=1.0 = termFreq=1.0
), product of:
    0.03382846, queryWeight, product of:
      4.701128, idf(docFreq=70, maxDocs=2875)
      0.0071958173, queryNorm
    1.175282, fieldWeight in 1289, product of:
      1.0, tf(freq=1.0), with freq of:
        1.0, termFreq=1.0
      4.701128, idf(docFreq=70, maxDocs=2875)
      0.25, fieldNorm(doc=1289)
```

Again, you might be terrified! Don't fret. We cover a theoretical backing for these numbers next, and after that, you'll be able to compare matches with ease. You'll be able to determine why some field matches seem to convey more strength than others.

3.6.2 *The vector-space model, the relevance explain, and you*

Much of the Lucene scoring formula derives from information retrieval. But the theoretical influence needs to be tempered mightily. Although the theoretical basis gives you context for solving a problem, in practice, relevance scoring uses theory-inspired heuristics based on applied experience of what works well. In many ways, aside from foundational concepts, relevance scoring is just as much an art as a science. Understanding the science will help you ensure that the search engine correctly measures the weight of features latent in the text, represented by terms.

To information retrieval, a search for multiple terms in a field (such as our over-view:basketbal overview:alien overview:cartoon against *Space Jam*) attempts to approximate a vector comparison between the query and matched document. Vectors? That's sounds like geometry for what seems like a language arts problem. Recall that a *vector* represents a magnitude and a direction in space. A vector is often represented as an arrow, pointing into space from the origin—say, to the Moon from Earth. Numerically, a vector is represented as a value for each dimension. Perhaps the vector <50,20> means "North 50 miles, East 20 miles." *Space* for a vector, however, need not relate to the physical world we move around in. For example, if the x-axis represents a fruit's juiciness, and the y-axis its size, you can define a *vector space* that captures some of the important features of fruitiness. Figure 3.2 shows this vector space.

Figure 3.2   Fruit in a two-dimensional vector space; the x-axis is size, and the y-axis is juiciness. Every fruit measured for size/juiciness can be represented as a vector, with similar fruit clumping together.

Here you see several pieces of fruit represented as vectors in the juiciness/size vector space. Some have a great deal of strength in the juiciness dimension, others in the size direction. You can easily see how similar fruit might clump together. For example, fruits in the upper right are most likely watermelon—very large and very juicy.

You can infer something about the similarity of two pieces of fruit by computing the *dot product* of their two vectors. In the fruit example, this means (1) multiplying the juiciness of each fruit together, (2) multiplying the size, and (3) summing the results. It turns out that the more properties fruit share in common, the higher the dot product.

```
dotprod(fruit1, fruit2) = juiciness(fruit1) x juiciness(fruit2) +
                          size(fruit1) x size(fruit2)
```

What does this have to do with text? To information retrieval, text (queries and documents) can also be represented as vectors. Instead of examining features such as juiciness or size, the dimensions in the text vector space represent words that might appear in the text. What if instead of fruit, you looked at a movie overview's mention of basketball, aliens, or cartoons, as in figure 3.3. Some text is definitely about aliens (for example, the overview for *Alien*), but not basketball nor cartoons. Other text (such as the overview of the Japanese anime film *Slam Dunk*) is about basketball and cartoons, but not aliens. We suspect that our target, *Space Jam*, should score highly in all the required dimensions.

In the same way that fruit has a "juiciness" feature, you can think of movie text as having an "alien-ness" feature based on the occurrence of alien words in the text. To generalize this idea of representing features, you'll define a *feature space* to mean a

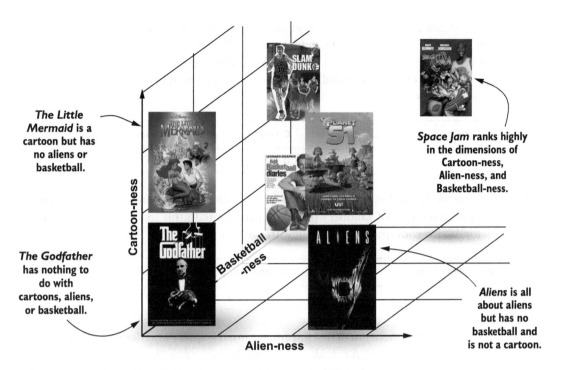

The Little Mermaid is a cartoon but has no aliens or basketball.

The Godfather has nothing to do with cartoons, aliens, or basketball.

Space Jam ranks highly in the dimensions of Cartoon-ness, Alien-ness, and Basketball-ness.

Aliens is all about aliens but has no basketball and is not a cartoon.

Cartoon-ness

Basketball-ness

Alien-ness

Figure 3.3 Movie overview text in a three-dimensional vector-space examining `basketball`, `cartoon`, and `alien`. Some movies are very much about cartoons and basketball (*Slam Dunk*). *Space Jam* is about all three!

vector space where dimensions represent features, regardless of whether you're talking about features of fruit, text, or anything else worth comparing.

Of course, movies are about far more than just basketballs, cartoons, and aliens. For text, the feature space is much larger than three dimensions. In what's known as the *bag of words* model of text, our vectors have a single dimension for each *possible* term. It's possible for there to be a dimension for every word in the English language! Naturally, any given document or query is unlikely to mention *every* word in the English language. You'll be hard pressed to find mention of Rome or history in the overview for *Space Jam*. Similarly, *Gladiator* is unlikely to mention Michael Jordan. Therefore, most dimensions in these document vectors are empty or zero. For this reason, they're known as *sparse vectors*.

After understanding that each vector dimension is a feature, the next step is measuring the strength or magnitude of that feature. In search, this value is known as a *weight*—a measure of how important that term is for the snippet of text. If `alien` is prominent, it should receive a high weight; otherwise, it should receive a low or zero weight. If you reexamine the previous explain, you can see Lucene's own weight measurement for the "alien" dimension in *Space Jam*:

```
0.03975798, weight(overview:alien in 1289)
```

Before digging into how Lucene computes this weight, let's walk through an example with a simpler definition. Let's define the weight for a particular term in text as 1 if the term is at all present, and 0 if not. With this definition, a snippet of text from Space Jam's overview, basketball game against alien, would be represented as this bag-of-words vector V_D:

a	alien	against	...	basketball	Cartoon	...	game	...	movie	narnia	...	zoo
0	1	1		1	0	0	1		0	0		0

This vector has a dimension for every word in the English language; we're showing you only a handful of English words. You can compare this to a similarly constructed vector, V_Q, for your query "basketball with cartoon aliens":

a	alien	against	...	basketball	cartoon	...	game	...	movie	narnia	...	zoo
0	1	0		1	1	0	0		0	0		0

How many components match? How similar are the query and document? Just as with the fruit example, you can calculate a dot product to arrive at a score. Recall that a dot product of two vectors multiplies corresponding components one by one. You then sum the components. So your score for this query would be calculated as follows:

```
score = V_D['a'] × V_Q['a'] + V_D['alien'] × V_Q['alien'] +
    ... + V_D['space'] × V_Q['space'] ...
```

When compared to the preceding explain breakdown, each multiplication factor represents a match score. In other words, `overview:alien` in the explain corresponds to the factor $V_D['alien'] \times V_Q['alien']$. The difference is that the explain reflects Lucene's own function for calculating a field or query weight, which we dive into next. The summation in the preceding dot product can be found in the behavior of the Boolean query that sums up matching clauses. You can see this in `sum of` from the previous explain:

```
3.19292, sum of:
      3.19292, weight(title:alien in 223) [PerFieldSimilarity]
```

3.6.3   *Practical caveats to the vector space model*

Although the vector space model provides a general framework for discussing Lucene's scoring, it's far from a complete picture. Numerous fudge factors have been shown to improve scoring in practice. Perhaps most fundamentally, the ways matches are combined by compound queries into a larger score isn't always a summation.

You've seen through the | symbol that the "max" of two fields is often taken. There's also often a *coord* factor that directly punishes compound matches missing some of their components (coord multiplies the resulting dot product by <the number of matches> / <the total query terms>). Many of the compound queries you'll encounter will perform various operations on the underlying queries, such as taking a max, summing, or taking a product. You also have tremendous freedom to arbitrarily calculate or boost scores with your own *function queries* that might combine match (or other) scores with other arbitrary factors. You'll explore many of these strategies in future chapters.

Another important note about this dot product is that it's often normalized by dividing the magnitude of each vector:

$$\text{score} = \frac{(V_D['a'] \times V_Q['a'] + V_D['alien'] \times V_Q['alien'] + \ldots + V_D['space'] \times V_Q['space'])}{(||V_Q|| \times ||V_D||)}$$

For dot products, normalization converts the score to a 0–1. This rebalances the equation to account for features that tend to have high weights, and those that tend to have smaller weights.[3] For search, given all the fudge factors in Lucene scoring and the peculiarities of field statistics, you should *never* attempt to compare scores between queries without a great deal of deep customization to make them comparable.

As stated previously, the sparse vector representation of text is known as the *bag of words* model. It's considered a "bag" because it reflects a decomposition of text that ignores the context of these terms. An important part of this context is the position the term occurs in to enable phrase matching. Luckily, Lucene also stores *positions* of each term's occurrence. Thus, you could view a document as a sparse vector that also includes every subphrase. This can be quite a large vector indeed! See the table below as an example. It's even larger when you open up the library of complex span queries!

a	an	alien	...	Basketball	lump	...	"basketball game"	"game against"	...
0	0	1		0	0		1	1	

3.6.4 *Scoring matches to measure relevance*

You're still trying to get to the bottom of why some of your movies are ranked suspiciously higher than the target *Space Jam*. You've explored the explain, and you see some match scores that concern you. You're almost there!

You need to understand how Lucene measures the weight of a term in a piece of document or query text in its vector calculation. You can then evaluate whether these weights correspond to your intuition of how strongly those matches should be weighted. Users, of course, don't think in terms of the math presented here. But these metrics have proven to experimentally approximate the user's broad sense of relevance. Let's see if it lines up with our expectations for our use case.

---

[3] Astute readers will recognize this as the *cosine similarity*.

Let's look at Lucene's weight computation for `alien` in *Space Jam* to suss out why a match on `alien` is relatively weak:

```
0.03975798, weight(overview:alien in 1289) [PerFieldSimilarity], result of:
  0.03975798, score(doc=1289,freq=1.0 = termFreq=1.0), product of:
    0.03382846, queryWeight, product of:
      4.701128, idf(docFreq=70, maxDocs=2875)
      0.0071958173, queryNorm
    1.175282, fieldWeight in 1289, product of:
      1.0, tf(freq=1.0), with freq of:
        1.0, termFreq=1.0
      4.701128, idf(docFreq=70, maxDocs=2875)
      0.25, fieldNorm(doc=1289)
```

How does Lucene's weight computation work? Looks like two weight components are multiplied together. The `fieldWeight` reflects how Lucene computes the importance of this term in the field text (in this case, `overview`). The `queryWeight` computes the weight of the term in the user's query.

This weight information can be translated from the explains into sparse vectors for the query and the two documents being scored (V_Q and V_D from the previous section). For example, if you compare the weight of `alien` in *Space Jam* with the corresponding entry in *Alien*:

```
0.15913194, weight(overview:alien in 223) [PerFieldSimilarity], result of:
  0.15913194, score(doc=223,freq=1.0 = termFreq=1.0), product of:
    0.033834733, queryWeight, product of:
      4.7032127, idf(docFreq=70, maxDocs=2881)
      0.0071939616, queryNorm
    4.7032127, fieldWeight in 223, product of:
      1.0, tf(freq=1.0), with freq of:
        1.0, termFreq=1.0
      4.7032127, idf(docFreq=70, maxDocs=2881)
      1.0, fieldNorm(doc=223)
```

You can represent these weights in a sparse vector. Here, you see the weight for `alien`.

Query or field	...	alien	...
Query: basketball with cartoon aliens (V_Q)		0.033834733	
overview field in Space Jam (V_D)		1.175282	
overview field in Alien (V_D)		4.7032127	

For some reason, the weight of the term `alien` is much higher in the `overview` field for *Alien* than it is for *Space Jam*. To us, this means that the feature of "alien-ness" is graded highly in this overview text.

3.6.5 *Computing weights with TF × IDF*

The rules for computing a term's weight in a field is driven by what Lucene calls a *similarity*. A similarity uses statistics recorded in the index for matched terms to assist a query in computing a numerical weight for the term. Lucene supports several similarity implementations, including letting you define your own.

Most similarities are based on the formula *TF × IDF*. This refers to the multiplication of two important term statistics extracted from the field and recorded in the inverted index by Lucene—*term frequency* (TF) and *inverse document frequency* (IDF). By default, terms have their importance weighed by multiplying these two statistics. As you may recall, these statistics were discussed at the end of chapter 2. Let's recap.

TF (`tf` in the preceding scoring) reflects how frequently a term occurs in a field. You can see it in the SimpleText version of the inverted index in earlier sections as `freq`. TF is extremely valuable in scoring a match. If a matched term occurs frequently in a particular field in a document (if the field mentions `alien` a lot), we consider that field's text much more likely to be about that term. (We consider it very likely to be about aliens.)

Conversely, IDF (`idf` in the preceding scoring) tells us how rare (and therefore valuable) a matched term is. Because IDF is the inverse of the document frequency, it's computed by taking 1 / document frequency, or 1 / DF. As you may recall, DF records the number of documents the term occurs in. If the term is common, it will have a high document frequency. Rare terms are considered valuable, and common ones less so. If the term `supercalifragilistic` occurs in a single document, it will receive a high IDF.

Raw TF × IDF weighs a term's importance in text by multiplying TF with IDF—or put another way, TF × (1 / DF), or TF / DF. This measures what proportion the index's overall use of that term is concentrated in this specific document.

Table 3.1 shows how TF × IDF works. In this example, when you weigh the importance of `lego`, there are relatively few movies about Legos. As you'd expect, the one movie that mentions Legos, *The Lego Movie*, receives a higher TF × IDF weight. Contrast this `lego` search with `love`. Movies that mention the term `love` are particularly common (everyone loves romantic comedies!). This causes occurrences of `love` in one particular romantic comedy, *Sleepless in Seattle*, to receive a lower weight than `lego` in *The Lego Movie*, despite having far more occurrences of `love` in *Sleepless*.

Table 3.1 Scoring `love` matches in *Sleepless In Seattle* versus `lego` in *The Lego Movie*. `lego` is rare and is mentioned only in *The Lego Movie*, thus yielding a higher score than the `love` match.

Movie	Matched term	DF	TF	TF × IDF (TF / DF)
Sleepless In Seattle	love	100	10	10 / 100 = 0.1
The Lego Movie	lego	1	3	3 / 1 = 3.0

The idea behind TF × IDF corresponds to most users' instincts about what matches should be considered important terms in text. Users perceive rare terms (such as `lego`) to be far more specific and targeted than common terms (`love`). Further, as a snippet of text mentions a term proportionally more than other text (as its TF increases), it's more likely that this text is going to be about the term being searched on.

Though broadly valuable, you'll see cases where these intuitions don't hold. Sometimes increased TF doesn't correspond to the user's notion of term importance. High TF matches on short text snippets like, for example, title fields (*Fire with Fire*) often don't correlate with our notion of increased term weight. Luckily, Elasticsearch gives us the ability to disable TF as needed.

3.6.6   *Lies, damned lies, and similarity*

Although you can see that TF × IDF seems to be an intuitive weighting formula, these raw statistics need additional tweaking to be optimal. Information retrieval research demonstrates that although a search term might occur 10 times more in a piece of text, that doesn't make it 10 times as relevant. More mentions of the term do correlate with relevance, but the relationship isn't linear. For this reason, Lucene dampens the impact of TF and IDF by using a *similarity* class.

This book uses Lucene's classic TF × IDF similarity (the defaults in Solr 5.x and Elasticsearch 2.0—see callout). Lucene's classic similarity dampens the impact of `tf` and `idf` when computing a weight:

```
TF Weight = sqrt(tf)
IDF Weight = log(numDocs / (df + 1)) + 1
```

You can see how these statistics are dampened in table 3.2.

Table 3.2   Term frequency and document frequencies dampened with default formulas (IDF calculated for 1,000 documents)

Raw TF	TF weight		Raw DF	IDF weight (for 1,000 docs)
1	1		1	7.215
2	1.414		2	6.809
5	2.236		10	5.510
15	3.872		50	2.976
50	7.071		1000	0.999
1,000	31.623			

Further, dampening TF × IDF by itself often isn't sufficient. Term frequency often must be considered relative to the number of total terms in a matched field. For example, does a single mention of `alien` in a 1,000-page book have the same weight as a single occurrence of `alien` in a three-sentence snippet? The shorter snippet with just one match is likely much more relevant for the term than the book that uses the term once. For this reason, in the preceding `fieldWeight` calculation, TF × IDF is multiplied by `fieldNorm`—a weight-normalization factor based on the length of the document. This normalization factor is calculated as follows:

```
fieldNorm =  1 / sqrt(fieldlength)
```

This normalization regulates the impact of TF and IDF on the term's weight by biasing occurrences in shorter fields. Norms are calculated at index time and take up space. Further, depending on the application and user base, they don't always correlate to our user's notion of term importance in a piece of text. Luckily, Lucene lets us disable the norms completely.

Taken together, Lucene's classic similarity measures a term's weight in a piece of text as follows:

```
TF weighted × IDF weighted × fieldNorm
```

Revisiting the `fieldWeight` calculation, you see this formula in play:

```
0.4414702, fieldWeight in 31, product of:
  1.4142135, tf(freq=2.0), with freq of:
    2.0, termFreq=2.0
  3.9957323, idf(docFreq=1, maxDocs=40)
  0.078125, fieldNorm(doc=31)
```

Lucene's next default similarity: BM25

Over the years, an alternate approach to computing a TF × IDF score has become prevalent in the information retrieval community: Okapi BM25. Because of its proven high performance on article-length text, Lucene's BM25 similarity will be rolling out as the default similarity for Solr/Elasticsearch, even as you read this book.

What is BM25? Instead of "fudge factors" as discussed previously, BM25 bases its TF × IDF "fudges" on more-robust information retrieval findings. This includes forcing the impact of TF to reach a saturation point. Instead of the impact of length (`field-Norms`) always increasing, its impact is computed relative to the average document length (above-average docs weighted down, below-average boosted). IDF is computed similarly to classic TF × IDF similarity.

Will BM25 help your relevance? It's not that simple. As we discussed in chapter 1, information retrieval focuses heavily on broad, incremental improvements to article-length pieces of text. BM25 may not matter for your specific definition of *relevance*. For this reason, we intentionally eschew the additional complexity of BM25 in this book. Lucene won't be deprecating classic TF × IDF at all; instead, it will become known as the *classic* similarity. Don't be shy about experimenting with both. As for this book's examples, you can re-create the scoring in future Elasticsearch versions by changing the similarity back to the classic similarity. Finally, every lesson you learn from this book applies, regardless of whether you choose BM25 or classic TF × IDF.

3.6.7   *Factoring in the search term's importance*

The computation of a query's weight (queryWeight) doesn't correspond to the same formula. More occurrences of a term in the query for nearly all search cases doesn't correspond to more importance for that term (users almost always list their query term once). Further, as queries are short, there's little need for length normalization. So this is also omitted. What's left from our preceding weight calculation is the IDF.

Additionally, queryWeight adds two factors:

- Query-time boosting
- Query normalization (queryNorm)

First we'll get queryNorm out of the way. The first thing to note is that without boosting, queryNorm doesn't matter. It's constant across all matches for our search. queryNorm attempts to make scores between the different matches outside this single search comparable, but it does a poor job. You should never attempt to compare scores across different fields outside a single search. So much variation in statistics like IDF and TF across fields and text makes relevance scores extremely relative. In fact, dropping this factor commonly comes up in Lucene's discussion list.[4]

What does matter in queryWeight is the boost factor. There's no boost in our query in overview, but we do boost on title matches. Unfortunately, at times the boost can be lost in the queryNorm calculation. Examining the queryNorm for our title match in *Alien* shows a different calculation than queryNorm in the corresponding match in the overview field by a factor of 10. You'll see how Elasticsearch allows you to boost different factors in future chapters.

3.6.8   *Fixing Space Jam vs. alien ranking*

Finally armed with mastery of Lucene's scoring, you can compare the *Space Jam* and *Alien* explains. *Alien* has two matches: a strong title match, and a much weaker match in the overview field. *Space Jam* has two matches in the overview field. If you zero in on what's driving the differences in how the matches are computed, you can see that scores for overview fields are in general always considerably weaker than scores in the title field.

You see this with a very high score for *Alien's* title match:

```
3.1940954, weight(title:alien in 223)
```

compared with the lower relevancy scores for an alien match in the overview field:

```
0.03975798, weight(overview:alien in 1289)
```

This difference is roughly two orders of magnitude! Wait, didn't we explicitly tell the search engine that title is only 10 times as important as overview via boosting? Sure,

---

[4] See "Whither Query Norm" at http://lucene.472066.n3.nabble.com/Whither-Query-Norm-td600443.html for more details.

although we did apply a boost, we also learned that scores between fields aren't at all comparable. They exist entirely in their own scoring universes. Comparing the `title` match for `Alien` with the `overview` match for `alien`, you can see this:

```
3.1940954, weight(title:alien in 223) [PerFieldSimilarity], result of:
  3.1940954, score(doc=223,freq=1.0 = termFreq=1.0
), product of:
  0.4793558, queryWeight, product of:
    6.6633077, idf(docFreq=9, maxDocs=2881)
    0.07193962, queryNorm
  6.6633077, fieldWeight in 223, product of:
    1.0, tf(freq=1.0), with freq of:
      1.0, termFreq=1.0
    6.6633077, idf(docFreq=9, maxDocs=2881)
    1.0, fieldNorm(doc=223)
0.03975798, weight(overview:alien in 1289) [PerFieldSimilarity], result of:
  0.03975798, score(doc=1289,freq=1.0 = termFreq=1.0), product of:
    0.03382846, queryWeight, product of:
      4.701128, idf(docFreq=70, maxDocs=2875)
      0.0071958173, queryNorm
    1.175282, fieldWeight in 1289, product of:
      1.0, tf(freq=1.0), with freq of:
        1.0, termFreq=1.0
      4.701128, idf(docFreq=70, maxDocs=2875)
      0.25, fieldNorm(doc=1289)
```

1 IDF is significantly lower for "alien" in overview, overview is also longer, giving it a higher field norm.

queryNorm is 1/10th the preceding queryNorm, reflecting title's boost.

Here you see the driver of the difference in the two match's `fieldWeight` scores **1**. These fields tend to take a different character. An overview is roughly paragraph length, whereas titles are just a few terms. This tends to drive the `fieldNorms` to be quite different. Further, the relative distribution of terms in `overview` fields doesn't mirror the term distribution in `title` fields.

These fields are often driven by how the authors of these fields chose to express themselves. What do movie marketers think when writing an overview? What words do they choose? How pithy or expansive is the writing? How does a movie studio choose a movie title? Do they tie it to existing brands (and thus terms) or are they always trying to be original? Often relevance with text requires both getting in the head of the author (why did the author choose certain language) and the searcher (why does the searcher use particular search terms).

For the math we have to fix, the main implication is that a good overview score may be significantly smaller than a good title score. A boost of 10 *doesn't* imply 10 times the importance to the search engine. It simply implies a multiple. When you take apart term matching, you can see this in stark relief, with overview scores always significantly lower than title scores. The appropriate way to use these field weights is to first dive into the rough timbre of these scores before deciding how to apply weights. It might be more appropriate to boost a title by 0.1, and this still may give significantly more weight to a title match than an overview match simply because of that field's particular character.

Let's rerun our query with a more reasonable title boost to see the impact.

Listing 3.14   Searching with an adjusted boost

```
query = {
    "query": {
        "multi_match": {                              User's
            "query": usersSearch,              ◁──┐  query
            "fields": ["title^0.1", "overview"],
        }}
}
search(query)
```

Results:

```
Num Relevance Score        Movie Title
1   1.0016364              Space Jam
2   0.29594672             Grown Ups
3   0.28491083             Speed Racer
4   0.28491083             The Flintstones
5   0.2536686              White Men Can't Jump
6   0.2536686              Coach Carter
7   0.21968345             Semi-Pro
8   0.20324169             The Thing
9   0.1724563              Meet Dave
10  0.16911241             Teen Wolf
```

Great! Now that looks much better.

3.7   *Solved? Our work is never over!*

You've made progress and pushed the ball forward, but have you really solved anything? You're left with several points for improvement.

First, recall how your query works from the preceding validation endpoint:

```
((title:basketbal title:cartoon title:alien)^10.0) | (overview:basketbal
overview:cartoon overview:alien)
```

Remember how the | is taking the maximum between the two field scores? You see this in the following explain too ❶, when looking only at the compound queries:

```
1.0643067, max of:                        ◁──┐  Why is this a maximum of two scores?
  1.0643067, product of:                   ❶  What purpose does this serve?
    3.19292, sum of:
      3.19292, weight(title:alien in 223) [PerFieldSimilarity], result of:

    0.33333334, coord(1/3)
  0.066263296, product of:
    0.19878988, sum of:
      0.19878988, weight(overview:alien in 223) [PerFieldSimilarity], result of:
```

By boosting overview and title more conscientiously, you've made it possible that overview might sometimes beat title when the query takes the maximum of the two fields. Why are you taking a maximum? Why is this strategy used by default? Are there other strategies you could use to combine these scores so that it's not all or nothing between strong title and strong overview matches? You may have solved the *Space Jam* problem, but what will this max do to other searches? When other searches create different scores, will we be back at square one?

Finally, you must ask whether your `fieldWeight` calculation could be improved. Do we truly care about `fieldNorms`? Is it important in this use case to bias toward shorter text or longer text? There's also the ever present struggle of the relevance engineer: do the terms themselves represent the right features latent in the text? If you looked at a snippet from *Space Jam*, you can ponder a few questions:

> Michael Jordan agrees to help the Looney Toons play a basketball game vs. alien slavers to determine their freedom.

Are all the features truly captured in this explain? We didn't see any weight for a match on cartoon in the explain; should `toons` or `looney toons` match `cartoon`? What about `Michael Jordan`? We humans associate him with basketball; should we amplify the weight of the `basketball` term by his name's presence?

Turning latent features into terms, and combining those features is the ever present struggle of the relevance engineer. In the next chapter, we cover this topic in great detail! You've begun with great promise here. In later chapters, you'll continue to explore these issues in greater depth, to maximize your use of the search engine's tools to match and rank in order to satisfy user and business needs.

3.8 Summary

- Not getting the expected search results requires debugging matching and ranking.
- To debug matching, examine how your search engine interprets and executes your query; with Elasticsearch, this corresponds to the query validation endpoint.
- Search engines require exacting, byte-for-byte term matching to include a document in the search results.
- Search engines need your help to determine which matches to include/omit (such as stop words) by choosing an appropriate analyzer.
- Search engines use TF × IDF scoring to rank results. You can see the scoring by using your search engine's relevance explain output.
- TF measures the term's importance in the document's text. IDF determines the rareness/specialness of a term across the whole corpus. Field norms (norms) bias scoring toward shorter text.
- Debugging search engine ranking requires understanding `fieldWeight` (how important search terms are in the text) and debugging `queryWeight` (how important search terms are in the search query).
- Relevance scores aren't easily compared, nor are they normalized. A poor score for a title field may be 10.0; a good search score for the overview field may be 0.01.
- Boost factors aren't field priorities. Instead, they let you rebalance relevance scoring. When scoring is balanced, you can prioritize one field or another.

Taming tokens

This chapter covers

- Tokenization to extract ideas rather than words
- The concepts of precision and recall in search
- Making trade-offs between precision and recall
- Controlling the specificity of matches
- Encoding non-textual data into the search engine

At this point, you have a good understanding of why relevance is critical for the success of a search application (chapter 1). You also have a working knowledge of search engine internals (chapter 2) and can debug relevance to pin down why documents match and why they're given a particular score (chapter 3).

Now, armed with motivation, knowledge, and tools, it's time to dive into the art of relevance engineering. In this chapter, we focus on text analysis. Proper analysis is the foundation of relevant search. As you saw in chapter 3, analysis controls matching. If analysis is performed correctly, users' queries will match only the documents that they seek. But if analysis is performed incorrectly, users' queries will match many irrelevant documents or maybe no documents at all!

4.1 *Tokens as document features*

Several times we've pointed out the relationship between relevance and classification. (Remember our fruit examples?) This relationship is perhaps most obvious when we talk about tokens, because just as the color, shape, and size of a fruit are *features* by which a fruit may be classified, the tokens pulled from a document are features by which the document can be classified.

Let's return to the fruit example. The most obvious features that come to mind are color, shape, and size. In reality, you could attempt to classify fruit by any number of features: weight, smell, price, number of freckles, sticker color, and distance from the Washington Monument. But as you can see in this list, some features are more useful to classification than others. And some features, like distance from the Washington Monument, are utterly useless for classification.

In the same way, we use text analysis to extract features—tokens—that anticipate the user's expectations and lead to highly relevant and targeted results. But when poorly configured, text analysis can lead to garbage features and a search experience that's mostly a waste of time. There's both an art and a science to text analysis. In chapter 2, we dealt mostly with the mechanics of analysis—the science, if you will. Our discussion here deals with the softer, more "artistic" side of analysis, which we call *feature modeling.*

With feature modeling, you take into consideration the user's *intent* as well the *ideas* conveyed in documents. You also ensure that the tokens produced by the analysis process represent descriptive, meaningful features of both the queries and the (as shown in figure 4.1).

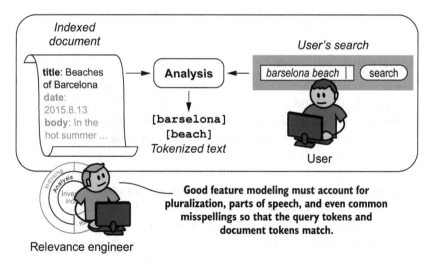

Figure 4.1 The relevance engineer makes sure that the tokens generated from documents match the tokens generated for queries. To accomplish this, the relevance engineer must understand the information in the documents and the intent of the users.

4.1.1 The matching process

Again with the fruit example … Let's say that you're hungry. And you're not hungry for just anything; you're hungry for a Red Delicious apple. So you head down to the corner fruit stand to satisfy your apple lust. When you arrive, you see many types of fruits:

- Long, yellow bananas; some with freckles, and some that are tinted green
- Small, round grapes; some that are light green, and some that are purple
- Giant, green and pink wedges of watermelon; some with seeds, and some without

But today you're *searching* for an apple. And in your mind, you have a clear template— a query, if you will—for what a Red Delicious apple should look like. It's a red, round fruit, about the size of your fist. Additionally, the really good Red Delicious apples are always *shiny*!

In the twinkling of an eye, you scan the selection of fruit and identify a subset that most closely matches your query. You approach the apple bin. And there on the top of the heap is the perfect, shiny, Red Delicious apple. Your search has brought you to the most relevant result in the available set. You purchase the apple and partake! (You won't notice until you're halfway through that the apple also has a worm. Maybe you should refine your search criteria next time!)

This scenario is a good approximation for what happens when a user searches for a document. When your users come to the search app, they have an information need and they supply the search engine with a set of search terms or a phrase that they feel most adequately describes their needs. The search engine, in turn, takes these terms and converts them into tokens via the analysis process described in chapter 2. Then the search engine quickly scans through the index and collects the documents that contain the same tokens as the query, organizes the document according to relevance, and provides the results back to the user.

4.1.2 Tokens, more than just words

It's important to notice here that the creation of tokens—*and thus the creation of features*—happens both to the query and to the documents. And a match can be made only if the features are generated consistently from the query documents. What's more, *relevant* matches can be made only if the features adequately capture the *meaning* of the documents and the user's query.

Those who are new to search typically think of analysis as the process of extracting an array of words from documents. And although tokens often directly correspond to words in the text, tokens can be much more than that. The various steps of analysis (character filtering, tokenization, and token filtering) anticipate the *intent* of your users. When properly performed, analysis extracts the *meaning* of a document beyond the words. Performing analysis with intent and meaning in mind greatly improves search relevance.

You'll see what we mean throughout this chapter. For example, it might come as a surprise that tokens don't have to correspond to words at all! As you'll soon see, meaningful tokens (features) can be extracted from things as diverse as geographic locations, images, and even whistled melodies.

4.2 Controlling precision and recall

Precision and recall are two fundamental measures of search relevance. Given a particular query and the set of documents returned by the search engine (the result set), these measures are defined as:

- *Precision*—The percentage of documents in the result set that are relevant.
- *Recall*—The percentage of relevant documents that are returned in the result set.

Admittedly, these definitions are a little hard to follow at first. They may even sound like the same thing. In the discussion that follows, we provide a thorough example that will help you understand these definitions and their differences. You'll also begin to see why it's so important to keep these concepts in mind when designing any application of search.

Additionally, we demonstrate how precision and recall are often at odds. Generally, the more you improve recall, the worse your precision becomes, and the more you improve precision, the worse your recall becomes. This implies a limit on the best you can achieve in search relevance. Fortunately, you can get around this limit. We explore the details in the discussion that follows.

4.2.1 Precision and recall by example

Let's lead with another example. And this time just to be different, let's use, oh, we don't know, *fruit*. After you recover from the wormy apple incident of the previous section, you go back to the fruit stand and consider the situation in more detail.

When you originally went to the fruit stand, you were looking for apples—but more specifically, your search criteria were "red, medium-sized fruit." These criteria led you to the search results indicated in figure 4.2.

Let's consider how this result set can be described in terms of precision and recall. Looking at the search results, you have three apples and three red, medium-sized fruits that aren't apples (a tomato, a bell pepper, and a pomegranate). Restating the previous definition, *precision* is the percentage of results that are correct. In this case, three of the six results are apples, so the precision of this result set is $(3 \div 6) \times 100$, or 50%. Furthermore, upon closer inspection of all the produce, you find that there are five apple choices among the thirteen fruit varieties available at the stand. *Recall* is the percentage of the correct items that are returned in the search results. In this case, there are five apples at the fruit stand, and three were returned in the results. The recall for your apple search is $(3 \div 5) \times 100$, or 60%.

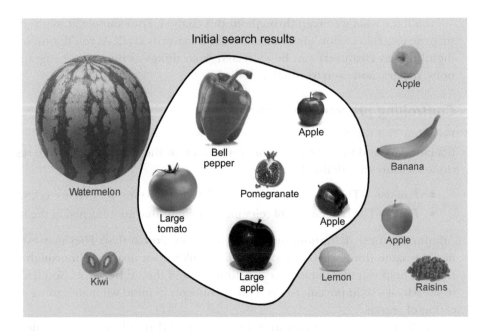

Figure 4.2   Illustration of documents and results in the search for apples

In the ideal case, precision and recall would both always be at 100%. But this is almost never possible. What's more, precision and recall are most often at odds with one another. If you improve recall, precision will suffer and your search response will include spurious results. On the other hand, if you improve precision, recall will suffer and your search response will omit relevant matches.

To better understand the warring nature of precision and recall, let's look at this phenomenon with our fruit example. If you want to improve recall, you must loosen the search requirements a bit. What if you do this by including fruit that's yellow? (Some apples are yellow, right?) As shown in figure 4.3, you do pick up another apple, thus improving recall to 80%. But because most apples aren't yellow, you've picked up two more erroneous results, decreasing precision to 44%.

Let's go the other way with our experiment. If you tighten the search criteria—for example, by narrowing the definition of *medium-sized*—results look like those in figure 4.4. Here precision increases to 67% because you've removed two slightly unmedium fruits. But in the process, you've also removed a slightly oversized apple, taking recall down to 40%.

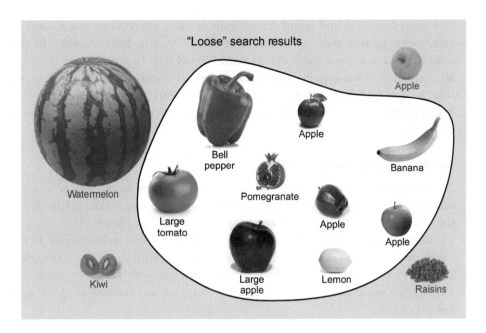

Figure 4.3 Example search result set when loosening the color-match requiremnts

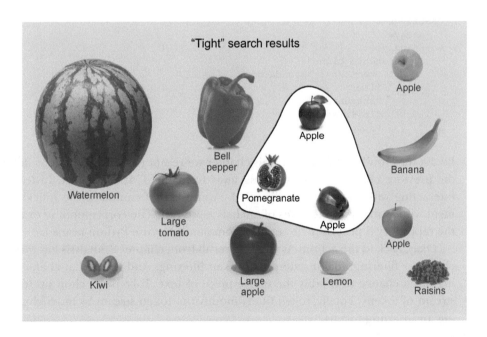

Figure 4.4 Example search result set when tightening the size requirements

Although precision and recall are typically at odds, there's one way to overcome the constraints of this trade-off: more features. If you include another field in your search, for flavor, then the tomato would be easy to rule out because it's not sweet at all. But, unfortunately, it's not always easy to identify new features to pull into search. And in this particular case, if you decide to go around flavor sampling the fruit in order to identify apples, you'll probably have an upset produce manager to contend with!

4.2.2 *Analysis for precision or recall*

But precision, recall, and fruit—what does this all have to do with text, tokens, and analysis? Plenty! By modifying the analysis chain, you can create tokens that balance the trade-off between precision and recall in any way you please.

To start, let's look at how text is analyzed in Elasticsearch by default. Let's say you create an index in Elasticsearch with no settings and then index a new document. That document's string fields will be analyzed using the default *standard analyzer.* Let's create our own clone of the standard analyzer to take a closer look at the analysis process.

Listing 4.1 Re-creating the standard analyzer

```
POST my_library
{
  "settings": {
    "analysis": {
      "analyzer": {
        "standard_clone": {
          "tokenizer": "standard",
          "filter": [
            "standard",
            "lowercase",
            "stop"]}}}}}
```

By the way, you'll notice that in this chapter we're not using the functions defined in the previous chapter. We're stepping away from the TMDB data set. Instead, we're interacting with Elasticsearch directly by using HTTP commands to quickly experiment with as many applications of analysis as we can. The corresponding examples in the repository repeat these lower-level commands but use Python instead.

Okay, back to the action! As you may recall from chapter 2, analysis has three steps: character filtering, tokenization, and token filtering. And recall that character filtering has a chance to modify the entire piece of text. Tokenizers chop up text into a stream of tokens. Finally, token filters modify the token stream by modifying, removing, or inserting tokens.

In listing 4.1, our `standard_clone` analyzer makes no use of any character filters, uses the `standard` tokenizer, and then is token filtered sequentially by `standard`, `lowercase`, and `stop`. Here's what each piece does:

- `standard` *tokenizer*—Splits text on whitespace and punctuation; this tends to work well for most European languages. Its widespread utility garners the name *standard*.
- `standard` *filter*—Does nothing! It currently serves as a placeholder should there ever be a need to implement token filtering that's associated with the `standard` tokenizer.
- `lowercase` *filter*—Lowercases all characters.
- `stop` *filter*—Removes common words that match a list of stop words. If the list that Elasticsearch uses by default isn't to your liking, you can also specify your own.

Now let's use the `_analyze` endpoint to examine the tokens produced from a sample sentence:

```
GET my_library/_analyze?analyzer=standard_clone&
    text="Dr. Strangelove: Or How I Learned to
        Stop Worrying and Love the Bomb"
```

In chapter 3, we showed how the analyzer can be used to gather the tokens, start and end offsets, token types, and positions, but here we're interested in only the tokens. In this case, the tokens produced are as follows:

```
[dr] [strangelove] [how] [i] [learned] [stop] [worrying] [love] [bomb]
```

And as expected, the tokens have been stripped of punctuation and lowercased, and the common words have been removed.

The standard analyzer is typically a good first draft for the analysis chain; search results will have high precision, and spurious results will be few. But recall may be poor, because a user's query must use *exactly* the same words that occurred in the document, or the document won't be returned. Consider the plight of a user who's clearly looking for this movie but has forgotten the exact title:

```
GET tmdb/movie/_search
{ "query": {
    "multi_match": {
      "query":
        "mr. weirdlove: don't worry, I'm learning to start loving bombs",
      "fields": ["title"] }}}
```

The query-time analysis tokenizes this as you'd expect:

```
[mr] [weirdlove] [don't] [worry] [i'm] [learning] [start] [loving] [bombs]
```

But not a single token from the query matches the tokens created from the movie title. Search engines are for finding things when users *don't* have all the information; otherwise, why would they even look? The fact that this query doesn't pull back the obvious document that the user is looking for is a failure of this feature-modeling approach.

We can do better! Recall again that a search engine is little more than a sophisticated token-matching system. A search engine knows nothing about the meaning of tokens; it knows only how to quickly find documents that have a particular set of tokens. It's the job of the relevance engineer to tokenize documents in such a way that *meaning* is captured. In principle, analysis shouldn't map words to tokens; it should map *meaning* and *user intent* to tokens.

Let's demonstrate this concept with a different analysis chain. An English text analyzer is less strict and helps ensure that tokens carry the English *meaning* of the words. Just like last time, Elasticsearch already comes equipped with an English analyzer, but to be explicit about what's happening, we'll clone the English analyzer. We'll go into more detail this time by cloning the token filters to teach you to customize the analysis chain to your choosing.

Listing 4.2   Re-creating the English analyzer in detail

```
POST my_library
{
  "settings": {
    "analysis": {
      "filter": {
        "english_stop": {
          "type":        "stop",
          "stopwords":   "_english_"},
        "english_keywords": {
          "type":        "keyword_marker",
          "keywords_path":   "/tmp/keywords.txt"},
        "english_stemmer": {
          "type":        "stemmer",
          "language":    "english"},
        "english_possessive_stemmer": {
          "type":        "stemmer",
          "language":    "possessive_english"}},
      "analyzer": {
        "english_clone": {
          "tokenizer":   "standard",
          "filter": [
            "english_possessive_stemmer",
            "lowercase",
            "english_stop",
            "english_keywords",
            "english_stemmer"]}}}}}
```

Let's take a moment to understand what the English analyzer is doing at each step of analysis:

- standard *tokenizer*—Here again we use the standard tokenizer because it does a good job of tokenizing European languages.
- english_possessive_stemmer filter—Removes the trailing *s* from words.
- lowercase filter—Lowercases all characters.
- english_stop filter—Removes common English words.
- english_keywords filter—"Protects" words from being mangled by the downstream stemmer (more on this in a moment).
- english_stemmer filter—Normalizes word endings so that, for instance, walking and walked map to the same token.

As you can see, there's a lot of overlap between what the standard analyzer and the English analyzer do. The "special sauce" of the English analyzer is in the english_ stemmer token filter. This filter takes the word tokens from the previous analysis steps and normalizes them by mapping words with the same root to the same token. For example, this shows that all of these terms map to the token flower:

```
GET my_library/_analyze?analyzer=english_clone&
    text="flower flowers flowering flowered flower"
```

And similarly for the following, all of these terms get mapped to the token silli:

```
GET my_library/_analyze?analyzer=english_clone&
    text="silly silliness sillied sillying"
```

You might notice that not all the words in the preceding example are real words. But english_stemmer doesn't mind. The stemmer isn't conferring with a dictionary to determine the word roots; it uses a heuristic for mapping words to root forms. The heuristic is correct enough to be useful, but sometimes the heuristic makes mistakes. For example, the word *Maine* (the state) will get stemmed down to main, confusing it with the common English word *main*. If this becomes a problem for you, don't sweat it! You can add the problematic term to the keywords file (/tmp/keywords.txt in listing 4.2), and this will signal any downstream stemmers to leave it unstemmed.

To bring the discussion back to the main point, stemming is a technique of feature modeling that sacrifices precision for increased recall. Using the English analyzer, our forgetful movie searcher will have better luck finding the movie. Let's demonstrate this by looking at the tokens produced from both the correct title and the incorrect query.

Listing 4.3   Tokenization of query and document text using the English analyzer

```
GET my_library/_analyze?analyzer=english_clone&
    text="Dr. Strangelove: Or How I Learned to Stop Worrying
          and Love the Bomb"

[dr] [strangelov] [how] [i] [learn] [stop] [worri] [love] [bomb]

GET my_library/_analyze?analyzer=english_clone&
    text="mr. weirdlove: don't worry, I'm learning to start loving bombs"

[mr] [weirdlov] [don't] [worri] [i'm] [learn] [start] [love] [bomb]
```

As indicated by the bold text, you've gone from zero matching tokens with the standard analyzer to four matching tokens when using the English analyzer. The document that originally wouldn't have been retrieved now would rank highly in search results.

4.2.3   *Taking recall to extremes*

You've seen a clear example of how sacrificing precision for improved recall can be a great way to improve overall search relevance. But beware that this can be taken to unhealthy extremes. Let's demonstrate with yet another analyzer, a phonetic analyzer, which maps words to tokens based on the way they sound. You'll use phonetic analysis to build search that's robust to misspellings. This is ostensibly a good thing because it improves recall and makes documents findable even if the document or the query contains misspellings. But we'll then demonstrate how this approach is often too heavy-handed.

For this demonstration, you *do* have to build the analyzer from scratch because Elasticsearch doesn't come with a prebuilt phonetic analyzer of its own. First you install the phonetic plugin[1] by entering the terminal, changing to the elasticsearch directory, and typing this at the prompt:

```
bin/plugin install analysis-phonetic
```

Once the plugin is installed, you can create a phonetic analyzer by providing Elasticsearch with the configuration in the following listing.

---

[1] You can find more information about the phonetic plugin at https://github.com/elastic/elasticsearch/tree/master/plugins/analysis-phonetic.

| Listing 4.4   Building a phonetic analyzer |

```
POST my_library
{ "settings": {
    "analysis": {
      "analyzer": {
        "phonetic": {
          "tokenizer": "standard",
          "filter": [
            "standard",
            "lowercase",
            "my_doublemetaphone"]}},
      "filter": {
        "my_doublemetaphone": {
          "type": "phonetic",
          "encoder": "doublemetaphone",
          "replace": true}}}}}
```

You should recognize several familiar components: the standard tokenizer, the
standard filter, and finally the lowercase filter. The new my_doublemetaphone filter
is where all the interesting action takes place this time. This filter takes the lowercased
words apple and banana and turns them into tokens that represent the basic sounds,
in this case APLS and PNNS, respectively. As you can see, the analysis is aggressive—all
but leading vowels are dropped, and certain sounds such as *ba* and *pa* are mapped to
the same symbol (in this case, P). But phonetic analysis works as advertised because a
terribly misspelled search for "oopuls" and "banunus" would indeed match on a document with apple and banana correctly spelled.

There's a problem, though, and it's best exemplified by looking at a search for
"message from Dalai Lama." Let's see how this and another phrase are tokenized:

```
GET my_library/_analyze?analyzer=phonetic&text=message from Dalai Lama
```

[MSJ],[MSK],[FRM],[TL],[LM]

```
GET my_library/_analyze?analyzer=phonetic&text=massage from tall llama
```

[MSJ],[MSK],[FRM],[TL],[LM]

Oops! It appears that through the eyes of the phonetic analyzer, message from Dalai
Lama is an exact match for massage from tall llama. (Oh, and how many souls have
been led astray by simple mistakes such as this!)

There's an important lesson here regarding the analysis process:

> To the extent possible, make sure that tokens represent not just words,
> but the *meaning of the words*.

This is why it's often a good practice to incorporate token stemming into analysis.
Stemming collapses multiple representations into a single form—transforming, as in
our earlier example, flower, flowers, flowering, and flowered all into a single root
form flower. Without stemming, these words would stand completely distinct. The

search engine would fail to recognize that they mean the same thing: searches for flowering wouldn't match flowers. Thus, without stemming, recall is greatly reduced. Precision may be improved, but it's improved to a degree that isn't useful to the typical search user.

At the other end of the spectrum, phonetic tokenization maximizes recall at the peril of precision. Here again consider how analysis maps tokens to meaning. With phonetic tokenization, the meaning associated with each token is too broad. Too many distinct meanings map to the same token. Precision is far too low: a search for the Dalai Lama finds the tall llama instead of the religious figure!

4.3 Precision and recall—have your cake and eat it too

The situation feels bleak. As a relevance engineer, you're faced with a hard decision: in order for documents to be indexed, the text must be analyzed. Yet your choice of analysis pins the relevance behavior to some fixed point on the precision-recall spectrum.

Fortunately, another aspect of search technology allows the relevance engineer to build search with good recall *and* good precision. In chapter 2, you saw the mechanical nature of the search engine. Another way of describing the search engine is as follows:

> A search engine is nothing more than a sophisticated token-matching system *and document-ranking system.*

It's that last part that sidesteps the fundamental precision/recall trade-off. Relevance ranking is how you cheat the system. Relevance ranking helps you improve precision for the top N results—the results that likely matter most to you users. The trick, as you'll see, is fine-tuning analysis to tightly control when various token representations map to an identical meaning.

4.3.1 Scoring strength of a feature in a single field

How exactly does relevance ranking sidestep the precision/recall trade-off? Analysis not only controls matching, but also manipulates TF × IDF relevance ranking to more accurately reflect the strength of a given feature in text (or any other form of tokenizable data).

Remember our good friend TF × IDF? A term's frequency (TF) counts how often the search term occurs in the document. Document frequency counts how many documents with the term occur across the whole corpus (IDF being its inverse). Together these factors work to score search relevance for matched text.

But can TF and IDF count different representations of the same idea? As an example, if you sat an English speaker in front of text and asked them to count the number of times run occurred, how would he proceed? Likely they'd sum the many forms of run (running, runs, run, perhaps ran) all together. Even if all forms of run were used, an English speaker could conclude the text as very much about running. The feature of running occurs prominently in the text, they might say, and should be scored highly for searches for "run," regardless of all the representations used.

As you've seen, the mechanical, dumb search engine doesn't count these different forms of run as the same without help. When alternate representations exist in the text, each representation is counted and scored separately. The search engine doesn't see a strong feature of "run-ness" here in its TF × IDF scoring. It sees isolated, weak mentions of different ideas: run, running, and runs. Luckily, you've seen how analysis helps normalize all these representations into a single term that can be counted and scored together.

Let's demonstrate how relevance ranking and analysis work together to fine-tune precision and recall. Let's start with a simple case—a query for a single word in a single field using the default standard analyzer over your test index, my_library:

```
POST my_library
{"settings": {
    "number_of_shards": 1}}
```

Then you can index some documents:

```
PUT my_library/example/1
{ "title":"apple apple apple apple apple"}
PUT my_library/example/2
{ "title":"apple apple apple banana banana"}
PUT my_library/example/3
{ "title":"apple banana blueberry coconut"}
```

And finally issue a simple search for apple in the field title:

```
GET my_library/example/_search
{ "explain": "true",
  "query": {
    "match": {
      "title": "apple"}}}
```

Here are the first three documents resulting from this query, along with corresponding explain text:

```
1.  {u'title': u'apple apple apple apple apple'}
    0.3001879, weight(title:apple in 0) [PerFieldSimilarity], result of:
      0.3001879, fieldWeight in 0, product of:
        2.236068, tf(freq=5.0), with freq of:
          5.0, termFreq=5.0
        0.30685282, idf(docFreq=1, maxDocs=1)
        0.4375, fieldNorm(doc=0)

2.  {u'title': u'apple apple apple banana banana'}
    0.23252454, weight(title:apple in 0) [PerFieldSimilarity], result of:
      0.23252454, fieldWeight in 0, product of:
        1.7320508, tf(freq=3.0), with freq of:
          3.0, termFreq=3.0
        0.30685282, idf(docFreq=1, maxDocs=1)
        0.4375, fieldNorm(doc=0)
```

```
3.  {u'title': u'apple banana blueberry coconut'}
   0.15342641, weight(title:apple in 0) [PerFieldSimilarity], result of:
      0.15342641, fieldWeight in 0, product of:
         1.0, tf(freq=1.0), with freq of:
            1.0, termFreq=1.0
         0.30685282, idf(docFreq=1, maxDocs=1)
         0.5, fieldNorm(doc=0)
```

The search engine's TF × IDF scoring heuristics order documents that feature the search term most prominently. Earlier we talked about shopping for fruit; based on whether it was shiny or red, you judged the fruit a Red Delicious apple or not. The examples considered these features binary. Is the fruit red—yes or no? Is it shiny—yes or no? The reality is that a feature such as "redness" exists on a spectrum from "not at all red" to "pinkish" to "bright, fire-truck red."

With TF × IDF, our apple documents also exist on a spectrum. Some matching documents are very much about `apples`. They have high term frequencies for `apple`. They're apple-y documents and mention few other concepts. Others mention other terms, with "apple" only as a side concept. These documents aren't apple-y at all. As such, their TF × IDF scores reflect this weak apple-y feature. Precision, at least for the top N, is improved by relevance ranking.

More important, analysis can improve the computation of TF and IDF by normalizing different representations of one idea! This improves the accuracy of scoring, aligning it to the user's intuitive notions of relevance.

For example, our current search has a prominent relevance-ranking bug! Say you indexed an additional document:

```
PUT my_library/example/4
{ "title":"apples apple"}
```

You might be surprised when the TF × IDF score for this document comes in as relatively low for a search on `apple`. Repeating the preceding search, you'd see it as near the end result of all the documents, despite being 100% composed of `apple` mentions:

```
3.  {'title': 'apples apple'}
   0.48553526, weight(title:apple in 0) [PerFieldSimilarity], result of:
      0.48553526, fieldWeight in 0, product of:
         1.0, tf(freq=1.0), with freq of:
            1.0, termFreq=1.0
         0.7768564, idf(docFreq=4, maxDocs=4)
         0.625, fieldNorm(doc=0)
```

Notice in the bolded section, the frequency of `apple` is 1. Yet two mentions of something apple-y exist here! Why can't TF × IDF see that?

You already know the answer. Because the standard analyzer is used, a query for apple *doesn't* match apples. The search engine won't understand that these ideas are the same, regardless of what an English speaker thinks. It's your job as a relevance engineer to use analysis techniques to manage equivalent representations of the same idea, normalizing and discriminating as needed so the search engine can make the right differentiations when scoring.

Simply using the English analyzer improves the TF × IDF scoring by normalizing apple forms to the stemmed appl. After applying the English analyzer and repeating indexing, the document moves up to position 2, with a term frequency for the stemmed appl increased to 2:

```
2. {u'title': u'apples apple'}
   0.6866506, weight(title:appl in 3) [PerFieldSimilarity], result of:
     0.6866506, fieldWeight in 3, product of:
       1.4142135, tf(freq=2.0), with freq of:
         2.0, termFreq=2.0
       0.7768564, idf(docFreq=4, maxDocs=4)
       0.625, fieldNorm(doc=3)
```

Tokens represent features prominent in text. You saw earlier the seemingly stark trade-off of precision and recall in these decisions. But as you see, manipulating relevance ranking can help make this trade-off less stark. You have the power, through analysis, to control both improved recall and TF × IDF relevance scoring! Analysis gives you the power to make matching *and* TF × IDF scoring as discriminating as you need.

4.3.2 *Scoring beyond TF × IDF: multiple search terms and multiple fields*

Unlike the previous example, users' searches rarely have only one search term. They use many ideas in their searches. You should use this in your favor to improve precision! Luckily, the *coordinating factor (coord)* is your ally. We discussed coord previously as a component of Lucene's Boolean search, but here we want to point out its role in biasing scoring toward more mentions of the searched-for ideas.

If you repeat the preceding search for apple banana, coord punishes the pure apple matches by multiplying the final score by 1/2. Only one out of two concepts matches the document, so it's summarily punished. You can see this in these explain snippets for the apple banana query (omitting the TF × IDF for brevity):

```
1. {u'title': u'apple apple apple banana banana'}
   0.9862758, sum of:
     0.30409503, weight(title:appl in 1) [PerFieldSimilarity], result of:
     0.68218076, weight(title:banana in 1) [PerFieldSimilarity], result of:

3. {'title': 'apple apple apple apple apple'}
   0.1962925, product of:
     0.392585, sum of:
       0.392585, weight(title:appl in 0) [PerFieldSimilarity], result of:
     0.5, coord(1/2)
```

While exploring query strategies in the next several chapters, you'll see coord's important role in promoting results with multiple matches more prominently.

Another way you'll sidestep the precision/recall trade-off is through searching over multiple fields, each with different forms of analysis. It may seem that forms of analysis are mutually exclusive: analyze via standard analysis *or* English stemming analysis *or* phonetic analysis. But you can use all of these together if you'd like. It's common to treat the same text differently with different analyzers, placing the result in different fields. In chapter 5 and on, you'll see how multiple fields can lend their own signals to improve the overall ranking function and improve the precision/recall trade-off.

4.4 Analysis strategies

To this point in the chapter, you've learned several important principles for using analysis to control relevance. First and foremost, you have an understanding of the foundational principles of *precision* and *recall*. We've discussed the interplay between these two concepts: an improvement in either precision or recall often causes degradation in the other. But in our discussion of document scoring, you can see that good recall *and* good precision are achievable, because search-engine scoring tends to sort the most relevant documents toward the top of the search results.

We've also established a couple of guiding principles when making analysis decisions. First, to the extent possible, tokens shouldn't map only to the terms in a document but to the *meanings* of the terms. You saw this in section 4.2.2, which explained how stemming helps ensure that the token captures the appropriate level of detail of each word's meaning. Second, analysis is an opportunity for the relevance engineer to anticipate the behavior and intent of search users. Section 4.2.3 describes how phonetic tokenization anticipates the possibility that users will occasionally misspell search terms.

In this section, we present more specific examples of using analysis to modify and control relevance. The examples aren't exhaustive; covering the great variety of search problems that readers might experience would be impossible. Instead, the following sections provide some quick examples to consider. When your own challenging problems arise, you'll have a better idea of what's achievable through proper analysis. Some of these examples are built around specific principles of relevance. Others focus on particular analysis features that can be applied to a variety of relevance problems.

4.4.1 Dealing with delimiters

Our previous examples used fields composed of text, with the words delimited on whitespace and punctuation. This needn't always be the case, and dealing inappropriately with delimiters can lead to poor search results. Consider the following examples, which focus on acronyms and phone numbers.

ACRONYMS

Sometimes acronyms use periods and sometimes they don't—for example, *I.B.M.* versus *IBM*. Analysis must normalize acronyms so that no matter the format, the resulting token will be the same. This is made easy enough with the `word_delimiter` filter. Here's an analysis chain that will create suitable tokens:

```
POST example
{
  "settings": {
    "analysis": {
      "filter": {
        "acronyms": {
          "type": "word_delimiter",
          "catenate_all": true,
          "generate_word_parts": false,
          "generate_number_parts": false}},
      "analyzer": {
        "standard_with_acronyms": {
          "tokenizer": "standard",
          "filter": ["standard","lowercase","acronyms"]}}}}}
```

This creates the acronyms filter of type `word_delimiter`. This token filter is designed to split tokens on many boundaries, including punctuation changes (Wi-Fi), change in case (wiFi), and changes between numeric and non-numeric (2016AD), to name a few. Rather than emitting the delimited parts as their own tokens, we have further choices to make. Here we've chosen to not `generate_word_parts` (otherwise, `I.B.M.` would become three tokens, i, b, m). We've also opted to `catenate_all`, which means that whatever parts are generated, we'll just stick them together and emit that as a token. Testing this out, you can see that the desired effect is achieved:

```
GET example/_analyze?analyzer=standard_with_acronyms
    &text=I.B.M. versus IBM versus ibm

[ibm] [versus] [ibm] [versus] [ibm]
```

So now, a user who searches for "IBM" or "I.B.M." finds a match. Be aware, though, that this could occasionally cause problems with acronyms that spell words (such as *N.E.W.*, which stands for *National Engineering Week*). In this case, the token produced would be new, a fairly poor text feature because it carries two meanings: National Engineering Week and something that isn't old. To help remedy the situation, you'd add `"preserve_original": true` to the acronyms filter. Then `N.E.W.` is tokenized both as new and `n.e.w.` In this case, a search for "new" will occasionally match on documents that contain the acronym `N.E.W.` That's OK because this might have been the user's intent, despite omitting the periods. And in this case a search for "N.E.W." will exactly match on the preserved original token, improving relevance greatly.

PHONE NUMBERS

Phone numbers—for example, 1(800)867-5209 versus 1.800.867.5309—are trickier. Although it's rare for delimiters to be removed from a phone number (you won't often see this number written as 18008675309), the variety of delimiters used in phone numbers can be broad. And users might search for a phone number with any of these formats.

Here again `word_delimiter` can help by effectively removing the delimiters, as shown in the previous example. There's a twist, though. Our two example numbers would both create tokens such as `18008675309`. But we must anticipate the users' expected behavior. Will the user always type in the full phone number, including the area code *and* the country code? Probably not. So let's add another filter that takes into account this behavior and creates two additional tokens: one is the last 7 digits (the local number), and one is the last 10 digits (the long-distance number):

```
POST my_library
{
  "settings": {
    "analysis": {
      "filter": {
        "phone_num_filter": {
          "type": "word_delimiter",
          "catenate_all": true,
          "generate_number_parts": false},
        "phone_num_parts": {
          "type": "pattern_capture",
          "patterns":["(\\d{7}$)","(\\d{10}$)"],
          "preserve_original": true}},
      "analyzer": {
        "phone_num": {
          "tokenizer": "keyword",
          "filter": ["phone_num_filter","phone_num_parts"]}}}}}
```

The important differences are highlighted in the preceding snippet. The first thing to note is that the tokenizer is now `keyword` rather than `standard`. The assumption here is that you're dealing with a `phone_number` field rather than a free-text field that happens to contain a phone number. The `keyword` tokenizer doesn't split the input into tokens, but creates a single token that contains the entire unaltered text of the field. "But why?" you ask. "Can't you just choose to not analyze this field at all?" Good question. You use the `keyword` tokenizer because it allows you to then use downstream filters to further modify the token.

In this case, `phone_num_parts` is the downstream filter. This is a `pattern_capture` filter that has two patterns, one to capture the last 7 digits of the input (the local number) and one to capture and last 10 digits (the long-distance number). The original token is also preserved. Let's test it out:

```
GET example/_analyze?analyzer=phone_num&text=1(800)867-5309
```

```
[18008675309] [8008675309] [8675309]
```

Based on this analysis scheme, a user's search for "800.867.5309" would get tokenized as `8008675309,8675309` and both of these tokens would match on a document containing the number `1(800)867-5309`. Perfect!

In both examples, you're shaping analysis to capture the most important features of the fields' data—*the meaning*. In this case, the meaning of an acronym and the meaning of a phone number aren't in their delimiters, but in the letters and numbers that compose them. Additionally, you're anticipating the *behavior* of users to use arbitrary delimiters, or even no delimiters at all. With phone numbers, capturing a meaningful subset of the numbers is a way of modeling the user intent, effectively acknowledging that the user will at times search for local numbers or national numbers. You want to provide the most relevant results possible, no matter which form the user uses.

4.4.2 Capturing meaning with synonyms

Synonyms often come in handy for fixing up corner-case relevance problems. Consider the plight of an online clothing retailer that's trying to fix problems with the query "dress shoes." To you, *dress shoes* probably conjures up images of leather men's footwear. But a beginner search engineer might be surprised to find that a search for "dress shoes" leads to a page full of sundresses and tennis shoes! The solution is once again to make sure that the token captures the *meaning* rather than just the terms.

How do you capture the meaning with synonyms? By noticing that, in the English language, whenever the term *dress* immediately precedes *shoes*, we're talking about a specific concept: dress shoes. You can use analysis to map this concept to a single token, like so:

```
POST retail
{
  "settings": {                                    English filters
    "analysis": {                                  from listing 4.2
      "filter": {
        <english filters omitted>          ◄─┘
        "retail_syn_filter": {                     ❶ Your new
          "type": "synonym",                          analyzer
          "synonyms": [
            "dress shoe,dress shoes => dress_shoe, shoe"
          ]}},
      "analyzer": {
        "retail_analyzer": {                   ◄─┐
          "tokenizer": "standard",
          "filter": [                              ❷ Here's where
            "english_possessive_stemmer",             the filter is
            "lowercase",                              used.
            "retail_syn_filter",
            "english_keywords",
            "english_stemmer"                    ◄─┘
          ]}}}},
  "mappings": {
    "items": {                                     ❸ Your desc
      "properties": {                                 field includes
        "desc": {                              ◄─┘    synonyms.
          "type": "string",
          "analyzer": "retail_analyzer"
}}}}}}
```

In this highlighted listing, you do the following:

- Create a `retail_syn_filter` filter ❶, which sets up the dress shoes synonym line
- Use that filter ❷ in a new `retail_analyzer`
- Make sure that this analyzer is used for `desc` field text ❸.

(Note that it's presumed that the `english_*` filters are defined similar to listing 4.2.)

One thing to consider is the placement of the `retail_syn_filter`. By placing it after the possessive stemming, plural stemming, and lowercasing, you've somewhat normalized the input to the synonym filter so that the expected synonyms will be created. For instance, if `retail_syn_filter` had been the first filter, then `dress shoe's` and `Dress shoes` wouldn't be picked up by the synonym filter. But it's important to place the synonyms filter before more drastic forms of normalization such as stemming or phonetic mapping because these filters change the tokens to such an extent that no synonym matches would be made.

Next let's take a look at the synonym line:

```
"dress shoe,dress shoes => dress_shoe, shoe"
```

This says, "Whenever you see either `dress shoe` or `dress shoes`, map that to two tokens: `dress_shoe` and `shoe`." It's important to include `shoe` here because a dress shoe is indeed a shoe, and you want them to be included in searches for "shoes."

Let's index some documents and see how it works:

```
POST retail/items/1  # "dress shoe" document
{ "desc": "bob's brand dress shoes are the bomb diggity"}
POST retail/items/2  # "dress" document
{ "desc": "this little black dress is sure to impress"}
POST retail/items/3  # "shoe" document
{ "desc": "tennis shoes... you know, for tennis"}
```

And then you make some queries:

```
    GET retail/items/_search?
{ "query": {
   "match": {
     "desc": "dress"}}}
```

This produces one result, the `dress` document. Perfect. Next you make a similar query for "shoes." Here, as expected, you receive both the `dress shoe` document and the `shoe` document. This is also what you should expect. One final test to close the loop: you make a query for "dress shoes" and expect to receive only the `dress shoe` document … and … hey! Why do both the `dress shoe` and the `shoe` document come back in the results?

Using the `_analyze` endpoint, it's not too difficult to get to the cause of the problem. Here's how the two documents in question are analyzed:

- dress shoe document: `bob, brand, dress_sho, shoe, bomb, diggiti`
- shoe document: `tenni, shoe, you, know, tenni`

And remember, the query gets analyzed as well and produces the tokens to be matched against the index. In this case, we have the following:

dress shoe search: dress_sho, **shoe**

As you can see, it's easy to overlook the implications of the fact that analysis happens both at index time and search time. Our synonym expansion of dress shoes causes two tokens to be generated—one of which is shoe, which is also included in both documents in question. Now the reason for the behavior is obvious.

Fortunately, there's an easy fix. Elasticsearch allows for different analyzers to be used at index time and query time. Here's how this can be used to remedy the problem at hand.

Listing 4.5 Index configuration for resolving the dress shoes problem

```
POST retail
{ "settings": {
    "analysis": {
      "filter": {
        "retail_syn_filter_index": {  # 1. new filter
          "type": "synonym",
          "synonyms": ["dress shoe,dress shoes => dress_shoe, shoe"]},
        "retail_syn_filter_search": {
          "type": "synonym",
          "synonyms": ["dress shoe,dress shoes => dress_shoe"]}},
      "analyzer": {
        "retail_analyzer_index": {  # 2. new analysers
          "tokenizer": "standard",
          "filter": [
            "english_possessive_stemmer",
            "lowercase",
              "retail_syn_filter_index",
              "english_stop",
            "english_keywords",
            "english_stemmer"]},
        "retail_analyzer_search": {
          "tokenizer": "standard",
          "filter": [
                "english_possessive_stemmer",
            "lowercase",
              "retail_syn_filter_search",
              "english_stop",
            "english_keywords",
            "english_stemmer"]}}}},
  "mappings": {
    "items": {
      "properties": {
        "desc": {
          "type": "string",
            # 3. two-sided analysis
          "analyzer": "retail_analyzer_index",
          "search_analyzer": "retail_analyzer_search"}}}}}
```

- **1** Index time synonym filter (same as listing 4.4)
- query time synonym filter forces "dress shoe" search to exactly **2** "dress_shoe"
- Creates different analyzers for search and index
- Creates analyzers for search and index
- Sets field to use different index and search analyzers
- set field to use different index and search analyzers

This might look complex, but all that you've done is split that analysis into index-time analysis ❶ (where `etail_syn_filter_index` creates two tokens for dress shoes: `dress_shoe` and `shoe`) and query-time analysis ❷ (where dress shoes maps to only one token, `dress_shoe`). And if you run through the queries again, you see that the results are as you'd hope they'd be. A query for "dress" returns the `dress` document, a query for "shoes" returns both the `dress shoe` and `shoe` document, and a query for "dress shoes" returns only the `dress shoe` document. The search now works because you've accurately captured the meaning of "dress shoe" and encoded it in such a way that the pertinent documents can be retrieved.

4.4.3 *Modeling specificity in search*

Wouldn't it be nice if you could search for an item like "dog" and pull back documents that contain terms like `poodle`, `terrier`, and `beagle`, even if those documents happen to not use the word `dog`? And go a step further. Wouldn't it be nice to do a search for "animal" and pull back results that contain `dog`, `poodle`, `cat`, and so forth, even if the word `animal` isn't included in the document? Well, you can! By using asymmetric analysis techniques, you can encode a notion of *specificity* into the search application. *Asymmetric analysis* means that the analysis applied at query time is different from the analysis applied at index time.

4.4.4 *Modeling specificity with synonyms*

How can you achieve this? Well, we secretly presented an example of this in the previous section. Not only did we use synonyms to make sure that `dress shoes` was tokenized as a semantic unit (`dress_shoe`), but we also generated the extra `shoe` token so that `dress shoes` would still match a search for `shoe`. This analysis was asymmetric. During index analysis we produce both tokens. At query time only a single token, `dress_shoe`, is produced so that our search matches strictly `dress shoes`.

To fully understand how asymmetric analysis may be used to encode specificity, let's look at an approachable example. Here we could use the preceding dog example, but that's boring. Let's use a more interesting example like, I don't know, fruit! Consider the fruit hierarchy shown in figure 4.5.

Based on this hierarchy, you can create the following entries in a synonyms file:

```
apple => apple, fruit
fuji => fuji, apple, fruit
mcintosh => mcintosh, apple, fruit
gala => gala, apple, fruit
banana => banana, fruit
orange => orange, fruit
```

Notice that the synonyms file maps terms to words of equal or greater generality. We call this *semantic expansion*. `fruit` and `apple`, for example, are of equal or greater generality than `apple`.

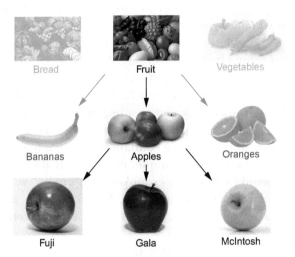

Bread

Fruit

Vegetables

Bananas

Apples

Oranges

Fuji

Gala

McIntosh

Figure 4.5 Fruit hierarchy focusing on apples

Next, consider the behavior of search if you apply synonym analysis only at index time, as depicted in table 4.1. As you can see, index-time synonym matching of terms to equal or more-general values has the desired behavior: queries match documents of equal or greater specificity. A query for "apple," for example, matches not only `apple` documents but also `fuji` documents.

Table 4.1 Semantic expansion at index time

Index		Query		
Doc contains	Tokens produced	Fruit	apple	fuji
Fruit	`Fruit`	*Match*	Miss	Miss
apple	`apple, fruit`	*Match*	*Match*	Miss
Fuji	`fuji, apple, fruit`	*Match*	*Match*	*Match*
orange	`orange, fruit`	*Match*	Miss	Miss

Conversely, consider the behavior of search if you use synonym analysis only at query time. In this case, you'll be able to make matches that *generalize* upon the query. In this case, such behavior is arguably not that useful, but it can come in handy at times.

As you can see here, index-time synonym matching of terms to equal or more-general values has the desired behavior: queries match documents of equal or greater specificity. A query for "apple," for example, matches not only `apple` documents but also `fuji` documents. And as an exercise for the reader, consider the behavior of search if you use synonym analysis only at query time. In this case, you'll be able to make matches that *generalize* upon the query. In this case, such behavior is arguably not that useful, but it can come in handy at times.

Although using synonyms to model semantic specificity can have some obvious benefits, it's not a pattern that should be used carelessly. Reflecting on the precision and recall conversation of section 4.2, this approach is guaranteed to improve recall, because results returned with this approach include all of the documents that would be returned without synonyms as well as other documents that contain more-specific concepts. But inevitably, this pattern will cause problems with precision. For one thing, there's more opportunity to conflate tokens that have the same representation but different meanings. For example, does `fuji` really refer to the apple? Or is it a city in Japan? And perhaps a user looking for "apples" wants documents that are near that level of specificity and wouldn't consider a document about the specific topic of `Fuji apple cultivation in Fujisaki Japan` to be all that relevant to the search.

The relevance engineer should also consider the implications on TF × IDF. Because the more general terms are replicated over and over, their doc frequency will be artificially inflated, and therefore matches on general terms will be penalized. This could work for or against you, depending on the situation. It might be worth turning off norms and term frequencies altogether and using a constant score query so that matches are scored equivalently, no matter the term frequency or doc frequency. This replication of terms also could increase the size of the index. Finally, using this method requires the collection and curation of an extra set of information—the synonyms themselves.

With all of these potential gotchas, is there ever a reason to use this pattern? Yes! This can be a tremendous tool for using a taxonomy to build semantic search. A great example is the Medical Subject Headings (MeSH), a rich taxonomy for medical concepts. Consider the task of building a search engine over medical literature. The documents might be tagged according to their *specific* MeSH topics. At index time, the synonyms file can make matches to more-general topics. For example you might expand the hypothetical MeSH concepts `depression`, `anxiety`, `schizophrenia` to also include their parent category: `mental illnesses`. With this done, it becomes possible to search for a subtopic such as schizophrenia and retrieve documents for any mental illnesses. If no schizophrenia results exist, the search engine would fall back to the broader concept in the corpus, in this case other mental illnesses.

This may seem like a silly fallback. But consider a medical researcher entering multiple search terms. For example they might hunt for a link between heart disease and schizophrenia with a query: "heart disease schizophrenia." Unfortunately, let's say, they find no direct matches linking `heart disease` and `schizophrenia`. Instead the corpus contains a large number of `heart disease` documents with a few of those mentioning some `mental illness`. Luckily our technique at least falls back on these pretty-close matches. The returned `heart disease mental illness` articles might be a good start for our researcher. They might have that small nugget of insight relating heart disease and mental illnesses that inspires their own creativity or improves their own research.

The takeaway is mapping concepts to varying degrees of specificity is very powerful. Keep this technique in mind especially if you need to lead searchers to new and powerful insights. The next section shows you an alternate method also applicable to taxonomies.

4.4.5 *Modeling specificity with paths*

Synonyms aren't the only way that specificity is modeled in search. And when you know where to look, specificity modeling pops up throughout common patterns of search. The underlying theme isn't synonyms, but the intentional asymmetry between query-time analysis and index-time analysis.

Let's demonstrate by looking at common search patterns involving paths. Let's say that you're building a filesystem search engine. As one of the features, you want the user to be able to find documents at or below a user-specified directory. For instance, if a user is searching for a document in /fruit/apples, the search should also include documents in /fruit/apples/fuji, /fruit/apples/gala, /fruit/apples/mcintosh, and so forth. (And *yes*, we're going with the fruit example again!)

Implementing this behavior is straightforward:

```
POST catalog
{ "settings": {
    "analysis": {
      "analyzer": {
        "path_hierarchy": {
          "tokenizer": "path_hierarchy"}}}},
  "mappings": {
      "item": {
        "properties": {
          "inventory_dir": {
            "type": "string",
            "analyzer": "path_hierarchy"}}}}}
```

First you set up a path_hierarchy analyzer, which expands a path such as */fruit/apples/fuji* into tokens /fruit, /fruit/apples, and /fruit/apples/fuji. Then you assign this analyzer to the inventory_dir field, which represents the directories that inventory-related files are stored in:

```
PUT catalog/item/1
{ "inventory_dir":"/fruit/apples/fuji",
  "description":"crisp, sweet-flavored, long shelf-life"}
PUT catalog/item/2
{ "inventory_dir": "/fruit/apples/gala",
  "description ":"sweet, pleasant apple"}
PUT catalog/item/3
{ "inventory_dir": "/fruit",
  "description ":"edible, seed-bearing portion of plants"}
```

Now you search for things in /fruit/apples/fuji:

```
GET catalog/_search
{ "query": {
    "bool": {
      "should":
        [{"match": {"description": "<whatever>"}}],
      "filter": [
        {"term": {"inventory_dir": "/fruit/apples/fuji"}}]}}}
```

And you get the `fuji` item back. If you do a similar search for items in /fruit/apples, you get back both of the more specific apple items, `fuji` and `gala`. And finally, if you search for items under /fruit, then all three documents are returned. (Hopefully, you're seeing parallels to last section's discussion on taxonomies—what we have here is our own little fruit taxonomy!)

You might notice that the `inventory_dir` configuration doesn't assign a different analyzer at index time and query time. So at first glance it may seem that somehow specificity is being modeled without asymmetric analysis. But this isn't the case. In Elasticsearch, the `term` filter doesn't perform analysis; it looks for tokens that exactly match the supplied text. Therefore, once again, you can see that specificity is modeled by asynchronous analysis.

To summarize the message of this section, consider the following rules:

- If the tokens in the index represent a generalization of the tokens produced at query time, search will retrieve items that are more specific than the search term.
- If the tokens produced at query time represent a generalization of the tokens in the index, search will retrieve items that are more general than the search term.

In this section, you've looked at a couple of ways that specificity can be modeled, first with synonyms and second with hierarchical paths. But as stated at the beginning of this conversation, this pattern arises throughout search. Case in point—numbers, and even geographic search! Read on …

4.4.6   *Tokenize the world!*

The focus of this chapter has been on analysis techniques used to convert text into tokens. But analysis is by no means limited to text. Any information containing features that can be mapped into discrete semantic units can also be represented as tokens, stored in an inverted index, and used in search. Here are some examples of information that can be tokenized, starting with the mundane and moving toward the more esoteric:

- Numerical data including integers, floating-point numbers, and dates
- Geographic information such as latitude/longitude points or geographic areas
- Images, shapes, sounds, textures … whatever

To apply search, you need to extract meaningful and discrete features from the information through analysis. This turns search into a far more general-purpose similarity system, allowing you to perform tasks such as image search or even classification. Let's look at some quick examples so that you can get an idea of the broad types of information that can be included in search applications.

4.4.7 *Tokenizing integers*

Let's consider numerical data, specifically integers. The best features to extract from an integer—the most semantically significant symbol for an integer—is the number itself! But search engines tokenize integers in a way that might initially seem surprising. Consider a search application that indexes historical events by year. In particular, consider 1945, the year that World War II ended. Rather than indexing one token for the year 1945, a search engine will also index tokens that represent lower-precision versions of the same number, for instance: 194, 19, and 1.

But why would a search engine do this? Well, consider what would be required to make a range query across this field. Naïvely, if you indexed only one token for the year, 1945, then in order to find all documents with years falling in that range, you'd have to scan through the term dictionary, find every term that falls in this range, and then do a Boolean SHOULD search for documents containing any of these terms. This could be millions of terms, which would obviously not scale. But because the years are indexed at several levels of precision, you don't have to look for every term; you can take advantage of the fact that the less-precise tokens cover ranges of terms.

Let's use this understanding to perform a range query for all interesting events in the range of 1776 to 2010. In this case, you wouldn't have to look for documents containing *any* of the 235 possible full-precision tokens from 1776 to 2010. As shown in the table 4.2, you can retrieve the appropriate documents by querying for the appropriate mixture of terms at varying levels of precision.

Table 4.2 Tokens used to represent numerical values and ranges

Token	1776	1777	1778	1779	18	19	200	2010
Range covered	1776	1777	1778	1779	1800–1899	1900–1999	2000–2009	2010

Will a query that ORs these terms together match a document for the year 1945? Yes, because that document was indexed with the less precise token 19, which is one of the terms in the query.

One more thing to notice here: the trick that search engines use for efficiently executing numerical-range queries relies on asymmetric tokenization. In particular, it tokenizes the number more generally during indexing than during query. This is exactly the pattern previously introduced for encoding specificity in search. We told you it would pop up again!

4.4.8   *Tokenizing geographic data*

Geo search uses a similar strategy, except that the tokens encode 2D information rather than linear 1D information. It may seem surprising that a search engine can encode 2D information. After all, the wheelhouse of search is text, and text is linear in nature. But besides the process of creating tokens, nothing is changed; the inverted index and the search algorithms work just the same as always.

Consider an application indexing funny or strangely named cities in the western United States. A simple method for encoding geo data across a flat, rectangular map is to use *Z-encoding*. What's *Z-encoding*? It's easier to show you via figure 4.6.

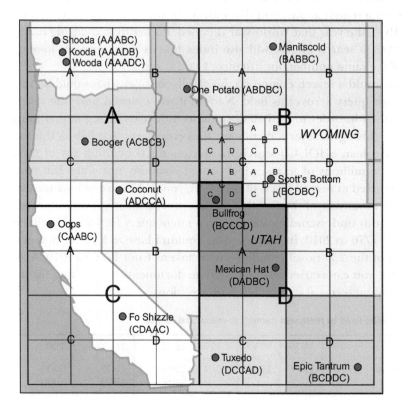

Figure 4.6   Example of several Z-encoded points on a rectangular map

This map is divided into four quadrants labeled A, B, C, and D. Each quadrant is then further divided into subquadrants that are also named A, B, C, and D. This process continues until the map is subdivided into small enough areas that the desired precision is achieved. Notice that the order of quadrants at each level follows a Z shape, thus the name. With this encoding, every point on the map can be translated into a sequence of symbols A, B, C, and D. For instance, direct your attention to Scott's Bottom (it's in Wyoming). The Z-encoding for this point is BCDBC, because the city is in B quadrant at the top level, the C quadrant at the next level, D at the following level, and so on.

When indexing geo points, you first find the Z-encoded representation of the point. Then, similar to the strategy for indexing numbers, you index the Z-encoded point at several levels of precision. For instance, the tokens produced from Scott's Bottom would include the highest-precision encoding of that location, BCDBC, followed by lower-precision representations BCDB, BCD, BC, and B. And in order to query for all points included in a specific area, you need to find the terms representing the appropriate areas of the map and place them into the same Boolean SHOULD query. For example, referring again to figure 4.6, a query for all towns with funny names in Utah can be accomplished by querying for the terms DA, BCCC, and BCCD. Referring to the map, you can see that both Bullfrog and Mexican Hat will match this query, because those cities have a token prefix that matches the Utah query terms. What terms would you use to find cities in Wyoming? And finally, do you notice the specificity pattern at play again? Geo search is effectively just a two-dimensional analogue to the pattern used for one-dimensional numerical-range queries.

4.4.9 Tokenizing melodies

Let's wrap up with an example of something esoteric that can be tokenized and incorporated into search: melodies, and in particular, whistled or hummed melodies. Let's say that you're required to create a search engine that allows people to whistle tunes and search for songs that are matches to the whistles.

To help in the process, the other side of the application development team has created a whistle encoder that can take audio input from a cell phone's microphone and for every whistled note determine whether this is higher pitch, lower pitch, or the same pitch as the previous note. Perfect! This is all you need to encode whistled tunes as tokens in an inverted index.

Here's how. Every note in an indexed tune or a whistled melody gets a symbol:

- If the note is higher in pitch than the previous note, its symbol is U for up.
- If the note is lower in pitch than the previous note, its symbol is D for down.
- If the note is the same pitch as the previous note, its symbol is R for repeat.
- The first note gets the symbol *, indicating that it's the start of a tune.

This notation, known as *Parsons Code for Melodic Contours*, was developed in 1975 for the explicit purpose of encoding and indexing melodies so that they could be searched. The beginning of the children's classic melody "Old MacDonald Had a Farm" can be encoded as *RRDURDURDRD, as shown in figure 4.7.

```
" ♪♫ "  Old MacDonald had a farm E-I   E-I   O  " ♫♪ "


   *----R--R      U---R       U-R
            \   /      \   /     \
             D          D        D-R
                                     \
                                      D
```

Figure 4.7   Parsons code for "Old MacDonald Had a Farm"

But you still have more work to do to turn this into useful, searchable tokens. As always, you need to identify meaningful features that can help discriminate one song from another. Certainly the entire melody encoding could be a meaningful feature, but it's subject to a couple of potential problems. For one thing, someone humming an entire tune will likely get a couple of notes wrong. It would be nice if our search application was resilient to user mistakes. The larger problem with using the entire encoding as a feature is that, although the index will hold the entire encoding, it's terribly unlikely that an individual would whistle the entire song. The user will likely whistle only the most memorable bits of the song. You still want this to match to songs in your index.

N-grams can come in handy here. An n-gram token filter takes each token and breaks it into smaller tokens that represent a windowed subset of the originals. For example, a 5-gram tokenization of the Parsons code for "Old MacDonald" (*RRDURDURDRD) is as follows:

[*RRDU] [RRDUR] [RDURD] [DURDU] [URDUR] [RDURD] [DURDR] [URDRD]

For the previous two sections, Elasticsearch uses specialized Java code for tokenizing numerical and geographic data. And internal to Lucene, this is done with byte arrays rather than with character arrays, as presented in the preceding simplified versions. Building similar functionality would therefore require you to build an Elasticsearch analysis plugin (remember, open source search can be plugged to the nth degree!). But for Parsons code, if you stick with the text representation, standard text-analysis techniques can be applied. In this case, an n-gramming analyzer can be set up as follows:

```
POST music
{ "settings": {
    "analysis": {
      "filter": {
        "parsons-ngram": {
          "type": "nGram",
          "min_gram": 5,
          "max_gram": 5}},
      "analyzer": {
        "parsons": {
          "tokenizer": "keyword",
          "filter": ["parsons-ngram"]}}}}}}
```

Here all you have to do is create a new analyzer called `parsons`, which internally uses a keyword tokenizer to create a single token of the input and then passes the token to an n-gram token filter. The n-gramming process is configured with the min and max gram length set to 5. This analyzer can be applied symmetrically. At index time, the Parsons code for an entire song would be 5-grammed. (Presumably, the Parsons code for the songs would have to be separately generated beforehand.) Then at query time a user's whistles or hums of partial songs can be transcribed into 5-grammed Parsons code using the same analysis.

Besides being an interesting example of using exotic information in applications of search, this is also a great example of choosing the appropriate features to represent and distinguish items stored in the index. 5-gramming Parsons code enables users to find songs without humming the entire tune, and even if they sing portions of the song incorrectly, this technique will still produce at least some tokens that will match to the song that the user seeks. What's more, the Parsons code itself encodes only the most basic notion of relative pitch—up, down, or repeated. Therefore, even if the user can't carry a tune, there's still a reasonable hope of finding the song he's looking for.

But we can do even better. It stands to reason that a match on a longer n-gram should be more meaningful than a match on a shorter n-gram. So you could increase both the `min_gram` and `max_gram` settings to, say, 7. But this isn't great, because if the user doesn't match on a longer n-gram, you still want to at least give him the most relevant songs based on matches with shorter n-grams. So, let's index n-grams of varying lengths. You can try this out by using a `min_gram` of 4 and a `max_gram` of 7. Then, "Yankee Doodle," which has a Parsons code of *RUUDUD (go ahead, hum aloud; we did) will produce the following tokens:

```
[*RUU] [*RUUD] [*RUUDU] [*RUUDUD] [RUUD] [RUUDU] [RUUDUD] [UUDU] [UUDUD]
```

An additional benefit of using various-length n-grams is that TF × IDF as presented in section 4.3.1 comes clearly into play here. Using the alphabet of *, U, D, and R, there are only 108 possible 4-gram tokens (4 × 3 × 3 × 3), whereas, by similar calculations, there are 2,916 possible 7-gram tokens. In all likelihood, the doc frequency will be much lower for 7-grams. Therefore, because of their rarity, anytime that the 7-gram tokens match, they'll be scored significantly higher than the shorter tokens. At this point, you have a good outline for how the whistle-search app can be implemented to have a relevant user experience.

Before moving on, reflect on the past three examples—numerical search, geo search, and melody search. The goal of these examples isn't to teach you specifically how to implement these three search applications. Numerical search and geo search are already built into Elasticsearch, and it's unlikely you'll ever need to index melodies by using Parsons code. The goal of these examples is to generalize your notions about where search technology can be applied. You've seen that search isn't limited to words and text. Search can be extended to any domain for which discriminative features can be extracted and encoded as tokens.

4.5   *Summary*

- Tokens express features latent in text and in any kind of tokenizable data.
- Analysis controls the formation of tokens, which controls the precision and recall trade-off across the set of all search results.
- Analysis transforms text and data into tokens that anticipate how users intuitively understand various representations of one idea (runs, running, run equate to forms of the idea of running).
- The precision/recall trade-off can be less stark than you might expect. One way to sidestep the trade-off is through relevance ranking.
- Manipulating analysis also controls how the search engine counts TF and IDF scoring statistics.
- Numerous strategies exist in Lucene to help you normalize many forms of data. We specifically covered the following:
  - Non-whitespace-delimited text
  - Synonyms to capture specific meanings
  - Path-based and synonym-based methods for capturing specificity: from broad terms (fruit) to narrow ones (fuji apple)
- You can tokenize locations, melodies, and many other kinds of data, turning the search engine into a general-purpose similarity system across many kinds of data.

Basic multifield search

5

Earlier we compared search to a book's index. Such an index lets you zero in on pages that discuss a subject you're interested in. If you're interested in the French Revolution, just browse to the back of your French history book and find the associated pages.

Similarly, a search engine can quickly identify documents that mention search terms by using an inverted index. Search for the term "revolution," and the search engine retrieves a list of documents that mention a revolution. In the previous chapter, your goal was to use analysis to optimize the terms in the inverted index and maximize precision and recall. You expressed features of content as tokens, going beyond the idea that tokens are always associated with words and instead associating tokens with the *meaning* contained in the documents.

If your boss is breathing down your neck with a tough relevance problem, you know there's far more to tuning search than optimizing analysis! You need to understand how search results are ranked using a broad range of criteria important to your business. Your documents almost certainly are composed of multiple fields. Each field has its own characteristics and quirks. Each field has its own expected influence on the search engine's ranking behavior based on the requirements of your business.

In this chapter, we begin to take an increasingly top-down view of search. A search engine is more than just an index in the back of your book; it's a highly scalable content-ranking system with tremendous power in expressing business and user priorities. In this chapter, we focus on layering in multiple fields in the ranking solution, as shown in figure 5.1. To do this, we peel back the ranking and scoring behavior of multifield search queries. Every multifield query has a purpose—a specific way of combining field scores that you can use to balance criteria critical to your business and users.

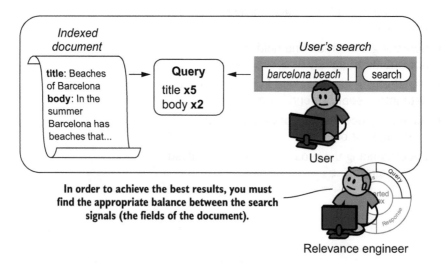

Figure 5.1   Relevance engineer prioritizing ranking criteria through fields when ranking

To master multifield search, you'll continue to manipulate individual field matching and scoring. Understanding, for example, something as simple as what a relevance score on a title or body field *means* to your users helps you pinpoint exactly how to combine those fields into a larger ranking function. In this chapter, you'll work to not only understand the meaning of fields when they're searched, but also to build fields expressly for the purpose of providing the right information to the overall search solution. This way, you can effectively program the ranking function to factor in criteria important to your business or users.

5.1 Signals and signal modeling

What does it take to express business ranking rules to a search engine? How can you treat the results ranking of a search engine as something programmable and not mystical?

First, let's reflect on something that feels mystical and intimidating, often to even experienced search developers. Throughout this book, you've had to stare at terrifying-looking relevancy explains such as this snippet:

```
2.555276, product of:
 3.1940954, sum of:
   3.1940954, weight(title:alien in 223)
 0.8, coord (4/5)
```

We're here to tell you: you can become the master of this big, ugly thing! Instead of seeing these scores as divined by the mystical search engine, you can transform your thinking into associating each number with a signal—an indication that there's something specifically meaningful or important about this document.

5.1.1 What is a signal?

What do we mean by signals? A *signal* is any component of the relevance-scoring calculation corresponding to meaningful, measurable user or business information. This could be any information you'd like to use in ranking, from "the movie sells well" or "the movie's overview text is about the user's query" or "the movie director's name is mentioned in the user's query."

You may not realize it, but if you've ever searched multiple fields, you've already begun to think in terms of signals. In chapter 3, you listed fields in a movie search that you thought were pertinent, such as the director's name or the overview text. By searching a director's name field, you're trying to measure the strength of the signal "the movie director's name is mentioned in the user's query" and give a hint to the search engine to use that fact in ranking. By searching a body's overview field, you're similarly trying to get at whether a movie's overview is about the user's search string. You're already groping toward the idea of getting the search engine to understand criteria important to your users, domain, or business.

To get beyond simply listing fields, you'll learn two techniques from this and future chapters that will put increasing power in your hands to create signals and control relevance ranking. What are these two ideas?

First, you'll *master signal modeling*. Instead of thinking of the relevance scores as incomprehensible, you control them! You exercised that power in the preceding chapter when manipulating features to model how users search. That effort continues with signal modeling. With signal modeling, you control every aspect of a field's relevance score to measure what you need. Your goal is to move closer and closer to signals that more precisely measure the desired information.

110   CHAPTER 5   *Basic multifield search*

Second, you'll *manipulate the ranking function.* This is a chapter about multifield search, after all. And multiple field scores—multiple signals—need to be combined into an overall relevance score to balance all the factors important to your users and business. This is the purpose of the ranking function. You combine signals into larger signals that quantify multiple pieces of information. You'll learn how to manipulate the ranking function in this and future chapters. The next two chapters focus primarily on the ranking function associated with specific uses of Elasticsearch's `multi_match` query. Future chapters show you how to manipulate the ranking function even deeper to boost, filter, and prioritize different pieces of information.

You can do quite a bit with just a search engine if you know exactly how to transform user and business criteria into meaningful ranking signals. After you understand how to use fields to put signals first, you can build any number of unique and intelligent search user experiences!

5.1.2   *Starting with the source data model*

Unfortunately, multifield search is often made complex because no signal modeling occurs. Instead, fields are directly copied from the source data without thought to how they'll be searched or the information they'll provide when scored. We refer to the *source data model* as the structure of the data as it lies in the originating system, be it a database, an API, or whatever else. Although this is an OK place to start, the source data model isn't optimized for search. It's optimized for concerns specific to the source system, such as database or application requirements. Instead of fields that give us specific, targeted signals during ranking, we get fields whose scores provide ambiguous information. This tends to create artificially obscure query-time logic, resulting in brittle and complex multifield search.

Take your company's employee database as an example. When placing employees in Elasticsearch, an obvious place to start is copying employee attributes from the source database directly into fields in the corresponding Elasticsearch document, as shown in figure 5.2. If your employee database table has `first_name`, `middle_initial`, and `last_name` columns, you place those exact `first_name`, `middle_initial`, and `last_name` fields directly into Elasticsearch without thinking about how you hope to search them later.

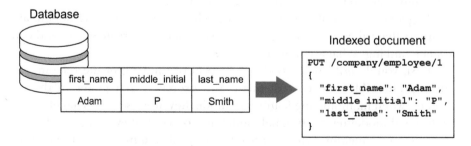

Figure 5.2 Directly indexing the source data model without transformation

With this field structure, you're left with many multifield search problems. How would you, for example, satisfy full-name searches in which the user enters searches of the form FirstName MiddleInitial LastName ("Adam P. Smith") into the search bar? In its current state, the best you could do is to search for each term in every possible field. If you applied `multi_match`, the search engine would need to execute something like the following listing.

Listing 5.1   Brittle multifield name search

```
usersSearch = "Adam P. Smith"
search = {
    "query": {
        "multi_match": { 1
            "query": usersSearch,
            "fields": ["first_name", "middle_initial", "last_name"],
        }
    }
}
```

The user's search terms ◄

Applies the user's query to first_name, middle_name, and last_name fields

As explained by the query validation endpoint (recalling Lucene query syntax from chapter 3), you can see how `multi_match` is likely to query each field for each search term:

```
(first_name:adam first_name:p first_name:smith) |
(middle_initial:adam middle_initial:p middle_initial:smith) |
(last_name:adam last_name:p last_name:smith)
```

This is a search for `Adam` in each field, a search for `P` in each field, and a search for `Smith` in each field. How does this turn into an overall relevance score? Each field is being scored against each of these terms. Recall from previous chapters, a TF × IDF score is calculated for a given term in a field (`first_name:Adam`), proportional to how frequently the term occurs for this document's field (TF) and how rarely the term occurs across all documents' instances of this field (IDF). The scores are combined to form an overall relevance score, the exact mechanics of which we present in more depth a bit later.

The preceding search seems like it might sort-of work. But there's a big problem. What happens when this query is scored against a document with an oddball employee with first name Smith and last name Adam—good ole "Smith P. Adam" in accounting?

Just looking at the search of the `first_name` field in isolation, you'll see a problem. Remember, *every* search term is searched against `first_name`, even those that aren't a first name:

```
first_name:Adam first_name:P first_name:Smith
```

The search for Adam in the first_name field is a fairly weak match; *Adam* is a common first name and thus the document frequency for Adam is high. The TF × IDF score for this match will be correspondingly low. What happens with our search for the term Smith in first_name? Well, only one employee has a first name of Smith—our friend "Smith P. Adam"! *Smith* is a rare first name, so the TF × IDF score for a first name of Smith will be correspondingly high. Suddenly and unexpectedly, due to a match of Smith in first_name, and similar match of Adam in last_name, Smith P. Adam far outranks Adam P. Smith in the search results.

There's a deep multifield search antipattern at play. There has been no reflection on what signals these fields provide based on how they're searched. You can see with your application of multi_match that each field is queried for each search term. In a name search, this results in field scores that provide ambiguous information. A first_name score, for instance, doesn't provide a signal about the relationship between a first name in the search string and the first_name in the document (which might be nice). Instead it provides vague information. It assumes that any search term might be a first name and scores accordingly. This isn't helpful when composing a ranking function.

Signal modeling builds fields that can be queried with less ambiguity, as you understand the questions to be answered by searched fields. When signal modeling, you must answer these questions:

1   How do users intend to search these fields to obtain the needed information?
2   What work needs to occur to improve or adjust that information?

Every problem differs. Name search has little resemblance to searches for restaurants or movie reviews. The fields that satisfy these searches are modeled differently. Instead of fretting over how hard multiple fields are to search, make fields an asset to your relevance solution. To the relevance engineer, fields exist to return a signal that measures information in the form of that field's relevance score. Fields are scorable units that you've constructed to generate a specific similarity score between a query and a document. In the rest of this chapter, you'll see numerous examples of multifield search that drive home this point. Only by understanding and controlling your fields can you build a relevance solution that accounts for multiple fields.

5.1.3 *Implementing a signal*

Let's explore a small signal modeling example. Revisiting the name search, you can see how this might help our problem. If you want to satisfy the expected FirstName MiddleInitial LastName search, the solution isn't just applying multi_match to a set of fields from your source data model, but instead creating a derived full_name field that provides the information you need at search time, as shown in figure 5.3.

If you know that users commonly search with the syntax FirstName MiddleInitial LastName, it may be valid to construct a derived field that appends names in this format. A multifield search solution might, in addition to searching each name in isolation,

Database

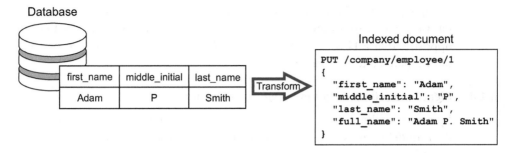

Figure 5.3   A transformation to a `full_name` field that creates a better signal when ranking

attempt to perform a phrase search against this `full_name` field. When users search exactly for "Adam P. Smith," this full-name phrase match can be used with other factors in a ranking function to bring users to the right employee. Perhaps the ranking function could look more like this:

```
max(first_name:Adam first_name:P first_name:Smith),
    (middle_initial:Adam middle_initial:P middle_initial:Smith),
    (last_name:Adam last_name:P last_name:Smith))
+ full_name:"Adam P. Smith"
```

You could accomplish this by using Elasticsearch's phrase query, and combining the impact with Elasticsearch's Boolean query. Although this is the first time you've seen Elasticsearch's Boolean query, you've seen Boolean search quite a bit. Recall from earlier chapters that SHOULD adds the scores of the contained queries, which is precisely what you do to create the needed ranking function.

Listing 5.2   Improved multifield name search

```
search = {
    "query": {
        "bool": {
            "should": [                                      Combines the two
                "multi_match": {                             scores with multiple
                    "query": usersSearch,                    SHOULD clauses
                    "fields": ["first_name", "middle_initial", "last_name"],
                },                                           The user's
                "match_phrase": {                            search terms
                    "full_name": usersSearch
        }]}}}                                                Applies the user's
                                                             query to first_name,
                    Queries full_name with a phrase          middle_initial, and
                    query, providing a signal that the       last_name fields
                    user's search is a complete
                    match to the full_name field.
```

When searched with a phrase query, the `full_name` field adds information to the overall relevance score that has a clear meaning. When a phrase query scores highly for this query, you know that the user has hit on a `full_name` field; you have a specific signal to use at search time. Conversely, no match for a phrase in this field means the opposite, that a FirstName MiddleInitial LastName search either wasn't executed or didn't match a user's exact name.

5.1.4   *Signal modeling: data modeling for relevance*

By querying the full name as in the previous example, you transcended your source data model to answer questions targeting search users. In other databases, data modeling is a task done to structure data in order to answer questions within the constraints of the data-retrieval system. You undergo data modeling to structure data to use the strengths of that system to answer questions.

This is no less true for a search engine. Signal modeling is just data modeling for relevance. A search engine has specific strengths as a data-retrieval system. These strengths imply that data modeling for relevance takes a different tack than your source data model. A search engine takes an index-first mentality to data. It allows text to be subdivided into terms likely to be searched efficiently in an inverted index. Most of the time, these terms correspond to words. But as you learned in the preceding chapter, this need not be the case. The terms you use need not correspond to words, or even text.

You can build terms to answer specific questions. By heeding the advice of signal modeling and the techniques of the previous chapter, you can construct fields that use the strengths of the search engine. You can apply fine control to how these fields will be searched. You can pick apart both the query and the field to engineer the relevance signal you need to answer important questions for your users.

If you can get past the idea that fields exist simply to store properties of data, and embrace the idea that you can manipulate data so it can be found as users expect it, then you can begin to effectively program relevance rules into the search engine.

5.2   *TMDB—search, the final frontier!*

Now that you've tasted a small sample of how signal modeling can improve multifield search, let's continue to explore various signal modeling scenarios with the TMDB (The Movie Database) data set that was introduced in chapter 3.

We're going to do something fun with this data set. It turns out you've been hired to build a movie search application for fans of the science-fiction franchise Star Trek! You've worked hard to load data from TMDB into the search engine. There's a beautifully designed futuristic UI that reminds users of the Starship Enterprise. All that's left is to plug in the search engine to get results, and you'll be finished! Right?

What you're about to learn is that users from Star Trek fandom have their own definition of *relevant*. But you'll need to undergo a bit of your own trek through the source data model to arrive at a relevance solution that can give you the right signals for what the Star Trek fan is looking for. In this and the next chapter, you'll apply the lessons of the previous section to create a ranking function and signals to satisfy user and business needs.

Your technical work in this and the next few chapters will be focused on technique, not process. You might feel that this avoids possibly even *harder* questions. (What *should* the search engine be doing? How do we figure out user requirements for search? Who defines them? How do we keep track and continuously retest to ensure that search hasn't deviated from our goals?) We cover these larger topics in depth in chapter 10. For now, it's more important to see some of the nitty-gritty of interacting with the search engine to solve targeted problems: the day-to-day technical work you'll do all the time as a relevance engineer.

Before we have fun, let's recall the Python functions from chapter 3 that you used to work with the TMDB data and Elasticsearch. You'll use these functions, listed in table 5.1, throughout this chapter and future ones when working with TMDB data and Elasticsearch.

Table 5.1 Primitives working with TMDB and Elasticsearch

Function	Description
extract	Returns a dictionary mapping movie ID to movie details from tmdb.json, reflecting the TMDB source data model
reindex	Reindexes into Elasticsearch with the passed-in TMDB movie dictionary, analysis settings, and field mappings
search	Searches the TMDB Elasticsearch index with the provided Elasticsearch Query DSL query

You're going to examine elements of the source data model related to the cast and crew of a movie. You're expecting that users will search for their favorite cast members and directors. Each movie in tmdb.json has the entries movie['directors'] and movie['cast'] that contain a list of records full of details about each cast member and director. If you'd like to see exactly how we've put together this data from TMDB's API, check out appendix A.

Recalling how to use our helper functions, you can easily get back to where you were in chapter 3. First you use extract to pull in TMDB data. Then you reindex and search, with English as the default analyzer for your text fields, as shown in the following listing.

Listing 5.3 Extraction, indexing, and search

```
movieDict = extract()              ⟵┐  Extracts data
                                      │  from TMDB into
analysis = {                          │  movieDict
   "analyzer" : {
      "default" : {
         "type" : "english"
         }}}
reindex(analysisSettings=analysis,  ⟵┐  Reindexes with the
      mappingSettings=None,             │  English analyzer
      movieDict=movieDict)             │  as default
```

```
usersSearch = 'basketball with cartoon aliens'        ◁┐  Runs your search
query = {                                                │  from chapter 3
    "query": {
        "multi_match": {
            "query": usersSearch,                     ◁┐  User's
            "fields": ["title^0.1", "overview"],        │  query
        }}}
search(query)
```

5.2.1 *Violating the prime directive*

Star Trek was notorious for having rules that brash starship captains routinely violated. Well, by indexing TMDB directly, you violated some advice we gave earlier. You directly placed the source data model into Elasticsearch. Shouldn't you have done some signal modeling? If you use this data directly to create a search index, won't you end up with relevance problems?

Well, yes, but that's for a good reason. Search is a place ripe for premature optimization. You're likely to reach the heat death of the universe before achieving a perfect search solution in *every* direction. You know there will be relevance problems, but you don't quite know what those are until you experiment with user searches. There are few areas that emphasize "fail fast" as much as search relevance. Load your data, get something basic working, find where it's broken, reconfigure, reindex if need be, requery, rinse, and repeat. Keep going until you've reached diminishing returns.

For the purpose of this chapter, this means solving where *exactly* the source data model falls apart, and where to spend careful time with signal modeling. When do you decide to perform feature modeling to extract specific, useful features into terms? You can do this work only when you've let your search fail for real search queries.

5.2.2 *Flattening nested docs*

The fact that you could pull the source data model down should seem suspicious from a pure "how could this work" perspective. You indexed a possibly deeply nested JSON movie object straight into Elasticsearch. Yet earlier in this book, we remarked that Lucene documents are a flat collection of fields. How does a hierarchical source data model get mapped into Elasticsearch? You'll need to know how Elasticsearch deals with hierarchical data in order to understand how to search data and iterate on signals focused on these subobjects.

Let's examine our old friend *Space Jam* to determine exactly how our documents look in Elasticsearch.

> **Listing 5.4 Snippet of *Space Jam* Elasticsearch document**

```
spaceJamId = 2300
httpResp = requests.get("http://localhost:9200/tmdb/movie/%s" % spaceJamId)
spaceJamDoc = json.loads(httpResp.text)
print json.dumps(spaceJamDoc['_source'], indent=True)
```

```
{                                                        ←┐ Output
 ...
 "overview": "Michael Jordan agrees to help the Looney Tunes play
              a basketball game against alien slavers to determine their
              freedom.",                    ←┐
 "video": false,                             │
 "id": 2300,                                 │
 "genres": [                                 │     We searched title and
  {                                          │     overview fields from
   "id": 16,                                 │     chapter 3.
   "name": "Animation"                       │
  }],                                        │
 "title": "Space Jam",                      ←┘
 "tagline": "Get ready to jam.",
 "cast": [                                              ←┐
  {                                                      │
   "name": "Michael Jordan",                            │
   "character": "Himself",                              │
   "order": 0,                                          │
   "cast_id": 2,                                        │     Cast and
   "credit_id": "52fe434bc3a36847f80496c9",             │     directors
   "profile_path": "/7y16frD57Ztzk2mY4JeI2pQQhan.jpg",  │     fields
   "id": 23678                                          │
  },                                                    │
  ...                                                   │
 ],                                                     │
 "directors": [                                        ←┘
  {
   "name": "Joe Pytka",
   "credit_id": "52fe434bc3a36847f80496c5",
   "job": "Director",
   "department": "Directing",
   "profile_path": "/c46Ah1Kx1fC4W8mHVrGDsJ7dMPJ.jpg",
   "id": 23677
  }]}
```

Several fields in this document reflect the flat structure native to Lucene. You can also see that the `cast` and `directors` fields are lists of people. You'll see various use cases in which users want to find specific people, and we'll model signals to address this criteria later.

How does Elasticsearch model these fields? How does Elasticsearch's behavior with nested fields inform your signal modeling work? The truth is that Elasticsearch layers a bit of syntactic sugar on your fields. A list of objects is translated to flattened fields with multiple values. Each cast member's name is flattened into a multivalue `cast.name` field, with multiple names. For example, this nested object

```
"cast": [
 {
  "name": "Michael Jordan",
  "character": "Himself",
  ...
 },
```

```
{
 "name": " Danny DeVito",
 "character": " Mr. Swackhammer (voice)",
 ...
},
```

is effectively translated into multiple flattened, parallel fields:

```
cast.name: ["Michael Jordan", "Danny DeVito", …]
cast.character: ["Himself", "Mr. Swackhammer (voice)", …]
```

Or in terms of the inverted index, the terms `Michael`, `Jordan`, `Danny`, and `DeVito` all exist in a `cast.name` field attached to the Lucene document. As `Michael` and `Jordan` exist in one instance, they'll be indexed as adjacent terms; the same with `Danny` and `DeVito`. It's as if the `name` or `character` field's text looks like this:

```
cast.character: Himself BLAH BLAH BLAH Mr. Swackhammer (voice) BLAH BLAH…
cast.name: Michael Jordan BLAH BLAH … BLAH Danny Devito BLAH BLAH BLAH…
```

This lets you search for names by listing the flattened `cast.name` in queries.

Elasticsearch calls this representation *inner objects*. It maintains some advantageous properties, but by flattening the fields, it loses the association of which child object each field belongs to. For example, this structure loses the connection between `Danny DeVito` and character `Mr. Swackhammer (voice)`, even though they're listed together. Both strings are simply terms in the parent document's fields.

Elasticsearch has other ways of modeling these relationships that preserve these connections. If you'd like to explore further, examine the Elasticsearch documentation on nested documents and parent-child documents, which provide a much more specific way of modeling relationships between multiple documents.[1] For now, let's proceed with the default data model in our signal modeling work.

Now that the pieces are in place, you can begin to work with TMDB to solve the relevance problems of Star Trek fandom. Exactly what use cases do you need to support? When do the fields in your source data model stop supporting relevance? What signal modeling might be required to satisfy the movie search needs of Star Trek fans?

5.3   *Signal modeling in field-centric search*

Let's get to work satisfying the movie curiosities of Star Trek fans! As we mentioned, you've already been delivered a slick, futuristic search UI for the Star Trek fan portal from your fellow developers. You've been hired to get the search to work. After all, what's a slick-looking search UI without relevant search results to drive the user experience?

---

[1] For more on this, read "Managing Relations" on Elastic's blog at www.elastic.co/blog/managing-relations-inside-elasticsearch.

To create a search solution that returns what Star Trek fans deem relevant, you have to think about what criteria are likely to be important to them. These inform your possible ranking signals. Certainly simple things such as title and overview matches continue to be important. Star Trek fans are also loyal to their favorite cast members. Thus matches on cast members are likely to be an important criterion. As many cast members often are directors of Star Trek films, director search is also an important ranking criterion.

All these factors may not be quite right, but that's OK. They're a reasonable starting point for crafting signals and a ranking function that answer these questions. You're sure to discover more criteria as you test your solution. Starting out, you can see fields in the source data model that could possibly generate signals that reflect these criteria when searched:

- `title`—A high score equates to a likely direct title match
- `overview`—A high score equates to a query that describes a movie
- `cast.name`—A high score equates to a likely cast member match
- `directors.name`—A high score equates to a likely director match

You haven't done any signal modeling yet, so it's likely the resulting signals aren't ideal. Yet you need to get started with an initial solution. What sort of ranking function should you start with that could create a sensible overall score? What's available to choose? In this section, you'll begin to explore the interplay between the ranking function and the signals. How do you craft a ranking function using the most basic multifield search capabilities? How do these ranking functions use the signals that are provided? How do you optimize field scoring in the context of a selected ranking function to improve the quality of search results?

Selecting a multifield ranking function dictates what shape your search results will take. It controls the general shape of your search results. Should your search, for example, be driven to one signal deemed most important among the menu of options? Or should your search take into account multiple factors equally when ranking?

Let's examine what options exist for multifield search. Lucene-based search applications take two general-purpose approaches to ranking multiple fields, as shown in figure 5.4.

Field-centric search runs the search string against each field, combining scores after each field is searched in isolation. *Term-centric* search works just the opposite, by searching each field on a term-by-term basis. The result is a per-term score that combines each field's influence for that term. For your first forays at our Star Trek search, you'll start with field-centric ranking functions. Field-centric queries are often the place to start, as they let you focus on each field in isolation and the signal that searching that field provides. We revisit term-centric approaches in the next chapter.

Elasticsearch bakes field-centric options into the `multi_match` query. You've seen `multi_match` a few times, but how exactly does it work? It runs the search against each field that's passed in. For each field, `multi_match` runs query-time analysis on the

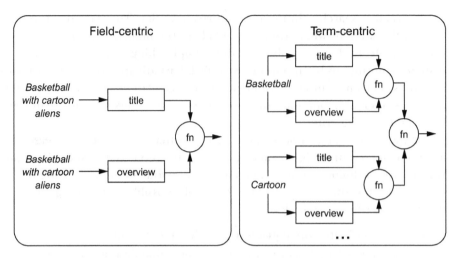

Figure 5.4   Field-centric versus term-centric search showing the fields `title` and `overview`. Field-centric searches each field in isolation; term-centric searches each field term by term.

search string, executing a Boolean search on the resulting tokens, each as a SHOULD clause. In other words, for a given field that uses the English analyzer, the search string goes through the process shown in figure 5.5.

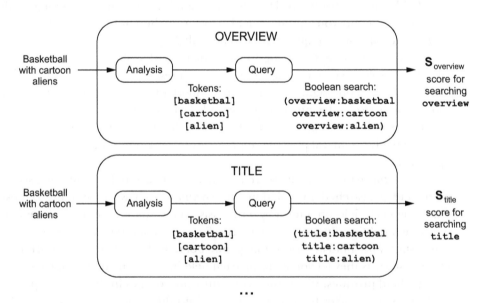

Figure 5.5   Match query over multiple fields (`multi_match`). Each field analyzes the search string and runs a Boolean OR query.

This way, `multi_match` searches each field in isolation, as a discrete unit, before combining field scores. How `multi_match` combines the result depends on the type of field-centric search. Let's examine the available ranking functions. If you denote the resulting score for a single-field search (`overview:basketbal overview:cartoon...`) as $S_{overview}$, you can see two main forms of field-centric search:

- `best_fields`—By default, take the highest-scoring field. If the `tie_breaker` parameter is specified (a value ranging from 0 to 1), the score of remaining fields is incorporated into the overall score. If `title` has the highest score, this math would look as follows:

```
score = Stitle + tie_breaker × (Soverview + Scast.name + Sdirectors.name)
```

- `most_fields`—Treat each match score as a clause in a Boolean query. Recall that a Boolean query is a summation, with a coordinating factor, or *coord*. Coord is the number of matching clauses / number of total clauses. Thus coord rewards Boolean queries with more matches:

```
score = (Soverview + Stitle + Scast.name + Sdirectors.name ) × coord
```

Figure 5.6 depicts this visually.

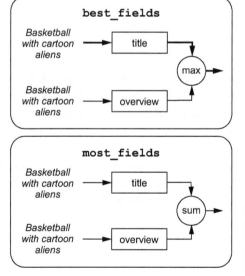

Figure 5.6 Contrasting `best_fields` **and** `most_fields`**. Here, the** `title` **field wins in** `best_fields`**, whereas** `most_fields` **takes a summation (coordinating factor not shown).**

Which ranking function might work for Star Trek searches? The two strategies live on opposite poles. The `best_fields` strategy works well when documents rarely have multiple fields that match the search string. This makes a *best field* easier to choose.

The `most_fields` approach works the opposite. It works when you expect multiple fields from a document to match the search string.

By picking the highest-scoring field that matches a search, `best_fields` decides, "This search must have been for that field." If your signal modeling is sound, and each field score is a signal, then `best_fields` selects the most appropriate signal as the resulting score. In a sense, `best_fields` is like a job interview—picking the field with the most credentials for the search terms. It ends up attempting to create a signal for each document that says, "This is a title search, and it's nothing else!" The `best_fields` strategy can be referred to as a *winner-takes-all search*. The winning field score is taken, and all other "runner-ups" get ignored or minimized—interpreted as spurious or lower priority.

In `most_fields`, fields work together like a team. More signals indicate increased relevance. This approach is all about synergy! You use `most_fields` by declaring a list of fields that all count toward increased relevance. As search terms match more of a document's fields, the document's resulting score increases, whereas fewer field matches punish the document's score. `most_fields` says, "The ideal search string contains a document's title, parts of the overview, and a cast member's name." In this way, `most_fields` rewards documents that have multiple field matches. The `most_fields` strategy can be referred to as *every field gets a vote*.

All that's the theory, at least! Anyone who's a fan of Star Trek knows that deep-space exploration can challenge the best of theories about how the universe is supposed to work! Let's get cracking on our TMDB search, and you'll see how your chosen ranking function and signal modeling work to deliver relevant search results.

5.3.1 *Starting out with best_fields*

Reflecting on our problem, it seems possible that sometimes Star Trek fans will search for specific movies by title or description, yet other times they'll search for actor or director names. Assuming that the scores for these fields correspond to these signals, you likely want to push the search toward one field score or another and ignore the rest. Could this be a use case for `best_fields`?

To try out a `best_fields` query, let's search for Star Trek actor "Patrick Stewart" and see if it behaves as we'd expect. You'd hope that `best_fields` might figure out we're searching for a cast member and choose that field as the best.

Listing 5.5 Star Trek query using content from chapter 3

```
usersSearch = "patrick stewart"
query = {
    "query": {
        "multi_match": {
            "query": usersSearch,
            "fields": ["title", "overview",
                       "cast.name", "directors.name"],
            "type": "best_fields"
        }
```

The user's search

Fields and boosts from chapter 3 (adding cast and director name)

```
        }
    }
search(query)
                                                           The search
Num   Relevance Score       Movie Title        ←┐         results
1     0.5308861             Legion
2     0.5308861             Halo 4: Forward Unto Dawn
3     0.5308861             Priest
4     0.5308861             Dark Skies
5     0.42397094            Drive Angry
```

Wow, right off the bat your initial attempt is doing poorly! The results show no Star Trek or Patrick Stewart movies. If this goes out, hordes of Star Trek fans will be knocking down your door! Better arm the photon torpedoes!

What's happening? Remember, best_fields picks a winning field. When you examine the explanation for your search queries, you see a particularly high score for a director named Stewart for the film *Legion:*

```
                                        Max component      Boolean query on
                                        of best_fields     directors.name field
                                                           (coord × sum of matches)
1.3460261, max of:                         ←┘                 ←┐
  1.3460261, product of:
    2.6920521, sum of:
      2.6920521, weight(directors.name:stewart in 868)   ←┐  Match on
    0.5, coord(1/2)                                           directors.name
                                                              field
```

Compare this explain for a film that stars actor Patrick Stewart, *Star Trek: Generations:*

```
                                        Max component              Expected matches
                                        of best_fields             on Patrick Stewart
0.38644278, max of:                        ←┘
  0.38644278, sum of:
    0.14300151, weight(cast.name:patrick in 533) [PerFieldSimilarity],   ←┐
    result of:
    0.24344127, weight(cast.name:stewart in 533) [PerFieldSimilarity], result
    of:
```

Director matches on Stewart appear to outscore the corresponding cast.name Stewart matches. The top results match the director, not the actor. This isn't intuitive. Why would the director matches be ranked so highly? Shouldn't it be clear that you're searching for the actor, not the director? The search results are lopsided, as in figure 5.7.

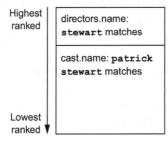

Highest ranked

directors.name: **stewart** matches

cast.name: **patrick stewart** matches

Lowest ranked

Figure 5.7 The director is chosen as the best field for many of our matches, and the Patrick Stewart actor matches score lower and are sorted to the bottom.

Fundamentally, you're not working with `best_field`'s strength. Search strings with names might match either the `directors.name` or `cast.name` fields. Without clear prioritization from you through boosting, `best_fields` appears to have the effect of shuffling one field's matches to the top. Without help from us, the shuffling won't be ideal or intuitive. This is for a couple of reasons.

First, field scores don't reliably line up. There's no absolute relevance scale for every TF × IDF score from, say, 0–100, where 0 means *irrelevant* and 100 means *relevant.* Therefore, you can't compare the preceding two field scores. You can truly compare field scores to only like field scores—a `cast.name` score to other `cast.name` scores. If you think about how scores work, you can see why. Term frequencies, document lengths, and inverse document frequencies all have different distributions among fields. All these factor into the field score, creating a scenario in which 2.0 might be a terrible `directors.name` score, but 0.2 might be a great `cast.name` score. These two scores are completely incomparable! In a sense, `best_field`'s mechanism for choosing the "best" (max) isn't that great. It's like choosing the "max" between a person's height in feet and height in meters! The two measurement systems are incompatible unless you manipulate the math to make them comparable.

Second, and perhaps more important, TF × IDF scoring is biased heavily against what the searcher is likely searching for. Remember, TF × IDF scores bias heavily toward rare terms (IDF correlates with rareness). But the user is more likely to be searching for a mundane, commonplace item. If you go to the grocery store and ask for coffee, you're more likely to be happy with being brought to the coffee aisle, where coffee is plentiful. You wouldn't be happy if brought to the ice-cream aisle, where a few tubs of coffee ice cream await you.

In the same way, the term `stewart` corresponds to a commonplace actor, but a rare director. For this reason, it's far more likely that the user is searching for the actor, *not* the director. Yet TF × IDF does the opposite. It rewards rareness. So the diamond-in-the-rough director scores more highly than the more likely candidate, the well-known but commonplace actor.

In other words, you're likely to get lopsided results—often in the direction you don't expect. This can create confusing search results for users as obscure field matches take precedence over common ones.

5.3.2   *Controlling field preference in search results*

In the previous section, `best_fields` created lopsided search results. First a director match is shown, followed by an actor, and so forth. Seemingly arbitrary lopsidedness feels unintuitive (why directors over actors?). But intentional lopsidedness might just be the ticket for your application! What if it's *very* important to bring films with our actors straight to the top of the search results and consider other matches secondary?

By using boosts, you *can* push `best_fields` to be lopsided in a preferred direction. For example, if you down-boost `directors.name`, you can deprioritize it with respect to other matches, as shown in the following listing. This gets more results with movies that star Patrick Stewart and deprioritizes the director field. Now, recall that you can't compare field scores, so the 0.1 down boost doesn't mean "10 times less important." The boost is just a multiple, chosen through experimentation, to ensure the desired lopsidedness.

Listing 5.6 Reducing the impact of `directors.name`

```
usersSearch = "patrick stewart"
query = {
    "query": {
        "multi_match": {                              User's
            "query": usersSearch,            ◄──────  query
            "fields": ["title", "overview",                    directors.name
                       "cast.name", "directors.name^0.1"],  ◄─ downboosted
        }                                                      by 0.1
    },
}
                                              Search
search(query)                                 results

Num  Relevance Score        Movie Title        ◄──┘
1    0.46373135             Vertigo
2    0.46373135             Star Trek: Insurrection       Patrick or
3    0.46373135             Gnomeo & Juliet               Stewart
4    0.46373135             Star Trek: First Contact      movies
5    0.46373135             Excalibur
```

Now your search is lopsided away from directors and toward actors, so your search results look better. The results appear to match actors named Patrick or Stewart, as shown in figure 5.8.

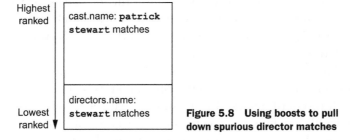

Figure 5.8 Using boosts to pull down spurious director matches

You should use `best_fields` when you'd like to create a lopsided ranking whereby results from one field dominate, followed by another. When there's more than one field match, you need to be assertive through boosting which field should take priority. In the preceding example, you pushed `directors.name` lower than `cast.name`; this flipped the search results upside down, dragging up results that were at the bottom, and pushing to the bottom results that were at the top.

Yet there remains a problem. *Vertigo*, for example, stars Jimmy Stewart, matching the "Stewart" part of our search. Another cast member has the first name Patrick, which matches "Patrick." So you're not exactly measuring what you want. The signal associated with the field score `cast.name` doesn't truly reflect a match on the exact actor Patrick Stewart. Instead you have matches on the individual search terms "Patrick" and "Stewart." So although you've modified the ranking function to perhaps fit your needs, the information being measured isn't precise. It's time to improve the signal!

5.3.3   *Better best_fields with more-precise signals?*

Even though you've flipped `best_fields` to your advantage, the results aren't quite what you want. The `cast.name` field has many spurious matches, because someone named Stewart and someone named Patrick happened to be in that movie. Recall that `multi _match` runs a SHOULD query on the field (`cast.name:patrick cast.name:stewart`). There's no notion that these terms ought to go together as a unit. If you could create a field that more definitively matched a name or didn't, you could dramatically improve the precision of the search. You'd likely remove many spurious results.

If you want to measure whether a name from the search matches a cast member, you'll need to perform some signal modeling on the field. What if instead of allowing matches on terms in isolation such as `Stewart` OR `Patrick`, you performed some signal modeling to force higher precision matching? What if you could force a field to score only exact matches on `Patrick Stewart`? Doing so would generate a precise signal that numerically conveys, "The search matches the person Patrick Stewart."

In the previous chapter, we talked about the degree of a term's specificity. Or in other words, how hard will the term be to match? How strict have you engineered the match? If the field has a pretty high hurdle to overcome (for example, exact matching `Patrick Stewart` instead of just `Stewart`), you know you've sharpened the precision of that field. This exactness misses out on alternate forms of names, which might reduce recall. Luckily, movie actors are referred to almost exclusively with the First-Name LastName form ("Patrick Stewart," never "Stewart Patrick"). So you might not need to match alternative name forms in this case.

Let's add a signal to improve the performance of `best_fields` queries. The shingle token filter can generate tokens from two-word subphrases. This can help you build a field to match two-word names. If you build an analyzer largely based on the English analyzer and add shingling, you'll generate what's known as a phrase index. A *phrase index* uses two- or three-word phrases as terms. In the phrase `Patrick Stewart Runs`, tokens extracted look something like `Patrick Stewart` and `Stewart Runs`. Remember that tokens and indexed terms need not be only single words! In this case, you've mapped terms to two-word pairs, or *bigrams*. The index will look something like this:

```
field cast.name.bigrammed
  term patrick stewart
    doc 0
      freq 1
      position 1
    doc 2
      ...
```

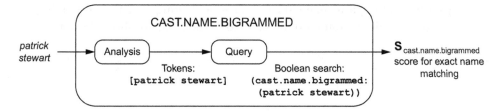

Figure 5.9 Searching `cast.name.bigrammed`**, which indexes bigrams. Searching such a field results in a more discerning signal than direct term matching.**

When Elasticsearch analyzes the search string, an identical analysis occurs, as depicted in figure 5.9.

Listing 5.7 modifies the TMDB index's analysis. The listing configures a shingle filter, `bigram_filter`, that generates bigrams. Using this filter, it also creates the `english_bigrams` analyzer that runs the same steps as the English analyzer, but finishes by generating bigrams instead of individual words. Once configured, the analyzer will be available for you to use in your field mappings.

Listing 5.7 Analysis extracting English bigrams

```
analysisSettings = {
   "analyzer" : {
      "default" : {
         "type" : "english"          English analyzer
      },                             customized to
      "english_bigrams": {          emit bigrams
         "type": "custom",
         "tokenizer": "standard",
         "filter": [
            "standard",
            "lowercase",
            "porter_stem",
            "bigram_filter"           Finishes with the
         ]                            bigram_filter to
      }                               generate bigrams
   },
  "filter": {
   "bigram_filter": {                 Our bigram_filter
      "type": "shingle",              that generates
      "max_shingle_size":2,          English bigrams
      "min_shingle_size":2,
      "output_unigrams":"false"
   }}}
```

Next, you need to use this analyzer for indexing and search. You can generate bigrammed versions of many of your fields using Elasticsearch's multifield feature. This feature lets you run two forms of analysis on a single field. The following listing provides your normal English analyzed `cast.name` field along with a corresponding `cast.name.bigrammed` field. (You'll do the same to `directors`, not shown here.)

```
mappingSettings = {
  "movie": {
    "properties": {
      "cast": {
        "properties": {
          "name": {
            "type": "string",
            "analyzer": "english",
            "fields": {
              "bigrammed": {
                "type": "string",
                "analyzer": "english_bigrams"
}}}}}}}}
reindex(analysisSettings, mappingSettings, movieDict)
```

Now the bigrammed fields should provide better discrimination when `best_fields` picks a score. Because of the analysis rules, the field is searched with two-word phrases. A search for "Patrick Stewart" will try to match the exact term [patrick stewart]. The documents with exactly Patrick Stewart also contain this term in the `*.bigrammed` fields. Let's repeat our search, now with bigrammed fields, as shown in the next listing.

```
usersSearch = "patrick stewart"
query = {
    "query": {                                   User's    Searches bigrammed
        "multi_match": {                         query     name fields instead
            "query": usersSearch,          ←               of non-bigrammed
            "fields": ["title", "overview",                versions
                       "cast.name.bigrammed", "directors.name.bigrammed"],  ←
        }
    },
}
search(query)
                                                 Search
                                                 results
Num  Relevance Score      Movie Title      ←
1    0.7239306            Star Trek: Insurrection
2    0.7239306            Gnomeo & Juliet
3    0.7239306            Star Trek: First Contact
4    0.7239306            Excalibur
5    0.6334393            Conspiracy Theory
```

This is a marked improvement! All of these movies star Patrick Stewart. By adding a specific signal that your ranking function could use, you've dramatically improved the precision of search results. If you use `best_fields`, it behooves you to provide precise signals—signals so precise that it's unlikely that the search string will match many documents. There's still a possibility that multiple fields will match. So you'll need to assert boosts that declare which fields you consider best. Even these bigrammed fields might need to be given boosts to prioritize cast matches over director matches. Actor Jonathan Frakes, for example, also directed many Star Trek movies. When there's conflict, you, as the relevance engineer, need to assert which is best via boosts. In this case, you likely still want to assert the cast matches over the director matches.

5.3.4 *Letting losers share the glory: calibrating best_fields*

A search such as "Patrick Stewart" is clearly a search for an entity that belongs in bucket A or bucket B. Using `best_fields` can work for these scenarios, as only a small set of fields will match this entity, pushing up the actor Patrick Stewart matches. What if the user searches for multiple entities, such as "Star Trek Patrick Stewart"? In this case, the searcher is specifying two pieces of criteria: the movie Star Trek and Patrick Stewart. One piece of criteria, "Star Trek," is a great match for the `title` field; and "Patrick Stewart" is a great match for `cast.name`. It's common for users to want to apply multiple criteria to their searches, expecting the search to account for all when searching.

To get at multiple user search criteria, you don't want a pure `best_fields` approach. In addition to the signal "this cast member was searched for," you'd also like to include other signals such as "this movie was searched for." Yet `best_fields` focuses on one field's relevance score over all others. If `title` scores higher, a match on `Patrick Stewart` will be completely ignored by `best_fields`. These searches begin to work against the strength of `best_fields`.

What if you want `best_fields` behavior, but with an influence from secondary fields as well? For example, it's likely that Star Trek searchers will consider movie title matches to be a primary signal when ranking. Other criteria, including cast names, director names, or description matches, ought to come second. In this way, you create a kind of *first-second sort*—preferring `best_field`'s chosen signal, but within that best field allowing other signals to have a small role. This is what `tie_breaker` does. Recall that `tie_breaker` lets you add some of the scores from matches that don't win to the result:

$$\text{score} = S_{\text{title}} + \text{tie\_breaker} \times (S_{\text{overview}} + S_{\text{cast.name}} + S_{\text{directors.name}})$$

This creates search results that look something like figure 5.10.

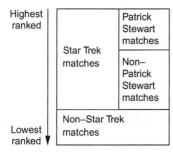

Figure 5.10 A first-second sort where `best_fields` still wins, but within that winner other criteria matches allow documents to bubble up.

Achieving the first-second effect requires you to carefully tweak field boosts and
tie_breaker. Remember, boosts *aren't* priorities. For TMDB, it turns out title scores
are extremely high (just as you saw in chapter 3). So you'll need to boost cast.name
.bigrammed's much smaller base score to push it into second place. In the following
query, a boost of 5 on cast.name.bigrammed and a tie_breaker of 0.4 gives the
desired best_fields competition: title in first place and cast.name.bigrammed in
second place:

```
usersSearch = "star trek patrick stewart"
query = {
    "query": {                                          User's
        "multi_match": {                                query        cast.name.bigrammed
            "query": usersSearch,          ◄────                          boosted by 5
            "fields": ["title", "overview",
                       "cast.name.bigrammed^5", "directors.name.bigrammed"],  ◄──┘
            "type": "best_fields",
            "tie_breaker": 0.4             ◄───┐  tie_breaker of 0.4
        }                                       used to incorporate
    }                                           other field scores
}
search(query)
                                                             Search
                                                ◄───         results
Num  Relevance Score      Movie Title
1    0.35363546           Star Trek: Insurrection
2    0.35363546           Star Trek: First Contact
3    0.34679613           Star Trek: Generations
4    0.34285474           Star Trek: Nemesis
5    0.33423716           Star Trek
```

Using best_fields prioritizes a title-matching signal and adds a bit of score from our
name-matching signal. You're left with every Star Trek movie. Within that grouping is
a secondary signal, indicating primarily whether the movie is a Patrick Stewart film.
These results get shifted to the top of your Star Trek group. Notably absent, and lan-
guishing toward the bottom of the results, far out of sight, are non–Star Trek or non–
Patrick Stewart movies.

The tie_breaker begins to push the best_fields search away from its primary
pole of either-or functionality. It lets you consider other signals in the score. In fact, if
you set tie_breaker to 1.0, you get a summation of all the field scores:

$$score = S_{title} + 1.0 \times (S_{overview} + S_{cast.name} + S_{directors.name})$$

This becomes the following:

$$score = S_{title} + S_{overview} + S_{cast.name} + S_{directors.name}$$

This begins to look like the summation in most_fields. You can see where such a
form might be enticing. What if you don't want lopsided results or first-second sort
behavior? What if you'd like to let each field have a contribution to the overall score?

5.3.5 *Counting multiple signals using most_fields*

best_fields is a fickle beast! We've covered how to use it to prioritize one match over another. With precise signals, best_fields can determine whether your search matches one field or another. You can use it to decide, "Is this a search for a person?" or "Is this a search for a movie?" by selecting one of those signals and ignoring all else. A lot depends on how precise your signals are at measuring these criteria. A great deal also depends on how assertive you are in establishing priorities among fields via boosts—keeping in mind the oddities and inconsistencies of field scoring.

When users specify multiple criteria, such as "Star Trek Patrick Stewart" or "Star Trek Patrick Stewart William Shatner," the search becomes more about the aggregate sum of multiple signals. If you choose one signal to emphasize, such as "this search mentions the movie title," you'll miss other criteria the user tells you about. You saw one way to begin to fix this, with the best_field parameter tie_breaker. Satisfying these use cases with best_fields and tie_breaker begins to look more like the behavior of most_fields. Remember, most_fields runs a Boolean query of each underlying field. This has the effect of summing the underlying signals:

$$score = (S_{title} + S_{overview} + S_{cast.name} + S_{directors.name}) \times coord$$

Thinking of most_fields as a set of Boolean SHOULD clauses helps you see how you ought to use it; these SHOULD clauses list all the criteria of the most relevant doc in terms of the signals that correspond to each field:

- The search string SHOULD mention the movie's title.
- The search string SHOULD mention text in the movie's overview.
- The search string SHOULD mention a movie cast member.
- The search string SHOULD mention a movie director's name.

The ideal document hits all four requirements. A search string matching title, overview, a cast member, and a director shoots to the top. A search string matching three signals comes next, and so on, as shown in figure 5.11.

Gone is the heavy focus on just one field, as in best_fields. Instead you let every field have a say in the final score. Let's see what happens when you switch to best_fields for your "Star Trek Patrick Stewart" search.

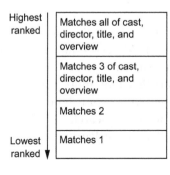

Figure 5.11 most_fields **heavily biases searches toward more matching fields.**

```
Listing 5.10   Searching for Star Trek Patrick Stewart
```

```
usersSearch = "star trek patrick stewart"
query = {
    "query": {
        "multi_match": {                              ┐ User's
            "query": usersSearch,            ◁────────┘ query
            "fields": ["title", "overview",
            "cast.name.bigrammed", "directors.name.bigrammed"],
            "type": "most_fields"                  ◁──┐
        }                                             │ Change to using
    }                                                 │ most_fields
}
search(query)                                      ┐ Search
                                          ◁────────┘ results
Num   Relevance Score       Movie Title
1     0.57795894            Star Trek: Generations
2     0.37984636            Star Trek: Insurrection
3     0.37984636            Star Trek: First Contact
4     0.37325242            Star Trek: Nemesis
5     0.20443419            Star Trek
```

Much like best_fields with tie_breaker, this brings up Star Trek movies that star Patrick Stewart. This is exactly what you want. You've used all the signals to drive up documents that meet your criteria, in this case surfacing the ideal document—one that stars Patrick Stewart *and* is a Star Trek film.

When users specify multiple criteria, ranking by combining the signals that match tends to better align with their expectations. Whereas best_fields would have worked hard to create lopsided results, most_fields creates a blend of all the provided field scores. When users' expectations don't prioritize one field or another, but rather prefer an ad hoc collection of multiple fields, most_fields is a great option. The ideal document in best_fields is one that matches one field over another. In the previous example, you pushed title to dominate the scoring. The most_fields strategy obsesses less about one field score, instead letting every field score have a say. When users don't have as clear of a "target" in terms of a specific kind of field to match, and instead list many criteria of equal importance, most_fields is the solution.

5.3.6   *Boosting in most_fields*

Though most_fields attempts to deliver results that match the most criteria, field scoring doesn't always cooperate. Remember, one field's score may naturally be an order of magnitude higher than another, for no particular reason. Because of wild scoring differences, you might have search results that look more like best_fields lopsidedness than the expected most_fields, "everyone contributes to the score" behavior. If you extend the search results for the preceding search further, you expect the second-level search results to be a mixed collection of Patrick Stewart and Star Trek titles. Unfortunately, they're not:

```
6    0.16354734             Star Trek: The Motion Picture
7    0.16354734             Star Trek Into Darkness
8    0.14310393             Star Trek VI: The Undiscovered Country
9    0.14310393             Star Trek V: The Final Frontier
10   0.14310393             Star Trek IV: The Voyage Home
11   0.14310393             Star Trek II: The Wrath of Khan
12   0.14310393             Star Trek III: The Search for Spock
13   0.10484329             Maps to the Stars
14   0.086285345            Star Wars: The Clone Wars
15   0.06411133             Star Wars: Episode VI - Return of the Jedi
```

These are all `Star Trek` or `Star` title matches! Why does this happen? Again, title scores, for whatever reason, tend to be higher than nontitle scores. A title score for `Star Trek VI` is as follows:

```
0.5196225, weight(title:star in 281)
```

In contrast, the comparable score for the nearest Patrick Stewart movie is *Ted*:

```
0.19781886, weight(cast.name.bigrammed:patrick stewart in 831)
```

Consider the summation associated with `most_fields`:

$$\text{score} = (S_{title} + S_{overview} + S_{cast.name} + S_{directors.name}) \times \text{coord}$$

Remember, scores for fields aren't *really* comparable. Despite the extensive bias toward multiple matches through coord, you'll need to boost accordingly to get a formula that gives you balanced behavior. With `most_fields`, you use boosts to balance this lopsided formula:

$$\text{score} = (S_{title} + S_{overview} + S_{cast.name} + S_{directors.name}) \times \text{coord}$$

Perhaps, for example, if you down-boosted `title`, or up-boosted `cast.name`, you might approach something closer to the target, as shown in the following listing.

Listing 5.11   Down-boosting title

```
usersSearch = "star trek patrick stewart"
query = {
    "query": {
        "multi_match": {
            "query": usersSearch,                                  User's query
            "fields": ["title^0.2", "overview",
            "cast.name.bigrammed", "directors.name.bigrammed"],     Downweight
            "type": "most_fields"                                  title to bring
        }                                                          scoring into
    },                                                             balance
}
search(query)
```

The resulting search results, beyond the Star Trek movies with Patrick Stewart, look much more like a mix of Star Trek and Patrick Stewart movies:

```
6     0.04985989          Ted
7     0.047840547         Star Trek
8     0.044039465         The Beaver
9     0.038272437         Star Trek: The Motion Picture
10    0.038272437         Star Trek Into Darkness
```

The takeaway is that you need to carefully tune boosts to make most_fields live up to its promise. Otherwise, with an arbitrarily strong field score, you'll end up with unexpectedly lopsided results. Whereas boosting in best_fields declares priority on which field matches should come first in expected lopsidedness, boosting in most_fields brings balance to the summed terms to restore a more blended score of weighted fields.

5.3.7 *When additional matches don't matter*

Before we leave most_fields, let's examine its Achilles' heel, which you'll likely run into. Though we describe the problem here, be forewarned that the solution waits for you in the next chapter. As in many Star Trek episodes, we'll leave you with a bit of a cliffhanger.

The most_fields strategy brings documents to the top that match all the criteria. This seems like a sane thing to do. But in many cases, having two strong signals shouldn't magnify a document's relevance. For example, consider this search:

```
usersSearch = "star trek patrick stewart william shatner"
query = {
    "query": {
        "multi_match": {                                   User's
            "query": usersSearch,                          query
            "fields": ["title", "overview",
                       "cast.name.bigrammed", "directors.name.bigrammed"],
            "type": "most_fields"
        }
    }
}
search(query)
```

Knowing something about Star Trek fans, you could guess that the query "Star Trek Patrick Stewart William Shatner" is likely seeking a Star Trek movie that stars both Patrick Stewart and William Shatner. Is this what most_fields delivers? Well, *mostly:*

```
Num  Relevance Score     Movie Title
1    0.5415871           Star Trek V: The Final Frontier
2    0.39785004          Star Trek: Generations
3    0.35108924          Star Trek IV: The Voyage Home
4    0.3037074           Star Trek: Nemesis
5    0.19542062          Star Trek: Insurrection
```

Why did a Star Trek movie that stars only William Shatner (*Star Trek V*) come up higher than the one that stars both William Shatner and Patrick Stewart (*Star Trek: Generations*)? It's because William Shatner both starred in and directed *Star Trek V: The Final Frontier*. Remember, `most_fields` describes the ideal document as follows:

- SHOULD match a *title* in the search string
- SHOULD match *directors* in the search string
- SHOULD mention *cast* members in the search string

For *Star Trek V,* a director and a cast member match, which fits the ideal document better. Two cast members match in *Star Trek: Generations,* which increases the strength of that signal.

The upshot is you're not quite describing the ideal document correctly. The signals listed don't line up with how users think about relevance ranking. To use `most_fields`, you need to think carefully about the "ideal document." Is the preceding specification correct? Maybe a better specification is as follows:

- SHOULD match a title in the search string
- SHOULD match *any person associated with the film* from the search string

Instead of having signals specific to "director" or "cast member," a more appropriate signal is "Is a person from the search string associated with the movie?" Perhaps our searchers don't care whether William Shatner is a director or a cast member, just that he's associated with the movie.

Term-centric search, as you'll see in the next chapter, provides an even more top-down view on search. Term-centric search helps you answer users' high-level questions even further removed from the source data model.

5.3.8 *What's the verdict on most_fields?*

`most_fields` gives you a way to specify what the ideal document looks like. But you must do so with care. With the right boosting and signals, `most_fields` can often create a better search solution for ad hoc searches. If you're not sure, for example, which of several signals ought to take precedence, `most_fields` is a good place to start. But you should avoid one antipattern of `most_fields`: adding signals for signals' sake. Many times, multiple field matches don't correlate with increased relevance.

5.4 *Summary*

- Users don't care about how your database stores data. They need data represented in a form that lends itself to searching.
- Signals map relevance scores to meaningful ranking criteria (the restaurant is close, the title is being searched for, and so forth).
- With signal modeling, you build fields that better map to criteria that's meaningful to users.

- Using the ranking function, you combine signals to arrive at the overall ranking of results.
- Field-centric search takes the entire query string to each field, combining the scores only at the end.
- A best_fields search takes a "winner takes all" point of view to search; the field that scores the highest is taken as the score.
- A most_fields search takes an "every field gets a vote" point of view to search, summing all field scores together.
- The best_fields parameter tie_breaker allows you to add the impact of other field scores, making best_fields a bit more like most_fields.

Term-centric search

6

This chapter covers

- Examining why field-centric search doesn't capture naïve expectations
- Exploring cases in which your source data model confuses search users
- Comparing the pros and cons of term-centric methods
- Explaining the tension between term-centric and field-centric methods
- Combining users' naïve search expectations with smarter capabilities

The previous chapter introduced you to signals and multifield search. Signals measure criteria such as "Is the search an exact title match?" or "Does the search mention a specific actor or director?" These sorts of signals depend on your ability to control querying and construct fields to model users' intent. We called this process *signal modeling*. Once fields correspond cleanly to signals, only then can you begin to balance them in a multifield search strategy.

The previous chapters focused heavily on fields as the central unit of relevance. But users don't think in terms of fields. Users think of their *search terms* as the central component to search. Users aren't mired in the details of your database or application. They've given you a few brief moments to satisfy them, and they expect you to meet them at their simpler understanding of search. Thus, *term-centric search* differs from other forms of multifield search by placing the search terms—not the structure of the content—front and center.

In this chapter, we introduce term-centric search techniques, depicted in figure 6.1. These techniques focus on the user's search terms above other considerations—even above considerations you might consider sensible! You'll see that term-centric search can often leave the carefully crafted fields of previous chapters in the back seat. The burly signals you crafted in previous chapters by manipulating field construction and analysis are replaced with a broader notion of relevance that prioritizes a user's simpler sense of document structure. Yet users are forever a contradiction; when you pin them down, they still prioritize intelligent matching of locations, ideas, and people in search. So in truth, the naïve behavior of term-centric search must be balanced and augmented with many of the smarter signals crafted in previous chapters.

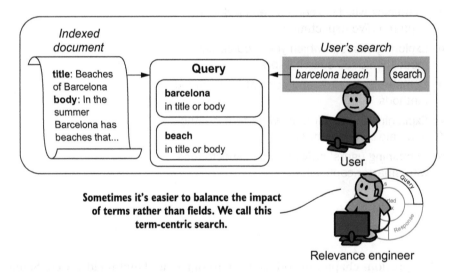

Figure 6.1   Term-centric search prioritizes the user's search terms above other considerations.

6.1   *What is term-centric search?*

Recall that field-centric search searches multiple fields by bringing the entire search string to each field, performing a search, and then combining each field score. Each field is expected to be its own special snowflake, measuring important business or user information with high precision—for example, "Is the movie's director mentioned in the search query?" or "Is the user searching for this specific movie's title?"

Term-centric search comes at search from a different point of view. Figure 6.2 illustrates the differences in this approach. Instead of searching every field with the full search string, *term-centric* search acts on the search string like a term-by-term matchmaker, finding each search term's ideal match. As each search term might find its ideal match in a different field, the final relevance score is the blended result of several field matches. A search for "basketball cartoon" might match basketball in a document's title field, and cartoon in the document's body field, yielding a blended term-by-term score of fields. This way, term-centric search focuses more on criteria specified by users and less on the specific fields. Users don't need fields; they just want their search terms to match something! Anything! After all, if every search term finds its ideal match, won't we reach search relevance nirvana?

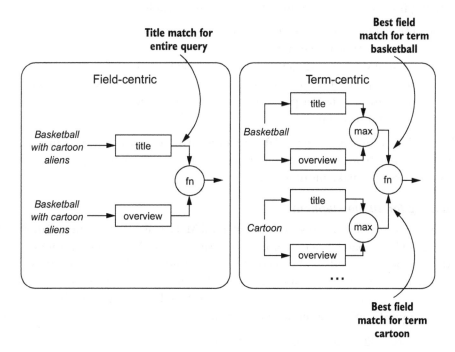

Figure 6.2   Term-centric search applies each search term to a combination of fields, ultimately generating a score that picks a blended, term-by-term score of fields in the document.

If only it were that simple! In reality, the promise of term-centric search carries a bit of a lie. Users think they don't care about fields, yet they still care about intelligently matching the various attributes associated with documents—people, locations, tags, and ideas. Users don't think about it, but they still need many parts of field-centric search. Term-centric and field-centric methods form an important yin and yang to search. As you'll see in this chapter, each has its limits and capabilities. The art of relevance is often applying a bit of both.

6.2   Why do you need term-centric search?

As we've stated, when users search, they typically don't care how documents decompose into individual fields. Many search users expect to work with documents as a single unit: the more of their search terms that match, the more relevant the document ought to be. It may surprise you to know that search engine features that implemented this idea were late to the party. Instead, Lucene-based multifield search depended on field-centric techniques. Instead of the search *terms*, field-centric search makes *field* scores the center of the ranking function. In this section, we explore exactly why field-centric approaches can create relevance issues. You'll see that having ranking functions centered on fields creates two problems:

- *The albino elephant problem*—A failure to give a higher rank to documents that match more search terms.
- *Signal discordance*—Relevance scoring based on unintuitive scoring of the constituent parts (title versus body) instead of scoring of the whole document or more intuitive larger parts, such as the entire article's text or the people associated with this film.

We explore these issues next. After reading this section, you'll be armed to identify exactly when field-centric search stops meeting your goals and when term-centric approaches may make more sense.

6.2.1   Hunting for albino elephants

How would you feel if you searched for "Paul McCartney Concert near San Francisco" and got a list of San Francisco music stores selling Paul McCartney music? Even worse, what if you navigated to the second page to find exactly what you wanted: a Paul McCartney concert near San Francisco! For whatever reason, the search engine ignored a big part of your search—the concert itself—instead bringing results to the top that satisfy only a subset of your criteria:

```
Search: Paul McCartney Concert Near San Francisco

Results:
1.   CDs R' Us, San Francisco - Paul McCartney
2.   MP3s By The Street Corner, San Francisco - Paul McCartney
...

Page 2:
19: Stubbys Music Emporium, San Francisco - Paul McCartney
20. Concert at Great American Music Hall, San Francisco - Paul McCartney
```

How disastrous would this sort of behavior be for your search application? A user gives you search terms, and you seem to ignore them! Unfortunately, field-centric search can cause this behavior. In 2004, engineer Chuck Williams saw this problem in his work with Lucene's field-centric search utilities. When using field-centric search, he noted that search results missing search terms counterintuitively outranked results matching every search term. This problem, known as the *albino elephant* problem, wreaks havoc on search solutions. It's the cause of quite a few relevance problems. When your boss comes to you concerned that your solution appears to ignore what users are searching for, albino elephant could be the problem, and term-centric search might be the solution.

Okay, what's with the weird name? The *albino elephant* reference comes from the canonical example that Chuck created to demonstrate the problem. Consider the following documents, indexed into Elasticsearch.

Listing 6.1 Indexing "albino elephant" documents

```
PUT albinoelephant/docs/1                          Document with title "albino"
{ "title":"albino", "body": "elephant"}   ◁──┘    and body "elephant"

PUT albinoelephant/docs/2                          title and body
{ "title":"elephant", "body": "elephant"}  ◁──┘   both "elephant"
```

Given the two documents, which will be scored higher for a field-centric `most_fields` search for "albino elephant" over the fields `title` and `body`? You likely expect document 1 (title `albino`, body `elephant`) to outrank the document that mentions only elephants. Executing the search, however, paints a different picture, as you can see in the following listing.

Listing 6.2 Searching for the infamous albino elephant

```
GET albinoelephant/docs/_search?               { "query": {
      "multi_match": {
            "query": "albino elephant",     ◁──   Field-centric search
            "type": "most_fields",                for "albino elephant"
            "fields": ["title", "body"]}}}

Score         Title       Body             ◁────  Summarized results
0.06365098    elephant    elephant      ◁──┐
0.06365098    albino      elephant         │
                                           Regular elephants the
                                           same as albino elephants
```

Wow, no extra points for the albino elephant! Why did this happen? Field-centric search doesn't let the `albino` match of one field team up with the `elephant` match of another field. `most_fields` scoring doesn't account for cases in which one search term occurs in one field while another occurs in a different field, as shown in figure 6.3.

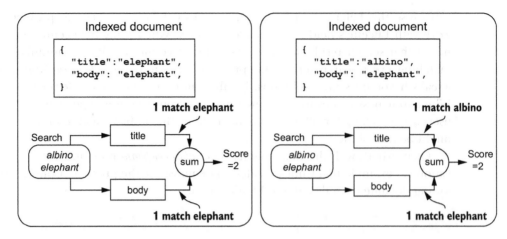

Figure 6.3 Field-centric search can fail to account for cases in which multiple search terms match.

Each field search occurs in isolation. Remember, field-centric search ships the entire search string to each field for scoring before combining the result. The title search (title:albino title:elephant) is computed independently from the body search (body:albino body:elephant), with no interaction between the two field searches. There's no difference between a match in which elephant matches both fields, and a match in which albino matches one field and elephant matches another. The ranking calculation from the two documents could be restated as follows (with bold font indicating the matching search clause):

```
(title:albino title:elephant) +
(body:albino body:elephant) == score for two matches

(title:albino title:elephant) +
(body:albino body:elephant) == score for two matches
```

In other words, field-centric search washes away any bias toward multiple search terms occurring across these two fields.

Understanding the albino elephant phenomenon is fundamental to honoring all of your users' search terms. Ignoring their search terms can make your search seem unintelligent to most users. As we dive into term-centric methods, you'll see how they can help solve the albino elephant problem, and thus help you avoid the hordes of angry users likely to knock down your door!

6.2.2 *Finding an albino elephant in the Star Trek example*

Speaking of angry hordes, it turns out that albino elephant directly impacts the relevance problem you were left with in the previous chapter. Recall that you were busy satisfying the movie curiosities of Star Trek aficionados with the TMDB data set. Your user searched TMDB for "Star Trek Patrick Stewart William Shatner," hoping to find *Star Trek: Generations*, a Star Trek movie starring actors William Shatner and Patrick Stewart.

Let's recap where you left off. You used a `most_fields` field-centric search in the hope that the movie with the most signals would score highest: a Star Trek movie, starring William Shatner and Patrick Stewart. Yet you were surprised when `most_fields` returned *Star Trek V: The Final Frontier*, a Star Trek movie that features William Shatner as both actor and director (and has nothing to do with Patrick Stewart!). "Patrick Stewart" was seemingly ignored. Is that because of the albino elephant problem? Let's revisit the field-centric technical details, and you'll soon see the problem!

In the preceding chapter, as you may recall, we stated that `most_fields` is an appropriate way to account for multiple signals. In combination with `most_fields`, you've done some intelligent signal and feature modeling. You improved the precision of cast and director name scoring with these fields:

- `cast.name.bigrammed`—When scored, indicates whether a cast member has been found
- `directors.name.bigrammed`—When scored, indicates whether a director has been found

Recall that the `*.bigrammed` field stores bigrams (two-word pairs) as tokens instead of individual words. This helps create a more accurate signal for finding people matching the term `patrick stewart` instead of the individual terms `patrick` and `stewart`. You also search the movie's `title` and `overview` fields to support finding the movie by name or description.

With that in mind, what happens when you reissue the `most_fields` search you left off with in the previous chapter? Why doesn't it work as your users might expect? Is there an albino elephant lurking?

Listing 6.3   Kirk and Picard visit the planet of albino elephants

```
usersSearch = "star trek patrick stewart william shatner"
query = {
    "query": {
        "multi_match": {                                         User's
            "query": usersSearch,                                query
            "fields": ["title", "overview",
  "cast.name.bigrammed", "directors.name.bigrammed"],            most_fields searches
            "type": "most_fields"                                over title, overview,
        }                                                        cast.name.bigrammed,
    },                                                           directors.name.bigrammed
    "size": 5,
    "explain": True
}
search(query)                                           Search        Search results
                                                         results       not accounting
                                                                       for "Patrick
Num  Relevance Score        Movie Title                               Stewart" match
1    0.5114776              Star Trek V: The Final Frontier
2    0.38542575             Star Trek: Generations
```

Yes, indeed, you're left with the albino elephant problem. When these two documents are scored, there's no bias toward documents containing more of the search terms (in this case, `patrick stewart` occurring in *Star Trek: Generations*). Breaking down the scoring as in the preceding listing (focused on the three matched fields), you have scores that result from these bold matches:

```
(title:star title:trek title:william title:shatner...) +
(... directors.name.bigrammed:william shatner ...) +
(... cast.name.bigrammed:william shatner ...)
== total score for four matches

(title:star title:trek title:william title:shatner...) +
(... directors.name.bigrammed...) +
(...cast.name.bigrammed:patrick stewart cast.name.bigrammed:william shatner
    ...) == total score for four matches
```

Just as in the albino elephant example, there's no differentiation between *Star Trek V* and *Star Trek: Generations* that takes into account all search criteria specified by the user—the occurrence of `patrick stewart`. Both take a total score from each field match, with no bias toward the document that matches all the search terms. You have quite an albino elephant to solve! You'll revisit this Star Trek search as you begin experimenting with term-centric methods, evaluating whether term-centric search has truly resolved your problems. But first we need to discuss the other major problem with field-centric search.

6.2.3 *Avoiding signal discordance*

If you searched a catalog of academic articles, would you focus on whether matches occurred in specific sections of an article? Would you prioritize a match in an article's introduction section over a match in its conclusion section, for example? What if instead of being broken up this way, the documents were subdivided into searchable fields by page (page 1, page 2, and so forth)? How would you prioritize each page? The point is that your database could arbitrarily break up article text any number of ways! But are those subdivisions appropriate for search? Do they map to your users' mental models of the content? The search user's expectations are likely far more general than the fine-grained subdivisions that originate from the systems feeding into your search engine.

Building signals that are in harmony with a user's understanding of the content is a major component to signal modeling, and a major feature of term-centric search. Users aren't mired in the details of your database, parser, or API. Your source data model, as you learned in the previous chapter, doesn't have fields built for search. There is, however, a more specific problem at play with the preceding article examples: signal discordance, illustrated in figure 6.4. *Signal discordance* is the disconnect between the signals generated from fine-grained, specific fields present in a search engine (as derived from a source data model) and a user's far more general mental-model of the content. Signal discordance, therefore, is a specific failure of signal modeling: a failure to express signals that measure the generalized ways users expect search

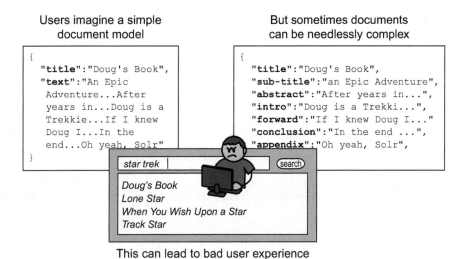

Figure 6.4 Signal discordance: not ranking with the user's sense of content structure might create odd results as field-centric search focuses on unfamiliar criteria.

to work, because you're still mired in the details of your database, API, parser or other source data model.

Working on a search-term by search-term basis, term-centric search can help solve signal discordance. Field-centric search, on the other hand, tends to amplify signal discordance. When derived fields closely reflect what's in the source data model, field-centric results don't match what users expect. By generalizing search scoring across multiple fields, term-centric search, as you'll see, helps measure relevance in a way that's much closer to our users' more naïve notions of document structure.

6.2.4 *Understanding the mechanics of signal discordance*

Let's take a moment to understand precisely how signal discordance manifests itself in the field-centric ranking function. Only with that appreciation can you evaluate the extent to which term-centric search helps your efforts.

Signal discordance manifests itself with field scores that don't map to the user's general expectations. As fields maintain their own statistics for ranking, such as a term's document frequency, having fields that don't map to our user's more general expectations deeply damages ranking.

If you examine the following explain for the broken "Star Trek Patrick Stewart William Shatner" search, you can see another major factor that drives movies directed by William Shatner straight to the top: he has directed only one movie, yet he has starred in many. The document frequency of william shatner in directors .name.bigrammed is exactly 1. The match of this term in this field drives that field's TF × IDF score way out of whack, which in turn drives the movie he directs straight to the top.

You can see how out-of-whack scoring gets because of signal discordance in the next listing.

> **Listing 6.4   Snippet of `directors.name:william shatner` vs. `cast.name`**

```
1.8605413, weight(directors.name.bigrammed:william shatner in 282)
   1.8605413, score(doc=282,freq=1.0), product of:
     0.22335224, queryWeight, product of:
       8.330077, idf(docFreq=1, maxDocs=3051)          William Shatner has
                                                        directed one movie

0.2568409, weight(cast.name.bigrammed:william shatner in 282)
   0.2568409, score(doc=282,freq=1.0), product of:
     0.1659712, queryWeight, product of:
       6.1900115, idf(docFreq=16, maxDocs=3051)         William Shatner has
                                                        starred in 16 movies
                                                        in our collection
```

Field-centric ranking functions amplify these anomalies. The ranking function has decided that the signal measuring whether the movie's director matches the search string is so strong that it should be heavily amplified. Scoring of this document then is completely dominated by the director's field, resulting in `most_fields` that scores as shown in figure 6.5.

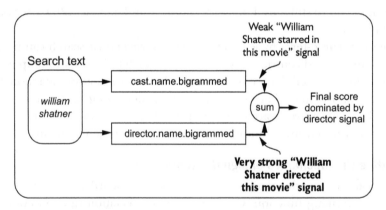

Figure 6.5   Field-centric methods over granular fields from the source data model result in scoring that doesn't correspond to user expectations.

But do users care? Is the score for `directors.name.bigrammed`—a score that ends up dominating the overall score—a reflection of how users would prioritize whether William Shatner directed a movie? Almost certainly not. Most Star Trek fans likely don't focus on the distinction between whether William Shatner directed or starred in a movie. Moreover, if they thought about it, they'd probably care more that he starred in a movie.

When fields come straight from the source data model, the TF × IDF calculations that result from searches don't neatly line up to user expectations. TF × IDF can be a poor metric when the field, and the underlying rough proportion of the underlying features, don't map to signals that users care about when ranking. When you search over dozens of fields, simply because "that's what's in the database," you end up with many of these scoring anomalies that don't at all correspond to user expectations.

Field-centric search amplifies signal discordance. By scoring each field in isolation, field-centric search is prone to heavily biasing search results in one direction or another. When you execute field-centric searches over dozens upon dozens of fields, all possible criteria from your database, you ask for trouble.

The source data model keeps you stuck in a bottom-up, source-data-model-first view of the searchable data. To undergo full signal modeling, you need to think top-down and user first. What do users care about when ranking? How can you craft fields from the source data model to compute these signals? What *should* the document frequency of william shatner be to reflect the user's sense of the term's rareness?

As you'll see, term-centric search can help provide this top-down perspective on signal modeling, helping solve signal discordance. You need not despair! Just as in Star Trek, the crew of the Enterprise always finds a way (often through creative and innovative engineering!). You can too! Let's embark on our journey to explore this strange, new universe of term-centric search!

6.3   *Performing your first term-centric searches*

You've seen the various problems that field-centric search can introduce. Now you'll get a chance to experience the completely different world of term-centric search, illustrated in figure 6.6.

Term-centric search solves the albino elephant problem and signal discordance by taking a top-down view of search: breaking up search terms, and querying each term one by one against a set of fields. You'll see how this simplifies aspects of signal modeling by prompting you to take the users' point of view, focusing on signals more closely tied to their query terms instead of just the fields. These resulting signals can answer broader, top-down questions more closely linked to your user's simpler

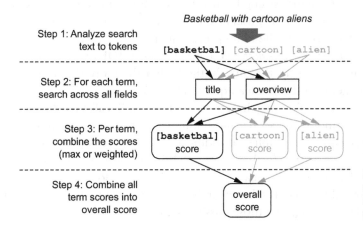

Step 1: Analyze search text to tokens

Step 2: For each term, search across all fields

Step 3: Per term, combine the scores (max or weighted)

Step 4: Combine all term scores into overall score

Figure 6.6   Term-centric search brings search terms to each field one by one to arrive at a score for that term.

understanding of the content rather than your source data model's structure. Term-centric search solves many of the problems it was created to solve, but it too has problems. As you near the end of this section, you'll begin to realize that a more hybrid approach is needed.

6.3.1 *Working with the term-centric ranking function*

To get started with term-centric search methods, you'll explore one of the original solutions to the problems of field-centric search: a term-centric query parser. Such a query parser implements term-centric search by parsing the query string and pulling out terms before searching each field. It's a method that's familiar to Solr users (Solr depends entirely on query parsers) and that has an Elasticsearch implementation in the `query_string` query.

Through exploring how a query parser works, you'll see how term-centric search works generally. What common underlying features do term-centric approaches have? From where does term-centric search derive its power? How does it bias search toward results that include more search terms? What's the cost of this benefit? Once you've explored the generalities of term-centric search, you can move on to its more modern forms.

Although often not used this way in modern search, query parsers harken back to a largely bygone era when everyday users searched frequently with a query syntax such as `"title:(star trek) +overview:shatner"`. This is the Lucene query syntax that you've seen throughout this book, though largely in a debugging context. In previous incarnations of Lucene-based search, query parsers let you pass the user's search on to the search engine itself, which transformed it into Lucene queries. But these days, users rarely specify fields or Boolean operators. Instead they issue more ad hoc queries (for instance, "Star Trek Patrick Stewart") and tend to expect the search engine to figure everything out. Query parsers have historically turned the ad hoc searches into a term-by-term Boolean query.

This emphasis on a search-term by search-term Boolean search is exactly the root of the query parser's term-centric strengths. If you have only a single field to be searched (the field `overview`, for example), users expect behavior commensurate with turning "Star Trek Patrick Stewart" into the more precise query `overview:star overview:trek overview:patrick overview:stewart` (a query with four SHOULD clauses). Users typically think that the more terms that match, the higher the score should be—which is precisely what you get with this Boolean query. These Boolean queries bias the scoring heavily toward documents that match more search terms. Recall that Boolean queries take the sum of the underlying scores and multiply that sum by a coordinating factor. The coordinating factor is a multiplier providing a heavy punishment to documents that don't satisfy all the clauses, thus further down-weighting documents that don't match all the search terms. Therefore, a Boolean search in which each Boolean clause is a search term creates powerful term-centric behavior, bringing up documents that match more search terms, and down-weighting those missing search terms.

In the preceding example, only the `overview` field is searched. What happens when more than one field is introduced? How does a query parser achieve term-centric search despite the occurrence of more than one field? The answer is the dismax query.

`DisjunctionMaximumQuery` (*dismax*, for short) provides the behavior underlying the `best_fields` multifield search strategy in the preceding chapter. In Lucene query syntax, you've seen several times by now that the | symbol means "pick the maximum score." But whereas `best_fields` uses the dismax behavior to choose the highest *field* score, our query-parser query uses dismax on a term-by-term basis to choose the best scoring field *per search term*. Similarly, the Boolean query—the query that biases heavily toward more clauses that match—remains just as in the preceding single-field example. It remains in the *outermost, per term* calculation in the ranking function, as shown in figure 6.7.

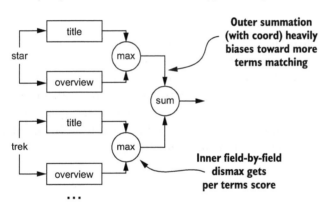

Query parser scoring
(template for other term-centric approaches)

Outer summation (with coord) heavily biases toward more terms matching

Inner field-by-field dismax gets per terms score

Figure 6.7 A query parser implementing term-centric search: inner field-by-field dismax with a term-by-term Boolean query biasing scoring toward more term matches.

Contrast this with a `best_fields` search in which the Boolean query is the *innermost* calculation done per field. This boosts only the scores of individual fields for having more terms, not the whole document.

Here's the `best_fields` search that runs two Boolean queries before evaluating the dismax:

```
(overview:star overview:trek overview:patrick overview:stewart) |
(title:star title:trek title:patrick title:stewart)
```

With the query parser, you instead get this term-by-term dismax search, which then runs the Boolean query on a term-by-term, not a field-by-field, basis:

```
(overview:star | title:star) (overview:trek | title:trek)
(overview:patrick | title:patrick) (overview:stewart | title:stewart)
```

This translates to a ranking function (letting S_{term} represent the result of the dismax operation for a term):

```
coord × (S_star + S_trek + S_patrick + S_stewart)
```

Conversely the `best_fields` method suffers from the albino elephant problem. You might match `star trek` in one field, and `patrick stewart` in another. Yet as `best_fields` returns only the best field score, one of those field matches will be ignored. This causes ranking to ignore cases where documents match more search terms.

Listing 6.5   `best_fields` suffering from albino elephant

> **best_fields chooses overview field scores as the resulting score**

```
(overview:star overview:trek overview:patrick overview:stewart) |
(title:star title:trek title:patrick title:patrick)
```

> **best_fields drops field with Star Trek matches**

Only by placing the Boolean query on a term-by-term basis do you arrive at solid footing for term-centric behavior that defeats the albino elephant. Each SHOULD clause adds to the score. Moreover, documents that fail to match all the terms are further diminished by the coordinating factor. This favors documents with more matches, regardless of the field matched, and defeats the albino elephant! Thus scenarios like the preceding albino elephant problem are avoided by each term being guaranteed an influence on the final search, as in the following listing.

Listing 6.6   Term-by-term dismax gives every search term influence

> **Star and Trek term have influence …**

```
(overview:star | title:star) (overview:trek | title:trek)
(overview:patrick | title:patrick) (overview:stewart | title:stewart)
```

> **… as do matches for Patrick and Stewart terms.**

This pattern, an inner field-by-field dismax with an outer Boolean query over all the terms, is a central pattern in term-centric search. It builds signals on a term-by-term basis, not based on the strength of a field as a whole. You'll see in sections ahead how this pattern can be both a benefit and curse of term-centric search. But maybe you can stop here? Does a query parser hold all the pieces to the puzzle? Can it satisfy the demands of Star Trek fans? Or does it fall short? Let's use test queries to demonstrate the issues.

6.3.2 *Running a term-centric query parser (into the ground)*

Now that you know something about how a query parser's ranking function operates, let's see if it's an amazing panacea. Let's get back to our Star Trek TMDB example. Perhaps a query parser can satisfy the demands of Star Trek fandom? What happens when you rerun your troublesome query, but switch from a field-centric `multi_match` query to a term-centric query parser? You're soon to encounter a nasty surprise—one that can dramatically limit the utility of not just query parsers, but term-centric search in general.

Let's try our troublesome "Star Trek Patrick Stewart William Shatner" search with the Elasticsearch `query_string` query. This query is Elasticsearch's implementation of a query parser with term-centric behavior. As you see in the next listing, this query has an interface similar to `multi_match`.

Listing 6.7 Running a query-parser query

```
usersSearch = "star trek patrick stewart william shatner"
query = {
    "query": {
        "query_string": {                          Uses query_string query parser
            "query": usersSearch,                  for term-by-term dismax
            "fields": ["title", "overview",
                       "cast.name.bigrammed",      User's
                       "directors.name.bigrammed"],  query
        }
    },
    "size": 5,
    "explain": True
}
search(query)

Results
Num  Relevance Score       Movie Title
1    1.5344285             Star Trek IV: The Voyage Home
2    1.0545591             Star Trek: Nemesis
3    0.7853979             Star Trek
4    0.6283183             Star Trek: The Motion Picture
5    0.6283183             Star Trek: Insurrection
```

Looking at these results, our Star Trek fans complain that something is way off the mark! Remember that your users are likely hunting for *Star Trek: Generations*, a movie that stars both Patrick Stewart and William Shatner. What went wrong? Examining the query validation endpoint certainly shows a term-centric search. But, shockingly, you're missing the expected fields:

```
(title:star | overview:star) (title:trek | overview:trek)
(title:patrick | overview:patrick) (title:stewart | overview:stewart)
(title:william | overview:william) (title:shatner | overview:shatner)
```

You explicitly told the `query_string` query to search the bigrammed `cast.name` and `directors.name` fields as well. Yet they don't appear to have been searched. Why? What failed and where?

6.3.3 *Understanding field synchronicity*

If you think about it, how could that work? Remember, to the `*.bigrammed` fields, search terms take on a completely different character from text fields. To the bigrammed fields, the two-word unit `william shatner` is a search term, not `william` or `shatner`, as would be the case in a text field. So how could the query parser figure out what to do? Can you keep the bigram nature of the `*.bigrammed` fields along with the term-centric solution?

Let's think through it. One naïve solution might be that the query parser could *try* to search with each individual text term, something like this:

```
...  (title:william | overview:william | directors.name.bigrammed:william)
```

But that doesn't make sense. Here `william` is certain to *not* be a match in the bigrammed field. You built `*.bigrammed` fields explicitly to be searched with bigrams, to lend a specific signal to search. Yet by hobbling the field by avoiding bigrams, term-centric search is eliminating the valuable work you did to build this field in the first place!

What if you figured out a way to search the bigrammed field on terms it expected? What if something like the following were possible:

```
...  (title:william | overview:william |
     directors.name.bigrammed:william shatner) ....
```

But that's not an apples-to-apples search-term comparison! That's not term-centric search! The point of term-centric search is to isolate each search term such as `william`. Here, the `william` search terms are conflated with `shatner` in the `directors.name` bigram query. Influence from the `shatner` term bleeds over into the score for the `william` term.

So in reality, a term-centric query-parser enforces identical search terms for each field. We call this property *field synchronicity*, the capability to query multiple fields with identical search terms—or put a different way, the restriction that they *must* be searched in the same way. In this case, Elasticsearch elided the fields that failed to share a common query analyzer, choosing to drop the bigrammed fields. This way, it could ensure that it searched fields in a consistent, term-centric manner. This is a common, and perhaps the safest, form of solving this problem (though one could quibble with the lack of helpful error message).

6.3.4 *Field synchronicity and signal modeling*

What are the implications of requiring field synchronicity? In previous chapters, we emphasized using analysis to generate fields with ranking signals you could use. You worked hard with signal modeling to make the search engine measure important user-ranking criteria. Every field, we taught, could be its own special snowflake, offering its own unique signal to the ranking function when searched in its own special way. You saw several examples of this in chapter 4, as many analysis tricks were shown to create unique fields that measured the users' intent. With term-centric search forcing every field to behave identically, does that cripple your ability to use signal modeling?

Yes, this can be a problem. You're told term-centric search is necessary to solve the problems of field-centric search. Yet you need fields that act intelligently on their own. How else can you match geographical places? People's names? Ideas? Taxonomies or any of the other entities you're asked to work with as a relevance engineer? Is the search engine stuck between these two unintelligent polar ends—one that lets you search in a vanilla, term-by-term way that can kill a field's power to create signals, and the other that's field-centric with its silly albino elephant and signal discordance?

Is there a way to have your cake and eat it too? Is the choice entirely binary? Or can you have a little from column A and a little from column B—blending the strengths of both into a solution tailored to your needs?

This is the fundamental yin and yang of term-centric versus field-centric search. It's both a feature and a bug. For now, we leave this as an open question. Consider this conflict a bit of a final frontier. Just as on Star Trek, we'll figure out how to bring opposing ideologies together to build something more harmonious and useful!

6.3.5 *Query parsers and signal discordance*

Given your ignorance of field synchronicity, your earlier work was a bit of a false start. Let's try again and see how term-centric search operates. Maybe it's not so terrible to match directly on the nonbigrammed, regular text name fields, as shown in the following listing.

Listing 6.8 Searching fields that work in sync

```
usersSearch = "star trek patrick stewart william shatner"
query = {
    "query": {
        "query_string": {                              ←┐ User's
            "query": usersSearch,                       ← │ query
            "fields": ["title", "overview",
                        "cast.name", "directors.name"], ←┐ Search
        }                                                │ nonbigrammed
    }                                                    │ fields
}
search(query)

Results:
Num  Relevance Score      Movie Title
1    3.03831              Star Trek V: The Final Frontier
2    2.282416             Star Trek: Generations
3    1.7969469            Star Trek: Nemesis
4    1.4064612            Star Trek IV: The Voyage Home
5    1.3728689            Star Trek: The Motion Picture
```

This is slightly better but still misses the mark. Our target result, *Star Trek: Generations,* is at number 2, but surprisingly a non–Patrick Stewart film is at spot 1. Is this due to an albino elephant? Are you emphasizing documents that include more search terms? Examining the query validation endpoint and the explain reveals additional weight given to the documents with more search terms. You *are* solving the albino elephant problem. The query validation endpoint shows this by demonstrating the expected term-by-term Boolean queries:

```
(title:star | overview:star | cast.name:star | directors.name:star)
(title:trek | overview:trek | cast.name:trek | directors.name:trek)
(title:patrick | overview:patrick |
                    cast.name:patrick |    directors.name:patrick) ...
```

The summarized explain for our desired result, *Star Trek: Generations,* shows the expected calculation:

```
2.282416, sum of:
  0.78420293, max of:
    0.78420293, weight(title:star in 847)
    0.12733683, weight(overview:star in 847)
  0.9435517, max of:
    0.9435517, weight(title:trek in 847)
  0.08256196, max of:
    0.08256196, weight(cast.name:patrick in 847)
  0.14055088, max of:
    0.14055088, weight(cast.name:stewart in 847)
  0.060675804, max of:
    0.060675804, weight(cast.name:william in 847)
  0.2708729, max of:
    0.2708729, weight(cast.name:shatner in 847
```

Yet despite the higher number of matches, this document still lost in the ranking calculation. What gives? Even when you examine *Star Trek V: The Final Frontier,* you see a coord that punishes the score for not matching all the search terms. Something else must be going on:

```
3.03831, product of:
  4.557465, sum of:
    0.68617755, max of:
      0.68617755, weight(title:star in 210)
    0.8256078, max of:
      0.8256078, weight(title:trek in 210)
    1.0834916, max of:
      0.07281096, weight(cast.name:william in 210)
      1.0834916, weight(directors.name:william in 210)
    1.9621884, max of:
      0.32504746, weight(cast.name:shatner in 210)
      1.9621884, weight(directors.name:shatner in 210)
  0.6666667, coord(4/6)
```

Coord punishes for only 4 out of 6 matching

Director matches for "william" and "shatner" score surprisingly high

It turns out the primary difference here is the match of william shatner in the directors.name field. Recall our discussion of signal discordance? You saw this exact problem: users likely don't care that William Shatner was a director. Yet because he was a director in only one movie, the resulting TF × IDF score for a director match is extremely high compared to the other matches. Despite the Boolean query's heavy punishment for failing to match all the query terms, the TF × IDF scores for directors.name cause the overall field score to be high.

This happens because although a query parser solves the albino elephant problem, it doesn't do anything about signal discordance. No consideration is made to adjust the overall term score based on the document frequency of each field. There's no direct adjustment to correct the document frequency of directors.name to more closely align with what users expect. The signal being used in the ranking function doesn't map to users' more general expectations for those terms. They're mired in the specifics of the source data model.

6.3.6 *Tuning term-centric search*

As you may recall from the previous chapter, one possible solution to inconsistent field scoring in best_fields search is to assert an explicit field preference through boosting. Let's take a moment to visit the topic of tuning. Does term-centric search have similar knobs and dials that let you modify the ranking function to your needs? You'll see that because of similarities between term-centric methods, tuning lessons from one method can usually be applied to another. With that in mind, how can you get closer to expressing signals the user wants, perhaps by simply stomping over the signal discordance problem entirely?

Looking at the term-centric ranking function, it doesn't appear that you can have much impact on any of the parameters:

$$\text{coord} \times (S_{star} + S_{trek} + S_{patrick} + S_{stewart} + S_{william} + S_{shatner})$$

But there must be some opportunity to tune this equation to solve signal discordance. And there certainly is. Remember that within each term's signal (S_{star}) is a dismax over every field being searched. Remembering the behavior of best_fields from the previous chapter, you know that this ranking function allows tuning with tie_breaker and per-field boosts. Luckily, those knobs and dials are available here as well. Here B indicates a boost, and S indicates a score:

$$S_{star} = B_{title} \times S_{title} + \text{tie\_breaker} \times (B_{overview} \times S_{overview} + \dots)$$

So for search-term scoring calculations, you can decide whether:

- To include the score of the nonwinning fields in the dismax equation by setting tie_breaker (defaults to 0)
- To weight (or perhaps rebalance) the influence of each field via boosts ($B_{overview}$)

Tuning term-centric search focuses on tweaking the dismax calculation inside each term score. The same tuning decisions you made for field-centric search in the previous chapter continue to apply here. Do you compute an individual term's score based on the "best field" for your terms (forcing a preference with a boost as needed)? Or do you manipulate the dismax calculation toward most_fields—increasing the score as multiple fields match the term?

In our example with signal discordance, you could use boosts to force a preference for one field's score over another—just as you did with best_fields in the previous chapter. In the following listing, you'll boost cast.name to overwhelm the directors .name score, enforcing a preference of cast matches over director matches.

Listing 6.9   Tuning term-centric search

```
usersSearch = 'star trek patrick stewart william shatner'
query = {
    "query": {
        "query_string": {
            "query": usersSearch,                       ⟵  User's query
            "fields": ["title", "overview",
                       "cast.name^10", "directors.name"],  ⟵  Boosts cast.name by 10
        }
    },
}
search(query)

Results:
Num  Relevance Score          Movie Title
1    1.0714334                Star Trek: Generations
2    0.8237567                Star Trek V: The Final Frontier
3    0.5298387                Star Trek II: The Wrath of Khan
4    0.52354753               Star Trek IV: The Voyage Home
5    0.502342                 Star Trek: Nemesis
```

This is exactly what you want! But is this the best way to solve signal discordance? You've hit the score over the head with a hammer, forcing it toward your field preference. Is this a sustainable solution?

Although this is one possible way to solve the problem of signal discordance, it's an unsatisfying (and possibly brittle) way. Instead of directly attacking the problem of document frequencies that don't truly measure term rareness, boosting forcefully pushes the score of one field over another. What if the user had searched for a director that only once appeared as a cast member? This solution would drive up that director's one cast occurrence pushing down that director's directorial films. Not at all what users expect.

Still, these tuning techniques *are* portable to other forms of term-centric search when you need to assert a preference. Much like our discussion in the previous chapter, there continues to be a dichotomy (here through tie_breaker) between how much you'd like to bias search scores toward the best field for that search term, or toward a behavior closer to `most_fields`.

With these signal discordance issues, this is where we'll get off the query-parser train. Term-centric query parsers were invented to solve the albino elephant problem. They can get you far. But because they leave us short of a proper solution to signal discordance, we'll begin to focus on two other methods of term-centric search.

6.4 Solving signal discordance in term-centric search

Although dismax-style query parsers demonstrate the fundamental behaviors of term-centric techniques, often two other solutions are used. These two term-centric methods, which solve both the albino elephant and signal discordance problems, are *custom all fields* and `cross_fields`. Custom all fields combine other fields together at index time into one `all` field, an inflexible arrangement, but one that certainly works. A `cross_fields` search, on the other hand, works at query time by attempting to directly compensate for signal discordance by patching the document frequency of fields prior to searching them. This, as you'll see, yields greater flexibility at the cost of introducing inaccuracy and inscrutability.

6.4.1 Combining fields into custom all fields

Custom all fields solve the problem of term-centric search at index time. The approach does this by directly combining the fields you'd like to search into a single field. After all, you can't have problems with multifield, field-centric search if you have only one field! The name *all fields* comes from the idea that you can copy fields together into a single field referred to as an *all field*. This has also been called *copy fields* in the Solr and Elasticsearch communities. For example, you could combine our troublesome name fields `cast.name` and `directors.name` into a more general `people.name` field by using the search engine's ability to append multiple fields together at index time.

Seems a bit odd to do, though; what does this buy you? Well, consider your troublesome actor/director William Shatner, who has directed one movie yet starred in many. This signal discordance causes `directors.name` matches to score unexpectedly high. This doesn't jibe well with your users' more general expectations of how documents are structured. By combining `directors.name` and `cast.name` into a broader, derived `people.name` field, the signal becomes far more general, and perhaps much closer to what your users imagine when they search. This generality manifests itself mechanically in the scoring. Suddenly, by searching `people.name`, there's no particular bias toward whether William Shatner directed a movie or starred in one. The difference is washed away! The document frequencies for the associated terms are combined and reflect a more general notion of how common William Shatner is as a person associated with a movie instead of as a director or cast member, as shown in the table 6.1.

Table 6.1 Relative document frequencies of the phrase `william shatner` **in two source fields and the combined** `people` **custom all field**

	`william shatner` **document frequency**
`directors.name`	1
`cast.name`	16
`people.name` (custom all field)	16

This field is searched just as any field would be searched by itself, using a Boolean query of SHOULD clauses. Remember that this form favors documents that include more results, thus continuing to defeat the dreaded albino elephant:

```
people.name:william people.name:shatner
```

Let's demonstrate by adding such a custom all field to our documents. You'll see that by eliminating the difference between cast and director, search results get closer to users' expectations.

To set up a custom all field, first you need to define the new field in the mapping. You define the field `people` just as you do any other. Then, in the mapping entry for each field that feeds into `people`, you use the `copy_to` option to copy the contents of the source field to a destination field. The mapping gets verbose, so we'll show you each one at a time. First there's the mapping for the `people` field, which looks just like the other `name` field mapping you saw in the previous chapter. We even leave in the bigram version of this field, as shown in the following listing.

Listing 6.10 Mapping for custom all field— `people`

```
mappingSettings = {
  "movie": {
    "properties": {
      "people": {              ◁——  Destination people field,
                                     defined like any other
        "properties": {
          "name": {            ◁——  people expects to receive src
                                     fields with a "name" property
            "type": "string",
            "analyzer": "english",
            "fields": {        ◁——  people continues to preserve
              "bigrammed": {         the "bigrammed" property
                "type": "string",
                "analyzer": "english_bigrams"
}}}}},
```

Continuing the mapping, you copy the `cast.name` field over to the `people.name` field. You do the same for directors. The following listing adds `copy_to` to the cast mapping.

Listing 6.11   Adding `copy_to` **from** `cast.name` **to** `people.name`

```
"cast": {
    "properties": {
      "name": {
        "type": "string",
        "analyzer": "english",
        "copy_to": "people.name",        ⟵  Appending this field
        "fields": {                            to people.name
          "bigrammed": {
            "type": "string",
            "analyzer": "english_bigrams"
          }
}} }}},
```

you'll need to reindex all your data:

```
reindex(analysisSettings, mappingSettings, movieDict)
```

Great! Now what happens when you search this new field? With a new field, your options are exceedingly flexible. You can use it anywhere you'd list a field to be searched. For now, though, to see the utility of just this field, notice what happens in the following listing when you directly search only this new `people.name` field for our two actors.

Listing 6.12   Simple use of a custom all field

```
usersSearch = 'patrick stewart william shatner'
query = {
    "query": {                              match query
        "match": {                          (searches a single
            "people.name": usersSearch,     field, people.name)
        }                            ⟵
    }                                       User's
}                                           query
search(query)
```

```
Num   Relevance Score         Movie Title
1     1.3773818               Star Trek: Generations
2     0.6629994               Showtime
3     0.65602106              The Wild
4     0.5989805               Bill & Ted's Bogus Journey
5     0.58601415              Star Trek V: The Final Frontier
```

First you notice that *Star Trek: Generations*, the movie containing both actors, comes to the top of the search results. Nothing surprising here; the Boolean query for the two actors continues to promote results that contain more search terms. The fact that the search occurs over a single field ensures that you don't encounter the albino elephant problem.

Signal discordance is solved in this case; the document frequency for a match on william shatner in *Star Trek V* for people.name is identical to the document frequency for *Star Trek: Generations*. So the scores come out closer to what users expect. The fact that William Shatner directed *Star Trek V* gets mostly washed away by the people.name field's combined document frequency. Also, notice how much higher the score is for *Star Trek: Generations*, a movie that satisfies all search criteria. The Boolean search of the combined fields amplifies the document that contains all the user's search terms.

How far should you take this? Should every field be copied into an all field ? Elasticsearch takes the approach far. By default, every field is copied to an overarching field called _all. Searching the _all field returns good results for our use case.

> **Listing 6.13   Searching _all**

```
usersSearch = "star trek patrick stewart william shatner"
query = {
    "query": {
        "match": {                          User's
            "_all": usersSearch,        ←   query
        }
    }
}
search(query)

Num  Relevance Score          Movie Title
1    0.9441141                Star Trek: Generations
2    0.577018                 Star Trek: Insurrection
3    0.577018                 Star Trek: First Contact
4    0.56560814               Star Trek V: The Final Frontier
5    0.5166054                Star Trek: Nemesis
```

Yet, repeat the same search with just patrick stewart, and the top result has nothing to do with Patrick Stewart:

```
1    0.4262765                Panic Room
2    0.33741575               Conspiracy Theory
3    0.33741575               The Wolverine
4    0.33741575               Vertigo
5    0.33741575               Star Trek: Insurrection
```

This happens because somewhere in the combined _all field of panic room, the text patrick is mentioned, and so is stewart. The signal generated from an _all search is vague, and doesn't map to meaningful information your users would recognize. The signal for the more carefully created people.name is probably closer to the user's sense of meaningful criteria; it measures relevance scores for people associated with a movie. Custom all fields that vacuum up all the text (such as the _all field) tend to be far too general, and should generally be avoided.

Again, term-centric search isn't a panacea. Users likely *do* care about *what* is matching. To tightly control what is matching per field, you often focus on field-centric methods and the lessons in chapters 4 and 5. Later in this chapter, you'll begin to see how to have your cake and eat it too.

6.4.2 *Solving signal discordance with cross_fields*

Custom all fields are static, created as documents are being indexed. In contrast, a `cross_fields` search is dynamic, addressing signal discordance at query time. It does this by becoming a dismax-style query parser on steroids. The ranking function of `cross_fields` remains identical to the query parser approach, with one important modification: the `cross_fields` query temporarily modifies the search term's document frequency, field by field, before searching. If the term `shatner` is particularly common in the fields being searched, except for one troublesome field such as `directors.name`, then that troublesome field will be lied to and given a larger document frequency. This attempts to solve signal discordance, albeit in a way that could be less accurate than an all field.

Say that instead of using a dismal query parser field, you execute a `cross_fields` search. So instead of something like this dismax

```
(cast.name:william | directors.name:william)
(cast.name:shatner | directors.name:shatner)
```

you get what's referenced by Elasticsearch with this `Blended` explain syntax, which blends the document frequencies of the listed fields before executing the search:

```
Blended(cast.name:william, directors.name:william)
Blended(cast.name:shatner, directors.name:shatner)
```

What would a `cross_fields` search combining all of these fields look like? It's a `multi_match` query that uses the `cross_fields` query type. `cross_fields` uses the field's common query analyzer. Much like the dismax query parser, `cross_fields` continues to suffer from field synchronicity. If fields don't share the same analyzer, `cross_fields` returns an error. With that in mind, you know that most of your fields have versions analyzed as English text. So you should be able to use `cross_fields` search over these English-language-analyzed results.

Running `cross_fields` with this in mind gets at our needed search results, as shown in the following listing.

Listing 6.14 `cross_fields` search over useful fields

```
usersSearch = 'star trek patrick stewart william shatner'
query = {
    "query": {                                                      User's
        "multi_match": {                                            query
            "query": usersSearch,                        ◁──┘
            "fields": ["title", "overview", "cast.name", "directors.name"],
```

```
            "type": "cross_fields",        ◁─┐ Uses a cross
        }                                     │ field search
    }
}
search(query)

Results
Num   Relevance Score        Movie Title
1     1.9040859              Star Trek: Generations
2     1.6575186              Star Trek V: The Final Frontier
3     1.3508359              Star Trek: Nemesis
4     1.1206487              Star Trek: The Motion Picture
5     1.0781065              Star Trek: Insurrection
```

The results aren't identical to the preceding _all field search. It turns out you can't exactly calculate the combined document frequency of multiple fields at query time. The fields have limited information for this approximation. The cross_fields query can access only each term's document frequency for a field. It then must attempt to sensibly combine them, which can't be guaranteed to be exactly correct. Let's say shatner has a document frequency of 16 in cast.name and 1 in directors.name. By knowing those two facts, you can't tell whether the single occurrence of the term shatner in directors.name occurs in a film where William Shatner also stars, or if it occurs in a movie directed by Shatner but not starring him. In the former case, the combined document frequency would be 16. But in the latter, the true document frequency should be the result of summing the two fields' document frequencies: 17. The cross_fields approach takes the safe route, picking the max of the two fields' document frequencies: 16.

A custom all field that physically combines fields would capture the document frequency more accurately. A combined people.name field would have the term shatner exactly once, regardless of whether or not he directed. But this accuracy comes at a cost. All fields are built exactly once at index time. You can't decide at search time to combine another set of fields. Moreover, the space requirements sometimes aren't tolerable, especially in large-scale systems. Although not as accurate, cross_fields allows more ad hoc flexibility in blending fields. Moreover, cross_fields is fundamentally a term-by-term dismax query—the same as you saw with the previous query parser. So tuning options, field boosting, and the tie_breaker parameter continue to be available to you! Unfortunately, the same field synchronicity issues also apply.

6.5   Combining field-centric and term-centric strategies: having your cake and eating it too

You've seen that field-centric search often ignores users' basic search expectations. Yet term-centric search, because of field synchronicity, has its own problems. It puts strict enforcements on the underlying fields. And for this reason, delivers basic, unsophisticated relevance functionality. To put things in context: you spent chapter 4 using analyzers to build special-snowflake fields, capable of modeling anything that can be tokenized. In chapter 5 you learned how to use those with field-centric search. And here you've learned that all that work is incompatible with term-centric search!

Sadly, there's no silver bullet. Mastering how to combine both approaches is an ongoing struggle. In this section, we discuss strategies for trying to balance the strengths of both techniques to create relevance solutions that satisfy and delight. You'll see that the way you use the two strategies together depends entirely on making the right compromises for your data and users. The struggle to get the balance right is a huge part of your ongoing tuning work as a relevance engineer.

6.5.1 Grouping "like fields" together

In this section, we examine one strategy for combining field-centric and term-centric effects: grouping similar, or *like*, fields together with a term-centric effect. These groupings are themselves combined with an outer field-centric search. Artfully grouping fields can be a way to sidestep field-centric search problems with just enough of a term-centric effect to prioritize more matches within the fields prone to albino elephant and signal discordance problems.

Note that if a user's search term can match only a single field, then the problems of field-centric search go away. You can't have albino elephant or signal discordance if search terms always find their ideal field. For example, a match for "Star Trek Patrick Stewart William Shatner" would be fine with field-centric search if you could guarantee that star trek matched in exactly one field (let's call it text), while name-related terms such as patrick stewart and william shatner matched only in a field about people.

We call these groupings *like fields*. As we've discussed, your source data model doesn't come with these straightforward groupings. It's your job when signal modeling to group fields in such a way that albino elephant and signal discordance have little effect on the final solution. Your job too is to map signals to users' general search expectations. By grouping like fields, you more closely approximate the higher-level signals users care about.

One way that a user is likely to think about ranking Star Trek matches, for example, is in groupings of like fields indicating that the ideal document

- SHOULD match people mentioned in the search string
  (inner term-centric people:term1 people term2 ...)
- SHOULD match text mentioned in the search string
  (inner term-centric text:term1 text:term2...)

Given this specification, you can express the ideal document to Elasticsearch for your Star Trek search. One simple improvement, shown in the following listing, is to group people to more closely match the preceding specification by using the custom all field people.name as part of a most_fields search. You'll note in the listing that we're searching the non-bigrammed field to demonstrate the basic idea. Further precision could also be gained searching the bigrammed field.

Listing 6.15   Search combining term-centric all field (`people.name`) with other fields

```
usersSearch = "star trek patrick stewart william shatner"
query = {
    "query": {                                               User's
        "multi_match": {                                     query
            "query": usersSearch,
            "fields": ["title", "overview", "people.name"],     Searches
            "type": "most_fields",                              non-bigrammed
        }                                                       people.name
    }                                                           field
}
search(query)

Num   Relevance Score        Movie Title
1     0.7104292              Star Trek: Generations
2     0.5998383              Star Trek IV: The Voyage Home
3     0.50374436             Star Trek: Nemesis
4     0.35599363             Star Trek
5     0.3373023              Star Trek: The Motion Picture
```

This is an improvement. By grouping people fields with other people fields (`directors.name` + `cast.name` -> `people.name`), you've eliminated a class of likely problems. Now you can search in a field-centric fashion, but with a term-centric effect on the custom all field. You carefully combined the various fields about people into a single field that provides a specific signal.

6.5.2   *Understanding the limits of like fields*

Is this it, then? Is this the solution to your search problems? Is grouping like fields the right way to balance the two approaches? The unfortunate reality is that search terms do spuriously crop up in fields we don't expect them to. So grouping like fields can't always save you. As we said, unfortunately there's no silver bullet to the yin and yang of field-centric and term-centric search. Like most programming problems, there are only carefully honed compromises based on the nature of your data and the demands of your users.

You can modify the strategy to account for reality. In our movie search, for example, names of actors crop up in movie descriptions. There are probably people named Star and even Trek that would score rather highly because of how rare they are as names. In the same way, names such as William could appear in titles or overview text. Grouping fields into like fields might not always be feasible.

Let's demonstrate the problem. Here `cross_fields` search is used instead of a custom all field to group text fields with text fields, and people fields with people fields. This is the strategy we described previously. Recall that `most_fields` expects a list of *fields* to search, not a list of *queries*. So to use `most_fields` with an inner `cross_fields` query, you need to implement the `most_fields` scoring behavior on your own. This is what the outer Boolean query does in the following listing.

Listing 6.16   Searching two field groupings—people and text

```
usersSearch = "star trek patrick stewart william shatner"
query = {
    "query": {
        "bool": {                                    Boolean SHOULD clauses,
            "should": [                              replicating "most_fields"
                {
                    "multi_match": {
                        "query": usersSearch,
                        "fields": ["directors.name", "cast.name"],      Grouping of
                        "type": "cross_fields"                          like people
                    }                                                   fields into a
        User's  }                                                       term-centric
        query },                                                        search
                {
                    "multi_match": {
                        "query": usersSearch,
                        "fields": ["overview", "title"],       Grouping of like
                        "type": "cross_fields"                 text fields into a
                    }                                          term-centric
                }                                              search
            ]
        }
    }
}
search(query)
```

```
Num   Relevance Score        Movie Title
1     1.1444862              Star Trek IV: The Voyage Home
2     0.75206727             Star Trek: Nemesis
3     0.7318188              Star Trek V: The Final Frontier
4     0.72360706             Star Trek: Generations
5     0.5002059              Star Trek
```

This, unfortunately, doesn't have the impact you want. For some reason, *Star Trek IV* shoots to the top of the list. Why? If you examine the explain, you'll see that surprisingly, william shatner is mentioned in the overview field of *Star Trek IV*:

```
0.18140785, max of:
    0.18140785, weight(overview:william in 474)
0.34648207, max of:
    0.34648207, weight(overview:shatner in 474)
```

As we suspected, names often crop up in many fields. You usually can't cleanly separate fields into like fields. The idea that "search terms will always be in bucket A or B" doesn't work always with our messy, unstructured data sets. Moreover, as the text-based cross_fields query gets biased heavily when more search terms match, the fact that names like William Shatner or Patrick Stewart do match these fields further amplifies the distortion of unexpected matches.

6.5.3   *Combining greedy naïve search and conservative amplifiers*

We said that term-centric search often satisfies but rarely delights. Another strategy combining term-centric and field-centric methods is to base relevance on a term-centric foundation. Using that baseline, smarter and discriminating per-field signals can be brought in to amplify documents in ways you feel confident will delight the user. You already know how to craft fields that when matched meet certain criteria with high confidence—for example, criteria such as "the user is searching for a person" or "the user is searching for a location." Using this criteria, you can think of the ideal document for your TMDB example as follows.

The ideal document

- SHOULD have all search terms match the superset of fields being searched
- SHOULD have searched-for names match the people associated with the film

The first SHOULD serves as a basic text score over a superset of the plain-text versions of fields that occur in all other clauses. It matches rather greedily. The second SHOULD clause is much less greedy. It's highly discriminating and searches only a subset of the fields from the first clause grouped into like fields (such as people, places, or things) in order to get specific signals.

Two factors are important with this approach:

- Any document that matches the second discriminating clause also matched the first "greedy" clause. This way, every document being considered has a base score.
- The nongreedy clauses should be high-quality signals erring on the conservative side to avoid overriding the base score with an unexpected match.

By having one wide-net base score and carefully selected discriminating amplifiers, you're more likely to arrive at a place that at the very least satisfies the user. As your secondary signals improve, you can continue to use those as amplifiers with high confidence—sussing out additional highly discriminating signals. The secondary signals are conservative for important reasons: If those secondary signals are unintelligent, or let something "sneak in" such as a non-name match, you may override the user's base assumptions of all their search terms matching, resulting in something rather silly. But if you miss the mark and don't quite get to the precise match on the person named William Shatner, at least the basic term-centric search is backing you up so that you don't arrive at something utterly terrible.

Let's try that out, with a base `cross_fields` term-centric search over the text version of each field, and an additional SHOULD that brings up documents that match the subset of those fields corresponding to people's names, modeled using the bigram analyzers.

Listing 6.17   Greedy term-centric paired with highly discriminating like fields

```
usersSearch = "star trek patrick stewart william shatner"
query = {
    "query": {
        "bool": {
            "should": [
                {
                    "multi_match": {
                        "query": usersSearch,
                        "fields": ["directors.name.bigrammed",
                                   "cast.name.bigrammed"],
                        "type": "cross_fields"
                    }
                },
                {
                    "multi_match": {
                        "query": usersSearch,
                        "fields": ["overview", "title",
                                   "directors.name", "cast.name"],
                        "type": "cross_fields"
                    }
                }
            ]
        }
    }
}
search(query)
1    1.6669365          Star Trek: Generations
2    1.5123603          Star Trek V: The Final Frontier
3    1.0779369          Star Trek: Nemesis
4    0.9057324          Star Trek: The Motion Picture
5    0.8793935          Star Trek: Insurrection
```

> **Outer Boolean query biases toward all matches of both general text and full people bigrammed names.**

> **User's query**

> **Searches names by bigrammed, discriminating like fields**

> **Computes base text score over all searched fields**

Now you're getting somewhere! There are refinements to be made, but this pattern is a good start. The score for *Star Trek V* is close to that of *Star Trek: Generations*. Is it because the term frequency for the bigram william shatner is 2 (as we know he acts and directs)? Users don't care that there are two mentions of William Shatner! You could keep improving the quality of this signal, enhancing how much it measures the association of a person with a field. You could disable term frequency and get even closer to the ideal signal (or as you'll see in the next chapter, use a constant_score query to completely eliminate TF × IDF).

Another question is how much of a foundation should the base term-centric search create? How much should it impact the score as compared to these more specialized signals? What is the impact of the less specialized term-centric clause? With increasing SHOULD field-centric clauses, could you get back into an albino elephant scenario in which many of the nonfoundational, field-centric, special snowflake fields match strongly, but not all individual search terms match in the term-centric search? Yes, you can. And continuing to wrestle with the yin and yang of term-centric and field-centric search takes a large portion of the relevance engineer's time. Luckily, every query in Elasticsearch can be boosted, tweaking the overall score toward whichever end—yin or yang—you need scoring to go.

6.5.4   *Term-centric vs. field-centric, and precision vs. recall*

The pattern in the previous section should remind you of the ever-present struggle between precision and recall. As you learned in chapter 4, high recall ensures that all the right matches are in the search results, and high precision ensures that few false-positive matches are included. You can modify the definition of precision and recall to think just about the top N (say, top 10) results that you'll show on the first page of search results. Practically speaking, this is what's important to get right!

A greedy term-centric search gives you high recall. It casts its net wide, ensuring that you've captured all the right search results. Your first search page contains a list of possibly relevant results—likely, a reasonable mix of fairly simple matches, though nothing particularly smart. Left alone, your users are likely to go through pages of search results every now and then, being forced to scan for what they want. Adding in highly discriminating field-centric signals improves the precision of the search results. It promotes increasingly more promising candidates to the first page only when certain exacting criteria are met.

What's great about the pattern from the previous section is that it lets you control how much term-centric or how much field-centric impact you'd like to have. If precise matching is more important, you can fine-tune those specific matches with boosts, letting those scores bubble up more easily. If this is less important, boosting field-centric signals matters much less than focusing on recall.

6.5.5   *Considering filtering, boosting, and reranking*

Although the pattern mentioned previously is a good starting point, the Query DSL is always being used in new and interesting ways. In the next chapter, you'll see how to carefully and explicitly use signals to manipulate ranking even further. You might, for example, want to fine-tune the base term-centric pattern discussed previously by filtering out results that don't match a minimum number of search criteria. Or figure out a way to make the number of search terms that match a primary sort, and call out the field-centric signals to be more of an inner reranking criteria. Often field-centric approaches can precisely let you filter or boost by using a specific signal. Perhaps you'd like to give an explicit nudge to restaurants close to the user, or to filter out restaurants far away. At the core, you may have a general relevance score. On the fringes, you massage and prod the relevance score with more carefully modeled signals.

6.6   *Summary*

- Because of the albino elephant problem, field-centric search doesn't satisfy users' relatively naïve sense of relevance, which relies on the premise that documents matching more of your search terms ought to be considered more relevant.

- Signal discordance creates unexpected ranking behavior as the search engine decomposes documents into many fields that are scored independently.

- Term-centric search pushes scoring toward users' naïve sense of relevance (prioritizing documents that match more search terms).

- Term-centric query parsers, such as `query_string` or Solr's edismax, solve the albino elephant problem, but not signal discordance.

- Creating a custom all field solves both the albino elephant problem and signal discordance most accurately, but increases the index size.

- Blended term-centric search methods solve the albino elephant problem and signal discordance at query time, but not as accurately as a custom all field.

- Term-centric search requires the search string to be analyzed before fields are searched. This eliminates the ability to specialize each field to measure different, smarter signals.

- Balancing generic term-centric scoring with smarter field-centric scoring requires careful work.

- Several strategies aim to take advantage of the strengths of field-centric and term-centric search (including like fields and highly discriminating boosts).

- Another way to look at term-centric versus field-centric search is that term-centric focuses on high recall, whereas field-centric is a tool to get higher precision.

Shaping the
relevance function

This chapter covers

- Bringing up relevant content through boosting
- Knowing when to use different forms of boosting
- Improving the ranking of popular or recent content
- Filtering out irrelevant or noisy content from search results
- Stoking your own creative uses of the search engine's querying features

As a relevance engineer, you tailor your users' search experience to their many unspoken ranking expectations. Unpacking, understanding, and finally implementing these expectations are key parts of your job. For example, almost everyone has a sense that a news search should show up-to-date articles about breaking events. Or that a restaurant search shouldn't take into account only the user's query but also the proximity of that user to the restaurant. Your search will probably have unique ranking needs that go beyond text matching. For instance, what if you're building a local news search? Should it focus on both proximity *and* freshness?

Or what about a global restaurant search for the jet-setting crowd? Should it focus on cities with major airports?

Previous chapters have shown you how to control the general form of results for common forms of search. In this chapter, you'll snip, craft, and shape the ranking function to get at your users' unique criteria. You'll see that you can become a master of your search engine's Query DSL, truly programming every corner of search ranking, in order to carefully boost, filter, rerank, and sort in exacting ways to implement unique ranking requirements.

This chapter is the search relevancy power hour, but our goal isn't to comprehensively teach you every trick for manipulating search. The number of permutations of every option of every query is far too large! Instead, we want to show you techniques to move the gears of your imagination. You'll see that using your search engine's Query DSL *is* programming. It's not a handful of knobs and dials to just tune. It's a language for customizing search ranking—with new techniques being constantly discovered! Indeed, if we're reading your blog post or book and learning a new technique from you in the years ahead, we'll have done our job in this chapter.

7.1 What do we mean by score shaping?

With *score shaping*, depicted in figure 7.1, relevance begins to take on the character of true programming. You use the tools within the Query DSL to snip the ranking function closer to your needs. The most important tools in the Query DSL for programming ranking are *boosting* and *filtering*. We've used these terms loosely in previous chapters, but they take on special importance in this chapter.

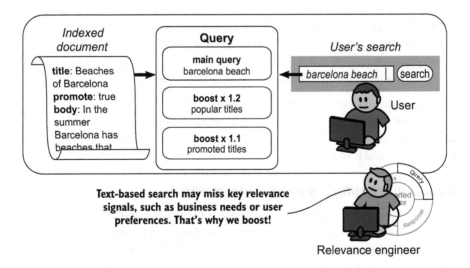

Figure 7.1 Relevance engineers use score-shaping techniques to carefully craft the ranking, thus implementing custom, application-specific ranking rules.

So let's tighten up our definitions:

- *Boosting*—Given a base set of search results, boosting increases the relevance score of a subset of those search results.
- *Filtering*—Given the entire corpus of possible search results, filtering removes a subset of those documents from consideration by specifying a filter query.

Defining the subset of search results for boosting and filtering, and deciding how they modify relevance ranking, extends the skills you learned in the previous chapter:

- *Signals*—Signals measure important ranking criteria at search time. In this chapter, signals take a more quantitative tone: How recently was an article published? How close is the restaurant to me? The presence of a signal indicates when to filter or boost; the magnitude of the signal might control a boosting factor.
- *Ranking function*—Filtering and boosting directly adjust the ranking function. For example, a boost might apply a multiplier proportional to how recently a movie was released. A filter might limit the subset of search results that the ranking function is run against.

Although boosting and filtering are the core techniques that we cover in this chapter, quite a few methods are available to shape scores. Other methods of score shaping include:

- *Modifying the sort criteria* to not strictly be based on the relevance score, but based on other values—such as date, popularity, distance, or computed values
- *Negative boosting*, which drives down a set of search results (in contrast to standard, positive boosting)
- *Rescoring* or *reranking* by adding a second stage to ranking to tweak the order of the top *N* set of results with additional signals
- *Scripting the score via a custom score query*, which allows you to use a script to completely take control of the scoring for a base set of search results

Honing your expressive ability with the Query DSL will stoke your creative abilities as a relevance engineer. As you examine these techniques, remember: the goal is not just to explore all of these ideas, but as all algebra teachers tell their students, you learn this stuff to "teach you how to think."

7.2   *Boosting: shaping by promoting results*

Boosting gives you the power to mathematically prioritize specific documents as more relevant than others. Carefully selecting the documents you'd like to boost and calibrating the impact of those boosts are key skills for programming relevance. How much you boost can be based on any number of criteria, including secondary text-relevance scores, simple constants, or content-quality metrics such as popularity, recency of publication, or user ratings.

You may recall that we discussed the boosts associated with various fields when going over multifield search in previous chapters. In those chapters, we spent time calibrating the relative weight of, say, a title or a body match in a multifield search. To be clear: those weights (what we refer to as *boost weights*) aren't what we mean here. The boosting work you'll see in this chapter isn't (just) tuning weights. Here you'll use secondary queries, or *boost queries*, to modify the overall ranking function.

For the boost to truly reflect an important, meaningful relevance signal, all the skills from previous chapters continue to matter a great deal. After all, without good signals to boost, you won't be shaping the score so much as polluting it with noisy scoring that promotes unexpected results to the top.

In this section, we'll introduce you to your first boost queries. You'll see the subdivisions used to break up forms of boosting. Initially, we'll teach you the basic forms of each. Knowing these basic forms is foundational for enhancing your boost-fu. Later sections demonstrate how to flex your skills to create search results that answer more real-world ranking questions through boosting.

7.2.1 *Boosting: the final frontier*

You're about to go on a wild boosting expedition, but before we tinker, explore, and prod, you need to pick up a basic example to drive your work.

What example should we choose? Well, boosting and score shaping is a bit of a final frontier—always ripe for discovery! So it makes sense to go back to the Star Trek fan movie search from previous chapters. One use case we haven't considered is a user's omission of "Star Trek" from the search. Fans who search for just "William Shatner" probably won't be happy with the TV show *TJ Hooker* as the first search result. Let's boost "Star Trek" titles to the top to get a feel for boosting basics.

First you need a base query. In the preceding chapter, you learned how cross_ fields search forms a reasonable starting point for relevance, so let's start with it here. In the following listing, you're searching for "William Shatner Patrick Stewart," hunting for the film that stars both of them.

Listing 7.1   Base query to boost

```
usersSearch = "william shatner patrick stewart"
query = {
    "query": {
        "multi_match": {                              User's
            "query": usersSearch,              ⟵┘    query
            "fields": ["overview", "title",
                       "directors.name", "cast.name"],
            "type": "cross_fields"
        }
    }
}
search(query)
```

```
Results
Num  Relevance Score        Movie Title
1    0.79947156             Star Trek V: The Final Frontier
2    0.67931885             Star Trek: Generations
3    0.4375222              The Wild
4    0.38154808             Dark Skies
5    0.32485005             Showtime
```

The results aren't perfect. *Star Trek: Generations* ought to be number one (recall that in the last chapter, we tweaked this a bit further). For our purposes, though, we're focused on a different problem. For the Star Trek fan, the last three results should be Star Trek movies. You need to boost Star Trek films! Let's explore the options.

7.2.2 *When boosting—add or multiply? Boolean or function query?*

You've seen a minor problem that requires boosting. Time to get to work bending the ranking function to your will! Where do you start? Let's make sense of the boosting landscape before deciding exactly how you'll bring (beam?) up those Star Trek title matches.

In particular, you'll see that when boosting, you need to make two key decisions:

- *The math used to boost*—Should you add or multiply the boost score to the base query?
- *The query used to boost*—Some queries are explicitly geared toward boosting, but which should you use?

Let's discuss the math first. A document matching the boost query (Star Trek films, in our case) will have its score combined with the base query's. What are the consequences of choosing addition or multiplication?

- An *additive boost stacks* the boost on top of the base query. To be effective, the boost must layer on just enough oomph to matter in the final calculation. A 0.01 boost added to a base query score of 4 will hardly matter. A 100.0 boost added to that base query will effectively override the base query.
- A *multiplicative boosts scales* the base query. A simple boost multiplier of 1.2 ensures, regardless of how the base query's score behaves, that boosted documents will get 20% more oomph than unboosted documents.

Figure 7.2 shows the implications of this choice. With the multiplicative boost, think of a document as a balloon. A multiplicative boost "inflates" the boosted balloon by the appropriate amount. Additive boosting forces you to consider how much you layer on the impact of a boost.

The second important decision is choosing the query to boost with. This choice dictates the form of the ranking function and the tools you'll have available to shape it to your needs.

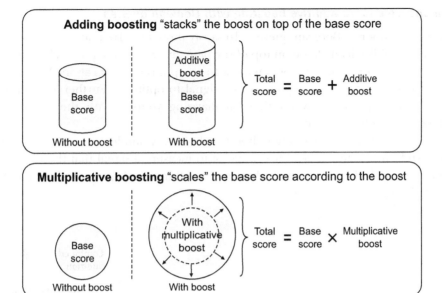

Figure 7.2 Additive boosting layers on extra criteria; multiplicative boosting inflates/ deflates through multiplication.

With Elasticsearch, two queries are used for boosting:

- With a *Boolean query*, you boost via an additional Boolean clause on top of the base query, using Elasticsearch's `bool` query.
- With a *function query*, you boost by directly modifying the ranking function by using Elasticsearch's `function_score` query.

By using Boolean queries, much is abstracted away for you. Adding a boost means adding a simple SHOULD clause on top of the base query and tweaking a few weights. The ranking math is baked in (Boolean queries are always *additive boosts*), with a few knobs and dials to manipulate.

Function queries give you direct control of the ranking function. You combine the base query and any boost queries in mathematically arbitrary forms. There's no baked-in "formula" as in Boolean queries. Therefore, function queries can't cleanly be categorized as multiplicative or additive. Function queries are simply math! Given the lower level of control, there are things only function queries can accomplish.

Let's get back to our problem. Where were we? Oh, right! You have an important search problem to solve with hordes of Trek fans raring to break down your door. Better choose a solution fast! Do you go through door A and solve your problem by applying an additional Boolean clause? Or do you go through door B and begin to get your hands dirty with function queries? Let's see the consequences of both decisions.

176   CHAPTER 7   *Shaping the relevance function*

7.2.3   *You choose door A: additive boosting with Boolean queries*

You choose door A: Boolean queries. To satisfy those Star Trek fans, you'll boost with an additional Boolean clause on top of the base `cross_fields` query. This will ask the search engine to prioritize documents with the phrase `star trek` in the title. You'll begin to see how to treat any boost as a signal to optimize. Further, combining the boost signal appropriately requires familiarizing yourself with the additive math underlying the Boolean query.

Let's see what a Boolean query boost looks like. A simple `match_phrase` query on "Star Trek" in the title is your first attempt to measure a signal that the film is a Star Trek film. Apply this alongside the base query within a `bool` query, as shown in the following listing.

Listing 7.2   Boosting with an additional Boolean clause

```
usersSearch = "william shatner patrick stewart"      ❸ Combined through
query = {                                               addition
    "query": {
        "bool": {                                      ❶ Base query—measures
            "should": [                                  signal that more query
                {"multi_match": {                        terms match
                    "query": usersSearch,
                    "fields": ["overview", "title",
                            "directors.name", "cast.name"],   User's
                    "type": "cross_fields"                     query
                }},
                {
                    "match_phrase": {                  Boost query—
                        "title": {                     measures signal
                            "query": "star trek",      that the film is a
                }}}                                    ❷ Star Trek film
            ]
        }
    },
}
search(query)
```

Before we reveal the final search results, let's walk through what happens when the search engine scores this query. This will reveal exactly how and where you can modify the ranking function and boosting to your needs.

OPTIMIZING BOOSTS IN ISOLATION
With a Boolean query, first the boost and base scores are run in isolation (❶ and ❷ in listing 7.2). Your boosting can be only as good as the underlying queries. In our case, your queries attempt to measure two signals:

- *Boost*—Is the film a Star Trek film? (❶ in listing 7.2)
- *Base*—Are all the query terms featured in the searched fields? (❷ in listing 7.2)

Do these queries accurately measure the needed signals? For instance, the boost query, a phrase query against the title field, relies on TF × IDF scoring of phrases. Does that score help to measure whether a film is a Star Trek film? Is TF × IDF appropriate to answer what seems to be a yes/no question?

What about the base query? Is this `cross_fields` search the right strategy? Are all the fields appropriately weighted? Should other fields be searched? What about other parameters of `cross_fields`, such as `tie_breaker`? The point is that all of these options are up for tweaking and experimentation. As a relevance engineer, you never rest when optimizing the signals underlying your queries.

COMBINING BOOST AND BASE QUERY

The next step to consider is how the Boolean query combines these queries' scores (❸ in listing 7.2). Boolean queries do a bit more than add the scores of their component clauses. Additive boosting means you need to layer on the boost's influence carefully to not overwhelm or underwhelm the base query score.

You know by now that Boolean queries do more than add. You also need to concern yourself with the coordinating factor (coord)—that strong bias toward documents that match all the clauses (here, both the boost and base queries). This can be disabled with the `disable_coord` option if you don't want this bias. You might want to do this if the boost query is more "extra credit" than "required."

Finally, with all these factors, each clause has been scored and combined. Let's examine the search results from listing 7.2 to see whether they match our expectations:

```
Num   Relevance Score       Movie Title
1     4.363374              Star Trek
2     4.0461645             Star Trek: Generations
3     3.7096446             Star Trek V: The Final Frontier
4     3.6913855             Star Trek: Nemesis
5     3.653065              Star Trek: The Motion Picture
```

It definitely looks better! But recall that our search is for "William Shatner Patrick Stewart." The first result doesn't star William Shatner or Patrick Stewart. Maybe the boost didn't work?

Examining these results, it appears that the Star Trek boost might be layered on too thick. You'll notice that instead of the desired result, *Star Trek: Generations*, we seem to be heavily favoring the shorter Star Trek match. This is suspicious, and leads us to think that perhaps the TF × IDF relevance score of the Star Trek phrase-matching clause isn't quite measuring the right signal. Why might we think this? Recall, TF × IDF has a strong bias toward shorter fields through field normalization, which scores the short Star Trek title match highly. Figure 7.3 shows the impact of each layer, with the Star Trek title boost overwhelming relevance scoring.

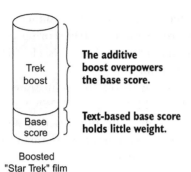

The additive boost overpowers the base score.

Text-based base score holds little weight.

Trek boost

Base score

Boosted "Star Trek" film

Figure 7.3   The Star Trek title boost is layered on too thick, and needs to be tuned down so the base relevance score can contribute more appropriately.

There's too much boosting going on, and that boosting is based on factors you don't care about! The boost clause doesn't measure the right signal. You could correct this in various ways. The simplest option most reach for is to reduce the boost weight, lowering the boost from 1 to perhaps 0.25 or 0.1. This dampens the wonky TF × IDF scoring. Let's examine the result of reweighting our boost to be more carefully applied (here we simply show the modified `match_phrase` clause):

```
{
  "match_phrase": {
     "title": {
         "query": "star trek",
         "boost": 0.1
}}}
```

This brings the results to a saner place. Notice how our top two results mirror the `cross_fields` search from our base search earlier. But what's improved is that subsequent matches bring up the Star Trek titles:

```
Num  Relevance Score        Movie Title
1    1.1662666              Star Trek V: The Final Frontier
2    1.0990597              Star Trek: Generations
3    0.6702043              Star Trek: Nemesis
4    0.62388283             Star Trek: The Motion Picture
5    0.6117288              Star Trek II: The Wrath of Khan
```

Nevertheless, this is a fragile solution. Simply tweaking a boost weight may postpone a problem for another search. Another, more sound option is to improve the precision of the signal associated with the Star Trek title matching. One way to do this is to disable field normalization for this field, trying to even out the Star Trek scoring.

The bigger question, however, is whether TF × IDF even matters here. Users think of a "Star Trek" movie query as more of a yes/no, 1/0 sort of question. So TF× IDF might not measure this signal correctly. We won't solve that problem right now. Later, when you dive into boosting strategies, you'll see one way to step away from TF × IDF to get to yes/no scoring.

7.2.4 *You choose door B: function queries using math for ranking*

Time to try a different strategy: door B, function queries! In your work, you'll likely need numerical attributes, such as a product's profitability or an article's popularity, in relevance ranking. To incorporate these factors, you need to directly control the ranking function. Function queries give you this power. With function queries, you directly define the ranking function based on a combination of quantitative factors (such as popularity, publication date, and profitability) and other search queries.

Before solving our "star trek" problem, let's look at a classic example: prioritizing recently published news articles over old ones. When users search for "bad apple harvest" on a news site, a recent bad apple harvest is likely what they're after. Unfortunately, out of the box, the search engine has no notion that the recency of publication is an important factor. The apple harvest of 1901 could easily outrank the apple harvest of 2011!

You need to tell the search engine to prioritize news articles published recently. You need to get inside users' heads, modeling their expectations by using math.

To define a relationship between recency and the user's notion of relevance, let's start with a simple, relatively naïve formula, shown in figure 7.4. Let's define a function, *R(m)*, as *1 / m*, where m is the months into the past this article was published. Let's use this function as a multiplicative boost: a single month into the past multiplies relevance by 1, two months knocks it down 1/2 (half as relevant), three months 1/3, and so forth.

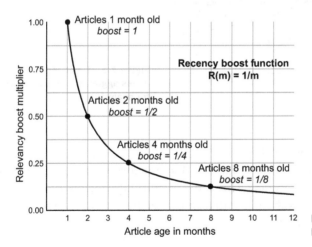

Figure 7.4 Naïve recency boost for news articles

Now, as is often the case, this first pass might not model how news users prioritize this recency signal. Knocking down news four months old by a multiple of 1/4 might be far too aggressive. Then again, it might not be aggressive enough!

Just as when boosting with Boolean queries, the signal you're building might be inaccurate. To optimize the signal, you're tweaking the math itself, not just TF × IDF and other text-scoring factors (what you might call *fudge factors*, we call *score shaping*).

Yet even with the increased mathematical freedom, the imperatives are the same: you need to make sure your signals are accurate too. Here the pertinent questions are as follows: Does the recency effect degrade too fast into the past? Or too aggressively? Is the boost a large enough multiple? Should it degrade using a different mathematical formula? All of these questions matter in measuring how users are likely to prioritize recency.

For example, you may have learned that your users are news analysts. They prioritize recency but still need to occasionally research older news stories. The bad apple harvest last year still matters. Through some tweaking (and fudging!), perhaps a recency function such as $R(m) = 8 / (5 + 3m)$ works better to make the recency signal less aggressive, and more attuned to the needs of your news analysts, as shown in figure 7.5.

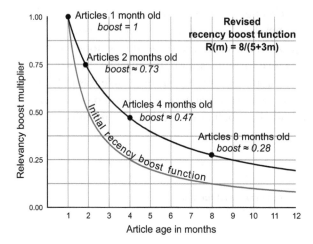

Figure 7.5   Tuned recency boost: a less aggressive recency boost for analysts

Manipulating math to arrive at the correct signal comes with many of the same burdens as manipulating other relevance factors. Does the formula account for how users and the business prioritize recency? This is the identical discussion as in the Boolean query boosting, only the possibilities with arbitrary math become far more open, creating many more decision points.

7.2.5   *Hands-on with function queries: simple multiplicative boosting*

Let's switch back to our Star Trek example to get our hands dirty with function queries in the Query DSL. You need to see a function query in the context of something basic before tackling larger mathematical problems. To ease you in, we'll give you a starting point: solving our Star Trek title boost. Later in this chapter, you'll begin to tackle a larger, more challenging problem that extends beyond the simple function presented here.

In this case, you want documents with Star Trek titles to be multiplied by a factor of 2.5. The function you'd like to implement applies a straightforward multiplicative boost that, expressed mathematically, looks something like this:

$$B(title) = \text{"star trak" in title?} \begin{cases} no: 1 \\ yes: 2.5 \end{cases}$$

This straightforward function returns one value when a particular match occurs, and another when it doesn't.

Let's get to work! Elasticsearch's function queries are known as `function_score` `_query`, as shown in listing 7.3. At the heart of the `function_score_query` is the base query query parameter ❶—another full-fledged Query DSL query. Being combined with that query's relevance score are mathematical functions ❸. Here the only function is our simple `star trek` function ❷. By specifying a weight and a filter as shown in listing 7.3, all documents that satisfy the filter (in this case, a phrase query for `star trek` in the title) receive a value of `weight` (here, 2.5) for this function. The `function_score_query` lets you specify how to combine the functions, but here we leave it as the default: multiplication of all `functions` with the base query score.

Let's execute this listing and see what shakes out.

Listing 7.3 Applying a multiplier for Star Trek movies

```
usersSearch = "william shatner patrick stewart"
query = {
    "query": {                                          ❶ Base
        "function_score": {                                query
            "query": {
                "multi_match": {
                    "query": usersSearch,               User's
                    "fields": ["overview", "title",     query
                            "directors.name", "cast.name"],
                    "type": "cross_fields"
                }
            },                                          ❸ Functions applied
            "functions": [                                 to the base query
                {
                    "weight": 2.5,                      Function multiplier:
                    "filter": {                         base score × 2.5 when
                        "query": {                      the phrase "star trek"
                            "match_phrase": {        ❷ occurs in a title
                                "title": "star trek"
                }}}}]
    }}}
search(query)
Results:
Num   Relevance Score        Movie Title
1     1.9986789              Star Trek V: The Final Frontier      5.4
2     1.6982971              Star Trek: Generations               6.5
```

3	0.6236526	Star Trek: Nemesis	6.3
4	0.60909384	Star Trek II: The Wrath of Khan	7.1
5	0.5075782	Star Trek IV: The Voyage Home	6.7

The end result is a reasonable boosting effect: Star Trek movies are brought to the top. You'll also notice that whereas in the additive boosting example you had to struggle with whether the TF × IDF score of the boost query made any sense, here that score isn't taken into account. In some ways, though more power and responsibility is in your hands, the end result is much simpler.

7.2.6   *Boosting basics: signals, signals everywhere*

You've seen the basic forms of boosting. One constant remains, regardless of the query form you choose to work with: the essential power of signals. Your signal modeling work is fundamental to relevance. With boosting, this is especially true. Does the boost for Star Trek layer on enough "oomph" to matter? Does TF × IDF scoring measure what's important to users? Is the right query being used? The right mathematical function? Do these factors map to a user's intuitive priorities?

The better you get at shaping the features and signals to measure this information, the stronger your ability to solve ranking in terms that humans, not search engines, understand.

7.3   *Filtering: shaping by excluding results*

The final basic ingredient when shaping scores is *excluding* search results. Users often don't want to see certain results, and your job is to ensure that they're excluded. You carefully craft queries to express what should be excluded, and then use finely honed signals to control those exclusions. This way, you tune the precision by excluding known classes of irrelevant results. This section briefly introduces filters and their role in the overall ranking function.

You often think of filtering when implementing user-experience features. Filters remove a set of results from consideration. You can think of them as tools to declutter search. Allowing users to manually select filters helps guide them to relevant content through the user interface. Perhaps they self-selected a category, such as deciding to limit themselves to seeing only the DVDs in a movie search, preferring to ignore the digital streaming or Blu-ray options. Or they might filter down when shopping for a TV to a particular set of criteria: 50-inch, plasma, free shipping. Guiding users toward relevant content with filters is a topic of the next chapter.

Yet filters aren't simply a matter of controlling the user experience. Filters act as a gate. A carefully implemented filter helps more precisely control the precision of search results, eliminating content you've expressly declared as irrelevant.

A simple example can be taken from our Star Trek search. In the previous section, we focused on boosting the Star Trek results to the top. Another way to think about this is to remove search results that aren't Star Trek results. What would this look like?

In Elasticsearch, filters take the form of a filter clause within a Boolean query. Within the filter, you can define how you'd like to restrict the document set; in the following listing, we're doing it by using a phrase query.

> **Listing 7.4 Filtering instead of boosting Star Trek results**

```
usersSearch = "william shatner patrick stewart"
query = {
    "query": {
        "bool": {
            "should": [
                {    "multi_match": {                          ← User's query
                    "query": usersSearch,
                    "fields": ["overview", "title",
                                "directors.name", "cast.name"],
                    "type": "cross_fields"
                }
            }],
            "filter": [{                          ← Include only "Star Trek" results
                "query": {
                    "match_phrase": {
                        "title": "star trek"
                    }
                }
            }]
        }
    }
}
search(query)
```

When scoring doesn't matter, and you only want to show or not show a set of search results, filtering can be a simpler solution. By scoring only a more limited set of search results, filtering allows your boosting to work with more precision. You eliminate obviously irrelevant results, letting you avoid corner cases in your relevance.

You ought to think about how you filter just as you think about boosting: in terms of signals. The queries you use to filter need to measure user and business criteria with high confidence. In the previous section, you concerned yourself with whether that phrase query measures the right criteria. The same is true here. If, for some reason, this isn't the right way to measure the signal "this is a star trek film," then you need to think through these queries. Filter queries can get as complex as boosting, as they try to include and exclude results.

As you continue to think through ranking problems in your career, be aware of all the tools in your toolbox. In some cases, other solutions aside from boosting might provide more straightforward functionality.

7.4 Score-shaping strategies for satisfying business needs

How should you use score-shaping tools like boosting and filtering to solve your specific problems? Remember, this chapter is about bending the Query DSL to your will. But in reality, it's not *your* will that you should be concerned about; it's all those challenging user and business ranking requirements you need to solve! This section helps you tackle real business and user needs with the tools you've learned thus far.

Score-shaping problems involve translating human, plain-English ranking priorities into boosts, filters, and queries that control the ranking function. Nontechnical bosses, content curators, and other colleagues like to ask for things such as "bring the movies with an exact-title match straight to the top" or "boost movies that came out in the last five years." Your job requires translating these plain-English expectations into "search-engineese" by incorporating the right data and mastering your search engine's features.

In this section, you'll explore strategies for manipulating the search engine to answer these questions. We introduce a framework for thinking through score-shaping problems based on two components.

First, our framework rests on a bedrock of high-precision boosting signals that rank based on questions in terms our users are familiar with: "the movie is an exact-title match" or "the movie came out > 5 years ago." To build these signals, you incorporate the right data, carefully control the composition of fields, and govern how they're queried and scored.

Second, our framework considers how you combine expectations into a larger solution. You might want to override ranking one way based on the strength of a particular signal, otherwise falling back to a base query. On the other hand, you might have little nudge or tie-breaker boosts—nice-to-have, lower-priority boosts that nudge relevance up or down.

These two phases, shown in figure 7.6, are highly interdependent.

How much your boost nudges or overrides might depend exactly on the precision of the signal. Perhaps it's a text-based relevancy nudge. Or a nudge based on multiplying

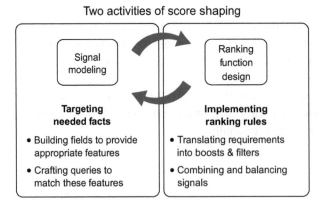

Figure 7.6 Two activities of score shaping are signal modeling (measuring pieces of ranking information) and the ranking function (combining the influence of different signals to implement business logic).

a carefully crafted function. You're always traversing both layers, optimizing signals, thinking how they'll be used, and modifying the ranking function accordingly. Search is highly iterative. With boosts, you have deep control over the ranking function—so this is where the iterations become fun. Let's see this philosophy in action by solving a real problem!

7.4.1 *Search all the movies!*

To flex the full power of this fully functional search engine, you're going to switch gears. You've done such a good job implementing search for those Star Trek fans that you've been promoted! Your next job is to implement movie search for everyone. You'll get a chance to implement some even more sophisticated ranking criteria to serve this broader audience. Let's take a second to consider what you're being told to implement for your search solution. Then you'll get your hands dirty with an interesting, nontrivial search solution that will mirror the tricky problems you're sure to face at your real job.

You've been told by your boss, "To get this search right, I think you generally need to implement the following logic in that search engine thing of yours. Here ya go:"

1 If the user's query is a full, *exact*-title match, such as a search for "Star Trek Generations," then that exact-title match should come straight to the top of the search results.

2 If the user's query is a full, *exact*-name match, such as a search for "William Shatner," then order results based on how recent and well rated the movie is.

3 Prioritize search results that include a person's full name, such as the query "William Shatner Star Trek."

4 Otherwise, base your scoring on a general text-based relevance of the user and a query.

Figure 7.7 captures these rules as a flowchart.

There's quite a bit to unpack. The first two criteria make it important to measure exact matches with high precision. You'll have to craft fields that can capture this ranking signal. Implementing step 2, the exact-name match, is interesting. You'll likely match many films when searching for a person, so your boss is thinking ahead when they

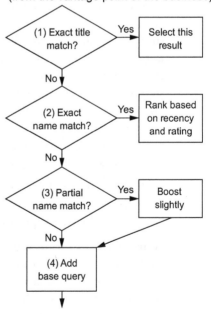

Flowchart of movie search ranking rules (from the vantage point of the business)

Figure 7.7 Flowchart representation of the custom business ranking rules as understood/specified by the business

come up with how these ought to be ranked. Users, your boss is thinking, may want to see the latest and best offerings for that actor or director. You've been working on step 3 for about two chapters by now. So your boss must continue to have confidence in your abilities. You'll see how you can use this to boost relevance for a narrow set of matches, similar, as you may recall, to what you worked with at the end of the preceding chapter. Finally, step 4, your base relevance score, measures how many search terms match the overall document. Recall from the previous chapter, term-centric search implements this functionality.

Sounds like great marching orders, but hopefully alarm bells are going off in your head. How does the business know these are the right criteria? Why should these be the priorities for your ranking solution? These are important issues, but fret not, in future chapters you'll get answers to those precise questions. Getting the criteria right *is* important! But so is knowing how to translate these plain-English ranking rules to search-engineese, which you get to focus on in this chapter.

Let's get started! Your first step when given this criteria is looking at your fields to see whether you can implement the required signals. Once you have confidence that you can support the required signals—that your fields can turn into facts—then you begin to work on the second piece of boosting: crafting the ranking function to your needs.

7.4.2　*Modeling your boosting signals*

As a relevance engineer, when you're told to boost by something like "when the search is an *exact* match for the title," your next question ought to be, how exactly do I measure *that?* That's what you'll tackle in this section. You'll translate the whims of human language into an implementation of a particular signal that you can work with in a larger ranking function. You've done this a few times already in this book. Yet this step is fundamental to being able to program relevance ranking rules. Without actionable information, how do you know whether your ranking function is prioritizing the right documents?

To implement your business requirements, you need to make sure that you can answer these important questions before crafting the overall ranking function:

- Is the user's query a full, exact match to the title?
- Is the user's query a full, exact match to the full name of an actor or director?
- Does the user's query contain the full name of an actor or director?

Your goal is to create highly discriminating signals. You need signals that act like snobby wine critics—carefully letting the essence of each document waft under their discerning noses and accepting a document only after careful consideration. You've begun this process: you have reasonable name-matching fields based on bigrams from previous chapters. These address your third criteria—whether part of the query matches a person on the film with high precision. We'll get back to our old name-matching friend, but first let's look at how to measure the other ranking criteria.

Two of these signals require exact, not partial, matching. To accomplish this, you can't simply wrap the user's query text into a phrase query. A search for the phrase "Star Trek" will match any document with Star Trek in the title, including *Star Trek: Generations*. This isn't an exact match between query and title. No, you want to boost *only* when the terms from the query line up exactly to the text in the title.

So now it's time for more signal modeling! You need to build a field that can measure this information with high precision. Astute readers might be thinking—exact matches? That's easy! Disable tokenization or use the keyword tokenizer to search on the exact-title string. This would generate exact tokens such as `star trek` or `star trek: insurrection`. Yes, that might work, but it rarely returns what you want. You want *some* analysis, even when doing so-called exact matching. For example, you'd like to remove that pesky colon in `star trek: insurrection` to help the user searching without the colon. You might also want some amount of stemming or any other form of per-term normalization.

Instead of disabling tokenization, you'll use a technique referred to as *sentinel tokens*. Sentinel tokens represent important boundary features in the text (perhaps a sentence, paragraph, or begin/end point). In this case, you'll inject the following begin and end sentinels into the title text:

```
"SENTINEL_BEGIN Star Trek SENTINEL_END"
```

These sentinels are tokens representing the beginning and end of the string. Then, when you search, you include the sentinels in the query, searching for the phrase query "SENTINEL_BEGIN <user query> SENTINEL_END." The result is a document that matches only when the phrase query matches *and* the correct sentinels are in the right place (in this case, when the beginning of the text and end of the text coincide).

You could implement this in a couple of ways. One intelligent way is to write a plugin for your search engine. As you may recall from chapter 4, token filters intercept and modify the token stream during analysis. You *can* write your own Lucene token filters to inject boundary features. Pick up a great Solr, Elasticsearch, or Lucene book to show you how. For brevity, you'll take the simpler road, injecting the sentinels outside the search engine.

First, you'll modify your TMDB index function to inject the sentinel characters before and after the title in a new field you'll call `title_exact_match`. To do this, you'll modify your TMDB `reindex` function to call a `transform` function before indexing. This will be your little hook to manipulate the document before going off to Elasticsearch.

```
for id, movie in movieDict.iteritems():
    ...
    esDoc  = movie
    transform(esDoc)
    ...
```

Next, you'll define the transform function to create the field you need to answer our question with the sentinel tokens included.

Listing 7.5   Injecting begin/end sentinels for exact matching

```
SENTINEL_BEGIN = 'SENTINEL_BEGIN'
SENTINEL_END = 'SENTINEL_END'
def transform(esDoc):
    esDoc['title_exact_match'] = SENTINEL_BEGIN + ' ' + \
                                     esDoc['title'] + ' ' + SENTINEL_END

reindex(analysisSettings, mappingSettings, movieDict)
```

I hope your head is swimming with all kinds of questions about how well this will work. Are all these settings, analysis, mappings, and so forth appropriate to measure this signal? There are many possible optimizations to think about. Remember the default analyzer? It's the entity whose job it is to break the string into tokens. We're set up to default to the English analyzer. Is that appropriate? The English analyzer will match "Stary Trek" to star trek because of stemming—do you want this behavior? Or do you want something as close as possible to character-by-character exact match? Your job is to sweat many of these details to ensure that you're measuring the ranking signal important to your users.

For now, let's see what happens when you issue a query for this exact-match signal. Does searching using the sentinels against this field give you the signal you need?

Listing 7.6   Isolated testing of your exact-match signal

```
usersSearch = "star trek"
query = {
    "query": {
        "match_phrase": {
            "title_exact_match": {                              ← User's
                "query": SENTINEL_BEGIN + ' ' + \                  query with
                        usersSearch + ' ' + SENTINEL_END,       ← sentinels
                "boost": 0.1
}}}}
search(query)
Num  Relevance Score        Movie Title
1    7.172676               Star Trek
```

Great, this works! You've built a field expressly for exact matching. As you grow in your skills, you'll keep being nagged by questions. Is TF × IDF scoring important here? Will I use it as a signal of something? Likely not. As your skill increases, so will your awareness of all the factors that can impact the signal you're measuring.

Finally, you'll repeat the same process for your name field. For this field, you'll create a non-bigrammed, regular old text field, just like the preceding one.

Listing 7.7   Name and title exact-match fields

```
SENTINEL_BEGIN = 'SENTINEL_BEGIN'                                    Adds title exact
SENTINEL_END = 'SENTINEL_END'                                          match field
def transform(esDoc):                                               with sentinels
    esDoc['title_exact_match'] = SENTINEL_BEGIN + ' ' + \
                                 esDoc['title'] + ' ' + SENTINEL_END  ◁
    esDoc['names_exact_match'] = []
    for person in esDoc['cast'] + esDoc['directors']:                 Adds name
        esDoc['names_exact_match'].append(SENTINEL_BEGIN + ' ' +      exact match
                                          person['name'] + ' ' +   ◁  field with
                                          SENTINEL_END)                sentinels
```

Now you have some ingredients to work with in your larger relevance solution. You've built and tested relevance signals in isolation. Next you'll look at how to incorporate the name and title exact matching signal into the larger ranking function. You can always come back to this piece if you need to improve any aspect of your ranking (or come up with a signal completely anew).

7.4.3   *Building the ranking function: adding high-value tiers*

With the pieces in place, the next step is to ask precisely how to combine them into a larger ranking function. The ranking function is where signals collide—hopefully into a harmonious whole, not a train wreck!

This section introduces one of our favorite shaping techniques: building *scoring tiers*. It's often useful to express ranking in terms of tiers based on your confidence in the information provided in the boosting signals. Particular signals that provide unequivocal information about what's being searched should not simply be "layered in" or "balanced against other factors." If you have truly high-precision, discerning signals that definitively point at what's being searched for, then to even consider much else would be foolish. Instead, in this technique you let these higher-value matches sit on their own highly scoring tier, pushing their scores into a class all their own. Scoring at those tiers is dictated by what's important for those sets of search results, such as the exact matches of the previous section.

Figure 7.8 shows two kinds of scores. First there are the base, black scores. These match the base query. This query pulls in a wide net of possibly relevant results. In our example, you'll reuse the term-centric search from earlier in this chapter. Second there are enhanced, white bars. These results have been heavily boosted.

You could implement this high-value tier with a variety of boosting techniques. Listing 7.8 uses a Boolean query; you can see the boost query as the first Boolean

Creating a high-value tier of results

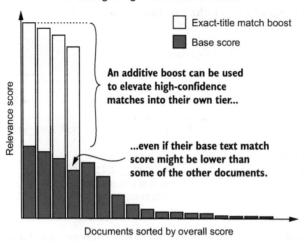

☐ Exact-title match boost

■ Base score

An additive boost can be used to elevate high-confidence matches into their own tier...

...even if their base text match score might be lower than some of the other documents.

Relevance score

Documents sorted by overall score

Figure 7.8 High-recall base query in black augmented with a high-precision tier of unequivocally more valuable search results

clause. Notice how the boost weight ❸ is set astronomically high—all the way to 1,000.

Listing 7.8 Boolean boost on exact-title matching

```
query = {
    "query": {
        "bool": {
            "disable_coord": True,
            "should": [
                {"match_phrase": {
                    "title_exact_match": {
                        "query": SENTINEL_BEGIN + " " + \
                            usersSearch + " " + SENTINEL_END,
                        "boost": 1000,
                    }
                }},
                {"multi_match": {
                    "query": usersSearch,
                    "fields": ["overview", "title",
                        "directors.name", "cast.name"],
                    "type": "cross_fields"
                }},

            ]
        }
    }
}
search(query)
```

❶ Boosting query— exact movie title match

❸ High boost to create an overriding effect

❷ Base query

User's query

You can see that the results for a search for "Star Trek" are promising, bringing the target straight to the top:

```
Num  Relevance Score      Movie Title
1    7.1752715            Star Trek
2    0.0020790964         Star Trek: The Motion Picture
3    0.0020790964         Star Trek: Nemesis
4    0.0020790964         Star Trek: Insurrection
5    0.0020790964         Star Trek: First Contact
```

And here's a search for "Good Will Hunting":

```
Num  Relevance Score      Movie Title
1    7.914943             Good Will Hunting
2    0.0016986724         The Hunt
3    0.0012753583         Good Night, and Good Luck.
4    0.0011116106         As Good as It Gets
5    0.00058992894        Saw V
```

Here you've added a little rule to your ranking function that should work well for a common use case—exact-title matching. As you move forward with your problem, we'll begin to call out specific patterns in the boosting.

ADDING A NEW TIER FOR MEDIUM-CONFIDENCE BOOSTS (THE BIGRAMS STRIKE BACK!)

So far you've added one tier to the larger Boolean query: the exact matches. Let's examine another precise but less exacting case: a search that contains a full name as *part* of the search. This case calls for some prioritization, in its own tier, but not quite as much as exact-name matches. To incorporate this boost, you'll work from two directions:

- You'll use a smaller boost of 100 to create an intermediate tier.
- You'll optimize the signal in the bigram matching, to ensure that you measure what's important.

The second point is the most pressing. Let's start with the bigram name matching from the previous chapter. You used a `cross_fields` search over `cast.name.bigrammed` and `directors.name.bigrammed`. In the following listing, we use this query as a boost alongside the base query. Unfortunately, it turns out that running the combined query doesn't always end up with great results, as in this search for "Star Trek Patrick Stewart."

Listing 7.9 Adding a clause for bigrammed matches (base query not shown)

```
'query': {
      'bool': {
          'should': [
              {'multi_match': {                    Base query
                  'query': usersSearch,
                  'fields': ['overview', 'title',
                             'directors.name', 'cast.name'],   User's query
                  'type': 'cross_fields'
              }},
              {'multi_match': {                    Mid-tier layer for name matching
                  'query': usersSearch,
```

```
            'fields': ['directors.name.bigrammed',
                        'cast.name.bigrammed'],
            'type': 'cross_fields',
            'boost': 100
        }}]}}
```

1	0.21988437	Star Trek: Insurrection	6.3	1998-12-10
2	0.21988437	Star Trek: First Contact	6.9	1996-11-21
3	0.19890885	Gnomeo & Juliet	5.9	2011-01-13
4	0.19890885	Excalibur	6.7	1981-04-10
5	0.19462639	Star Trek: Nemesis	6.3	2002-12-12

It's odd that *Gnomeo & Juliet* and *Excalibur* rank higher than *Star Trek* results. Why do these non–*Star Trek* Patrick Stewart results override the *Star Trek* ones? Turning to the explain, you see that, oddly, the *Excalibur* match on "Patrick Stewart" gets scored higher than *Star Trek: Nemesis*.

Here's *Excalibur*'s score:

```
0.5910474, weight(cast.name.bigrammed:patrick stewart in 315)
```

The *Star Trek: Nemesis* match receives a lower score:

```
0.5171665, weight(cast.name.bigrammed:patrick stewart in 631)
```

So why the difference? The *Excalibur* match receives a higher score because of the field norms. Remember this bias toward shorter fields? *Excalibur* has a smaller crew, so matches here appear more relevant to the search engine. But our users don't care about this; that factor doesn't matter in answering the question, "Does the movie star Patrick Stewart?"

Time to do more signal modeling. Just as with the previous sentinel tokens, you'll need to tightly control field matching and scoring. You can revisit the mapping, reindex with norms disabled, and rerun the search query. First, dig back into the deeply nested mapping to disable norms and reindex the movies:

```
mappingSettings['movie']['properties'] \
        ['cast']['properties'] \
        ['name']['fields']['bigrammed']['norms'] = {'enabled': False}

reindex(analysisSettings, mappingSettings, movieDict)
```

Searching again, you see that the intermediate tier makes more sense:

1	0.03920228	Star Trek: Insurrection	6.3	1998-12-10
2	0.03920228	Star Trek: First Contact	6.9	1996-11-21
3	0.03917096	Star Trek: Nemesis	6.3	2002-12-12
4	0.03917096	Star Trek: Generations	6.5	1994-11-17
5	0.03820324	Gnomeo & Juliet	5.9	2011-01-13

All Patrick Stewart movies move to the top. Within that set, the base query for "Star Trek Patrick Stewart" ranks more precisely.

BUILDING A TIERED RELEVANCE LAYER CAKE

In the preceding examples, you implemented part of the ranking criteria asked for by your business. Exact-title matches were so compelling that your boss told you to ignore all other considerations. Placing exact-title matches in a higher-scoring tier does this. Similarly, name matches were compelling, but less overwhelmingly so.

Both of these boosts work well because you optimized their queries to more closely align to the needed signals. The boost query is assigned a boost weight in these situations not because the query has that level of priority, but because the signals are so unbelievably precise and discriminating. Matching each means winning the relevance lotto. For once, you happen to know exactly what's being searched for, so take advantage of that! You'll use another high-value strata in the next section as you think through exact-name-matching criteria, but the focus will shift to a more mathematical modeling of users' goals.

7.4.4 High-value tier scored with a function query

The next major challenge requires you to flex even deeper muscle in programming the ranking function. As you program relevance, you'll learn increasingly sophisticated techniques that build on each other. In this section, you'll take the high-value tier from the previous section and combine it with a second technique: the careful incorporation of a finely tuned function query based on features of the film.

The business has asked for specific ranking criteria when there's an exact-cast-name match. In these cases, your boss wants to show a combination of popular and recently released films. Doing this requires you to flex two sets of ranking muscles simultaneously, as depicted in figure 7.9.

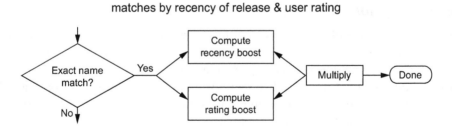

Figure 7.9 Flowchart representing the custom business ranking rules for exact-name (cast/director) matching

First, you need to bring those high-confidence, exact-name matches up into their own scoring tier. You know that these exact-name matches stand above the rest, so they should be selected aggressively. Second, and new to this section, that scoring tier needs its own method of ranking. It needs to be based on two features of the films associated with those actors: the recency of their release and their user ratings.

You'll incorporate three parts in this next component of your query:

- The *exact-name matching* itself, used to trigger recency and rating
- The *recency* of the film, based on the release date
- The *user rating*, the 1–10 average rating from all the users' individual ratings of the movie (1 meaning terrible, 10 meaning best ever)

Your job in this section is to combine the influence of the latter two, but only when the first criteria (the exact-name matching) triggers.

As you build this part of the query, you'll become aware of how large these queries can get! You may be about to build one of the largest Query DSL queries you've ever worked with. Yet you're learning to cope with these behemoths in the same way you think through any large piece of code. Each scoring component has a purpose, a signal that it's lending to the overall ranking function. If you feel overwhelmed in your work, never hesitate to bring it down to a simpler level: working with the component queries in isolation before combining them.

How will you go about adding this functionality to the larger query? This query will be built into the Boolean query from the preceding section. You'll end up with three clauses: two you've already introduced, and a third, your new Boolean query. This Boolean query will look something like this:

- SHOULD: Base query (listing 7.8 ❷)
- SHOULD: Full query exactly matches a title, boost 1,000 (listing 7.8 ❶)
- SHOULD: Query contains full name, boost 100 (listing 7.9)
- SHOULD: Full query exactly matches a name (new to this section)

7.4.5 *Ignoring TF × IDF*

You want to rank a film by its user rating and recency of release, but only when the query is an exact-name match. This ranking doesn't depend, at all, on the TF × IDF of the exact-name text query. This isn't uncommon: frankly, many times you need a simple yes/no instead of the TF × IDF score. You saw this earlier when working with the star trek title boost. Let's begin to dig into the exact-name function query, demonstrating a technique for omitting TF × IDF.

As you might guess, because scoring for this query will be dominated by two numerical factors, recency and user ratings, you'll use a function_score query. Recall that with a function query, you specify a base query with the query argument. Your first attempt could be to insert the exact-name-matching phrase query as the base query:

```
query = {
    "query": {
        "function_score": {
            "query": {
                "match_phrase": {
```

```
            "names_exact_match": SENTINEL_BEGIN + \
                                 " william shatner " + \
                                 SENTINEL_END
    }},
...
```

You need to make one change here; you need to consider the fact that the TF × IDF score of this query is unlikely to be useful. Remember, by default the `function_score` query will take the score for the `query` and multiply it by the resulting `functions`. This means multiplying the TF × IDF score of the exact-name matching by the `functions`. In some cases, you need a way to ignore the TF × IDF scoring. To do this, you can wrap your query in a `constant_score` query. This lets you hardcode the resulting query's score to a constant (the boost value). As you're focused on bumping this score into a discriminating higher tier, let's set this constant to a very high 1,000:

```
"function_score": {
    "query": {
        "constant_score": {
            "query": {
                "match_phrase": {
                    "names_exact_match": SENTINEL_BEGIN + \
                                         " william shatner " + \
                                         SENTINEL_END
                }
            },
            "boost": 1000.0}}
```

Great! So now your base relevance score will be constant when the user's query matches exactly with an actor or director name.

To complete this query, you need to think through the functions themselves. You need to balance two considerations: the user rating and the recency. Each provides a signal to tune in isolation. So for a bit, you'll work on these in isolation. You'll see how each signal takes advantage of its own set of techniques to line up its influence with user expectations. Getting these signals precise and lined up to user expectations is crucial.

7.4.6 Capturing general-quality metrics

First, let's consider a boost on user rating. It's time to get back to thinking mathematically. The user rating field (called `vote_average`) is an example of a document property that directly measures the content's value. You'll often boost on other similar direct indications of quality: profitability, popularity, page views, and other factors. In this section, as you hone this signal, you'll explore what it means to include these general-quality features. Should you take its value directly or modify it somehow? Perhaps temper it down? Or should it be magnified? What do users think of the importance of this quality metric?

Incorporating `vote_average` depends on Elasticsearch's `field_value_factor` function. This function lets you take a field's value and use it directly. Optionally, you can apply a few simple modifiers and functions. In the following listing, for example, you take the square root of `vote_average` and multiply by 2.

Listing 7.10 Factoring in user's ratings of the movies

```
query = {
    "query": {
        "function_score": {
            "query": {
                "match_all": {}
            },
            "functions": [
                {
                    "field_value_factor": {
                    "field": "vote_average",
                    "modifier": "sqrt",
                    "factor": 2
                }}]
    }}}
```

This can be visualized in the graph shown in figure 7.10.

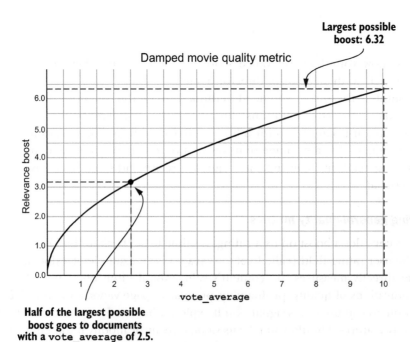

Figure 7.10   Boosting user rating, an indication of content quality. The square root is taken to dampen the effect in line with how users perceive this metric's value.

Why take the square root? You're aiming for a signal that measures how important the user considers movie ratings. If you took the value directly, a rating-10 movie would be considered twice as valuable as a rating-5 movie. Users rarely perceive the influence of quality factors so starkly and directly. Taking the square root, as you can see by examining the graph, roughly ranks a rating-3 movie as half as important as a rating-10 movie.

These quality metrics are tricky, as you rarely want to incorporate them directly as a signal. Just as you did here, you have to ask how users perceive the value as a function of these features. For example, what if instead of a 1–10 user rating, this quality metric had been something like the number of page views of the movie's TMDB home page? Most pages have single-digit page views. A fractional amount have several hundred. A small handful get thousands, and one or two get millions of page views. Is a page that gets a million views a million times higher quality? No! It might be more reasonable to your users to measure it as twice as important. How you tone down the influence of these factors can be crucial. Users' considerations are more subtle than simply hammering in the quality metric directly.

7.4.7   Achieving users' recency goals

You're still working on creating custom ranking rules when users match exactly on cast or director names. The second signal to consider for this case is the user's perception of the importance of a movie's recency. You'll see in this section that ranking is often about modeling how far a result is from an expressed goal. For example, users want to rank news items close to the present, or restaurants close to their home, or perhaps televisions near their target price. Elasticsearch's built-in *decay functions* rank based on how far documents are from target goals. You'll see in this section how to think through modeling a simple goal-based ranking problem based on a TMDB film's recency.

At the core, though, is how you express goals to the search engine with three primary variables: origin, decay, and scale. The *origin* is meant to indicate the user's goal (or ideal). At the origin point, scoring is at the highest (a 1.0). The *scale* is also a point, off in the distance. At this location, you can imagine the user declaring, "At this point from my goal, I consider the document this much less valuable." It's as if the user were saying, "If I have to drive 20 minutes from home to pick up food, that food is now half as interesting to me." How do you declare how much less valuable? Well, that's the *decay* parameter's job. It states the value at a certain location, given the scale. Taken together, you could rephrase the user's restaurant statement: "If I have to drive <SCALE> minutes from <ORIGIN> to pick up food, that food is now <DECAY> less interesting to me."

Given our query, you'll start by stating that movies released 900 days ago (Elasticsearch helps with same-date syntax) will have roughly a score of 0.5, or be considered half as valuable to users. This is expressed in the following isolated query.

Listing 7.11   Gaussian decay from the user's recency goal

```
query = {
    "query": {
        "function_score": {
            "query": {
                "match_all": {}
            },
            "functions": [
                {
                    "gauss": {
                        "release_date": {
                            "origin": "now",
                            "scale": "900d",
                            "decay": 0.5
                        }}}]
        }}}
```

The equation for this Gaussian decay is complex, but to give you an idea of how it behaves, we've included the graph in figure 7.11. This graph demonstrates the user's perceived value for an actor's or director's film as a function of days into the past, showing that films 900 days into the past are half as valuable. As movies move five to six years into the past, the influence of this function begins to approach 0—near worthless!

Here, you might ask whether the decay function is too aggressive. Perhaps scale is too close in. Why's that? Consider one possible use case: a user searching for an actor

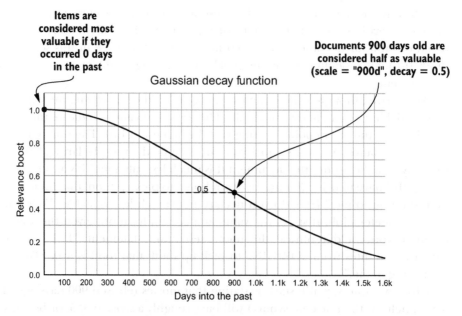

Figure 7.11   A multiplicative boost controlling the impact of distance from your user's goal; here the goal is movies released "now," with movies released 900 days into the past considered half as valuable.

wants not only recent films but also films considered classics for that actor. You need to apply a careful balancing act between the conflicting goals of users who want the most recent films and those who want an understanding of what the really great films are, regardless of the recency.

Now this is an interesting point, because not all users are the same. As we discuss in a later chapter, one option could be to suss out which users have which priorities. For the purposes of this chapter, however, let's come up with a reasonable, generic solution. The proposed function considers films from even five to six years ago near worthless, approaching 0. It's unlikely, you decide, that the average user considers films from not this long ago that invaluable. For now, let's extend how far into the past this function decays. Instead of a scale of 900 days, let's use something far more conservative: 15 years.

The graph in figure 7.12 demonstrates this modified function. The x-axis measures thousands of days. The decay happens gradually, over the course of decades, instead of quickly over the course of a few short years.

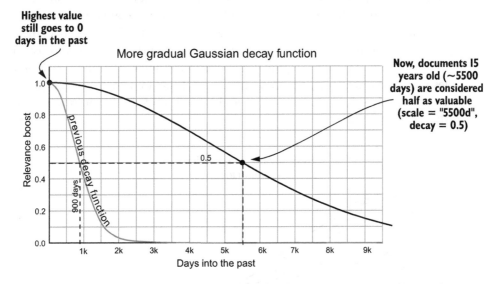

Figure 7.12 A tweaked multiplicative boost for movies; movies released 15 years into the past are deemed half as valuable.

This function, you decide, is probably a better model of the average user's recency goals when matching on cast/director names. Now you've modeled the user as thinking that films released 15 years into the past are half as valuable. As is true with any signal, this is a starting point. You can always revisit this signal in isolation to assess whether it's still too aggressive. (Plenty of amazing movies came out more than 15 years ago!) Fine-tuning these knobs to generate the right signal is a matter of readjusting your understanding of the goals. Luckily you now have all the tools you need to calibrate relevance to users' goals.

These decay functions give you the ability to generate a signal based on how far an item is from a user's goal. This is a common pattern, not just something limited to dates and geography. Consider a real estate search in which ranking is based entirely on whether a home meets a user's goals. Factors such as school quality, commuting distance, price range, and proximity to parks can be ranked by how far an item is from where a user ideally would like to be. Sometimes these ranking problems aren't seen as search, but as more of a kind of machine-learning problem. But here the lines begin to blur. You're seeing how search engines are a framework for programming all kinds of ranking capabilities, based on far more than just text factors.

7.4.8   *Combining the function queries*

It's time to start building back up to our main query. Remember, you've been going down a path trying to model two signals that matter to users who search for exact actor/director names. You've been trying to consider how much the movie's rating and its distance into the past might matter to users. It's time to get back to programming the main ranking function. To do that, let's consider the impact of combining these two curves.

You need to visualize how multiplying these two variables will impact the relevance score to determine whether their influence is appropriate. One way to visualize this is to draw a cool 3D graph. Yet sometimes overlaying a few 2D graphs, each of which varies one of the variables, can be a more useful way to answer critical questions. The graph in figure 7.13 represents the multiplication of the movie rating function and the decay function.

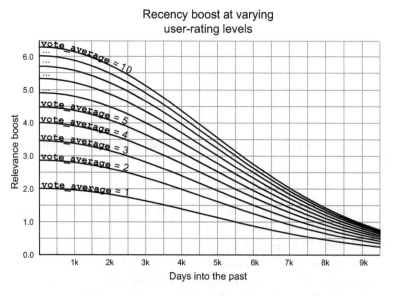

Figure 7.13   Recency curves based on the user rating (`vote_average`) field for a movie, demonstrating how both recency and user rating impact the relevance score for exact-name matches.

The bottommost line corresponds to the recency graph of movies with a rating of 1. The topmost corresponds to movies with a rating of 10. What does this tell us about the combination of these two factors? One thing to notice is how movies of rating 1 relate to movies of rating 10. At what point into the past does a movie with a rating of 10 become less relevant than a movie with a rating of 1? This happens a little past day 6,000, or roughly 16.5 years from now.

You can reflect on the combination of these two factors. How do they work together to signal relevance? This is particularly true here: these functions *are* the relevance calculation for this case. Isolating how they work together can help you reason through their impact. Do these two factors have the right priority? What could be improved? Perhaps the recency should have a floor; users may want a slight nudge toward recent films, and care little about the difference between 80s and 70s films, for instance. Reflecting on and evaluating all of these factors is your constant job—and as you'll see in chapter 10, the whole organization's job!

Finally, with these functions taken together, let's complete the person exact-matching query. This in turn will be folded into the larger query.

Listing 7.12 Clause for exact-name matching, ranking based on recency and user rating

```
usersQuery = "patrick stewart"
query = {
    "query": {
        "function_score": {
            "query": {                          Base query, score simply
                "constant_score": {             taken as the "boost"
                    "query": {
                        "match_phrase": {
                            "names_exact_match": SENTINEL_BEGIN + " " + \
                                                 usersSearch + " " + \
                                                 SENTINEL_END
                    }},
                    "boost": 1000.0
            }},
            "functions": [                      Boost for
            {                                   recency
                "gauss": {
                    "release_date": {
                        "origin": "now",
                        "scale": "5500d",
                        "decay": 0.5
            }}},
            {                                   Boost for
                                                rating
                "field_value_factor": {
                "field": "vote_average",
                "modifier": "sqrt"
            }}
}}}
search(query)
```

```
Results:
Num  Relevance Score         Movie Title            vote_average release_date
1    2.762838                X-Men: Days of Future Past  7.7     2014-05-23
2    2.4984634               The Wolverine               6.4     2013-07-25
3    2.4377568               Ted                         6.3     2012-06-29
4    2.2800508               Gnomeo & Juliet             5.9     2011-01-13
5    1.9779315               TMNT                        6.0     2007-03-22
```

Interestingly, our search for "Patrick Stewart" results first in a relatively high-rated film that was released relatively recently. Notice too the difference between the fourth and fifth results. A 5.9-rated movie released in 2011 outranks a 6.0 released in 2007. These expectations seem to correspond to the preceding graph that demonstrates the impact of different ratings.

7.4.9   *Putting it all together!*

This query is simply a single clause in an even larger query! Yet we'll spare you from seeing the full thing (you can view the examples on GitHub to see the full query in all its glory). Nevertheless, outlined in your overall query is a set of four Boolean clauses, including these criteria:

- SHOULD have full query exactly matching the title (listing 7.8, ❶)
- SHOULD have full query, exactly matching a director's or cast member's full name, scored by popularity and recency (listing 7.12)
- SHOULD have part of the query match a director's or cast member's full name (listing 7.9)
- SHOULD have all the user's query terms match somewhere in the document (listing 7.8, ❷)

Combining these four SHOULD clauses in one `bool` query, you've done it! You've solved a particularly complex ranking problem. You've taken thoughts, whims, and requirements expressed in English and brought them to the search engine—bending the search engine to your will!

Now you can begin to ask some of the bigger questions. Just as in real programming, once you realize that you know *how* to program, you suddenly become conscious of the larger question: exactly *what* should you be programming? In the same way, as you become increasingly confident with programming relevancy, you'll begin to see that this challenge applies to relevance as well. As you move into future chapters, finding the right ranking requirements will become front and center. How do you define what requirements/use cases are important to your search? How do you test to make sure you're continuing to meet requirements? Here they've been given to you—a technical challenge. As you'll see in future chapters, real life is never so simple!

7.5 *Summary*

- Score shaping, including techniques such as boosting and filtering, is about programming results ranking to satisfy your business/user needs.

- Boosting comes in several forms: Boolean and function queries, additive and multiplicative approaches.

- Boolean queries abstract ranking for you, providing a simple means to add a boost. Calibrating them correctly layering on additive boosts.

- Function queries allow you to take control of ranking math by boosting in arbitrary forms. Calibrating them means modeling user priorities mathematically.

- Filters often provide an alternative to boosting, removing low-priority results instead of trying to promote high-priority results.

- Score shaping depends on your ability to implement high-quality signals and incorporate them in the ranking function based on business rules.

- High-quality signals can be prioritized by placing them in their own scoring tier.

- You can implement a broad range of ranking forms, including modeling user goals, incorporating content quality metrics, and the like.

Providing relevance feedback

8

To this point, we've discussed how to deeply manipulate relevance ranking. In this chapter, you'll see that relevance ranking isn't the only way to guide users to relevant content. Search enables a multifaceted conversation between the user and the search engine. Because the relevance portion of this conversation is never perfect, your users will always thank you for additional guidance toward relevant content. In this chapter, you'll steer the many layers of the search conversation beyond relevance ranking by building features that do the following:

- Explain to users how their query is being interpreted
- Correct mistakes such as typos and misspellings
- Suggest other searches that will provide better results
- Convey an understanding of how documents are distributed in the corpus
- Help users understand why a particular document is a match
- Help users efficiently understand the result set

We term these conversational aids *relevance feedback*. In this chapter, we provide an overview of relevance feedback across three areas of search user experience: the search box, browsing and filtering, and the search results. Figure 8.1 shows the activities covered in this chapter; the relevance engineer implements supporting capabilities to guide the user toward relevant content in the various parts of the search application.

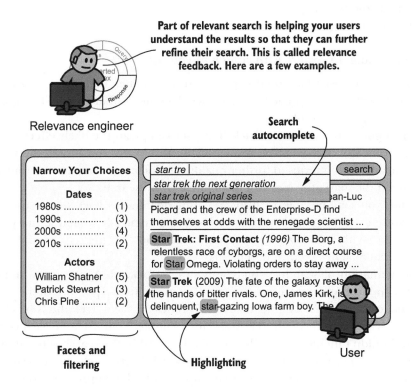

Figure 8.1   Relevance feedback helps users refine their searches and find the information they seek.

In your work, you'll see that guiding the user's search behavior can be an easier problem to solve than perfect relevance ranking. In this chapter, you'll find alternate paths for the user to reach relevant content. We won't be exhaustive. There are innumerable forms of relevance feedback, and countless methods for implementing them. Rather, we hope to get you started down a crucial path of the relevance engineer: enabling the two-way search conversation through any means possible.

8.1 Relevance feedback at the search box

The user and search application first interact at the search box. You may be surprised by the extent to which search box interactions provide the user with relevance feedback. By providing information to users while they type and immediately after they submit a query, you enable users to refine the query or sometimes even find what they need before submitting it. This section covers three common forms of relevance feedback at the search box:

- Search-as-you-type
- Search completion
- Postsearch suggestion

8.1.1 Providing immediate results with search-as-you-type

Search-as-you-type is just what you'd expect from the name: as the user types in keywords, the search engine proactively provides documents that match. The goals for search-as-you-type are twofold.

The first goal is relevance feedback. The user can glean the likely effectiveness of the query from search-as-you-type results. If the results are too broad, the user will continue to add search terms to further qualify the documents he wants to find. If the results are off the mark, the user can revise the current search.

Second, you may be able to bring relevant documents back to the user more quickly. Without search-as-you-type, users have to consciously submit a query before seeing results. With search-as-you-type, users can choose to quit typing and select a document that matches their requirements.

Implementation of search-as-you-type is straightforward. As the name indicates, the search application issues a series of searches as the user types. But there's at least a little nuance here. For example, if a user searches for "Star Trek the Next Generation" and types halfway through a keyword (for example, "Star Trek the Next Gener"), then you shouldn't include the trailing partial keyword in the search without indicating that it's a prefix rather than a completed word. Fortunately, Elasticsearch provides a `match_phrase_prefix` query that implements this approach. Consider the following query:

```
{ "query": {
    "match_phrase_prefix" : {
      "title" : "star trek the next gener"}}}
```

If this query is provided to the /_validate/query?explain endpoint, the query explanation shows that, as expected, the query is interpreted as a phrase query with the last term expanded via a trailing wildcard:

```
"explanation": "title:\"star trek the next gener*\""
```

As displayed in figure 8.2, applications typically present search-as-you-type matches concisely in a drop-down menu. This menu enables the user to easily select matching documents.

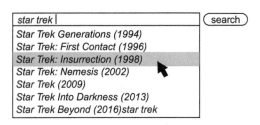

Figure 8.2 Search-as-you-type is a means of providing users with immediate results. It's often presented as a drop-down menu below the search box.

But the drop-down menu presents some UI/UX challenges. For one thing, this area may be needed to provide suggested search terms to the user (search completions, described in the next section). Having both features share space can confuse users who must differentiate between two types of feedback. Also, the drop-down menu's limited space makes it impossible to give much information on a matching document. Unless search matches only titles, users won't always be able to determine why documents are relevant. Finally, the drop-down lacks application state. For instance, if a user selects a document from the drop-down menu and then immediately realizes that this document isn't relevant, how do they switch back to the previous search-as-you-type view? Typically this isn't possible, or is clumsy at best.

Google's search application uses an interesting search-as-you-type approach that avoids these problems. Rather than placing search-as-you-type results in a drop-down menu, Google presents them in the normal space for search results. This pattern helps eliminate possible user confusion. Placing results in their normal location reserves the drop-down menu for search-completion suggestions. Therefore, the user can focus attention on either the search results or search-completion suggestions. With search results in their normal location, there's more room to provide richer information per result than could be provided in a drop-down menu.

8.1.2 *Helping users find the best query with search completion*

Search completions usher users to better search queries and keywords. In effect, the search application brainstorms with the user about what they're looking for: "User, you typed *robots are*, do you want to search for *robots are our friends*? How about *robots are awesome?*" If you finely tune this interaction, it becomes almost subconscious, with users iteratively typing, reformulating, and occasionally selecting the resulting completions.

As illustrated in figure 8.3, search applications usually present completions in a drop-down menu below the search box. Selecting any of the drop-down items will add the selected text to the current query.

Figure 8.3   Search completions are typically presented in a drop-down menu below the search box. Selecting an item from the drop-down replaces the current query with the selection text.

Implementing search completion can be challenging. Users expect search completions to return shortly after they begin typing. If completions are too slow, users won't recognize that completions are available. The user then misses out on your guidance, searching unaided. Completions must also be highly relevant. Users will learn to ignore irrelevant suggestions and instead forge ahead unaided. Similarly, if users select a completion, but it leads to unexpected or 0 results, then the user will feel misguided.

As with most features discussed in this chapter, you can implement search completions in many ways. In the following discussion, we present three methods.

BUILDING COMPLETIONS FROM USER INPUT

As you prepare to build search completions, the first question you must ask yourself is "From what data source should I pull the completion text?" With enough traffic, you could base completions on past users' queries. This makes sense: allowing users to search with past users' searches should assure the current user that they are not far off the beaten path, right?

Maybe—but be careful; you need to consider a few gotchas. First, let's look at the assumption that you have enough traffic. Is your application a *short-tail* search application where a handful of queries (hundreds, perhaps) represent the majority of your search traffic? Or is yours a *long-tail* application where thousands of queries represent only a small portion of the search traffic? With too few queries, you may have insufficient data to build a satisfactory completion experience. Too many queries, and you'll have to prioritize what's most important from a large, diverse set of completion candidates.

Also consider whether old search traffic becomes obsolete for your application. Consider search completions for an e-commerce application that frequently changes inventory. Searches important a month ago may no longer match currently available products.

Finally, and perhaps most damagingly, old user queries are a distinct data set from the corpus. It's easy to find user queries that return 0 results! Suggesting such a query as a search completion would befuddle your users. If search completions lead to poor experiences, the user learns not to trust the search application.

Search completion based on past user queries *can* provide a good user experience; but the search engineer must ensure that the user's queries provide sufficiently rich and timely completions. Additionally, the search user should be reasonably assured that the completion will lead to relevant search results.

BUILDING COMPLETIONS FROM THE DOCUMENTS BEING SEARCHED

A more straightforward approach for building search completions uses the text of the content being searched. This approach ensures that any completion recommended to the user corresponds to text in the corpus.

Let's look at how search completion might be implemented using the text in the TMDB data set. In your work, you'll first need to consider which fields could be used for completion. For TMDB, let's consider two: `title` and `overview`. Some users look for movies by their name. For these users, the `title` field has obvious utility. Other users, however, search by typing movie details. The richer `overview` provides better content for these users' search completions.

But with richer text comes complications. With so much text, the `overview` field contains quite a bit of variety and noise. The user might be disappointed with seemingly arbitrary completions pulled from overview text. For these verbose fields, you'll have to seek strategies for prioritizing which search completions ought to come first, which in itself is its own ranking and relevance problem. For now, let's keep things simple by using only the `title` field for a source of completion text.

The next thing to consider is how the text should be analyzed. In chapter 4, you explored several strategies for analyzing text in order to help users find what they're looking for. There, you used stemming or another form of token mutation to collapse several words, such as `happy`, `happier`, `happiest` into a single token: `happi`. These tokens won't suit as a search-completion data source. A user entering the partial word "happ" would be presented with the completion `happi`, which isn't a word!

Instead you'll preserve readability during analysis, as shown in the following listing.

Listing 8.1 Analysis setup for 2-gram completions

```
"settings": {
  "analysis": {
    "filter": {
      "shingle_2": {
        "type":"shingle",
        "output_unigrams":"false"}},
```

❶ Shingle filter for two-word bigrams

```
    "analyzer": {
      "completion_analyzer": {        ◄——┐  Completion analyzer
        "tokenizer":                        for generating
          "standard",                       completion text
        "filter": [
          "standard",
          "lowercase",
          "shingle_2"]}}}}
```

You create an analyzer called completion_analyzer. The analyzer splits the text on punctuation and whitespace (using the *standard* tokenizer) and then lowercases the tokens. The lowercasing helps match/suggest regardless of the case of the content or search string. As an additional step, to support phrase suggestions, you use a shingle filter ❶ to generate two-word phrases. The analyzer transforms the string star trek: into darkness into the tokens star trek, trek into, into darkness.

Now that you have your completion_analyzer, let's use it on the title text. To do so, you'll copy the title field into a completion field that uses the completion_analyzer, as shown next.

Listing 8.2 Mappings for title-based completions

```
"mappings": {
  "movie": {
    "properties": {
      "title": {
        "type": "string",
        "analyzer": "english",             Duplicates title field
        "copy_to":["completion"]},   ◄——   to completion field
      "completion": {              ◄——  Completion field
        "type": "string",                for holding
        "analyzer": "completion_analyzer"}}}}}   completion text
```

And finally, after you index the documents, you're ready to construct your completion search. This search yields the most common two-word phrases that match the already typed query.

Listing 8.3 Query used to generate completions

```
{ "query": {
    "match_phrase_prefix": {      ❶  Limits candidates to
      "title": {                      titles that match the
        "query": user_input}}},   ◄—  user's query so far
  "aggregations": {
    "completion": {               ❷  Suggests search completions
      "terms": {              ◄——     from title text
        "field": "completion",
        "include": completion_prefix + ".*"}}}}   ◄—  Limits suggested completions
                                                      to those that begin with
                                                   ❸  "completion prefix"
```

Let's walk through how listing 8.3 works to deliver completions. Notice the two variables, user_input ❶ and completion_prefix ❸.

The user_input variable holds the full query string typed by the user. If the user types "Star Tr," user_input is then star tr. You place user_input into the same match_phrase_prefix query ❶ introduced earlier for search-as-you-type. This query forces completions to use titles that match the user's query. In our example, this prevents you from using star wa movies to suggest completions to Star Trek fans.

The completion prefix ❸ is the word currently being typed. For "Star Trek," this is tr. This limits completions to phrases the user could be trying to type (phrases that start with tr). Sometimes, especially when the last word typed is too short, it helps to include the previous term to limit further (phrases that start with star tr). If there's not even enough text for that (if the user just started typing), you may wish to omit completions altogether. There's too little context to aid the user.

Referring again to listing 8.3, you retrieve search completions by using an Elasticsearch *terms aggregation* ❷. Given a query (in this case, the match_phrase_prefix query), a terms aggregation collects a list of all terms that exist in the documents matching this query. Elasticsearch returns the list of terms, sorted according to the number of documents that contain the term. At ❸, you tell Elasticsearch to limit this to include only those terms that begin with completion_prefix (tr).

This strategy results in a list of the most common title phrases that match the already typed query. The response returned after issuing the search in listing 8.3 includes a completion section that looks like the following.

> **Listing 8.4 Example response for aggregation-based search completion**

```
{'completion': {'buckets': [
  {'doc_count': 1, 'key': 'trek 3'},
  {'doc_count': 1, 'key': 'trek axanar'},
  {'doc_count': 1, 'key': 'trek first'},
  {'doc_count': 1, 'key': 'trek generations'},
  {'doc_count': 1, 'key': 'trek horizon'},
  {'doc_count': 1, 'key': 'trek ii'},
  {'doc_count': 1, 'key': 'trek iii'},
  {'doc_count': 1, 'key': 'trek insurrection'},
  {'doc_count': 1, 'key': 'trek into'},
  {'doc_count': 1, 'key': 'trek iv'}
], 'doc_count_error_upper_bound': 0, 'sum_other_doc_count': 4}}
```

Using aggregations to generate completions guarantees that completions match your documents within the context of what the user has typed. For instance, if a user supplies the partial query "Star Tre," the completion prefix in this case will be tre*. Based on only this prefix, you could return completions such as treasure island and treading water, but neither has anything to do with star. Because aggregations take the search context into account, the completions returned for star tre will include only context-appropriate items such as trek generations and trek insurrection.

Table 8.1 shows examples of completions that would be made as a user searches for a Star Trek movie.

Table 8.1   Completions for a user searching for a Star Trek movie

User input	Completion prefix	Completions
st	(Not used—too little context)	(Not applicable)
star	star	star wars star trek starship troopers
star t	star t	star trek
star tr	tr	trek 3 trek axanar trek first trek generations

Another nice side-benefit of this method is that it can be easily combined with search-as-you-type because, as you can see in listing 8.3, you're indeed issuing searches as the user types via the `match_phrase_prefix` ❶.

You can definitely improve this approach. The current strategy limits completions to two words. It could be more ideal to complete an entire movie title. This could be accomplished with a different tokenization strategy that generates longer completions. For instance, you could tokenize titles by using the `path_hierarchy` tokenizer with `delimiter` set to the space character and with `reverse` set to `true`. This splits movie titles on whitespace and saves the ends of movies as tokens. For example, *Star Trek: The Motion Picture* would be tokenized as `star trek the motion picture`, `trek the motion picture`, `the motion picture`, `motion picture`, and `picture`. These sound like great completions!

This approach has one sticking point, though: the single-word tokens are going to be much more prevalent than the longer tokens. But by reversing the terms aggregation to return completions from least to most prevalent, you can provide the user with the most specific and often the longest completion available.

Before you implement aggregation-based search completions, be aware that this method comes with drawbacks. First, heavy aggregations over large text fields can tax the search engine, especially in an application that uses distributed search. If you choose to use this method, ensure that response times are acceptably low; otherwise, your completions won't keep up with users' keystrokes. For this reason, this approach works best with smaller corpuses and with text fields with a relatively small set of unique terms.

Second, by default this method returns completion suggestions ordered from most commonly occurring to least commonly occurring. This isn't always an appropriate metric. For instance, referring to listing 8.4, notice that all possible completions occur exactly once in the index. Therefore, in this case it isn't possible to establish an ordering for the completions based on their prevalence in the index. To address these problems, we introduce our final search-completion strategy: specialized completion indexes.

BUILDING FAST COMPLETIONS VIA SPECIALIZED SEARCH INDEXES

Because completion is such an important element of relevance feedback, Elasticsearch introduced a specialized component called the *completion suggester*. This component circumvents the performance problem referenced previously and allows for custom sorting of completion results (rather than sorting by occurrence). Effectively, the completion suggester is a specialized search index that's stored in parallel with the normal search index. It's backed by a compact data structure (a *finite state transducer*) that provides a fast prefix-lookup capability. In many ways, this approach is the ideal solution for completion, but as you'll see in a moment, it introduces a couple of problems of its own.

Setting up the completion suggester is simple: you just declare one of the fields to be of type `completion`.

Listing 8.5   Setting up Elasticsearch's completion suggester

```
{ "mappings": {
    "movie": {
      "properties": {
        "title": {
          "type": "string",
          "analyzer": "english"},       Field of type "completion"
        "completion": {                 to use Elasticsearch's
          "type": "completion"}}}}}     completion suggester
```

In principle, you could copy the `title` field to the `completion` field and index the documents in the same way as demonstrated in the preceding section. But if you do, you forego one of the main benefits of using the completion suggester: the ability to directly specify the weight of the completion. This weight affects the order in which completions are suggested. In the following listing, we enrich the given document with a new `completion` field that uses the movie's title for completion text and the movie's popularity as the completion weight.

Listing 8.6   Enriching documents with a completion field using popularity for weight

```
doc = {                                      Original
    "title": "Star Trek Into Darkness",      document
    "popularity": 32.15,
    /*...other fields*/  }

doc["completion"] = {                  Document
    "input": [doc["title"]],           enrichment
    "weight": int(doc["popularity"])}     Weights must
                                          be integers
```

After you index these enriched documents, you can query for the completion. In the following listing, you use Elasticsearch's _suggest endpoint rather than the _search endpoint you used before. (Though if you like, you can include a suggest clause within a normal Elasticsearch search and get suggestions along with search results.)

Listing 8.7 Retrieving search completions via the _suggest endpoint

```
GET /tmdb/_suggest
{ "title_completion": {
    "text": "star tr",
     "completion" : { "field": "completion"}}}
```

In this example, you search for a completion to the prefix text star tr. As in the previous case, the results are a list of Star Trek movies, but this time you sort by popularity rather than occurrence counts. This provides the user with much more relevant results. Additionally, the completion suggester can be configured to perform fuzzy matches so that appropriate completions can be returned despite a certain degree of user error.

The benefits of the completion suggester come at a cost. Because the completion suggester is implemented as a separate index internal to Elasticsearch, it isn't aware of the full context of search. For instance, consider a user who wants to find the Star Trek movie in which Spock dies (sorry, spoiler alert). What if the user searches for "Spock Dies Star Trek"? Obviously, no title completion will start with spock dies star, so a good completion implementation attempts to find completions starting with the second term—dies star—again, no completions. The completion implementation then moves on to find completions beginning with just star. Here, based on the context of the entire query, it would be unreasonable to return anything but Star Trek movies. But in the case of the Elasticsearch completion suggester, the top completion result is *Star Wars: Episode IV—A New Hope*. This demonstrates that the completion suggester is unaware of the search context.

Another unfortunate consequence with using a finite state transducer to back completion is that the data structure is immutable. If a document is deleted from the index, the completions for that document will still exist. Currently, the only remedy for this situation is a full-index optimization, which effectively rebuilds the completion index from scratch.

Despite the possible pitfalls, the completion suggester is an important tool for relevance feedback. The Elasticsearch completion suggester can occasionally lead users astray, but, it allows you to specify the criteria by which completions are sorted (in this case, popularity). And the completion suggester is typically the fastest method for retrieving completion suggestions. This rapid feedback to users can become an almost subconscious aid, helping to direct them to more targeted searches and ultimately to the documents that they're looking for.

WHICH SEARCH-COMPLETION METHOD IS BEST

In the preceding sections, we covered three search-completion methods: completions based on user input, completions based on the text in the index, and completions based on specialized indexes. Each technique helps bring your users closer to the information they seek. But as you've seen, there's no silver bullet; each technique has its share of benefits and drawbacks. Equipped with this knowledge, you'll at least have a better starting point for building your own completion solution.

8.1.3   *Correcting typos and misspellings with search suggestions*

Search completions provide suggestions to users as they type. But another opportunity to provide relevance feedback arises immediately after the user's query is submitted. Users make mistakes—misspellings or typos—while entering their searches. After they submit a malformed query, the search engine can provide suggestions to modify and improve the query.

Here again Google serves as a good example of how post-search suggestion can provide relevance feedback to users. As displayed in figure 8.4, if Google receives a query that contains an obvious typo, it replaces the user's query with the correction that the user likely intended. Similarly, if the user's query likely contains a typo, but the situation is more ambiguous, then Google retrieves results corresponding to the user's original search, but also suggests a different query likely more aligned with the user's goals. In either case, the presentation of this information is paramount. If users are unaware that their query has been replaced, they may become disoriented and begin to mistrust the search application. Conversely, if users are never made aware of a typo mistake, they may similarly be disappointed, believing that the search application isn't able to find the anticipated results.

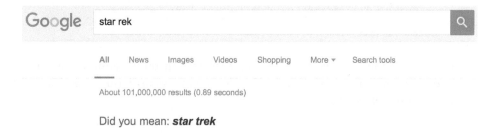

Figure 8.4   Google uses post-search suggestions to provide users with relevance feedback.

You can implement post-search suggestions by using Elasticsearch's phrase suggester. To set up the phrase suggester, the mapping must contain a field specifically set aside for suggestion. Similar to the completions discussed previously, this field must be tokenized so that the tokens are still readable, correctly spelled words. For this example, you'll copy the title field into a suggestion field and use the default standard analysis chain:

```
"mappings": {
  "movie": {
    "properties": {
      "genres": {
        "properties": {
          "name": {
            "type": "string",
            "index": "not_analyzed"}}},
      "title": {
        "type": "string",
        "analyzer": "english",
        "copy_to":["suggestion"]},
      "suggestion": {
        "type": "string"}}}}
```

To pull back suggestions, you again use the _suggest endpoint:

```
GET /tmdb/_suggest
{ "title_suggestion": {
    "text": "star trec",
    "phrase": {
        "field": "suggestion"}}}
```

This returns suggestions that look like this:

```
{'title_completion': [{'length': 9, 'offset': 0,
  'options': [
    {'score': 0.0020846569, 'text': 'star three'},
    {'score': 0.0019600056, 'text': 'star trek'},
    {'score': 0.0016883487, 'text': 'star trip'},
    {'score': 0.0016621534, 'text': 'star they'},
    {'score': 0.0016162122, 'text': 'star tree'}],
  'text': u'star trec'}]}
```

Each suggestion is scored, representing how strongly the suggestion matches the user's intended query. But as seen here, this doesn't always work out—*star trek* isn't the first suggestion. Let's make some improvements.

Listing 8.8 Retrieving post-search suggestions in the context of a user's search

```
{ "fields": ["title"],
    "query": {
      "match": {"star trec"}},
    "suggest": {
      "title_suggestion": {
        "text": "star trec",
        "phrase": {
          "field": "suggestion",
          "collate": {
            "query": {
```

❶ Collation added to main query

```
"inline": {
  "match_phrase": {
    "title" : "{{suggestion}}"}}}}}}}}
```
← ❷ **Alternate query to issue for each suggestion**

In this listing, you include the suggestion in the body of the corresponding search so that you don't have to make two separate requests. But you also address the problem of the poor suggestions by using collation ❶. With *collation*, the search engine is performing a sort of mini-search using each of the suggestions and then removing the suggestions that don't have a match. Within the collate section, you specify the search that determines which suggestions are returned; if documents match a suggestion, that suggestion will be included in the suggestions passed back to the user. Here Elasticsearch replaces the special {{suggestion}} parameter with the text of each suggestion.

Notice that you use a match_phrase query for the collation query. You do this to more tightly constrain the possible suggestions to phrases that exist in the index. For instance, if you had used the match query at ❷ for the collation, then the suggestion star three would have remained in the suggest response, because some documents contain either star *or* three, even though none include the phrase star three. By filtering out weaker suggestions, you ensure that the user is presented only with suggestions that lead to meaningful results.

We present the final result of star trec query suggestions in the following listing.

```
{ 'title_completion': [{'length': 9, 'offset': 0, 'options': [
  {'score': 0.0019600056, 'text': 'star trek'},
  {'score': 0.0016621534, 'text': 'star they'}]}]}
```

There are several things to note here. First, notice that several of the previous suggestions have been removed because of the collation match_phrase search. Also notice that the top-ranking suggestion is now the most appropriate suggestion for this search.

Another tough question: what should the application do with the suggestions? Should it outright replace the user's query with the highest-scoring suggestion? Or should you present the suggestion as a "did you mean" suggestion? Unfortunately, the answer is rarely clear-cut. The suggestions provided by the phrase suggester are scored as a function of the text edit distance and the frequency of the suggested terms. But just because a suggestion is in some sense "more likely" than the user's query, the user's query isn't necessarily incorrect; the user might be looking for something very specific.

Practically speaking, you can never read the mind of an individual user. Therefore, a good solution will involve reading up on all of the Elasticsearch phrase suggester parameters, building a solution, and watching how it performs. But as a rule of thumb, it's usually safer to direct users toward a better search with a "did you mean" suggestion rather than replacing a search without asking them.

There is, however, one big exception to this rule: if the user's query returns no results, it's always better to provide results that might be relevant rather than leaving the user with no results at all. And in either case (search replacement or post-search suggestion), make sure that the UI readily conveys what's happening so that users won't become disoriented by an interaction that falls short of their expectations.

8.2   Relevance feedback while browsing

We've discussed several aspects of relevance feedback that can occur in or around the search box. But interaction at the search box is only a small part of the conversation between the search user and the search application. This section focuses on the *browse experience.*

A user can browse through the results of a search by selectively filtering those results, narrowing down to a small set that's most relevant to that user's information needs. Sometimes the user may even *start* by browsing through the documents rather than with a text query. The browse experience is different from interactions with the search box. Whereas search-box interactions provide subtle relevance feedback to users, the browse experience gives users a broad overview of how documents are distributed in the corpus. This lets users make intentional choices about how to filter through the documents.

Faceted browsing is the predominant method for facilitating browse behavior. Visit almost any e-commerce website and you'll see the same pattern: At the top of the page is the search box. Below the search box, and typically to the left side of the screen, is a list of categories. Within each category are items that can be selected to filter the results. These menu items are called *facets* (introduced in chapter 2). Often the facets include a count of the documents that match a particular filter. If a user selects a certain facet, the results are filtered according to that selection. As shown in figure 8.5, Zappos provides a great example of a faceted browsing interface.

Here a search for "leather sandals" returns a mix of sandals—mostly women's sandals, but you can also see a toddler's sandal. I (John) happen to be a grown man, so I'm uninterested in these. But looking at the categories on the left side of the screen, I see that I can filter these results according to product type, gender, and brand. Furthermore, within gender the products are divided into four groups: *Women, Men, Girls,* and *Boys,* and although the great majority of the products matching *leather sandals* are for women (4010 items), there are 530 items that I might be interested in. If I hadn't been presented with this information, I might have seen this initial set of products and assumed that Zappos wasn't into men's fashion. If I click the *Men* facet, the results will be filtered so that only men's sandals are displayed. From there, I may choose to further narrow my results by brand or by shoe size or by any other criteria that I choose.

Consider the great amount of relevance feedback that the faceted browsing interface is providing to users. With a quick scan of the information in the sidebar, users

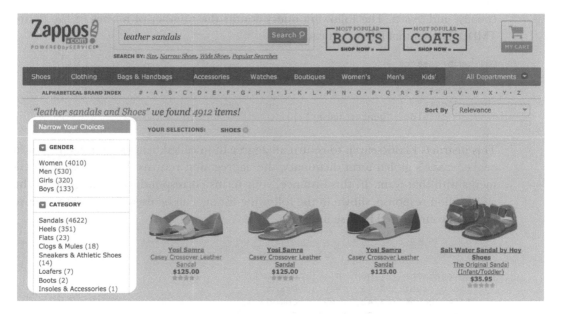

Figure 8.5   Faceted browsing helps Zappos users slice and dice the inventory and narrow the result set to include only items that most closely match their search goals.

gain a deep understanding of the products in the catalog and the metadata associated with these products. By looking at the document counts, users can also get a sense of how these documents are distributed within the categories. Finally, and most important, users can act on this knowledge by clicking a facet and narrowing the search results. In an e-commerce search, the ability for customers to quickly navigate the data and find the items they're looking for increases the likelihood that they'll make the purchase. These techniques also help you sidestep and simplify the relevance process. By giving users more options to guide themselves to what they want, you fret less about complex ranking and trying to read the user's mind.

In the following subsections, we discuss how faceted browsing is implemented in Elasticsearch. We also cover a couple of related topics. In the breadcrumb navigation section, we introduce a simple UI feature that helps users remain aware of the current facets they've selected. And in the result ordering section, we discuss how users can more closely control relevance ranking priorities.

8.2.1   Building faceted browsing

You can implement facets by using Elasticsearch's aggregation feature. For the purposes of this discussion, aggregations return a count for specific subdivisions of the current search results. Let's consider an example from TMDB—movie genre. All movies in the TMDB set contain a field `genres.name` that includes tags such as Adventure,

Comedy, and Drama. The following query counts the number of movies in the entire TMDB data set that fall within each genre:

```
GET tmdb/_search
{ "aggregations": {
    "genres": {
      "terms": {
        "field": "genres.name"}}}}
```

This instructs Elasticsearch to return an aggregation called genres. For each term in genres.name's global term dictionary, the aggregation returns the number of documents with that term. In this instance, your terms correspond to movie genres. The aggregation response, shown in the following listing, can be used to populate a genre menu in your faceted browse interface.

Listing 8.10   Facet counts for movie genres

```
{ 'aggregations': {'genres': {'buckets': [
    {'doc_count': 7546, 'key': 'Drama'},
    {'doc_count': 5342, 'key': 'Comedy'},
    {'doc_count': 3878, 'key': 'Thriller'},
    {'doc_count': 3753, 'key': 'Action'},
    {'doc_count': 2623, 'key': 'Romance'},
    {'doc_count': 2165, 'key': 'Adventure'},
    {'doc_count': 1981, 'key': 'Horror'},
    {'doc_count': 1861, 'key': 'Crime'},
    {'doc_count': 1640, 'key': 'Family'},
    {'doc_count': 1597, 'key': 'Science Fiction'}],
    'sum_other_doc_count': 7479}
```

Scanning over this list, you can see that most movies in our set are labeled as dramas, followed by comedies, thrillers, and so forth. What's more, you can look at the sum_other_doc_count and see that 7,479 movies are in genres not listed in the top 10.

It's important to again draw attention to the analysis process. As in the previous sections in this chapter, you tokenize the documents so that the raw tokens can be presented back to the user. For this particular instance, it's important to *not* use the default standard analysis because it splits the input on whitespace. Splitting on whitespace would cause *science* and *fiction* to be considered as two different genres, which is clearly incorrect.

In this query, you don't constrain the document set, so the counts represent the distribution of all movies within the genres. This is fine; it's a great data set to present to users who haven't yet specified any other information. Users coming to the movie search application for the first time can quickly scan the distribution of movies across genres to decide where to look next.

But as users continue to interact with the search application, what do they do next? Presuming that they don't decide to leave (always a possibility), there are two options: search via the search box or click a facet item to narrow the focus. In either case, the effective result is the same; they've narrowed the relevant documents to a subset of the corpus. The neat thing about aggregations is that the counts associated with each facet will be calculated based on this filtered set.

So let's say that the user clicks the Science Fiction genre, indicating a desire to see only movies tagged as science fiction. You can then filter the results set accordingly:

```
GET tmdb/_search
{"query": {
    "bool": {
      "filter": [{
        "term": {
          "genres.name": "Science Fiction"}}]}},
  "aggs": {
    "genres": {
      "terms": {"field": "genres.name"}}}}
```

With this addition, the new search response contains updated facet counts corresponding to movies tagged as science fiction:

```
{ 'aggregations': {'genres': {'buckets': [
    {'doc_count': 1597,'key': 'Science Fiction'},
    {'doc_count': 753, 'key': 'Action'},
    {'doc_count': 502, 'key': 'Thriller'},
    {'doc_count': 466, 'key': 'Adventure'},
    {'doc_count': 337, 'key': 'Drama'},
    {'doc_count': 336, 'key': 'Fantasy'},
    {'doc_count': 327, 'key': 'Horror'},
    {'doc_count': 299, 'key': 'Comedy'},
    {'doc_count': 188, 'key': 'Animation'},
    {'doc_count': 164, 'key': 'Family'}],
  'doc_count_error_upper_bound': 0,
  'sum_other_doc_count': 361}}}
```

And not only do the facet counts change, but the search results update to include only science fiction movies. Where do users go from here? Anywhere they please. They may choose to filter again within the same category by selecting another genre. They may filter based on other criteria, such as release date. Once they get an idea of what they're looking for, they may even abandon the browse interaction in favor of using the text box. No matter the case, the facet counts and the documents presented in the results will guide users to understand what's available and where to find it.

8.2.2 Providing breadcrumb navigation

You'll often want to give users feedback about how they've filtered the results. Without feedback, the user may be unaware that certain filters are still in place and therefore surprised to find no search results. *Breadcrumb navigation* is a commonly used technique for guarding against this problem. As shown in figure 8.6, breadcrumb navigation is typically presented at the top of the result set as a list of the currently selected

Figure 8.6   Zappos uses breadcrumb navigation to remind users of the currently selected facets and allow them to easily deselect filters.

facets. Here we use the previous Zappos "leather sandals" search example. This time the result set is further filtered by men's, under $100, and brown.

As you can see, the breadcrumb navigation not only provides users with an awareness of which filters are in place, but also serves as an intuitive interface enabling users to remove filters of their choice.

8.2.3   *Selecting alternative results ordering*

During a browsing style search, what's the appropriate ordering for the result set? Throughout the rest of this book, the focus has been on presenting results according to relevance. But when the user hasn't yet specified a textual query, relevance has little meaning. Instead it's up to the search application to define a default ordering. Depending on the domain, this may be based on popularity, location proximity, recency, or any number of things. The choice for the default ordering might even be a good opportunity for the search application to incorporate business concerns by, for instance, subtly promoting high-margin items toward the top.

You can also give the user control over the ordering of results. This is as simple as placing a drop-down selection box at the top of the result set. This commonly appears toward the right side of the search results, as again exemplified by Zappos search, shown in figure 8.7.

Zappos allows customers to sort results by the newest items, customer rating, popularity, and price. Allowing users to manipulate sort criteria is an excellent form

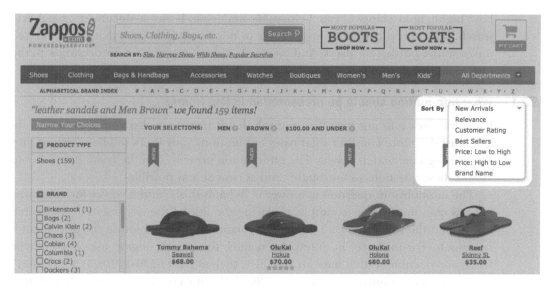

Figure 8.7   Zappos allows users to sort results according to various criteria.

of relevance feedback. This gives users a better understanding of the results and provides a means for users to organize the results to match their current search goals.

You might not always want to directly sort on these factors. A user requesting a sort on "popularity" may only want popular items prioritized: but not so strong that it overrides their search criteria. For example, a user searching for stylish "leather sandals" likely won't be pleased if they see very popular flip flops. Refer to the boosting lessons of chapter 7 should you need to implement sorting this way.

8.3   *Relevance feedback in the search results listing*

In this chapter, you've followed the typical path of a user through a search application, starting with interactions at the search box and moving on to browsing and filtering with faceted search. These techniques give users many alternate paths to relevant content. Finally, let's discuss relevance feedback and guidance in the search results themselves. Here users get an overview of the documents that the search application deems relevant. If users find a particular item interesting, they click through and investigate, hoping to find what they've been looking for. If users glance through the results listing and don't find what they need, they'll either modify their search and try again, or they'll abandon it entirely.

The results listing is therefore an important part of relevance feedback. The items in this listing must convey the most important aspects of matching documents. This allows the user to judge whether to investigate further. In the sections that follow, you'll consider what questions users ask when looking at results. You'll examine how to answer those questions before users click into the search results. You'll also see how highlighted snippets can help users understand why a document matches a search. We cover a couple of approaches to document grouping that help decrease the cognitive burden for users. And we briefly discuss approaches for dealing with the case of no search results.

8.3.1 *What information should be presented in listing items?*

Users will click a listing item if they think that it may meet their information needs. You must therefore consider what types of questions your users will be asking as they scan through the search results. The information presented in the result items should answer these questions as thoroughly and as concisely as possible.

The most obvious question to answer is "What is this?"; and if you're lucky, answering this question may be as simple as placing the title of the document in the search results. But the title often isn't a reliable semantic representation of the document it represents. For instance, in enterprise realms, the search engine may hold official forms and documents that have arcane titles, such as *Form I-130* or *401(k),* which don't readily convey the purpose of the form. Similarly, in e-commerce, products are often given titles intended to draw attention and convey a feeling, but not necessarily convey an accurate representation of the item. For instance, Oakley has a prominent line of women's sunglasses call *Little Black Dress*—a funny name for sunglasses.

If you find yourself in a situation where there's no meaningful title, you must look for other ways to convey information to the user. To answer the question "What is this?" in the realm of e-commerce, photos are often better than a title (or any other text, for that matter). A user seeking a certain product can glance through a page of images and quickly narrow the results that require more-focused attention. Even enterprise document retrieval can benefit by including imagery in the search results. For instance, including a small scanned image of the document in the search results could help users pinpoint a document that they've seen and used in the past.

Short descriptions also help the user answer "What is this?" But caution is warranted here. With too much text competing for users' attention, they might miss important details, or worse yet, become overwhelmed by the surplus of information and abandon search altogether. But if the available title doesn't readily convey an understanding of the item, a short description might be just the thing you need. If neither meaningful titles nor short descriptions are available, consider going back to the content provider and asking for a short description. If the content being searched is user provided, maybe you can place a required field for a short description. If an upstream vendor provides the content, perhaps you can work together to generate this extra bit of information that will make their products more saleable.

Besides the big question "What is this?" consider other questions that your users will ask. Are you building an e-commerce application? Then your users will be interested in knowing the price of a product. Does your search application revolve around events? Then date, time and location will be important. Place this information prominently in the search results so that users won't have to bounce in and out of results to judge whether a result is relevant. And if your search domain includes several subdomains, consider the questions important to users searching in those subdomains as well. If you know that users are shopping for cameras, place helpful camera-related details in the search results so that users can compare available choices in the results page itself.

8.3.2 *Relevance feedback through snippets and highlighting*

When the search domain involves text-heavy documents, snippets and highlighting provide an important form of relevance feedback. Snippets and highlighting mean exactly what you might imagine. If a user submits a keyword search, *snippets* are fragments of text from the matching documents that include the search keywords. *Highlights* are the keywords matches within the snippets, literally highlighted to the user. This can be done using bold text or altering the background color on the keyword match. Some search interfaces go as far as to use a different highlighting style per keyword.

The relevance feedback goal of snippet highlighting is to tell users why a particular document matches their query and where the match occurs. Users, especially search power users, will appreciate the ability to quickly read through matches in the context that they occurred. Without having to click into a particular search result, users get a sense of whether a document is a good match for their information needs. Furthermore, users may start to see patterns in the matching text and choose to further refine their search so that the appropriate documents will match. And occasionally, the answer to a user's question might be made immediately available in the snippets, thereby removing the need to even click through and look at the document where the match occurred.

Throughout this book, we've discussed considerations regarding text analysis. In chapter 4 we showed how to craft analysis to capture a semantic understanding of the words in a document. At various points, this chapter has seemingly reversed that notion to support human-readable tokens in facets and suggestions. With highlighting, we can safely return to the notion that tokens capture meaning. In other words, highlighted tokens don't have to be human readable. This is made possible by the fact that Elasticsearch—or more accurately, Lucene—tracks starting and ending character offsets of the original word prior to tokenization. During highlighting, Lucene can match on the token, look up the original character positions, and place the highlight appropriately in the original, stored text.

Elasticsearch provides three modes of highlighting that come with various trade-offs:

- The basic highlighter (the default mode)
- The postings highlighter
- The fast vector highlighter

The *basic highlighter* (the default mode) requires no special setup; you simply request with your search that Elasticsearch return highlighted snippets. The highlighted snippets will then be returned along with the search results. Unfortunately, the default implementation must reanalyze documents in order to find the location of the matching terms within the document. For small documents, the time required to reanalyze the text is miniscule. But for larger documents (pages of text), this reprocessing comes with a significant performance hit.

The *postings highlighter* and the *fast vector highlighter* avoid query-time processing by storing extra information at index time. This comes at the cost of increasing the index size. But these two methods come with certain advantages. For instance, the postings highlighter is especially useful with natural language text (sentences and paragraphs as opposed to titles or single-term fields). It automatically breaks the input text such that snippets are returned to the user as complete sentences. The fast vector highlighter can highlight matching terms independently, allowing each keyword to be highlighted in its own color or style.

To demonstrate the utility of snippet highlighting, the following listing shows one of the highlighters, the fast vector highlighter. This listing showcases some of the interesting features that make highlighting a great source of relevance feedback.

Listing 8.11 Submitting a query with highlighting enabled

```
GET tmdb/_search
{    "fields":["title","overview"],
     "query":{
        "match":{
            "title": "star trek"}},          ❹ Highlight
        "highlight": {                           request
            "fields": {
               "title": {                     ❶ Fields to be
                 "number_of_fragments": 0},      highlighted
               "overview": {
                 "fragment_size": 100,
                 "number_of_fragments": 5,                        ❷ Tags to
                 "no_match_size": 200 }                             mark up
            },                                                      matches
            "pre_tags": ["<em class=\"hlt1\">","<em class=\"hlt2\">"],
            "post_tags": ["</em>"],
            "order": "score"}}           ❸ Optional ordering
                                            of snippets
```

Prior to submitting this query, the documents were indexed with term vectors enabled for both the `title` and `overview` fields. (You do this by placing `"term_vector"`: `"with_positions_offsets"` in the field mappings.) Let's now take a look at some of the details in this query.

To enable highlighting, a new *highlighting* section is included ❹. In the `fields` section of the highlight body ❶, you specify the fields you want to highlight along with any other parameters you need per field. (You'll look more closely at these momentarily.) The optional `pre_tags` and `post_tags` parameters ❷ specify how to annotate the highlighted keywords in the results. By specifying several tags, you can style each

keyword in different ways. For instance, each keyword can be given its own color. This
will allow users to glance at search results and quickly understand just why a given document matches their query. The final order parameter ❸ is particularly useful for
search involving large documents. Ordering the snippets by score causes highlighting
to take the extra step of sorting the snippets so that the best matching snippets are
returned first.

Now that highlighting has been enabled, let's take a look at a portion of the result
for the "Star Trek" query in the following listing.

Listing 8.12 Partial response for a search for "Star Trek" with highlighting enabled

```
{ '_id': '193', '_index': 'tmdb',
  '_score': 5.0279865, '_type': 'movie',
  'fields': {
    'overview': ['Captain Jean-Luc Picard ...'],
    'title': ['Star Trek: Generations']},
  'highlight': {
    'overview': ['renegade scientist Soran who is destroying entire
                <em class="hlt1">star</em> systems. Only one man
                can help Picard stop Soran\'s'],
    'title': ['<em class="hlt1">Star</em> <em class="hlt2">Trek</em>:
              Generations']}},
{'_id': '201', '_index': 'tmdb',
 '_score': 5.0279865, '_type': 'movie',
'fields': {
   'overview': ['En route to the honeymoon of William Riker ...'],
   'title': ['Star Trek: Nemesis']},
  'highlight': {
    'overview': ['En route to the honeymoon of William Riker to Deanna Troi
               on her home planet of Betazed, Captain Jean-Luc'],
     'title': ['<em class="hlt1">Star</em> <em class="hlt2">Trek</em>:
               Nemesis']}}
```

In this response, the new highlight sections of each listing item are shown in bold
text. The first thing to notice is that, thanks to the use of the *fast vector highlighter* with
the specified pre- and post-tags, the keyword star and the keyword trek are encapsu-
lated in different tags.

Now, referring to listing 8.11, let's dig into some of those field-level highlighting
specifications. For short fields, such as the title, you don't want just a snippet to come
back; you want the entire text. By specifying number_of_fragments returned to be 0,
you signal Elasticsearch to highlight and return the entire text of the field. Next, with
the overview field, you see that the length and number of snippets can be specified
via the fragment_size and num_of_fragments parameters, respectively.

The next parameter, no_match_size, can be particularly useful. Often a document
that's a perfectly good match for a search may not have a match in the field you're
using for highlighting. And, typically, this means that no snippets will be returned for
this field. But rather than returning nothing, why not at least return a portion of the

leading text in the field so that the user receives some context. This is precisely where the no_match_size parameter comes in handy. After specifying no_match_size to be 200 here, any document that has no keyword matches in the overview field will return the first 200 characters rounded down to the nearest whole word. Notice that this is exactly the case with the second document in listing 8.12. Because neither star nor trek occur in this field, the first portion is returned instead.

One final thing to note about listing 8.12: the snippets are broken at arbitrary locations. If you opted to use the *postings highlighter* rather than the *fast vector highlighter*, the snippets would be broken at sentence boundaries, which arguably provides a better user experience by making more-understandable snippets. But the postings highlighter can't differentiate between the keywords so that they can be presented differently in the search results. Thus, as is so often the case, you must understand and carefully weigh the trade-offs when choosing one implementation over another.

8.3.3   *Grouping similar documents*

Within the results listing, another way to provide users with relevance feedback is to group documents in such a way that the information is easier for users to process. This comes in two flavors: document grouping and field collapsing.

First, concerning document grouping, documents often fall into several natural buckets within the corpus. For example, the movies in the TMDB corpus have a status field indicating where the movies are in the production pipeline: *rumored, planned, in production*, and *released*. For certain conceivable search applications, it may be helpful to present search results pregrouped according to the available buckets. If your users think first in terms of document groupings, then this feature can greatly reduce their cognitive burden.

Document grouping can be accomplished with the use of aggregation—in this case, a combination of *terms* aggregation and *top hits* aggregation.

Listing 8.13   Using a combination of terms and top hits aggregation for doc grouping

```
GET /tmdb/_search
{ "query":{
      "match":{
          "title": "star trek"}},
   "aggs": {
      "statuses": {
          "terms": {"field":"status"},
          "aggs": {
              "hits": {
                  "top_hits": {}}}}}}
```

This query instructs Elasticsearch to find all documents matching Star Trek and then group the documents according to status. The corresponding result set will contain a buckets section that looks like the following listing.

Listing 8.14 Documents grouped with a combination of terms and top hits aggregation

```
{ 'buckets': [
  { 'doc_count': 82,
    'key':  'released',
      'hits': { 'hits': { 'hits': [
        { '_id':  '13475',
          '_index':  'tmdb',
          '_score': 6.032624,
          '_source': {
            'name':  'Star Trek: Alternate Reality Collection',
            'popularity': 2.73003887701698, ... },
                  /* more documents */ },
  { 'doc_count': 4,
    'key':  'in production',
      'hits': { 'hits': { 'hits': [
        { '_id':  '13475',
          '_index':  'tmdb',
          '_score': 6.032624,
          '_source': {
            'name':  'Star Trek: Axanar',
            'popularity': 3.794237016983887, ... },
              /* more documents */ },
        /* more groups */],
  'doc_count_error_upper_bound': 0,
  'sum_other_doc_count': 0}
```

A note on group ordering: by default, the terms aggregations are sorted according to the number of matching documents, in descending order. If the default top-level sorting isn't appropriate for your application, take some time to read through the Elasticsearch documentation and see if you can construct a more appropriate ordering for the top-level groups. (Listing 8.15 demonstrates an example of implementing a custom sorting of the top-level groups.)

The other common form of document grouping is known as *field collapsing*. Say you have several documents that are near duplicates of one another. For instance, what if the TMDB collection contains multiple, separate entries for the *Star Trek* movie, one for each language that the movie has been translated into? Rather than filling a user's search results with page after page of effectively the same result, you can use field collapsing to group near-duplicate documents and then present the user with only an exemplar document from this set.

To build such a search response, you again use a combination of terms and top hits aggregation. Getting the details right takes finesse. A bit of setup is required for field collapsing: you need a field that indicates which documents are near duplicates of one another. Though the TMDB set doesn't have a good example, let's again assume that the *Star Trek* movie has multiple, separate entries, one for each language that the movie has been translated into. Furthermore, presume that no matter the language, each entry contains a unique identifier for the original English version. This unique identifier field is a good candidate for field collapsing. By combining all movies with the same value in this field, you'll have successfully de-duplicated the movies that have multiple translations.

The next finicky bit is modifying top-level group ordering. Recall that the top-level groups are by default sorted according to the number of documents that they contain. In this case, the top-level groups correspond to the original version of movies, and you want the results to still be sorted according to relevance. To achieve this, sort the top-level groups by the score of each group's most relevant document. The following listing is similar to listing 8.13, but it highlights the changes necessary to correctly implement field collapsing.

Listing 8.15   Sorting groups according to the most relevant document in the group

```
GET /tmdb/_search
{
    "query":{
        "match":{
            "title": "star trek"}},
    "aggs": {
        "original_versions": {
            "terms": {
                "field":"original_id",
                "order": {"top_score": "desc"}},          1 Collapses on
            "aggs": {                                        original_id,
                "hits": {                                    ordered by
                    "top_hits": {"size":1}},                 top_score
                "top_score": {
                    "max": { "script": "_score"}}}}}}
```

In particular, the top-level terms aggregation now refers to the `original_id` field; the terms aggregation is ordered according to `top_score`; and adjacent to the top hits aggregation, the `top_score` **1** is defined as the maximum scoring document associated with each top-level bucket.

8.3.4   *Helping the user when there are no results*

Sometimes your users make a request for which no results can be found. This can either be because they make a mistake such as a misspelling in the request or because they have so constrained the request that no documents are available. In this situation, the worst thing that you can do is to present the user with an empty results page. This leaves the user with no recourse other than to abandon search and fulfill their needs elsewhere.

To guard against this, always consider backup methods to bring users closer to satisfying their search goals. In section 2.1.3 we discussed how to use suggestions to correct user mistakes. If there are no search results, you can take this a step further by replacing the user's query with the best suggestion. Or, if there's no obvious mistake on the part of the user, perhaps you can automatically remove the user's last filter so that the search will be less constrained. Finally, if you have nothing else to go on, show users popular documents. Whatever the case may be, if the search application modifies the search on behalf of the user, make sure to inform the user about how the search has been changed so that the user won't become disoriented with results that don't match expectations.

8.4 Summary

- Relevance feedback facilitates a conversation between the search application and the user.
- When designing the search experience, consider the users' typical workflow. They often start with a text search and then, as they review the results, they engage in filtering and refining their criteria. Finally, they find items of interest and click through to see the details page.
- Help users find items more quickly by updating search results as they type.
- Assist users in building successful queries by suggesting search completions.
- Correct user mistakes with "did you mean" suggestions.
- Faceted search helps users understand the distribution of items in the index and allows them to filter and drill down to the subset of the results that they want.
- The breadcrumb UI component can make users aware of how their results are being filtered. It also gives them an obvious way to remove existing filters.
- Highlighted search results and details pages draw the users' attention to *why* a particular item is deemed important.
- Result grouping and sorting can reduce user cognitive load by allowing users to focus on the most interesting results.
- Relevance feedback makes it easier for users to engage with search and find what they're looking for.

Designing
a relevance-focused
search application

This chapter covers

- Gathering information before building a new search application
- Designing and implementing a complete search application
- Designing a query as a composite of subqueries
- Balancing query parameters
- Deploying, monitoring, and improving search
- Knowing when further relevance tuning is no longer advantageous

In the previous chapters, we laid out all the ingredients for good search:

- Extracting features from the text of the documents through proper tokenization
- Defining important signals and creating search fields to represent them
- Crafting queries that take into account both user needs and business requirements
- Providing feedback to users in order to guide them to more-relevant results

Now, this chapter is the rest of the recipe—the set of instructions that organizes these ingredients and lays out the methodology for building a relevance-focused search application.

Previously, we looked deep into the details of the search engine itself and described how to provide users with a relevant search experience. In this chapter (and the chapters beyond), we shift from low-level details to a higher-level view of search application development. In this chapter, we present a systematic approach for building a search application based on the simple flowchart in figure 9.1. At a high level, designing a search application requires three steps: gathering search requirements, designing the application, and maintaining a deployed application. In the subsequent sections, we provide a detailed understanding of each step so that, upon completing this chapter, you'll have a solid framework to build your own search application.

As with all of our chapters, we motivate the discussion with a fun example. And having completely wrung all educational and comedic value from the Star Trek examples, we turn to a different one. You're going to build a new and exciting start-up called *Yowl*, and search will be its central feature.

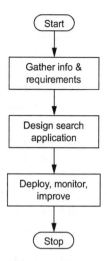

Figure 9.1   Relevant search is built in three phases: information gathering, design, and deployment. This chapter covers all three phases in detail.

9.1   *Yowl! The awesome new start-up!*

First things first, you need a tough problem to start to solve, as in figure 9.2.

Luckily, Doug has come up with a great idea! Just imagine it: you hop off a plane in a city you've never been to before and, having subsisted on pretzels and ginger ale for the past five hours, you're dying for something more substantive—a big, juicy hamburger. But how do you find a good burger joint? There's no product on the market that can help you find good restaurants nearby.

Yowl to the rescue! With Yowl's smartphone application, you can search for and quickly find nearby restaurants fit for your cravings. Or maybe you're not in a new city, but you're interested in exploring the foodscape in your hometown. Yowl will help you discover restaurants that you never knew

Figure 9.2   At the start of any good search application is a problem that needs to be solved. Identifying and thinking through that problem is an important step in building the search application.

existed. Yowl will find restaurants perfectly matched to your tastes. Yowl will even help you explore new tastes! The possibilities are endless.

Though you might have to do some legwork up front, you hope that as Yowl catches on, all the restaurant data will come from restaurant patrons and owners. The restaurant patrons will write reviews for restaurants they've dined at. And restaurant owners, encouraged by the new traffic created by Yowl, will update their restaurant data so that their restaurant can easily be found.

And the best thing is that Yowl has absolutely no competition in this market. Amazing, right? How has no one thought of this before? *Doug said he looked for it on Google, and nothing came up!* Yelp, folks, as soon as we get this new search application built, we're all going to be rich. Oh, and a final note on the name; you might think that Yowl is the sound that a cat makes when you step on its tail. Maybe so. But we think it's catchy. Think of Yowl as the sound that your stomach makes when you're really, really, *really* hungry. So when you're most hungry, you'll immediately think of our app!

9.2   *Gathering information and requirements*

Before building a search application, take time to consider the needs and expectations of all stakeholders. This is the next step in our process, as shown in figure 9.3. Most obviously, search should be easy to use and helpful for users. But Yowl is a search-driven business, so it must also meet business needs. In this section, we look at both user and business needs. We identify the information required to meet these needs and we describe potential sources for this information.

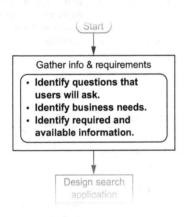

Figure 9.3   **Before building search, consider the needs of all parties involved, identify the information required to fulfill those needs, and determine where this information can be found.**

9.2.1   *Understand users and their information needs*

A useful exercise is to create personas for the various types of users who are expected to interact with the application. A *persona* is a description of a fictional character that epitomizes a particular type of user behavior. Here's our first cut at Yowl user personas:

- *Jet-setter Jenny*—Jenny regularly travels and looks to Yowl to find places to eat when she's in a new city. Sometimes she's looking for a quick and convenient bite; other times she wants to find a fancier restaurant for meals with business associates.
- *Connoisseur Courtney*—Courtney is interested in the finer things in life, and when it comes to food, she has exacting tastes. One night she'll seek the finest French cuisine. Another night she'll look for the restaurant that serves the best Chirashizushi (a Japanese dish).

- *Explorer Evan*—Evan has a broad palate and is always interested in trying something new. This includes new types of food, new restaurants, and new parts of town.
- *Discount Danny*—Danny is a price-conscious user. When choosing a restaurant, he wants to find the best value possible. He's looking for low prices and high ratings. If there's a discount or meal deal available, he'll use it. He prefers nearby restaurants—you know, to save on gas.

Building out user personas might seem artificial at first, but they make it possible to identify with users on a more concrete level. Personas also form a shared vocabulary that allow you to more easily discuss the entire spectrum of user behaviors. When creating personas for your project, make sure to cover all of the predominant behaviors you expect to see, and try to avoid overlapping behaviors.

Let's use the preceding personas to get to know your users. You can do this by enumerating the questions that these imaginary users might ask of your service. Three of your consumers are interested in restaurant location, though in different ways. They might ask the following questions:

- Jet-setter Jenny: "Where are all the nearby delis?"
- Discount Danny: "Where are the nearest restaurants that have discounts?"
- Explorer Evan is still interested in location but rather than "nearby" or "nearest," he's interested in a slightly different question: "What areas of town have new and highly reviewed restaurants?"

The next most prevalent concern appears to be the users' tastes for a particular type of cuisine. Here, the questions are as follows:

- Jet-setter Jenny may require only a generic representation of cuisine type. She may ask, "I'm heading out with business colleagues for dinner; what Italian restaurants are nearby?"

  Or perhaps, being in an unfamiliar city, Jet-setter Jenny might long for familiar chain restaurants where she knows what she can expect: "My tummy has the grumblies for cheap Mexican. Is there a Taco Belly nearby?"

- Connoisseur Courtney needs Yowl to understand cuisine with the acumen of a professional chef. She won't ask for Chinese food; instead she'll ask more specifically: "Where's the finest Szechuan dining in the city?"

  This indicates that you might need to keep track of cuisine types as a hierarchy—for instance, with Hunan and Szechuan cuisines being a subtype of Chinese cuisine. But Courtney, being a true connoisseur, may even go so far as to ask for specific dishes: "Where can I find the Szechuan dish called *bon bon chicken?*"

- Explorer Evan, having a broad palate, won't constrain search results by a particular cuisine, but he's interested in knowing what types of food are available. He'll ask exploratory questions, such as "What kinds of restaurants are located in this part of the city?"

Finally, all of the personas appear to have additional criteria that they might use to filter their results:

- Explorer Evan is interested in "What's new?"
- Connoisseur Courtney is interested in "What's highly reviewed?"
- Discount Danny is interested in "What's cheap and yummy (low price, high rating)?"

Danny might also appreciate knowing about any available discounts. Hmm ... you might even use the discount thing as a business angle.

Identifying your typical users and their information needs gives you a good start at identifying the information necessary to satisfy these requirements. Read back through your users' questions and consider: What types of information will you need in order to answer all of your users' questions? Where will you get this information? Before getting to the bottom of this, let's look at the other side of the equation: the needs of the business itself.

9.2.2 *Understand business needs*

If Yowl is going to help users for very long, you need a sustainable business model; someone has to pay you for the service you provide. No sweat—you have the perfect idea: restaurants will pay a subscription fee in order to become one of Yowl's *promoted restaurants*. Whenever a user searches for a type of cuisine or a dish that's a match for a promoted restaurant, that restaurant will get an extra boost in its relevance score, which will ensure that the restaurant is listed higher in the search results. On top of this, you'll further boost promoted restaurants that have available discounts.

There are also nonmonetary aspects to the business. Yowl is a content-driven company, and by and large you'll depend on restaurants to provide information. Therefore, whenever a restaurant provides Yowl with useful information, Yowl will temporarily provide it with a boost as a *thank you* for the help.

Notice that at this point you have several competing concerns to balance. If you boost too far in favor of the restaurants, you'll lose users because the search results will be less relevant. If you boost too far in favor of the users, you offer no benefit to promoted restaurants and will soon lose them as customers. Relevance engineering is tricky!

9.2.3 *Identify required and available information*

Having considered both user needs and business needs, let's boil all this knowledge down. You're looking to answer three main questions right now:

- What information is required?
- What will the information be used for?
- How do you get it?

After answering, you'll have a clearer understanding of the application. And you can identify feasibility risks that may arise as a result of hard-to-get information or information that doesn't quite answer your users' questions.

Let's first consider the content being searched—restaurants. At a minimum, a restaurant is represented as a name and an address. Usually this information is publicly available. Restaurant names and addresses that are more accurate and machine readable can be purchased from a business database provider.

Restaurant names will be of obvious use, both in search and in the presentation to the user on the details page. You need to use the address for location information. You'll use a geolocation service to convert restaurant addresses into their corresponding latitude-longitude coordinates. At search time, the latitude-longitude location will be useful for filtering, for finding all restaurants within a given bounding box. And the latitude-longitude coordinates will also be useful in boosting restaurants that are located close to the user making the search request.

Even more than location, Yowl users want to know about the food that restaurants serve. Often users will search for restaurants by cuisine (Mexican, Italian, Chinese, and so forth). Some users will come to Yowl looking for a particular dish. And when users review search results, they'll appreciate having cuisine and menu information nearby so that they can be sure their search is on the right track. Gathering this information is tricky. You do expect users to provide restaurant reviews; maybe you can also ask them to provide missing details about the restaurants. And once you bring significant users to more restaurants, the restaurant owners will have the incentive to provide this information. But for now, you'll probably have to roll up your sleeves and research and enter this information yourself.

After location and cuisine, users will filter and sort results according to secondary criteria: price, review rating, and whether a discount is available. The overall price and rating will come from the users. And the discounts will be supplied by the restaurants. Restaurants can also provide descriptions of themselves. This will be nice to present to users in the details pages, but it might also carry rich, searchable text.

And finally, don't forget that Yowl's success depends on subscribed restaurants. This is a simple Boolean value that controls whether restaurants will get an extra nudge toward the top of the search results. Similarly, for a limited time, you're boosting *engaged* restaurants—those that are helping you by providing information.

In review, the information you need, the sources you'll draw this information from, and the uses for this information are presented in table 9.1.

Table 9.1   Yowl information requirements, sources, and uses

Information	Example	Source	Uses
Restaurant name	Taco Belly	Public	Search, display (listing, details)
Address	1234 Cordon Ave. Blacksburg TN 23913	Public	Source of location, display (details)
Location (lat/long)	35° 24′ 30″ N 88° 31′ 20″ W	Geolocated from address	Filtering, display, source for distance

Table 9.1   Yowl information requirements, sources, and uses *(continued)*

Information	Example	Source	Uses
Distance	12 mi	Calculated from user and restaurant locations	Boosting, sorting, display (listing)
Cuisine	Mexican; fast food	Restaurant, user	Search
Menu items	Burrito Ultimate $4.95	Restaurant	Search, display (details), source of price information
Price	$, $$, $$$,$$$$	Menu items, user	Filter, display (listing)
Review rating	★,★★,★★★,★★★★	User	Filter, display (listing)
Discounts	(Varies)	Restaurant	Filter, display (listing, details)
Promoted restaurants	Boolean	Restaurant	Boost
Completed form	Boolean	Restaurant	Boost
Description	"Tasty, Fast, Cheap, Addictive"	Restaurant	Display (listing, details), search

9.3   *Designing the search application*

With all of the ingredients assembled, it's time to pull together your recipe for restaurant search. As indicated in figure 9.4, you'll first design the user experience based on expected user needs. Next you'll rely on knowledge of the available information to identify the fields that you need to index; these will serve as your base signals. You'll determine analysis requirements to ensure that the text is properly tokenized and the appropriate features are extracted. Once you're sure that the base signals function well in isolation, you'll build a query that balances the signals together.

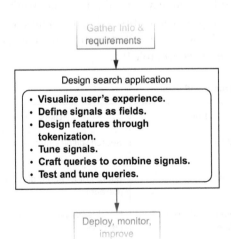

Figure 9.4   A systematic approach for designing a search application involves creating the appropriate fields and queries so that the users' questions are met.

9.3.1 *Visualize the user's experience*

Leaning on our understanding of user and business needs, let's think through the user experience. From a search relevance perspective, you have two goals. The primary goal is to help users fulfill their information needs as quickly as possible (this is the goal of the book, after all). The secondary goal is to provide users with relevance feedback (as in chapter 8) to help them understand why they're seeing the current search results and how to adjust their searches accordingly.

When users come to Yowl, they immediately begin browsing for restaurants through a user interface similar to the one shown in figure 9.5.

Some users start with a text search and enter a restaurant name, a cuisine type, or specific dish. Users with less-specific needs filter nearby restaurants according to price or rating. Many users search and filter. As users modify their search text or their filter selections, the map updates with markers for nearby restaurants that meet the search criteria. The map itself can be used as a location-based filter of restaurants, and users can pan and zoom to various parts of the map in order to see restaurants in a different location.

After you satisfy users' search criteria, they move on to one of the two search result displays. The first display, the map view, is part of the browse interface. As shown in figure 9.6, the browse components can be dismissed to reveal a full-size map.

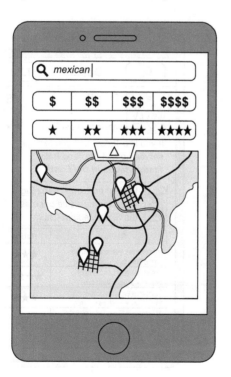

Figure 9.5 Yowl's browse interface

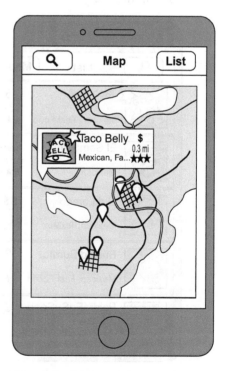

Figure 9.6 Yowl's map view, one of the two search result displays

The visual presentation of a map provides relevance feedback, assuring users that they're searching in the correct location. When a user clicks a restaurant marker, a restaurant card appears, displaying relevant information:

- Restaurant name
- Distance from the user to the restaurant
- Rating (by number of stars)
- Price (by number of $ characters)
- Cuisine type
- An image for the restaurant

The goal of the restaurant cards is to present the most critical information as compactly as possible on the screen. This allows the user to efficiently scan the display and click through to the details only when the restaurant is a good match.

As shown in figure 9.7, you also present search results as a tabular listing of matching restaurants. The list view presents each search result as a restaurant card that looks just like the restaurant cards used in the map view. The list view isn't as good as the map view for displaying location information, but it allows users to focus on the other metadata—cuisine type, rating, price, and distance. The results can be sorted by relevance or distance; and in order to retrieve more results, the user can scroll further down in the list.

Figure 9.7   The list view, a tabular view of the search results

Figure 9.8   Yowl's restaurant details view

Finally, if a user clicks a restaurant listing, you present the restaurant details view, shown in figure 9.8. This page provides rich information for that restaurant, including:

- Everything from the restaurant card (restaurant name, distance, rating, price, and so forth)
- Restaurant description
- User reviews
- Details about available deals
- A link to the menu
- Hours that the restaurant is open
- Address and phone number

9.3.2 Define fields and model signals

You now know what information is available and how it will be used within Yowl. It's finally time to start building this search application! This starts with defining your fields. Table 9.2 uses the information from table 9.1 to describe how each piece of information will be analyzed and indexed into its own field. Nothing should be too surprising here; everything is a straightforward application of the ideas discussed in chapter 4.

Although we're brushing over some details, don't be fooled into thinking that modeling the signals is an easy task. In practice, defining fields can be iterative. You'll often run into unexpected behavior and have to go back and tune the analysis to handle the corner cases as they pop up.

Table 9.2 Given the required information, you form fields and determine how to appropriately analyze the content.

Field name	Information (from table 9.1)	Analysis
`location`	Location (lat/long)	`geo_point` (geolocated from address)
`name`	Restaurant name	Standard tokenized, possessive and plural stemmed, lowercased, diacritics removed
`cuisine_hifi`	Cuisine (from restaurants/curators)	Standard tokenized, synonyms (used to normalize the vocabulary)
`cuisine_lofi`	Cuisine (from user)	
`menu`	Menu items	Standard tokenized, lowercased, bigram shingled, multivalued (ETL will involve OCR and curation)
`description`	Restaurant description	English tokenization and stemming, lowercased
`price`	Price	One of {$,$$,$$$,$$$$} as determined from menu items or user reviews

Table 9.2 Given the required information, you form fields and determine how to appropriately analyze the content. *(continued)*

Field name	Information (from table 9.1)	Analysis
`rating`	Review rating	One of {★,★★,★★★,★★★★} as determined by average user reviews
`has_discount`	Discounts	Boolean
`promoted`	Promoted restaurants	Boolean
`engaged`	Completed form	Boolean

At this point, it's good to start thinking about how base signals (the fields in table 9.2) naturally group together. Later, when it's time to build your queries, you can think about these groups as logical chunks rather than having to consider each base signal as a completely independent entity. A few sections from now, you're going to build out Yowl's main query. You'll see that thinking of fields in groups greatly simplifies the process of balancing signals and tuning the overall query.

As you can see in table 9.2, Yowl's fields fall into four fairly natural groups: location, content, user preferences, and business concerns. These are defined as follows:

- *Location*—The `location` field is just that: a `geo_point`-encoded set of latitude-longitude pairs.
- *Content*—This includes text fields: `name`, `cuisine_hifi`, `cuisine_lofi`, `menu`, and `description`. Note that you split your cuisine information into two fields: a high-fidelity field, `cuisine_hifi`, for cuisine information supplied by Yowl curators and restaurant owners; and a low-fidelity field, `cuisine_lofi`, for information that comes from users reviewing the restaurants.
- *User preference*—User preference is represented in the `price` and `rating` fields. Both fields have similar UI/UX that allows users to filter through the restaurants. Both fields are represented similarly in the index. They differ only in meaning.
- *Business concerns*—This includes `has_discount`, `promoted`, and `engaged` fields. These Boolean fields define groups of restaurants that Yowl wants to boost as part of your business strategy.

9.3.3 *Combine and balance signals*

By this point, you're confident that fields correctly capture the important features from the data that they encode. You're now ready for the sometimes-arduous task of creating queries that combine and balance these signals. In this section, we lay out a bottom-up approach whereby the base signals (fields) combine according to their logical grouping. Once these higher-level signals are in place, you combine them to create the final query used for Yowl search.

BUILDING QUERIES FOR RELATED SIGNALS

You've already seen how the fields naturally group into location, content, user preferences, and business concerns. Now let's consider how each of these higher-level signals might be stated in terms of Elasticsearch queries.

First, let's look at the location signal. You need two queries to handle location. One is a bounding-box filter that will be used on the map screen to geographically limit the area that needs to be searched, as shown in the following listing.

Listing 9.1 Bounding-box geographic filter

```
{    "filter": {
        "geo_bounding_box": {
            "location": {
                "top_left": <northwest corner of user display>,
                "bottom_right": <southeast corner of user display>}}}}
```

The other location query scores the restaurants according to their geographic distance from the user's current location, as shown in the next listing.

Listing 9.2 Geo-query scoring restaurants near to the user more highly

```
{    "query": {
        "function_score": {
            "functions": [{
                "gauss": {
                    "location": {
                        "origin": {
                            "lat": <user-lat>,
                            "lon": <user-lon>},
                        "offset": "0km",
                        "scale":  "10km"}}}]}}}
```

This query ensures that nearby restaurants are boosted above the distant ones in Yowl's list view. Determining a score based on distance can be computationally expensive, so every time you use this query, you'll also apply the geo-filter of listing 9.1. Otherwise, you'll inadvertently be calculating distance scores for restaurants so far away that the users wouldn't be interested in them anyway.

As you build up the subqueries corresponding to your signals, it's important to test each query in isolation, as you did in chapter 7. This simplifies the work required when combining these pieces into an overarching query, because you'll be able to focus on the higher-level signal rather than worrying that the base signals aren't appropriately balanced. Test queries by indexing a realistic set of documents and then running through each query to ensure that it measures the expected information. In this case, you test the location filter and query by making sure that only restaurants within the bounding box are returned, and that they're returned in order of increasing distance.

Next, you'll build a query to handle the content signal. This is your main text-based query.

Listing 9.3 Query associated with content

```
{ "query": {
    "multi_match": {
        "query": <user query>,           ◁──┐   User's
        "fields": [                          │   search
            "name^10",
            "cuisine_hifi^10",
            "cuisine_lofi^4",
            "menu^2",
            "description^1"],
        "tie_breaker": 0.3}}}
```

As discussed in detail in the previous chapters, a lot of strategies are available for searching text fields: the query can be field-centric or term-centric, the scoring can be a simple summation of subscores or something more complicated such as a disjunction-maximum score with a tie parameter. Or you can forego all the complexity and just dump the text into a single content field and have a single score to worry about. In the preceding case, you use a field-centric approach by applying a multi_match query across the name, cuisine_hifi, cuisine_lofi, menu, and description fields. By default multi_match uses a best_fields approach, which is good here because the users will likely search for a restaurant name *or* a cuisine type *or* a menu item—but not all three at once. But to soften the best_fields behavior a bit, you'll also introduce a tie_breaker with a value of 0.3.

The fields in listing 9.3 are associated with boosts that indicate the level of importance placed on each field. It's good to think through these boosts and get a representative value down for each field. These boosts are subject to change as you fine-tune your relevance. Because the typical use-case involves users searching for a restaurant name or a cuisine type, these fields receive the highest boost. Recall that cuisine_lofi content is contributed directly by the user, so you trust it less than the curated cuisine_hifi field. Because of this, you give it a lower weight. The menu field is important for people searching for a particular dish, but you weigh it lower because you don't want cuisine types that happen to be in the menu trumping matches in the cuisine fields. Finally, the description field is given the lowest boost because it's intended to merely bolster the search content.

Test the content query by ensuring that it matches the expected documents. And test the scoring by making sure that the documents are returned in the appropriate order. This type of testing tends to be subjective. In a moment, you'll learn about test-driven relevance—a technique for making this type of testing as objective as possible.

Next, the user preference signal is the easiest portion of your search. When your users select a price point (number of dollar signs) or a rating (number of stars), they're asking to filter out all other results. Therefore, no scoring is involved; you only need a filter, as shown in the following listing.

Listing 9.4   User-preference filter to limit to matches according to price or rating

```
{    "query": {
        "bool": {
            "filter": [
                {"match":{
                    price: "D"}},
                {"match":{
                    rating: "S"}}]}
```

Here you're using D to represent a single dollar sign and S to represent a star. Testing this filter is easy; just make sure that the search results contain only restaurants that match both the specified price and rating.

Finally, you consider the business needs. The goal is to boost restaurants that are promoted members of your service, restaurants that advertise a discount through your service, or restaurants that are engaged (they're providing helpful information).

Listing 9.5   Business concerns query to promote paying and engaged customers

```
{    "query": {
        "function_score": {
            "functions": [{
                "filter": {
                    "bool": {
                        "should": [
                            { "term": { has_discount: True }},
                            { "term": { promoted: True }},
                            { "term": { engaged: True }}]}},
                "script_score" : {
                    "script": """
                    0.5*doc["promoted"].value +
                    0.3*doc["has_discount"].value +
                    0.2*doc["engaged"].value
                    """}}]}}}
```

For the sake of simplicity, you encode the scoring logic in a script score to give promoted restaurants the highest boost, followed by restaurants that have available discounts, followed by the nonpaying but highly engaged restaurants. Script scoring can be computationally expensive, so in order to limit the number of restaurants that have to be processed, you filter the data to include only restaurants that have at least one of promoted, has_discount, or engaged. Note that this *won't* filter out any results; it just filters the documents that will be processed by the script_score. Testing this query is simple: create a set of documents containing every combination of promoted, has_discount, or engaged and make sure that each gets the expected score.

COMBINING SUBQUERIES

At this point, you've constructed subqueries corresponding to each of the dominant signals in your search application. As you built each subquery, you also tested it to ensure that the correct documents were matched and the results were scored so that they reflected your relevance goals. In this section, you'll go up one level of abstraction by building the overarching query that backs Yowl's search. Let's first look at the composite query and then discuss the choices you'll make in its construction.

Listing 9.6 Composite query that incorporates all of the major signals

```
{    "filter": {
        "bool": {
            "filter": [                                    Location
                {                                          filter
                    "geo_bounding_box": {
                        location: { <user's bounding box> }}},
                {
                    "match":{                              User
                        "price": <user's price preference>}},   preference
                {
                    "match":{
                        "rating": <user's rating preference>}}]}},
    "query": {
        "function_score": {                      ❶ Sums the
            "score_mode": "sum",                   relevance scores
            "query": {
                "multi_match": {                   Content
                    "query": <user's search terms>,
                    "fields": [
                        "name^10",
                        "cuisine_hifi^10",
                        "cuisine_lofi^4",
                        "menu^2",
                        "description^1" ],
                    tie_breaker": 0.3}},
                "functions": [                     Business
                {                                  concerns
                    "weight": 1.2,
                    "filter": {
                        "bool": {
                            "should": [
                                { "term": { has_discount: True }},
                                { "term": { promoted: True }},
                                { "term": { engaged: True }}]}},
                    "script_score" : {
                        "script": """
                            0.3*doc["has_discount"].value +
                            0.5*doc["promoted"].value +
                            0.2*doc["engaged"].value
                        """}},
                {                                  Location
                    "weight": 2.1,
                    "gauss": {
```

```
            "location": {
                "origin": { <user's location> },
                "offset": "0km",
                "scale":  "4km", }}},
        {                                              Content weight
                                                       (mysterious!)
            "weight": 1.0}]}}}
```

This query has two top-level sections, filters and queries. The filter limits the result set to include restaurants only near the user's current location and (if specified) match the user's price and rating requirements. The query section is more complex. The first section is the content query. In the context of the entire query, the content query serves to further filter the restaurants to only those that contain the user's search terms. But more important, this query provides a base relevance score for each document. The other signals (location and business concerns) are intended to serve only as boosts—subtle nudges—on top of the base content score. The remainder of the query section contains functions (within a function_score query) that provide these boosts. Each function contains a weight parameter that allows you to balance the signals. You have three weights in total: a weight for the location, the business concerns, and the content. The user preferences don't have a weight because they merely serve to filter the content.

At this point, you can clearly see the importance of first creating subqueries for each high-level signal. The preceding query has only three knobs to turn in order to control relevance behavior—the three weights. If you hadn't started by building subqueries, you'd have to consider the interactions of all 11 fields simultaneously, and debugging a relevance problem would be nearly impossible.

UNDERSTANDING THE BEHAVIOR OF SIGNAL WEIGHTS

You might notice something strange about listing 9.6: the content subquery is separated from the associated content weight. Let's take a closer look at the structure of the query, in order to better understand the behavior of each weight. And at the end of this section, we take a step back and generalize the lessons learned so that you can apply the same reasoning to your own search projects.

In Elasticsearch, a function_score query has a query section and a function section. There's nothing special about the query; it matches and scores documents. The interesting part is how the score from the query interacts with the numerical values produced by the functions. By default, the values generated from each function are multiplied together, and the resulting value is then multiplied with the score of the main query. In equation form, this looks something like this:

```
TotalScore = (BusinessScore × LocationScore) × ContentScore
```

But by including 'score_mode':'sum' (❶ in listing 9.6), the behavior is modified so that the function values are summed together before finally being multiplied with the query score, as shown in the following listing.

Listing 9.7   Equation representing the calculation of the overall score

```
TotalScore = (wB × BusinessScore + wL × LocationScore + wC) × ContentScore
```

Here you include weights (w_B, w_L, and w_C) corresponding to the weights in listing 9.6. These correspond to the business, location, and content weights, respectively. At this level of abstraction, you no longer directly control the values of `BusinessScore`, `LocationScore`, and `ContentScore`. Those values are determined by the subqueries you put together earlier. But by adjusting the weights w_B, w_L, and w_C, you can carefully balance `BusinessScore`, `LocationScore`, and `ContentScore`, and thereby control the search relevance.

Notice that the signals aren't symmetric in this equation. The `ContentScore` is multiplied across the `BusinessScore` and `LocationScore`. In a sense, this gives the content score an advantage over the other signals; if content score is low, it will be difficult for the total score to be high. Say, on the other hand, that you make the equation more symmetric by adding in the content score:

```
TotalScore = wB × BusinessScore + wL × LocationScore + wC × ContentScore
```

Then it would be possible to have a high-scoring document that has a content score of *zero*! This would obviously lead to a horrible user experience. A user could search for "sushi," and the Yowl app would recommend the burger joint next door! To avoid this dynamic, multiplying the content score by the other factors works best.

Now what about that mysterious content weight from listing 9.6? Why is it necessary? To finally answer this, let's consider how search would behave if the content weight wasn't present. In terms of an equation, this would be just like the equation from listing 9.7, but with w_C removed:

```
TotalScore = (wB × BusinessScore + wL × LocationScore) × ContentScore
```

With this equation in mind, let's think about a degenerate case. Consider a restaurant that's a perfect match for the user's query, but is of no business value (not promoted, engaged, or offering any discounts). Additionally, the restaurant is located at the edge of the geo-bounding box and its location score is therefore quite low. If you use the equation without the content weight, then despite being a perfect match for content, the overall score of this restaurant will be low. Effectively, the business score and the location score are "teaming up" against the content score. *But*—if you add the content weight back in as shown in listing 9.7, you control the extent to which the business score and location score are allowed to team up against the content score. Therefore, when w_B, w_L, and w_C are properly tuned, the search results will retain an appropriate focus on the quality of the content and won't be overrun by the less important location or business signals.

Let's step back and generalize this discussion. As you develop your own search applications, your queries will likely be structured similarly to the Yowl query of listing 9.6.

They'll be composed of a `function_score` query in which the query clause matches and scores documents based on content and the function takes care of additional boosting logic. But even if you have more exotic queries, it's important to understand their structure in the same way that you now understand the Yowl query. Be able to write out an equation that explains how the high-level signals are combined to create the overall score. Consider extreme cases to guard users from poor behavior caused by unimportant signals overpowering the more important signals.

TUNING AND TESTING THE OVERALL SEARCH

With a well-structured query in hand, you have one final task: tuning the weights so that content, user, and business signals are properly balanced. But as simple as this task may sound, it's often the most frustrating and time-consuming job in all of relevance work. In this section, we present an organized approach for tuning query parameters.

You'll start by focusing on content-based relevance and ignoring other concerns such as user preferences or business requirements. After you've optimized content-based search, you layer in user preference. Finally, after the user experience has reached its peak performance, you introduce the business requirements into the query. As a result of this progression, you arrive at a search experience that prioritizes the user without neglecting the practical needs of the business. Again, you'll use the Yowl query, but the principles presented here can be applied to your own search projects.

Before you start tuning query parameters, you need to index a realistic set of documents to test against—and the larger the data set, the better. Ideally, you can take a snapshot of the production index and use that when tuning your query parameters. You'll also need a representative set of search requests. For an existing application, you can scan search logs to get an idea of typical requests.

Here you're building out Yowl search for the first time, so you'll have to be creative and infer the types of questions that users will ask. The important part is to have a small set of sample requests that exercise every typical use case. Because you've already created user personas, it might be a good idea to refer to their questions and make sure that you're at least covering all the use cases that you anticipate seeing.

The first thing to tune is the content subsearch. Remember this guy?

```
{ "query": {
    "multi_match": {
        "query": <user query>,
        "fields": [
            "name^10",
            "cuisine_hifi^10",
            "cuisine_lofi^4",
            "menu^2",
            "description^1"],
        "tie_breaker": 0.3}}}
```

Here you have six parameters to tune, one for each content field and one for the `tie_breaker` parameter. You tune these parameters by running through the exemplary search requests, looking through the results from each request, and modifying parameters to correct any problems you run into. As we've mentioned before, this is typically a subjective process. In the next section, we introduce *test-driven relevance*, which can make this process more organized and objective than the typical approach of "just trying a lot of queries and seeing how they look."

While tuning text queries like this, you'll inevitably run across results that are hard to explain. When this happens, remember to lean heavily on Elasticsearch's built-in query explain feature (activated by placing 'explain': true in the query). As discussed in chapter 3, the explain details are a little difficult to read at first but they're useful for understanding why documents match a particular query and how they're scored.

When you're happy with the content subquery, zoom back out to the full Yowl query presented in listing 9.6. (Naturally, you'll update the parameters of the content subquery to match the values you just arrived at.) From here on out, all you have to do is find appropriate values for the three weights: the content weight w_C, the location weight w_L, and the business weight w_B. Let's begin by setting w_C to 1.0 and w_L and w_B to 0.0. This serves as a baseline in which documents are scored solely on their content, and neither location nor business concerns affect the overall score. (Referring to the equation in listing 9.7, can you see why this is true?)

Because you're dealing with the overall query, you again have access to location, price, and rating filters. As a next step, you'll make this example search more realistic by including a location filter representative of your typical search requests. Immediately you'll see a drop in content-based relevance. Can you think of why this would be? The drop in relevance is caused by a decreased number of available documents. When you were looking at the entire index, there were plenty of restaurants to match. But as you narrow the focus to a particular locale, there might not be as many relevant results for a given query. Don't fret. You at least know that you're getting more realistic with your search. If the results are terrible at this point, no amount of query tuning will help; you simply need more restaurants in the index—and that's a business problem!

Next let's layer in the location. To do this, you gradually increase the location weight w_L while keeping an eye on the quality of the search results. At 0.0, the location query has no impact on search results. As you increase the value w_L, you observe the documents rearrange so that nearby restaurants are preferred above distant ones. And if you increase w_L too much, you'll begin to see less-relevant results pulling toward the top.

After you find an appropriate value for w_L, the content and location signals will be in balance. At this point, you've built as close to optimal search app for your users. Unfortunately, you're not yet meeting any of your own business needs! Therefore, it's time to layer in the business signal. The direct approach would be to slowly increase the business weight w_B from 0.0 until you start to see relevance drop. But you've just increased the location weight so high that any further influence from the business signal will likely cause the relevance to drop off quickly.

You need a different approach, one that treats the location signal and the business signal symmetrically. To achieve this effect, you start by temporarily turning off the location signal by setting w_L to 0.0. And then, using the same technique as before, you increase w_B until just before relevance starts to be noticeably affected. After finding an appropriate value for w_B, you restore the location weight w_L to the previously determined value. Because you've handled the location signal and the business signal symmetrically, they should now be reasonably well balanced with one another. But with influence now coming from both business *and* location, it's likely that the content signal is being overpowered. Fortunately, this isn't a problem, though you have one more knob to turn. By gradually increasing the content weight w_C until relevance is restored, you can reach an optimal balance between content, location, and business concerns.

Unfortunately, in real search applications, parameter tuning can get a lot messier than this idealized example. But it's important to at least aim for these ideals in order to avoid unnecessary complexity (for instance, attempting to tune all fields independently). Also, even when tuning gets messy, the preceding thought process still applies: you have to understand how signals interact so that you change the parameters appropriately.

YEAH … BUT HOW DO YOU TUNE RELEVANCE PARAMETERS?

You've probably noticed that in all of these steps you're doing a lot of fiddling around with parameter values. And at each step, we talk about making sure the search results "look good" before moving on to the next step. But we haven't talked about *how* to make sure your parameters are moving in the right direction.

For starters, our optimality criterion, "looks good," is vaguely defined. In order for the search results to be optimal, you have to understand what your users think is relevant. But this is difficult. One user searching for "taco" is looking for a restaurant that has *taco* in the title (perhaps the user forgot the name), whereas another user searching for "taco" seeks restaurants that serve tacos. Therefore, our notion of optimal relevance must be aware of the differing information needs of our users. Furthermore, "taco" is just one query; you have to make sure that relevance is maintained across any queries that users might make. If every user searched for "taco," you could simply tune the parameters until the *taco* search looked perfect. Instead, there are 100,000 other searches that need to look good too; and concentrating too heavily on any one of them will certainly be detrimental to the others.

So what should you do to nudge those parameters in the right direction? First you need a good set of typical queries to work with. This set should include popular queries, it should include queries from every imaginable use case, and it should even include some random queries—ideally, things you've plucked from a query log file.

Now, given a typical set of queries, you need to understand what "looks good" means for each of these queries. This can be as vague as "I know it when I see it," but ideally it should be more concretely defined. At an extreme, the field of information retrieval uses so-called *relevance judgments* to define "looks good." Here, given a fixed set of queries and a fixed set of documents, each query-document pair is graded on a 1-to-5 scale according to how well the document matches the corresponding query. Collectively, these graded query-document pairs are called the *judgments*.

When you have a set of queries and a reasonably good understanding of what "good" looks like, you're finally ready to start tuning the parameters. This process involves issuing *several* queries, looking through the results of *each* query simultaneously, and then identifying and diagnosing relevance issues as they arise. If you have a good understanding of how the query works, you should also have a good idea of how to modify search parameters. In the preceding Yowl example, if the first page of search results contains only nearby restaurants that are weak matches for the query, then the location signal should be given less weight.

Needless to say, gathering judgments is a labor-intensive process. If you find yourself revisiting relevance settings often, it may be worth spending time to automate this process. You could build a relatively simple application that allows a content curator to issue queries, view results, and mark results as either appropriate or inappropriate for the given search. When enough queries and documents have been annotated (when you have enough relevance judgments), you can automate relevance testing so that each time you modify search parameters, all test queries will be reissued and the new settings will be scored based on how good the results are across *all* test queries.

We call this automated approach *test-driven relevance*. With test-driven relevance, you no longer have to issue searches by hand, and more important, you no longer have to mentally keep track of the search behavior across all searches. Tools like Quepid (http://quepid.com) help simplify the process.

Ultimately, the ideal solution for tuning parameters is to push automation one step further. Many techniques automatically gather relevance judgments given sufficient user traffic. Armed with these judgments, a program can automatically adjust query parameters on your behalf. In the field of information retrieval, this highest level of automation is known as *learning to rank*. Learning to rank turns out to be a tricky problem to solve, but it has become a focus in information retrieval. So be on the lookout for improvements and breakthroughs in the near future.

We'll have more to say on learning to rank and test-driven relevance in the next chapter.

9.4   *Deploying, monitoring, and improving*

At long last, with your query parameters finely tuned, you're ready to go live with the Yowl restaurant search application! You've gone through a lot to get to this point in terms of planning, designing, and implementing the search application. You can breathe a sigh of relief as some of the hardest work is behind you. But, in many ways, deploying the search application means that you're just at the beginning of your *real* work. Now you enter into a cycle of monitoring, updating, and iteratively improving your search application, as shown in figure 9.9.

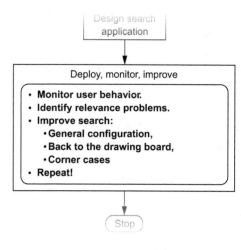

Figure 9.9　Deploying the search application is the start of a cycle of monitoring and iteratively improving search.

9.4.1　*Monitor*

In designing a search application, many of the choices are subjective—from the look-and-feel of the UI to the parameter values for your query, you rely on intuition to guide your decisions. But as soon as the application is launched, you have access to a new stream of information that reflects the quality of your search application. What's this new stream of information? User behavior.

If a user understands, enjoys, and gains value from Yowl, the behavior of your users will reflect this. And if users encounter problems with the application, you can analyze user behavior in order to track down and correct these problems. Similarly, if you make a change that introduces a new problem, you should be able to see a corresponding shift in user behavior. Therefore, from the moment the application is deployed, it's important to gather information from your users. There are many potential sources of behavioral information, but here we list just a few to get you thinking about the possibilities:

- *Time on page*—If users glance at search results and quickly leave, they aren't finding what they're looking for. Conversely, your relevance feedback may be so good users find answers instantly and leave.
- *Click-through rate*—You can tell that a user has found something interesting when they click through to find more details.
- *Conversion rate*—If a user buys a product (or in the case of Yowl, grabs a restaurant discount), search is working. This is *the bottom line.*
- *Retention*—If users come back to the app regularly, they find it useful.
- *Deep paging*—If users regularly need to go to the second or third page of search results, this may be a symptom of a relevance problem. Why aren't the results on page 1?
- *Pogo-sticking*—Users click a result but then quickly find out it's not what they want and return to the results listing. This reveals a problem with relevance

feedback. Ideally, the user should get a good sense of whether the document is worth looking at *before* clicking through to the details page.

- *Thrashing or reformatting*—Users change their search several times in a row because they're finding nothing that meets their information needs. This may indicate users have a complex information need and your relevance feedback is pointing them in the correct direction.

Whatever metrics you choose to track, the absolute value is often less important than the change in value over time. For instance, deep paging on an e-commerce site may indicate that a user isn't finding the item needed; but for legal or patent search, deep paging might indicate that the user has uncovered a rich vein of useful documents. Because we're often looking for telltale *changes* in behavior, it's important to gather and track baseline values for user-behavior metrics. Then, if you notice any sudden changes or degradations, you can investigate the problem further.

Search logs are another great source of information worth keeping an eye on. By reviewing the searches that your users are making, you can start to build a clearer understanding of users and how they're using your application.

9.4.2   *Identify problems and fix them!*

When tracking search history and user behavior, it's easier to spot search problems as they creep up. The easiest problem to spot is the zero-results search. You can almost always do better than "sorry—got nothin' for ya." And finding zero-results searches is as simple as grepping through the appropriate search log.

More generally, when you see an unexpected degradation in metrics, try to find the underlying pattern. Usually the search problems that arise from well-tuned search applications represent some sort of relevance corner-case. Can you find a pattern in the user strategies? Maybe Yowl users searching by cuisine find their restaurant, but users searching for a specific dish tend to get lost.

Maybe the underlying problem has to do with a particular topic or set of query keywords that are performing poorly. For instance, as users begin using Yowl, you notice that those seeking French cuisine appear to have a particularly bad experience. Among users who search for "French food," "French cooking," and the like, you see a good deal of thrashing, low click-through rate, and poor retention. By looking through the search log and trying some of the problem queries yourself, the reason for the bad user experience becomes clear: every result for a query containing the keyword french returns nothing but fast-food restaurants! You dig into the ranking with explain set to true and soon realize that *French fries* are the source of the troubles. Having isolated the root cause of the relevance problem, you can make the appropriate corrections.

As you isolate relevance problems, you may be required to fix them at any level of the search application. Here are some examples from each layer:

- *Configuration*—Indexes are typically sharded across several servers, so that each server holds just a portion of the documents. Because the number of documents will be different for each shard, relevance can sometimes be negatively impacted. A change to the index configurations can address this.

- *Text analysis*—In the preceding example with french fries, you might need to add an entry in the synonyms file to ensure that french fries aren't conflated with French cuisine. Another common fix is to add certain terms to a *protected words* file so that they don't get inappropriately stemmed.

- *Signal modeling*—Certain signals may be unnecessary or detrimental to search relevance. For instance, as you watch Yowl users, you might find that the description field is too noisy to be useful. After testing in production, you may choose to reduce the description field boost or to remove the field altogether. Alternatively, important signals are sometimes missing and need to be incorporated into search.

- *Query*—As the needs of users and the business change, you'll need to add or remove pieces of the query in order to affect the desired change. If Yowl decides to have tiered services, you may offer an extra boost to your premier members. This will involve dropping in a new function_score function and rebalancing the query.

- *Relevance feedback in the UI*—You need to watch your users interact with your application and make sure that they understand what they're seeing. They should be able to easily find what they seek and understand the results that they're provided. If they don't, you should address this by improving the relevance feedback that you provide. For instance, Yowl might provide users with keyword autocompletion in order to guide them toward fruitful searches.

Whenever you successfully address one tough relevance issue, be aware that many more are waiting to be found. Search application maintenance is a process of continual vigilance. Besides the problems yet to be discovered, each new document in the corpus, each new query, and each new business need holds the potential for introducing new relevance problems. But don't fret! A principled approach of monitoring behavior metrics, finding and fixing problems, and testing solutions will keep your search application on track and your users satisfied.

9.5 *Knowing when good is good enough*

Almost as important as building a great search app is to know *when to stop building* (see figure 9.10)! When building a search application, you're effectively building up a model for natural language. But natural languages are dirty, dirty things. English, for example, is full of words that can be used in different settings to mean different things. Some

Figure 9.10 It's important to build a highly relevant search application, but it's also important to know when to stop.

words in English even serve as *their own* antonyms! For example, consider *cleave*, which means *to split apart* and also means *to adhere to strongly.* See! English is dirty!

Therefore, be aware of this stark truth:

> When building and refining a search application, you'll eventually be met
> by the law of diminishing returns.

In developing the basic Yowl search, you were probably 50% of the way toward "perfect" search when you turned on the search engine and dumped in the restaurant data. By more carefully considering the characteristics of individual fields, and by building and tuning your queries, you jumped to 85%. After deploying search and identifying and resolving the obvious relevance issues, you moved to 93%. Anything beyond this takes considerable work and provides only incremental benefit. And furthermore, the more "perfectly" you configure search at any point in time, then implicitly the more brittle and resistant to change search becomes. You'll eventually arrive at a point where you're effectively overfitting the search application according to the narrow understanding that you have at a particular point in time. Any new documents or business requirements that contradict this understanding will cause new relevance problems to pop up.

Prevent overfitting your search by stepping back and asking yourself, "Is it worth it?" If you can make a change guaranteed to fix an important corner case, go for it. But if your search is already good and you wish to eke out just a little more performance, be cautious—you might be inadvertently making search brittle and resistant to change.

9.6   *Summary*

- Typical steps when developing a search application include modeling your users with personas, identifying users' typical needs, and designing an application that will meet those needs.
- Integrating new sources of information supports user and business relevance requirements.
- Transforming and cleaning data sources through transformation and analysis allow you to implement low-level user and business matching rules.
- Low-level signals can be grouped into higher-level signals that balance and combine different user and business ranking concerns.
- A search application, once deployed, should be monitored based on user interactions to identify new problems and unexpected use cases.
- Remember the nature of diminishing returns when resolving relevance corner cases. This should help guard against overfitting search according to the narrow understanding of requirements at a given point in time.

The relevance-centered enterprise

10

Our conversation up to this point has been about *how* to implement the technical requirements of search relevance. We've yet to discuss the fundamental *why* behind implementing these requirements. If you're a software developer, you know it's easy to toil for months on end on a feature or product. Only finally when you release it do you discover that the market has little interest in your work. Your careful craftsmanship is squandered as users' feedback renders a harsh verdict on what you've delivered.

257

Search relevance is no different. You might waste months of skilled work, carefully implementing supposedly correct ranking requirements. Only upon release do you realize that users aren't using search as you expect. Perhaps shoppers on e-commerce sites expect to search within product reviews, yet you've implemented only regular product search. Or perhaps a hospital system's search returns pages about diseases when users expect to find doctors who treat those diseases. Despite all our hard work, users surprise us all the time with what they expect from search, not neatly fitting into how we'd like them to behave.

Building a robust, cross-functional culture to discover what users want out of search is the central focus of this chapter. How do you build a business culture with accurate and fast feedback systems to correct your search application's requirements? How can your work be continuously informed or corrected to line up with users' expectations?

Much like chess, relevance is easy to get into—delivering a basic untuned solution is often simple. But discovering subtle user expectations accurately, and quickly responding to them with technical finesse, turns relevance into a frenetic game of speed chess. Luckily, unlike speed chess, relevance is a team sport. Skilled, key positions throughout the enterprise can help you understand what the user needs and respond appropriately. Figure 10.1 details a cast of characters: the roles (relevance engineer, content curator, boss, domain expert) and solutions (analytics, tests) that can deliver feedback to relevance work.

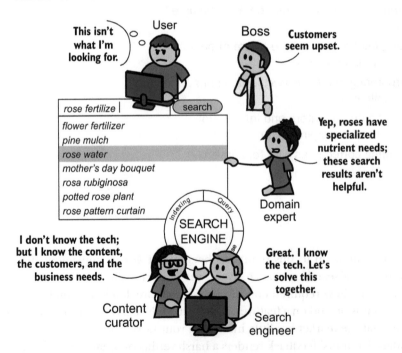

Figure 10.1 Forms of feedback to the relevance engineer, starting from most removed from the problem (the user, boss/manager types realizing search is bad) to those involved constantly (the content curator role and relevance testing)

10.1 Feedback: the bedrock of the relevance-centered enterprise

To figure out what users want out of search, you need to admit something that might feel uncomfortable. Despite holding the title *relevance* engineer, you likely don't know what users deem relevant. You probably have no idea how an eight-year-old will approach a searchable, kid-friendly database of dinosaurs. You almost certainly don't know how a doctor might use a medical search application to diagnose a patient. Or how mechanics might search for car parts. The reasons that users search are endless. Your capacity to understand users and their domain is limited. You operate in the dark, and failing to appreciate this might be your undoing.

Not knowing what users deem relevant is made worse by the inviting nature of search to tweak and prod. Most development work falls in the category of small alterations such as boosting, changing the types of queries, or modifying analyzer settings. Because these little changes alter everything about your search ranking, they have extremely broad ramifications. In your ignorance of your users' relevance needs, you can easily throw search completely out of whack. You might guess right and do something great! Or you might ruin existing, working use cases with the simplest of changes. It's like you're flying a giant Boeing 787 jet in the dark with a giant dashboard of easy-to-flip switches in front of you. Flipping one switch might help you, but when flying without feedback, you're just as likely to fly into turbulence or worse!

To account for your lack of understanding of what *relevant* means, we advocate strongly for a certain style of work. The best way to improve relevance is to deliver a solution, observe how it fails to some degree, and adjust accordingly. We refer to this style of work as *iterative* and *fail fast*. It's iterative in the sense that it focuses on delivering a real, interactive search solution quickly for evaluation. It's fail fast because it anticipates immediate, small failures as the best mechanism to adjust course and avoid more-catastrophic failures. Figure 10.2 illustrates the ideal iterative cycle: bite-sized

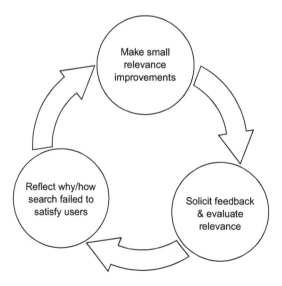

Figure 10.2 Ideal search relevance iteration: trying simple adjustments, soliciting feedback, and failing fast in order to continuously improve

changes are delivered for evaluation, feedback is observed, and the course is adjusted over and over.

Feedback is the most important ingredient. Obtaining and understanding search feedback needs to be your obsession. It ought to become your whole team's obsession. This chapter advocates a *user-focused culture*—one that bends over backward to bring relevance engineers accurate and precise user feedback to guide their work.

A user-focused culture recognizes several sources of feedback. First, it recognizes that domain experts in your organization can help you correct the direction of relevance work. Yet corrective feedback goes beyond these experts and becomes a full-time job for relevance engineers. You'll see that one role, which we call the *content curator*, becomes the high priest of search feedback. The content curator takes command, examining user behavioral data and the broader business, to understand search correctness. Ultimately, you'll see how you can speed up feedback in the form of test-driven relevancy. As discussed in the previous chapter, this form of feedback continuously evaluates search changes, highlighting where search is taking a slide for the worse.

Figure 10.3 outlines these increasingly more potent forms of user-focused culture. You'll move through this progression through the remainder of this chapter. Each loop in this diagram is a feedback loop—a style of iterative feedback associated with increasingly user-focused organizations. The organization starts on the outermost feedback loop: complete ignorance of the users' search needs. We discuss this phenomenon in section 10.2. From there, you move inward, evolving to correct the course of relevance development. As you move to more-evolved forms of user-focused culture, feedback arrives to the relevance engineer faster and more accurately.

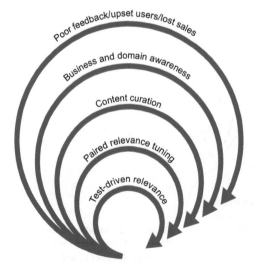

Figure 10.3   Various key feedback loops enable the relevance engineer to refine search relevance.

10.2   Why user-focused culture before data-driven culture?

Before working through the relevance feedback loops, let's discuss one common misperception you might have at this point. As an engineer, you might be thinking, given the problem of gathering relevance feedback, why not simply gather tons of data on what users think of search and just work with that?

In today's world of high-end user analytics and machine learning, it's tempting to sidestep cultural issues. Many discuss building a data-driven culture that bases user-experience decisions solely on user behavioral data. As you may recall, we discussed many such metrics ourselves. In the previous chapter, we introduced click tracking, deep paging, thrashing, and others. With search metrics like these, why bother consulting marketing, domain experts, and others in the organization? You can discern search relevance correctness directly from the data—right?

We believe user-focused culture must come *before* data-driven culture. For search, good user data is often unavailable or hard to interpret. When data is available, it often takes more than a relevance engineer to derive insight about whether a user is satisfied. Making scientifically valid claims from data, frankly, is hard. Making scientifically valid claims about how users think and feel can be doubly so. Let's consider this difficulty, because it speaks directly to why we place cultural issues so highly.

First, why would data be unavailable or not useful for search feedback? For most applications, the majority of individual search queries are special snowflakes. They're too rare to derive meaningful insights. Let's think about why this is. Consider the distribution of all user searches in your application. You probably have a handful of extremely common searches and an extremely large set of rare, special snowflake searches.

Let's think through an example for a garden supply e-commerce search application. The most common searches are for things such as hoses, flowers, and pots. These occur many times each minute. But after this handful of common searches, other searches become increasingly obscure. For instance, a search for "Rosa rubiginosa" (the scientific name for a type of rose) might occur twice a year. It's possible that these rare searches compose the bulk of the search traffic; each search item is rare, but there are just so darned many rare searches!

This search phenomenon has come to be called *long-tailed search.* As shown in figure 10.4, *long-tail* refers to the shape of the distribution of possible search items.

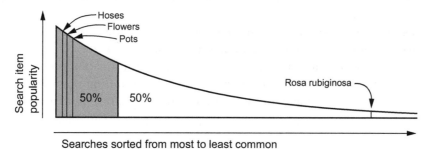

Figure 10.4   **For long-tailed search, a majority of traffic is associated with rare search items.**

Notice that a relatively small set of items (on the left side) compose 50% of the search traffic in this example. The remaining 50% of search traffic is attributed to a vastly larger number of relatively rare searches (on the right side). These searches form the long tail of search.

Search's long tail can make purely data-driven relevance feedback challenging. If your application has a long tail, you may need to rely on more indirect qualitative measures for relevance feedback. In our gardening example, user data for popular searches such as "Hoses," "Flowers," and "Pots" could be useful. But for most other searches ("Rosa rubiginosa", "Rosa rubiginosa Fertilizer"), user data may be a vague rubric. The long-tail data might tell you what use cases are important to users (such as searching on scientific names), but not much else.

The second problem you'll encounter is deriving information about user satisfaction from behavior data. How will you interpret when users are dissatisfied, for instance? You might assume that visiting page 2 (and beyond) of the search results is clearly a negative behavior. But your user population may want to exhaustively research all available results. It's common in patent or legal search to leave no stone unturned as every match is carefully examined.

The same problem exists when trying to identify results that users perceive as relevant. Users might appear to be satisfied by a search result because they purchased the found product or read through an article. But this conclusion is far from straightforward. Users may decide to purchase at a mediocre, barely relevant result if more-promising results never come to the top. If your users search for "Rosa rubiginosa", and you show them only daisies, the fact that they sometimes purchase daisies doesn't mean a certain kind of daisy is the most relevant result. Less absurdly, they may purchase a mediocre sweet briar rose product and decide that's all your gardening shop has to offer. Meanwhile, a stellar product is buried deep in the data and would result in more purchases if only it surfaced.

The point is, even with a pile of user behavioral data, the relevance engineer remains ill prepared to read the tea leaves. Search quality feedback isn't simply a matter of digesting use data. You need to understand user context, domain expertise, and business requirements to assess a random user's satisfaction with search through data. Just as with relevance, you don't hold the answers here. Your colleagues who better understand the domain, business, and users must help you interpret your application's usage data.

Good feedback goes beyond data. It's based on a broader, collaborative organization that can interpret both search correctness and user behavioral data together. Only then can data be a factor in providing you good information on how users perceive search. Instead of a data-driven culture being the starting point, it's in fact the most mature form of a collaborative, user-focused culture. By building a user-focused culture, you'll end up at a place where data plays its appropriate role.

10.3　*Flying relevance-blind*

You often start with a more mundane problem: your organization isn't aware of search relevance. Stakeholders don't see relevance as foundational to their success. Instead of iterations that fail fast, the only iteration you undergo is the painful process of developing a complete search solution, shipping it to users, and then painfully learning upon delivery how disappointed they are.

Unfortunately, many of your colleagues may assume that the search engine has some kind of built-in Google-like intelligence. They may think the search engine knows best, and isn't meant to be questioned, configured, or programmed. For many, the idea that users have specific relevance expectations unique to your application is a truly novel concept.

Lacking awareness of relevance, in what we call the *relevance-blind enterprise*, can be a dangerous place for your organization to be. Being here exposes you to the most extreme, outer feedback loop: sales losses and customer complaints, as shown in figure 10.5. In this phase, users stop performing desirable actions as a result of their searches (they stop purchasing things, for example). It's not uncommon in this state, shortly after releasing or updating the product, for the organization to come upon a sudden and unpleasant awareness of the importance of search relevance. Unfortunately, this awareness comes only after a sudden downturn in user engagement and product sales.

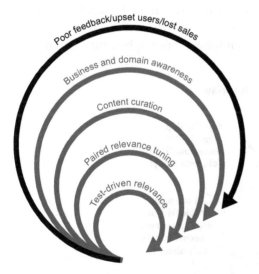

Figure 10.5　The organization lacks awareness of relevance as an issue. Your team may perceive poor search only through the outermost feedback loop: lost sales and disappointed customers.

How do you know your organization is in such a state? Generally, these relevance-blind organizations share several characteristics. The predominant pattern you'll notice is that search work involves no relevance work. Instead, the focus is on features, performance, and scaling. Instead of a *relevance engineer,* you may be seen as a back-end *search engineer* with no official relevance-tuning role. This is problematic when search is a core component of the user experience. Instead of helping create the user experience, you're seen as another back-end developer divorced from users and their concerns. Additionally, the organization may, to its peril, consciously keep you *away* from conversations that discuss user goals. Instead, they hope you'll make the search 10 milliseconds faster or figure out how to integrate another set of documents.

It's easy to see how this happens. Search engines appear to many as another datastore. Working with search engines shares many characteristics of working with something like a database: both must consistently store and retrieve data. They must remain available and high-performing, storing the data needed for our applications. Starting out, many may not want to question or think too hard about that weird, seemingly mystical ranking component inside the search engine. It doesn't fit how we think about other applications, and many would prefer to think of it in terms of the databases they're already familiar with.

Because of this ignorance, relevance ranking becomes a blind spot when working on the application. If you take a screenshot of a typical search application, you'll find search results presented smack-dab in the middle of the page. But in a relevance-blind organization, as shown in figure 10.6, the front-end developers and designers fine-tune components of the search application other than search relevance ranking. Most features and bugs revolve around items in the application typical of most development: logging in/out, look-and-feel, and other custom features. When focused on search, your team would rather improve easier-to-understand components of the application: faceting, filtering, and other browse capabilities. Or perhaps improve the presentation of the search results themselves—but not how they're ranked.

Search in a relevance-blind enterprise

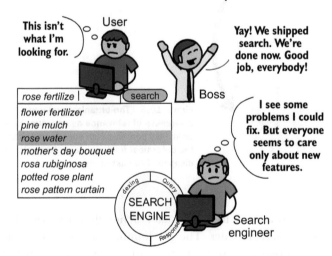

Figure 10.6   In a relevance-blind organization, nobody seems to see that searches return poor results. Instead the team is busy on other, more comfortable tasks.

These organizations often have a rude awakening when the app is released. Users type in their first searches and have a hard time finding what they want. In our consulting work, we've witnessed the aftermath of the relevance-blind enterprise over and over. The result is never pretty. Customers are disappointed, and users flock to competitors. Despite the hard work of application developers and designers, the overriding message that "search stinks" comes straight from users.

At this point, with the organization backed into a corner, the team turns to you, the search engineer, wondering what to do. Suddenly you aren't simply a back-end developer. You must take a central role in crafting the user experience! The problem we discussed earlier, enabling relevance engineers to get more-immediate feedback for their work, becomes crucial to the success of the application. Now begins your hunt for ways to fail fast. You'll need to identify ways to get accurate feedback on relevance before your organization suffers another embarrassing blunder.

10.4   Relevance feedback awakenings: domain experts and expert users

Being suddenly tasked with determining what users want out of search ranking can be daunting. As a relevance engineer, you won't be intimately familiar with what every group of users expects. New to relevance work, you might feel more comfortable in the realm of databases and code than user-experience concerns. Making matters worse, the users may be from a specialized domain, such as medicine or law. Searches like "Myocardial Infarction" might make little sense to you. Finally, it may turn out that the business itself has its own ranking expectations, hoping to steer users one way or another through search—perhaps toward more-profitable products or more-informative web pages. You need to seek feedback from the broader organization to adjust course.

To discover what *relevant* means for this application, you must become a champion for the cause. You'll need to get organizational buy-in to create the first relevance feedback loop. And you'll quickly realize that the information you need is scattered throughout the enterprise. Depending on the kind of organization, the definition of "what users want" may be spread among marketing, sales, QA, legal or medical analysts, management, and any number of groups. You must become a cross-functional champion of collaboration. Instead of gleefully hacking away on fun code, you must become a highly social mover. To figure out what the user expects from the search experience, you must break down organizational barriers and find the answers you seek.

What you're doing is constructing the next feedback loop, as highlighted in figure 10.7. This feedback loop is the organization's first attempt to validate relevance and adjust course before bad effects are seen by users.

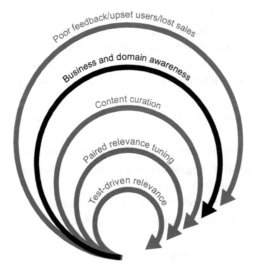

Figure 10.7   First feedback loop internal to the enterprise: relevance feedback is acquired ad hoc from QA, BA, and other specialized siloed teams.

Out of the various groups that study and engage users, you should first look to an expert user. An expert user was once a member of the user population and now works at the organization. If you're building search for a gardening site that caters to professional horticulturalists, then perhaps marketing, QA, or other groups in your organization staff horticulturalists. Expert users are a gold mine for search feedback. They can directly simulate the appropriate negative reaction that users will experience with irrelevant search. Yet unlike most users, they're deeply invested in your success. They're much more likely to give you detailed, constructive feedback. Figure 10.8 shows an expert user guiding a relevance engineer to better results.

Your organization might also perform usability testing. With *usability testing*, groups of target users are studied as they interact with the application. They may have their

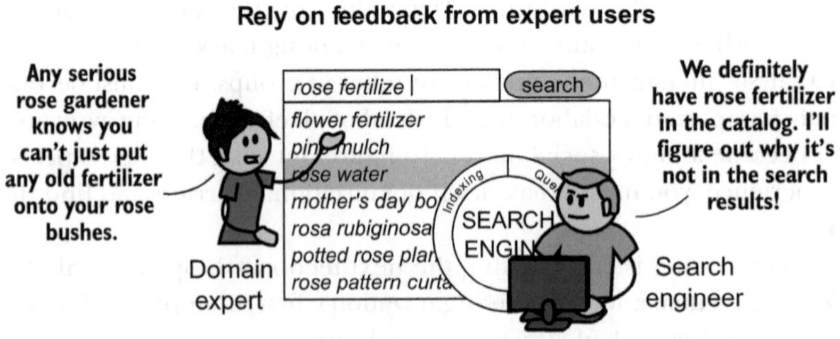

Rely on feedback from expert users

Figure 10.8   The relevance engineer receives feedback on the correctness of the relevance solution from domain experts.

behavior tracked to great depth—including eye tracking and expression monitoring. These users may also provide qualitative feedback about the application, answering questions about what they thought of it. You might be able to piggyback on such testing to get feedback about the application's search relevance. You may even be able to interact with such users, ascertaining what they found helpful with the relevance ranking and more important, what they didn't—getting the same rich feedback you obtained from the expert users.

Still, at this point, you're picking up relevance feedback through your own sleuthing work. None of these helpful but siloed groups have search as their central function. Other groups have other duties to attend to, and have only limited attention to give you. Thus your testing remains ad hoc, informal, and depends on the availability of members of other teams.

So even with persistence, this remains a low-information and slow feedback loop. The feedback given is sometimes deep and valuable and at other times limited. Although many problems are solved and avoided, others continue to get through. Still, the output of this phase can be crucial. By breaking out of the technical silo, you might be able to build powerful allies on other functional teams. Others begin to see the importance that search plays for users. Even with their spotty attention, you and your allies may begin to realize there's good reason for establishing a full-time role for managing the search quality.

10.5 *Relevance feedback maturing: content curation*

In the previous section, we discussed the relevance engineer as a champion for the cause of relevance feedback: taking down silos, wandering the halls, knocking on doors to identify how the organization defines relevance. This is a crude attempt to build an initial feedback loop to guide your work. Unfortunately, you can't sustain this level of feedback gathering and get your technical work done. Further, your colleagues don't always have time to give you sustained or high-quality search feedback.

More important, the answers you get from colleagues will grow increasingly inconsistent. More and more, finding the "right answer" will require reconciling multiple points of view on what search should do. The marketing department may push you to promote results based on advertisers and supplier relationships, while domain experts may advocate for the needs of high-end experts over lay users. Arriving at the "right answer" may depend on a subtle understanding of the domain, user expectations, office politics, and many other factors.

Instead of driving technical improvements, you may feel increasingly confused and bewildered. You're navigating an incoherent, alien world that requires many skills you may not have: an understanding of business needs, domain expertise, and user familiarity. Value may be gained initially as colleagues help point out what's obviously wrong with the search results, but making sense of how search ought to work beyond these obvious fixes becomes a job unto itself—a job that distracts you from the important technical work you're good at.

The organization solves this problem by adding a role responsible for search feedback: the *content curator* (as shown in figure 10.9).

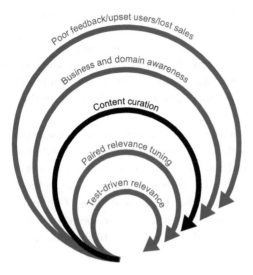

Figure 10.9   Content curation, the act of curating feedback from the broader enterprise for the relevance engineer

10.5.1   *The role of the content curator*

The content curator becomes responsible for accepting all forms of feedback, and determining the "right answer." The ideal content curator is someone with enough business/domain expertise, user familiarity, and seniority to own search correctness. Content curators think critically about how search ought to behave. They understand deeply how users will interact with the search application and translate that into actionable feedback for the relevance engineer to implement.

In this role, content curators work with the broader business. They also interpret whatever user behavioral data might be available. They understand what the business (not just users) need from search. They capture all of this feedback and expertise into an actionable set of feature enhancements and bugs. They reconcile multiple points of view with political finesse into a coherent road map for search relevance. In a sense, they act as *product owners* for search. In Agile terminology, a *product owner* represents the broader business and stakeholders to the team. They act as the engaged stakeholder, they know how search *should* work, and they provide the technical team—relevance engineer(s)—the broader direction on where search should go, as shown in figure 10.10.

Some content curators might also be somewhat technical, allowing a certain degree of relevance self-service. They may also help organize and manage information. These skills can add a ton of value to search. We discussed how to use synonyms

Bring content curators onto the team

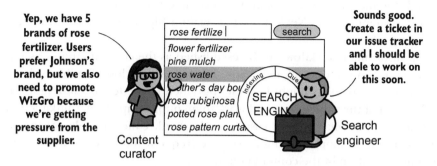

Figure 10.10   Content curator defines how search should behave based on feedback/consultation with the broader business and evaluation of user feedback.

and taxonomies in search in chapter 4. These tools can be used to dramatically improve the relevance of search results by relating different terms to each other. Because they have the right domain expertise, content curators can help manage these sorts of conceptual relationships.

A garden search engine that can understand that a "Reel Mower" is a kind of "Lawnmower" or that a "Lawnmower" is synonymous with a "Grass Cutter" can help a great deal in improving the relevance of search results. You don't likely have the right skills to relate these concepts in a taxonomy of lawn-care products. But a content curator may be able to catalog these relationships in a way that anticipates the jargon and terminology that your users might expect the search to understand.

Thus an ideal content curator also contributes to the relevance solution. This can go as far as letting the content curator control boosts and weights for various ranking factors. Recall in the previous chapter's Yowl example, you worked to balance the impact of content, restaurant location, price preference, and other factors. After the technical foundation is laid, who better to find the optimal balance between these factors than the content curator?

Adding a content curator to the team is a powerful multiplier for the effectiveness of your relevance efforts. Content curators allow the team to work toward their strengths instead of compensating for their weaknesses. They interface with the broader organization and listen carefully to user feedback. They're available to provide consistent, informed course correction on search, helping to paint a picture in broad strokes that you can color in with technical finesse. They let you focus on your technical skills instead of being mired in politics and interpreting deep domain requirements.

10.5.2 *The risk of miscommunication with the content curator*

Once a content curator is on the team, you may be tempted to permanently rejoin the other programmers in the server room. You may think you can get back to fun technical problems, and solve relevance problems as they arrive in the issue queue. Yet as you work, you'll quickly see that having a content curator on the team isn't a panacea. Instead, the most important communication line becomes the one between yourself and the content curator. Neglecting that relationship can create confusion and chaos for tuning efforts.

An unfortunate workflow can be established as the content curator assigns a new task to you: You rarely speak in person. Instead, a slow, lossy feedback channel over email and issue trackers might become ingrained in the team. You might take issues off the front of the work queue and work them until completion, thinking of the issue as relatively self-contained and easy to understand. Unfortunately, solving relevance issues is rarely so simple. Solutions require frequent follow-up communication, and ongoing evaluation by the content curator.

For example, if you're still in the business of building gardening search for horticulturalists, maybe you, as the relevance engineer, pick up a ticket that reads something like this:

> *Searches for plants by their scientific name (Rosa rubiginosa) should return the same search results as if the nonscientific name was searched for (sweet briar rose).*

Ah, simple enough! The content curator delivers term equivalences, and you add a few simple synonyms. After you declare the task done, in a few days you get another email from the content curator:

> *Hey relevance engineer,*
>
> *I'm seeing searches for "Rosa Rubiginosa" returning other rose species such as "Rosa Glauca," not just for a specific type of rose. Also, I sort of expected searches for generic "rosas" to show you a cross-section of different species, and instead they seem to be biased toward one species. Should "Rosa" also return the same results as "Rosas"? Is this possible? Let's discuss...*

There are important distinctions between these species of roses—and an avid gardener and a content curator will immediately pick up on this. Further, the content curator and the broader business have unspoken expectations. You may not understand these distinctions, how users will use these "Rose" scientific terms, or the underlying motivation in the use case. Even if they think you understand the issues, you continue to suffer from a limited ability to evaluate the correctness of the search solution in real time. You may think confidently, "I can do this!" yet learn there are more subtleties to horticulture than you appreciate!

10.6   *Relevance streamlined: engineer/curator pairing*

To appropriately tune search relevance, you need to have frequent, in-person conversations with the content curator to know how the search application is expected to behave. These communication lines need to run even deeper than the occasional chat. We advocate that you work side-by-side with the content curator when solving relevance problems.

You may have heard of *pair programming*, whereby two programmers work together to solve a programming problem. Here, the content curator and relevance engineer participate in *pair tuning*, working at the same desk to improve search relevance. This is our next level of feedback, as shown in figure 10.11.

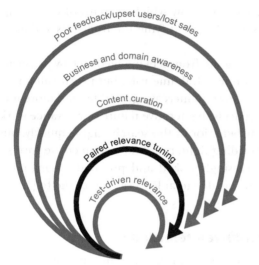

Figure 10.11 Next feedback loop: content curator and relevance engineer coworking

Through pair tuning, you both sit at the helm of the giant search-relevance jumbo jet! Your fine-tuning can be evaluated immediately by the content curator. Simple mistakes can be seen and fixed with simple course corrections, not after trying to exchange confusing and time-consuming emails that waste your time going far off course. Both sides begin to see tuning as a highly collaborative, iterative cycle requiring the careful application of two distinct forms of expertise. Figure 10.12 shows the content curator and relevance engineer working closely on relevance problems.

Pairing on relevance

Figure 10.12 The relevance engineer and content curator can quickly solve problems when they work side-by-side.

Most important, when pairing, the duo can discover what's possible instead of just working toward what's required. The content curator might express problems more deeply instead of simply assigning tasks. You may be able to think more carefully about the broader ecosystem of solutions in the search space that can solve broader classes of problems. The communication can also begin to move the other way: you can increasingly let the content curator know which search tasks are simple, and which are more involved projects, quickly identifying the trade-offs and easy wins in certain enhancements.

Looking at the big picture, you've gone from seeking feedback by pestering others for help to now advocating for not only a full-time role, but nearly full-time pairing. Our feedback loops are telescoping down to increasingly tighter and more immediate forms of feedback. This feedback reflects the iterative nature of relevance work. Often the relevance engineer can modify behavior of the search engine quickly, but failing fast and early is important. By providing tighter and more immediate forms of feedback, your work is becoming increasingly poked and prodded toward correctness. Now when flying that jumbo jet, you're able to at least see out of the fog and stay at a safe altitude.

10.7 Relevance accelerated: test-driven relevance

Pairing with the content curator solves important communication problems. Yet, quickly you realize that modifying relevance, even with the best intentions, tends to create new problems. Search tuning begins to feel like a game of Whac-a-Mole. You focus on a spate of problems. Solving those problems then causes existing, working searches to slide backward in quality. In our gardening example, for instance, you might thoroughly fix searches for scientific names ("Rosa rubiginosa"). Unfortunately, without knowing it, you might cause a popular search to return nonsensical results. A search for "Rose" might begin returning daisies! (A rose by any other name indeed!)

10.7.1 Understanding test-driven relevance

While tuning, you need efficient and real-time course correction for both you and your content curator copilot. What can you do to make feedback broad, instant, and quantitative?

The answer comes from the world of test-driven development in traditional software development. In these methodologies, you construct a set of automated unit tests that run your code. These tests evaluate the output of your code based on your understanding of application correctness. Failed tests then point you to broken functionality. With sufficient test coverage, you can implement new features and fix bugs, all while ensuring that old functionality continues to work.

Test-driven relevance, as shown in figure 10.13, solves the Whac-a-Mole problem by evaluating your search solution with automated tests as you tune. You still need the content curator and other colleagues to help define correctness. Ideally, these colleagues

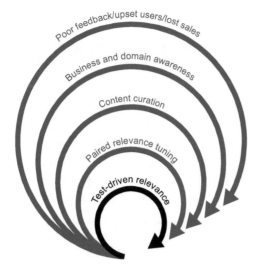

Figure 10.13 The most immediate form of relevance feedback: test-driven relevance

help you create the automated tests. These tests come in the form of important searches to programmatically run and evaluate for quality and correctness. This effectively puts the expert's brain in a box, letting you evaluate search against their expert feedback automatically.

With test-driven relevance, pair tuning takes on a new dimension. Instead of improving relevance followed by manual testing, you and the content curator become responsible for the maintenance of relevance testing. If a fix for "Rosa rubiginosa" breaks the "Rose" query, you'll see right away, and be able to make informed decisions based on the use cases that matter to your users and business.

What form do the relevance tests tend to take? For search relevance, testing tends to come in two forms:

- *Judgment lists*—For each search query, individual results are given a grade, or judgment. For example, a user search for "Rosa rubiginosa" might have `sweet briar rose` graded as an exact match. Other roses returned as matches might be graded as "OK" and all other results graded as "poor."
- *Assertion-based testing*—Instead of gathering explicit judgments, more ad hoc assertions are made in traditional unit tests. For example, assert that when a user searches for "Rosa rubiginosa," the first result is a sweet briar rose plant.

Figure 10.14 shows gathering relevance judgments using Quepid (disclosure: the Quepid application is developed by one of the authors). A content curator uses Quepid to grade a search result based on the relevance to a query. This results in an overall quality score for the query against the current search solution.

Maintaining these judgments, although ideal, comes with significant costs. As data changes, you must constantly make new judgments. The work becomes cumbersome.

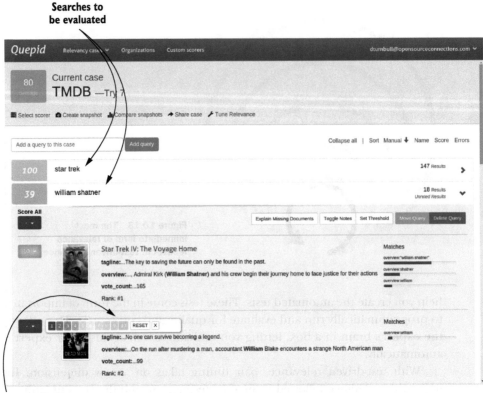

Searches to be evaluated

Content expert provides judgment of relevance of this result

Figure 10.14   Quepid (http://quepid.com), a test-driven relevance product for Solr and Elasticsearch, is seen here using judgments.

Moreover, it's not easily outsourced. Judgments require a basic level of domain expertise. Many organizations staff legions of relevance testers for the sole purpose of maintaining accurate relevance judgments.

In contrast to judgment lists, assertion-based tests allow more ad hoc and black-and-white testing. Traditional unit tests don't require the costly maintenance of accurate judgments. Rather, you simply specify correctness criteria. Many organizations get by on the simpler and easier-to-maintain unit tests. But simple tests can't as easily help you see fine gradations in relevance quality, query to query. There's no way to 75% pass a test, whereas with judgments you value knowing that a query is roughly 75% of the ideal. It could be that 75% is good enough!

From a political standpoint, tests have another important effect. They give content curators and other stakeholders a sense that they're also deeply involved in relevance efforts. By helping define tests, they gain a sense of control and investment in the relevance process. Further, as they ask for changes, they can instantly witness the impact of their requests. Instead of being an obscure, mystical component that only the relevance engineers understand, search tuning becomes increasingly transparent and collaborative. These stakeholders will feel increasingly empowered and informed to discuss the behavior of search and the associated trade-offs.

You can imagine being asked in a meeting to make a disruptive change to the relevance tuning. With a test-driven relevance tool, you could make the requested change and rerun the required tests right there in the meeting. This gives the team immediate insight into the impact of the changes without constant conversation, indecision, and chance for conflict. Thus despite seeming to be about moving away from collaboration, encoding wisdom in tests enables deeper and more thoughtful collaboration. Search stops feeling like guesswork throughout the organization because it's far easier to understand the consequences of decisions.

10.7.2 Using test-driven relevance with user behavioral data

The tests described in the previous section depend heavily on the expertise in your organization. The content curator must use the expertise of the broader organization to try to get inside the heads of users, and to then encode this information into the testing tool via judgment lists or tests. The content curator depends on these colleagues being correct, and not having their judgment clouded with misperceptions, ignorance, or selfish motivations.

Because your colleagues have their own misperceptions, consulting user behavioral data (for example, what users click or purchase) to derive judgment lists becomes increasingly attractive. In the previous chapter, we discussed particular user patterns in search that *might* indicate frustrated users: pogo sticking, thrashing, and so forth. Content curators may be able to work with these patterns to identify frustrated users. They may further be able to identify when users *converge*, or do something valuable (for the user or the business), such as purchase an item or subscribe to a newsletter. These bits of information can then be translated into relevance judgments, either manually or automatically.

This seems like an obvious path, but even with large amounts of data about how users work with your search app, challenges remain. Understanding how behavioral data translates to indications of search relevance or lack thereof continues to require expertise about your users. The same colleagues who contribute to judging what's relevant/not relevant often need to be brought in to determine what indicators are appropriate to determine when users are frustrated or satisfied.

So using behavioral data itself has its own catch-22. You need your human, imperfect colleagues to help get inside the heads of users through behavioral data. At the same time, you need the data to help realign your colleagues' understanding of what users expect from search.

There's no silver bullet! Data-driven feedback comes with plenty of human baggage. Even your well-meaning colleagues sometimes try to find data that fits their personal biases or beliefs. Deriving meaningful information from data means having a smart team willing to be humbled by what they find. You need colleagues who can leverage their expertise to interpret data while simultaneously allowing their expertise to be informed by surprising user antics.

With careful and hard work, you *can* use this data to inform search correctness, up to automating the collection of relevance judgments. Combining user data with your organization's user expertise is the gold standard of relevance feedback. Automated feedback from behavioral data must be constantly reevaluated by a cross-functional team. This lets the relevance engineer test with confidence with user data.

10.8   *Beyond test-driven relevance: learning to rank*

With the team working hard to derive information from data, additional automated practices to improve relevance become attractive. Advanced organizations can begin to use machine-learning techniques to predict when a search result will be relevant for a query. The practice of automating relevance is known as *learning to rank*.

With learning to rank, either human or automated relevance judgments are used to learn which of your content's features predict relevance globally. This cutting-edge field is increasingly finding its way out of the halls of information science research and into advanced search shops.[1]

In the feedback loops diagram, shown in figure 10.15, learning to rank becomes the red-hot center inside test-driven relevancy. It builds on every other external feedback loop: it depends on a user-focused organization that knows how to interpret user data to evaluate relevance. This is an important note, as learning to rank is a hot topic these days. It seems to many that you can sidestep the hard work of creating an organization that intimately knows its users. Unfortunately, there's no superhighway that sidesteps the work we discuss in this chapter. You still need an organization deeply focused on users' search needs: a team capable of finding markers in user behavioral data for relevance. Deriving real information from data—information relevant to *your* search user experience—remains a hard cultural and technical problem.

Finally, you need to combine all the insights from this chapter with cutting-edge information retrieval and machine learning. Often simpler relevance gains can be gathered with the straightforward techniques discussed earlier in this book. In our consulting work, we're often hired to implement an advanced solution when a far simpler adjustment can provide more immediate and less risky gains for an organization.

---

[1]   Solr readers may be interested in this patch, which proposes to add learning-to-rank features to Solr: https://issues.apache.org/jira/browse/SOLR-8542.

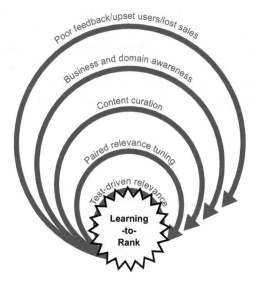

Figure 10.15 **Learning to rank is a cutting-edge method for relevance tuning that holds the promise of one day being able to automatically converge the ideal relevance parameters.**

You don't need data scientists to provide a simple tweak to an analyzer or query strategy that gains you a significant—and with test-driven relevancy—measurable improvement to search's bottom line.

Nevertheless, with the right expertise and data in place, learning to rank can be extremely powerful in helping push beyond the "diminishing returns" of relevance tuning. It iterates on search instantaneously based on user interactions that signal relevance or lack thereof. When you have the right pieces in place, you can begin to think about this exciting technique.

10.9 Summary

- Search relevance work is highly iterative, and works best when you seek feedback by failing fast.
- User behavioral data (such as clicks and purchases) isn't a panacea, and a user-focused culture should come before a data-driven culture.
- Relevance-blind organizations lack awareness of search relevance and are often surprised when poor relevance leads to lost sales and complaining users.
- The relevance engineer begins to correct relevance issues by seeking feedback from colleagues who understand the user in general: domain experts, QA, and sales.
- A content curator can help optimize search by bringing feedback to the relevance engineer. Ideally, the relevance engineer and content curator work together on relevance.

- Test-driven techniques can help automate relevance judgments, but these techniques still depend on content curators and other user-focused professionals.
- Incorporating search usage data requires careful interpretation, but this data can inform and correct the organization's understanding of how users use search.
- Learning-to-rank techniques automate parts of the feedback process, but continue to depend on maintaining and interpreting behavioral data.

Semantic and personalized search

11

This chapter covers

- Making search personalized for individual users
- Matching documents based on meaning rather than just words
- Implementing recommendation as a generalization of search

You're at the end of a long journey. You've learned to use search technology to build relevant search applications. But you're still just scratching the surface. In this final chapter, we look toward the horizon to explore some of the more novel—and experimental—ways to improve your users' search experience. In particular, we cover two related techniques that can provide better relevance:

- *Personalized search* provides search results customized to a user's particular tastes using knowledge about that user. User information can be gleaned from users' previous interactions as well as anything they tell us directly.
- *Concept search* ranks documents based on concepts extracted from text, not just words. Concept search relies on deep knowledge of the search domain, including jargon and the relations between concepts in that domain.

When used in tandem, the search solution understands users personal needs as well as the ideas latent in the content.

Building a good personalized search or concept search requires a considerable amount of work. You should treat the methods in this chapter as a conceptual starting point. But please realize that these methods bear some technical risks; they can be difficult to implement, and you often won't know how these methods will perform until after they've been implemented. Nevertheless, for established search applications, these methods are worth careful investigation because of the profound benefits that they may offer. In the discussion that follows, we present several ideas for implementing personalized and concept search. In both cases, we start with relatively simple methods and then outline more sophisticated approaches using machine learning.

In the process of laying out personalized search, we introduce *recommendations*. You can provide users with personalized content recommendations even before they've made a search. In addition, you'll see that a search engine can be a powerful platform for building a recommendation system. Figure 11.1 shows recommendations side-by-side with search, implemented by a relevance engineer.

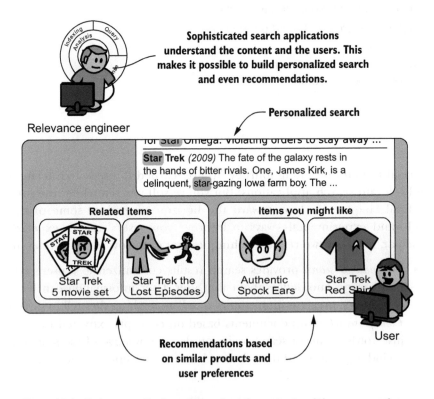

Figure 11.1   By incorporating knowledge about the content and the user, search can be extended to tasks such as personalized search and recommendations.

11.1 Personalizing search based on user profiles

Until now, we've defined *relevance* in terms of how well a search result matches a user's immediate information need. But over time, as you get to know users better, you should be able to incorporate their tastes and preferences into the search application itself. This is known as *personalized search.*

Throughout this book, we've emphasized that, at its core, a search engine is a sophisticated token-matching and document-ranking system. We discussed techniques to ensure that search matches and ranks documents to reflect your notion of relevance. As we move on to personalized search, the fundamental nature of a search engine doesn't change. No special magic or hidden feature makes personalization possible. Search is still about crafting useful signals, and modeling them with the search engine through queries and analysis. The main difference is that instead of drawing information exclusively from documents, you'll look to the users themselves as a new source of information.

With this in mind, we turn our attention to the first method of building personalized search: *profile-based personalization.* With this method, you track knowledge of individual users with *profiles.* At query time, you refer to the user profile and use its information to boost documents that correspond to the user's tastes. Figure 11.2 demonstrates profile-based personalization using our previous Star Trek examples.

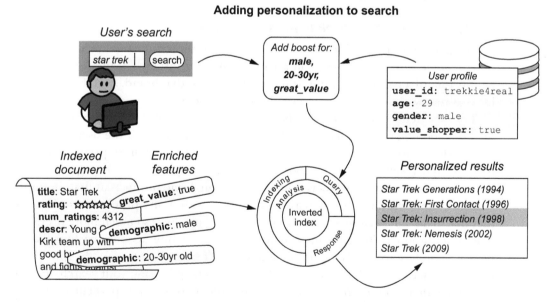

Figure 11.2 Adding personalization with user profile data, including demographics and preferences

11.1.1 *Gathering user profile information*

But how do you gather information for your user profiles? Well, if you're fortunate enough to have an engaged user base, you can create a profile page and wait for users to tell you about themselves. Be sure to provide incentives for users to fill out their profiles. For socially oriented sites, make the profiles public so your users can project their personality through the profile. Allow users to describe themselves in free text. Let them tag their profiles with categories that interest them. For private profiles, help users understand how creating a profile can provide a more personalized experience. For instance, you can directly ask users about their preferences and indicate that this will influence the behavior of the application. You can incentivize profile building with functionality; for example, by letting users bookmark items that they like, or share items with friends.

If you lack a profile page, you can still gather profile information from user interactions. By observing search behavior, underlying themes will reveal themselves over time. Perhaps a user has historically preferred certain brands. Maybe a user's choices indicate an interest in a particular domain such as photography or video games. By watching a user's interactions, you might identify demographics such as age, gender, and income level. The way that users filter searches often reveals *how* they make purchasing decisions. For instance, if users narrow search results by product reviews or price, you've learned something about that user's priorities. All of this information can be used to tune a user's search experience.

11.1.2 *Tying profile information back to the search index*

As you gather user profile information, consider how this can be used in a search solution. In some cases, the connection is easy to find. For instance, if the user shows an affinity toward a particular brand, you can subtly boost that brand. And if a user often looks at reviews, boost items with several positive reviews.

But be careful how you do this boosting, because you can create an unexpected feedback loop that can damage search relevance. For instance, if the user buys Acme Co. products more than once, you should probably boost Acme's presence in that user's search results. But if that boost is overwhelming, the search page might be flooded with only Acme products—and less relevant Acme products at that. In future searches, users will show an increased interaction with Acme products, not because they like them, but because your boost makes Acme products so much more prevalent than other products. To make the situation worse, these interactions may look like an increased preference for Acme products and drive further boosting. With Acme products everywhere, you might soon find that customers quit using your search application altogether. Therefore, it's best to alter the boosting for particular product categories only when you have definitive evidence of a preference for that category— such as a purchase rather than just a product page view.

Sometimes you'll need to add new signals to the index in order to match information from the user profile. If you know that a user prefers less expensive, "higher value" products, you can't simply boost all items below $20. A $20 blender is a great value, whereas a $20 can of beans is quite pricey. Instead, you should associate documents and users with some sort of general *value* rating scale ("cheap" to "boutique").

Demographic information such as age and gender can be another good set of information to pull into search. Let's say a profile indicates that the user is a young adult and male. If you know which products sell better in this demographic, give them a boost in the search results. To accomplish this, include a field in the indexed documents listing demographic groups with a high affinity to this item. The task of annotating this field with demographic information likely falls to the content curator. The information itself will probably come from marketing research.

With sufficiently heavy traffic, another source for demographic data is your search logs. Count the number of sales that occur within various demographics. The next time you reindex, add this information to the demographics field. Once this data is in the index, personalizing search is as easy as boosting using the current user's demographic data.

11.2 Personalizing search based on user behavior

In the previous section, we showed that you can learn about users by observing their behavior in the application. In this section, we take this notion to an extreme with *collaborative filtering*. This technique uses historical information about user-item interactions (views, ratings, purchases, and so forth) to find items that naturally clump together. For instance, collaborative filtering provides an algorithmic way to state that "users who purchase *Barbie dolls* will likely also be interested in *girls' dresses*." You can incorporate this information into search for an even more personalized search experience. We call this *behavior-based personalization*. In this section, you'll walk through a basic collaborative filtering example and see how to incorporate it into search.

11.2.1 Introducing collaborative filtering

For behavior-based personalization, you narrow your focus. Rather than considering user demographics, search histories, and profiles, you focus solely on user-item interactions. In this section, you'll look specifically at user-item purchases. In principle, interactions can be anything: item views, saves, ratings, shares, and so forth. Given the data set of user-item interactions, you'll use collaborative filtering to reveal hidden relationships among users and the items.

Collaborative filtering comes in many forms, from simple counting-based methods (which we introduce in a moment) to highly sophisticated matrix decomposition techniques (which are outside of the scope of this book). But no matter the technique, the input to collaborative filtering and the output from collaborative filtering follow the same pattern.

As shown in figure 11.3, the input is a matrix representing the users' interactions with items in the index. Each row corresponds to a user, and each column corresponds

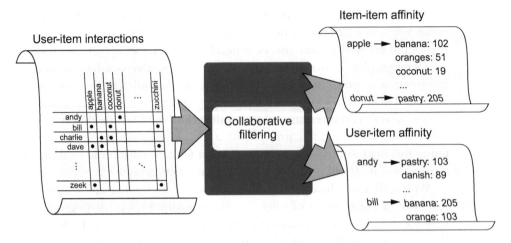

Figure 11.3   No matter the method used, collaborative filtering typically takes a user-to-item matrix and returns a model to quickly find user-to-item or item-to-item affinity.

to an item. The values in the matrix represent user interactions. For the simplest case, the values of the matrix represent whether an interaction has taken place. For instance, the user has viewed or purchased a particular item. In the more general case, the values of this matrix can represent how positive or negative the user-item interactions are. The values can represent a user's ratings of products purchased in the past, for example.

Collaborative filtering outputs a model that can find which items are most closely associated to a given user or item. So, given a source item such as apple, the collaborative filtering model might return a list of items, such as banana, orange, or grape, for which apple has a high affinity. Additionally, each item includes an affinity score. Consider the output banana:132, orange:32, grape:11. Here banana has a relatively high affinity for apple, grape a low affinity.

11.2.2 *Basic collaborative filtering using co-occurrence counting*

To better understand how collaborative filtering works, let's look at a simple example using a co-occurrence counting approach. The following algorithm is a bit naïve; we intend it to be introductory and don't recommend that you implement it in a production system. Nevertheless, it builds up a basic understanding of collaborative filtering, and it removes the feeling that collaborative filtering is somehow magic. As you'll see, many machine-learning algorithms are based on simple ideas, such as counting the number of times that items are purchased together.

Jumping into the example, let's say that you work for an e-commerce website and you have a log of all items purchased across all users. Table 11.1 shows a sample.

Table 11.1   Log tabulating users' purchases

Date	User	Item
2015-01-24 15:01:29	Allison	Tunisia Sadie dress
2015-01-26 05:13:58	Christina	Gordon Monk stiletto
2015-02-18 10:28:37	David	Ravelli aluminum tripod
2015-03-17 14:29:23	Frank	Nikon digital camera
2015-03-26 18:11:01	Christina	Georgette blouse
2015-04-06 21:50:18	David	Canon 24 mm lens
2015-04-15 10:21:44	Frank	Canon 24 mm lens
2015-04-15 21:53:25	Brenda	Tunisia Sadie dress
2015-07-26 08:08:25	Elise	Nikon digital camera
2015-08-25 20:29:44	Elise	Georgette blouse
2015-09-18 06:40:11	Allison	Georgette blouse
2015-10-15 17:29:32	Brenda	Gordon Monk stiletto
2015-12-15 18:51:19	David	Nikon digital camera
2015-12-20 22:07:16	Elise	Ravelli aluminum tripod

The first thing you must do is group all purchases according to user, as shown in table 11.2.

Table 11.2   The first step for determining item co-occurrence is grouping items by user. A dot (•) indicates a purchase.

	Tunisia Sadie dress	Gordon Monk stiletto	Georgette blouse	Nikon digital camera	Canon 24 mm lens	Ravelli aluminum tripod
Allison	•		•			
Brenda	•	•				
Christina		•	•			
David				•	•	•
Elise			•	•		•
Frank				•	•	

It's in this next step where all the "magic" happens. For any given item A, you count the number of times that the purchase of item A co-occurs with a purchase of any other item B by the same user. (Here, the term *co-occurs* doesn't imply that the purchases were made at the same time, but that they were made by the same user.) You perform this calculation for every pair of items encountered in the purchase history. After collecting all the co-occurrence counts, you have a measure of the *affinity* between any two items A and B.

As a specific example based on the information in table 11.2, consider the relationship between the Canon 24 mm lens and other items in the index. You can see that only one individual, David, has purchased both the Canon lens and the Ravelli tripod; therefore, these items receive a co-occurrence count of 1. But two individuals, David and Frank, purchased both the Canon lens and the Nikon camera. The co-occurrence count for this pair of items is 2. And finally, no user has purchased both the Canon lens and the Tunisia Sadie dress. Therefore, this co-occurrence count is 0. After performing this calculation for every pair of items in the index, you arrive at the matrix of results displayed in table 11.3.

Table 11.3   Item co-occurrence counts for every item in the purchase history

	Tunisia Sadie dress	Gordon Monk stiletto	Georgette blouse	Nikon digital camera	Canon 24 mm lens	Ravelli aluminum tripod
Tunisia Sadie dress	-	1	1	0	0	0
Gordon Monk stiletto	1	-	1	0	0	0
Georgette blouse	1	1	-	1	0	1
Nikon digital camera	0	0	1	-	2	2
Canon 24 mm lens	0	0	0	2	-	1
Ravelli aluminum tripod	0	0	1	2	1	-

These values indicate the strength of associations between every pair of items. Notice that in this example, as expected, fashion items co-occur more highly with other fashion items. Similarly, photography items co-occur more highly with other photography items. In some instances, fashion items and photography items co-occur. This also is to be expected, because a few users are interested in both fashion and photography at the same time.

Item-to-item affinities can be directly used for item-based recommendations. The data shown in table 11.3 can be saved to a key-value store. Then, when a user visits the details page for the Ravelli aluminum tripod, you look up this item in the key-value store, pull back an ordered set of the corresponding high-affinity items (the Nikon digital camera and the Canon 24 mm lens) and present these items to the user as recommendations. As shown in figure 11.4, this is what Amazon does when it shows you its version of related item recommendations.

Customers Who Bought This Item Also Bought

| Hamilton Beach 58149 Blender and Chopper ★★★★☆ 2,741 $26.49 ✓*Prime* | Crock-Pot SCCPVL600S Cook' N Carry 6-Quart Oval Manual Portable Slow Cooker, Stainless Steel ★★★★½ 1,409 $24.00 ✓*Prime* | Kitchen MissionTM Stainless Steel Mixing Bowls 1.5,3,4, and 5 quart. Plus Measuring Cup and... ★★★★½ 146 $21.99 ✓*Prime* | Cuisinart CTG-00-CCR7 Curve Crock with Tools, Set of 7 ★★★★½ 136 $25.49 ✓*Prime* |

Figure 11.4 Item-to-item affinities can be used to make "related item" recommendations. When the user lands on the page for a Frigidaire microwave, you can display items with high affinity to the microwave in a panel similar to these recommendations from Amazon.

Taking the analysis one step further, you can find the affinity between users and the products in your catalog. To do this, refer to the user-item purchases in table 11.2 and, for every purchase made by that user, collect the corresponding item-to-item affinity rows and add them together. For instance, Allison bought the Tunisia Sadie dress and the Georgette blouse. Table 11.4 shows the corresponding rows from the co-occurrence matrix along with the sum of those rows.

Table 11.4 User-to-item affinities can be generated by adding together rows of the item-to-item matrix that correspond to a user's purchases.

	Tunisia Sadie dress	Gordon Monk stiletto	Georgette blouse	Nikon digital camera	Canon 24 mm lens	Ravelli aluminum tripod
Allison purchases Tunisia Sadie dress	-	1	1	0	0	0
Allison purchases Georgette blouse	1	1	-	1	0	1
Summation	1	2	1	1	0	1

After you perform this summation for every user you're interested in, you end up with a matrix like that shown in table 11.5. The values represent each user's affinity to every item in the catalog.

Table 11.5   Complete user-to-item affinity matrix

	Tunisia Sadie dress	Gordon Monk stiletto	Georgette blouse	Nikon digital camera	Canon 24 mm lens	Ravelli aluminum tripod
Allison	1	2	1	1	0	1
Brenda	1	1	2	0	0	0
Christina	2	1	1	1	0	1
David	0	0	2	4	3	3
Elise	1	1	2	3	3	3
Frank	0	0	1	2	2	3

Because you started with item purchases, it isn't usually meaningful to track user affinities toward items that they've already purchased. It also isn't meaningful to keep track of products that users have 0 affinity toward; why would you recommend users something that you don't think they care about? So let's remove these values and have another look at the remaining user-item affinity data, shown in table 11.6.

Table 11.6   User-to-item affinity matrix with purchased items and zero-affinity items removed

	Tunisia Sadie dress	Gordon Monk stiletto	Georgette blouse	Nikon digital camera	Canon 24 mm lens	Ravelli aluminum tripod
Allison	-	2	-	1	-	1
Brenda	-	-	2	-	-	-
Christina	2	-	-	1	-	1
David	-	-	2	-	-	-
Elise	1	1	-	-	3	-
Frank	-	-	1	-	-	3

With the clutter removed, it's easy to see that collaborative filtering works well. Just as in the previous item-to-item case, this information can be used directly for personalized recommendations. *If only there was some way to incorporate this into your search application!* Don't worry; you'll get there soon.

Looking at the data, you can see that fashion shoppers have highest affinity toward fashion items, and that photography shoppers have highest affinity toward photography items. But because one of the users, Elise, has interests in both photography and fashion, crossover recommendations exist between fashion and photography. Because of this, David will probably be confused when he gets a recommendation for the

Georgette blouse. Fortunately, as the input data becomes richer (more items and more purchases per item), crossover recommendations such as this will become less prominent, and the user-item affinities will be dominated by the statistically significant co-occurrences.

Furthermore, in richer data sets, when unusual crossovers like this *do* exist, they're often fortuitous because they point out a latent relationship among the catalog items. For instance, about the only thing that Mentos has in common with Diet Coke is that they're both food (sort of). But toward the end of 2005, when the Mentos + Diet Coke experiment became viral on the internet, it became highly likely that these two items would show a spike in purchasing co-occurrence. This highlights the fact that collaborative filtering can identify connections that wouldn't be obvious by looking only at the textual content of the documents.

As alluded to earlier, finding affinities in this way is a fairly naïve approach. For example, you haven't normalized products that are extremely popular. Consider socks. No matter whether you're interested in fashion, photography, or any other field you can think of, you still regularly purchase socks. Therefore, the co-occurrence count between socks and every item in the index will be very large; everybody will be recommended socks. To resolve this issue, you'd need to divide the co-occurrence values by a notion of popularity for each pair of items.

Co-occurrence-based collaborative filtering isn't the only option for generating item-to-item or user-to-item affinities. If you're considering building your own recommendations, make sure to review the various matrix-based collaborative-filtering methods such as truncated singular-value decomposition, non-negative matrix factorization, and alternating least squares (made famous in the Netflix movie recommendation challenge). These methods are less intuitive than the simple co-occurrence counting method presented here, and they tend to be more challenging to implement. But they often provide better results, because they employ a more holistic understanding of item-user relationships. To dive deeper into recommendation systems, we recommend *Practical Recommender Systems* by Kim Falk (Manning, 2016). And no matter the method you choose, keep in mind that the end result is a model that lets you quickly find the item-to-item or user-to-item affinities. This understanding is important as we explain how collaborative filtering results can be used in the context of search.

11.2.3 *Tying user behavior information back to the search index*

In the previous section, we demonstrated how to build a simple recommendation system. But we're supposed to be talking about personalized search! In this section, we return to search and explain how the output of collaborative filtering can be used to build a more personalized search experience. We also point out some pitfalls to be aware of.

You can pull collaborative filtering information into search in several ways. The three strategies demonstrated here are related in that they take a standard, text-only search and incorporate collaborative filtering as a multiplicative boost. Here's how it works: Consider an example base query in which you take the user's query "Summer Dress" and search across two fields, `title` and `description`, as shown in the following listing.

Listing 11.1   Base query

```
{ "query": {
    "multi_match": {
      "query": "summer dress",
      "fields": ["title^3", "description"]}}}
```

Given this base query, you incorporate collaborative filtering by applying a multiplicative boost using a `function_score` query, as shown next.

Listing 11.2   A multiplicative boost can be used to incorporate collaborative filtering

```
{  "query": {
       "function_score": {
           "query": {
               "multi_match": {
                   "query": "summer dress",
                   "fields": ["title^3", "description"]}},
           "functions": [{
               "filter": { COLLAB_FILTER },
               "weight": 1.1}]}}}
```

In this simple implementation, the documents that get the collaborative filtering boost are determined by the contents of your `COLLAB_FILTER` filter (which we discuss in a moment). Notice that this filter doesn't filter out any documents from the result set. Instead, documents matching this filter are given a multiplicative boost of 1.1, as indicated by the `weight` parameter. The query of listing 11.2 returns the same documents as the query of listing 11.1, but any documents also matching the `COLLAB_FILTER` get a 10% boost over the score of the base query. This subtly affects the ordering of the search results so that users making the query will see results that are more aligned with their previous behavior. *This is the goal of personalized search.*

QUERY-TIME PERSONALIZATION

With the basic structure in place, we can discuss the three strategies for incorporating collaborative filtering, each of which corresponds to a different `COLLAB_FILTER` and indexing strategy. For now, assume that the output of our collaborative filtering process is a set of user-to-item affinities—things like "Elise likes Tunisia Sadie dresses, Gordon Monk stilettos, and Canon 24 mm lenses." But because we're talking to machines here, Elise is `user381634`, the Tunisia Sadie dress is `item4816`, the Gordon Monk stiletto is `item3326`, and the Canon 24 mm lens is `item9432`. Further, assume that you have similar information for all users and all the products in your catalog.

Given this data set, the most straightforward approach for incorporating collaborative filtering is as follows: Start by storing collaborative filtering data in a key-value
store (outside the search engine). Let's say that Elise, user381634, has high-affinity
items: item4816, item3326, and item9432. Now, next time Elise uses the search
engine, the first step is to retrieve her high-affinity items from the data store, and then
referring again to listing 11.2, replace COLLAB_FILTER with a filter to directly boost her
high-affinity items by ID:

```
COLLAB_FILTER = {
  "terms": {
    "id": ["item4816", "item3326", "item9432"]
  }
}
```

Then any item matching Elise's high-affinity items will be driven further toward the
top of the search results.

Although this is the most obvious approach, it might become computationally
expensive at query time. In the preceding example, Elise has only three high-affinity
items. In a more realistic implementation, a user could have hundreds or poten-
tially thousands of high-affinity items. And at some point, having too many terms
ORed together like this makes for slow queries. But you might be surprised with
the extent to which this approach *will* scale. For instance, consider that Lucene
does quite well with geo search. But as we discussed in chapter 4, under the hood
geo search is implemented by ORing together many, possibly hundreds, of terms
that represent a geographic area. Besides, in many personalized search applications, you won't need thousands of high-affinity items anyway; a user's searches will
often tend toward a relatively small domain of interest. A few few hundred high-
affinity items in this domain will likely provide users with a noticeably personalized
search experience.

INDEX-TIME PERSONALIZATION

If your application can't afford the performance hit at query time, the next approach
places the burden on the index size. A benefit of this technique is that there's no need
for an external key-value store, because you'll save collaborative filtering information
directly to the index.

To do this, you add a new field to the documents being indexed named
users_who_might_like. As the name indicates, this field contains a list of all users
who might like a given item. For example, when you index the Gordon Monk stiletto,
you include all the typical information that you need for search: title, description,
price, and so forth. But this time you also include a users_who_might_like field,
which is a list of all users showing a high affinity to this item. Referring to table 11.6,
you can see that both Allison (user121212) and Elise (user989898) have a high
affinity to this item. In this case, the users_who_might_like field will be the list
user121212, user989898.

After all documents are indexed with their corresponding `users_who_might_like` field, the rest is easy. At query time, when Allison (`user121212`) makes a search, you issue her query along with a simple boosting filter:

```
COLLAB_FILTER = {
  "term": {
    "users_who_might_like": "user121212"
  }
}
```

Again, this returns the same results as the base query, but any document that includes Allison as a "user who might like" gets a 10% boost—pushing it toward the top of the search results. You can see that this query is much easier on the search engine at query time, because there's only one extra term. But with this method, you must be watchful of the index size. As a frame of reference, in a modest Lucene index of 500,000 one-page English text documents, you might expect something like 1 million unique terms in the index. With this approach, each unique user ID represents another term in the index. So you should expect this approach to scale well for hundreds of thousands of users. But if you have millions of users, your index may outgrow its servers. Fortunately, this method scales well horizontally. You can create shards that represent a portion of your customers. If you have millions of users, you probably have the resources for this.

INDEX- AND QUERY-TIME PERSONALIZATION

Our final approach splits the difference between the two preceding approaches. Previously, you used user-to-item affinities, but for this last approach you'll assume that the output of the collaborative filtering is a set of item-to-item affinities like those shown in table 11.3. In this new approach, the search engine calculates user-to-item affinity implicitly at the time of the query.

The setup for this approach is more involved than in the other approaches. You'll again require a key-value store to look up user-related information. But this time rather than storing user-to-item affinities, you store the users' most recent purchases. You also add a new field, `related_items`, to the index. As the name suggests, this field will contain a list of IDs for high-affinity items. At query time when Frank makes a search, you first pull his recent purchases—a Nikon digital camera (`item1234`) and a Canon 24 mm lens (`item9432`)—and then you issue his query along with the following boosting filter:

```
COLLAB_FILTER = {
  "terms": {
    "related_items": ["item1234", "item9432"]
  }
}
```

You query using a list of IDs just as in the first method, but it's a much shorter list. And as in the second method, you're required to index an extra field with a list of IDs, but unless you have millions of items, this will also be much less information than in the previous method.

As mentioned at the opening of this section, the preceding methods are just a few of the many ways that collaborative filtering can be incorporated into search. And you can improve these methods in many ways. For instance, you probably noticed that we didn't mention the affinity values in any of these solutions. Instead we lumped items into two groups: high-affinity items (matching the COLLAB_FILTER filter) and lower-affinity items. You can modify these methods to take the individual affinity values into account, but this requires creativity involving payloads and scripting or possibly even a custom search-engine plugin.

11.3 Basic methods for building concept search

Personalized search is just one of the many possible directions to explore outside the more standard approaches presented in the previous chapters. Another interesting extension of search is *concept search*. Before reading this book, you probably thought of search as the process of finding documents that match user-supplied keywords and filters. Hopefully, you've come to realize that a good search application works to infer the user's intent and provide documents that carry the *information* that the user seeks. Concept search takes this notion to an extreme.

The goal of concept search is to augment a search application so that it in some sense *understands the meaning* of the user's query. And because of this understanding, the documents returned from a concept search may not match *any* of the user's search keywords, but will nevertheless contain meaningful information that the user is looking for. To borrow a phrase coined by Google, the goal of concept search is to allow users to "search for *things*, not strings."

Perhaps an example will help bring home the need for concept search. Consider a search application for medical journals. Using a typical string-based approach, a search for "Heart Attack" would fall short of the ideal. Why? Because medical literature uses various words for *heart attack*, such as *myocardial infarction, cardiac arrest, coronary thrombosis*, and many more. Plenty of articles about heart attacks won't mention *heart attack* at all. Concept search provides the user with an augmented search experience by bringing back documents that talk about heart attack even if they happen to not contain that specific phrase.

Still—and we can't emphasize this enough—a search engine at its core is a sophisticated token-matching and document-scoring system. The crux of concept search isn't magic; it involves augmenting queries and documents to take advantage of new relevance signals that increase search recall. By carefully balancing these new *concept* signals, you can ensure that search results retain a high level of precision. In this section, we cover several human-driven methods for augmenting your search application to take on a more *conceptual* nature.

11.3.1 *Building concept signals*

Initially, you may reach toward human-powered document tagging to implement concept search. You can create a field that will serve as a dumping ground for terms and phrases that answer the question "What is this document about?" This field will be the home of your new concept signal.

With this approach, when users of the medical journal application search for "Heart Attack" but miss an important article, you add the phrase heart attack to your concept field. Thereafter the document will be a match. This approach also helps fine-tune a document's score. For instance, let's say you have an important article about heart attacks. It may even contain the phrase *heart attack*. Unfortunately, it shows up on the second page of search results. Rather than attempt to solve the problem globally, add the phrase heart attack to the concept field (maybe even add it multiple times). This nudges the score for that document just a little bit higher whenever the user searches for "Heart Attack."

But be forewarned that human curation can be challenging and resource consuming. Accurate tagging requires extensive domain expertise and rigorous consistency. For example, should the heart attack query also be tagged with heart? In the domain of your users, does acute heart attack differ from heart attack? Should a document receive both tags? Only trained, domain-aware content curators can make these fine-grained distinctions. Tagging also takes a lot of human effort. It may require deep reading of the content, which may not scale to cover realistic data sets.

One way to reduce the curation workload is by looking to your users as a possible way to crowd-source the concept signal. Do you recall the conversation about thrashing behavior in chapter 9? When thrashing, an unsatisfied search user quickly moves from one search to another, indicating that the search results don't match their intent. Imagine that a user searches for "Myocardial Infarction," spends about 20 seconds on the results page, and then makes a new search for "Cardiac Arrest." It's obvious that this user isn't finding what they are looking for.

But often these users do finally find a relevant search result. Once there, it's as if the user tells you, "Hey, remember all that other stuff I was searching for? *This* is what I meant!" Imagine that in our example, the user still doesn't find anything interesting in the *cardiac arrest* results and submits a third query—this time for "Heart Attack." Upon seeing the results, the user clicks the second document in the result set and then doesn't return to search. This user implicitly tells us that the phrases *heart attack, cardiac arrest*, and *myocardial infarction* are somehow related. Therefore, why not take the thrashing search terms and add them to the concept field for the document that finally satisfies the user's information need? This way, the next time someone follows the same path as our thrashing user, they will more likely find what they need in their first set of search results.

Again, the main goal of the new concept field is to increase search recall. But you should be careful to not ignore the impact made upon precision. In the preceding example, if the user initially searches for "Cardiac Arrest" but then changes to "Gall

Bladder," your concept signal may become noisy. Make sure to properly balance the concept signal with the existing signals. If the concept field is human curated, it's more likely to be high quality than a user-generated field and should be more strongly represented in the relevance score.

11.3.2 *Augmenting content with synonyms*

Synonym analysis is another useful way to inject deeper conceptual understanding into search. The first time you open the synonym file and add an entry such as the following, you're building out concept search:

```
TV, T.V., television
```

When the user asks the search application for a "TV," the search application answers back, "I have documents with TV—but I bet you're also interested in these other documents that have words like T.V. and television, right?"

Initially, synonym augmentation of the documents takes place somewhat manually. Content curators may hand-generate an extensive synonym list customized to the jargon of a field. In larger domains—medicine is again a good example—it may be possible to repurpose a publically available taxonomy such as the Medical Subject Headings (MeSH) for use during synonym analysis.

One thing to think about when using synonyms is whether to encode hierarchical structuring with the synonyms. For instance, in the preceding simple case with *television*, all the synonym entries are semantically on the same level; they truly are synonyms. But, as discussed in chapter 4, it's common to use synonyms to encode a notion of specificity into the indexed terms. For instance, consider the following synonym entries:

```
marigold => yellow, bright_color
canary => yellow, bright_color
yellow => bright_color
```

This encodes a hierarchy for yellow things (and you can imagine what a much larger synonym set for all colors would look like). When used correctly, synonyms like this will serve to expand a user's narrow query, for instance "Canary," to a broader notion: yellow. This improves recall, allowing the user to find items that use more-general terminology.

As always, recall and precision must be balanced. Fortunately, the natural TF × IDF scoring works in this case. Namely, after synonym analysis has been applied, specific terms such as marigold will occur much less often in the index than terms like yellow and bright_color. Therefore, when a user searches for a specific term such as "Marigold," both marigold and yellow documents will be returned, but marigold documents will be scored above the more general yellow documents.

As a final note, synonym augmentation and concept fields are complementary approaches. Synonym analysis usually dumps the synonyms back in the same field as the source text that was analyzed. But if you're concerned that your synonyms are noisy, it might be a good idea to stick them into a separate field so that they can be given a lower weight. Another good combination of concept fields and synonym augmentation occurs in document tagging. In this scenario, you can greatly reduce the burden placed on the people doing the tagging by having them apply only the most specific tags. Then hierarchically structured synonyms can be used to automatically augment the documents with less specific tags.

11.4   *Building concept search using machine learning*

In the earlier sections, we introduced personalized search using simple methods and then moved on to more sophisticated, machine-learning approaches. Here we follow this same route, moving from human-powered concept management to a machine-learning approach that we call *content augmentation*.

Just as before, the goal is to include a new content signal into the documents to improve search recall. In particular, you'll use machine learning to automatically generate *pseudo-content* to be added back into the indexed document. This content won't be new paragraphs of human-readable text. Rather, the pseudo-content will be a dump of terms that aren't in the original document but that, in some statistically justifiable sense, should be present because they pertain to the concepts in that document.

To generate the new pseudo-content, you algorithmically model the statistical relationship between words based on the documents that contain them. For instance, consider a medical journal article that contains the word cardiac. There's a high probability that the same article will also contain words like heart, arrest, surgery, and circulatory; these words are related to the *cardiac* topic. But it's unlikely that the same article will contain the words clown, banana, pajamas, and Spock; these words have little in common with the *cardiac* topic. By looking at the co-occurrence of words, you can begin to understand how they're interrelated. And once you have a good model of these relationships, you can take any given document and generate a set of words that in some sense should be in that document.

Let's look at an extremely simplified example. Consider the small set of documents displayed in listing 11.3. Each document is a sentence ostensibly about dogs or cats. If you put these documents through analysis, you can split out the tokens, normalize them (by lowercasing and stemming), and filter out the common stop words. The end result can be represented in matrix form, as shown in table 11.7. Here a dot (•) indicates that the term (represented in that column) has occurred one or more times in the document (represented in that row).

Listing 11.3   Simple documents illustrating term co-occurrence

```
doc1: The dog is happy.
doc2: A friendly dog is a happy dog.
doc3: He is a dog.
doc4: Cats are sly.
doc5: Fluffy cats are friendly.
doc6: The sly cat is sly.
```

Table 11.7 Matrix representation of the words and the documents that contain them. (Stop words have been removed and plural words have been stemmed. Additionally, the columns are arranged to draw attention to statistically clustered words.)

	dog	happy	friendly	cat	fluffy	sly
doc1	•	•				
doc2	•	•	•			
doc3	•					
doc4				•		•
doc5			•	•	•	
doc6				•		•

You may notice that this term-document matrix resembles table 11.2's user-items matrix. This is no coincidence. The problem of identifying related items based on user interactions is nearly identical to the problem of identifying related terms based on document co-occurrence. Whereas the earlier personalization example revealed natural clustering among fashion items and photography items, table 11.7 reveals a clustering among dog terms and another clustering among cat terms. In principle, you could even use the same co-occurrence counting method to identify closely related terms. But in practice, more-sophisticated methods are used such as latent semantic analysis, latent Dirichlet allocation, or the recently popular Word2vec algorithm. Though these methods are well beyond the scope of this book, the models generated from these algorithms allow you to "recommend" pseudo-content for documents in much the same way that section 11.2.2 showed how to recommend products based on user-to-item and item-to-item affinity.

After automatically generated pseudo-content is indexed with each document, queries can match documents that didn't originally contain the user's search terms. Nevertheless, these documents *will* be strongly associated with the keywords based on statistical term co-occurrence. In the preceding example, a search for "Cat" may return a document that talks about a sly fluffy animal even if that document doesn't contain the word *cat*.

11.4.1 The importance of phrases in concept search

We haven't discussed an important component of concept search: phrases. Often phrases carry meaning that's more specific than the terms that compose the phrase. Case in point: *software developer*. A software developer isn't software, but a person who develops software. Additionally, there are many types of developers, and a *land developer*, for example, has nothing to do with software development.

Therefore, prior to *content augmentation*, it's useful to first identify statistically significant phrases within the text. These phrases can be added to the columns of the term-document matrix so that during content augmentation these conceptually precise phrases will be included in the newly generated content.

Collocation extraction is a common technique for identifying statistically significant phrases. The text of the documents is split into n-grams (commonly bigrams). Then statistical analysis is used to determine which n-grams occur frequently enough to be considered statistically significant. As is often the case, this analysis is a glorified counting algorithm. For instance, if your document set contains 1,000 occurrences of the term `developer`, and if 25% of the time the term `developer` is preceded by the term `software`, the bigram `software developer` should probably be marked as a significant phrase.

11.5 *The personalized search—concept search connection*

As we earlier indicated, a strong relationship exists between personalization and concept search. Both rely on crafting new signals to improve precision and recall. Both use similar machine-learning approaches. But the relationship goes even deeper because these methods can be used *together* to improve relevance even further.

Consider the *cold-start* problem. Let's say that you're trying to build personalized search based on collaborative filtering. What happens when a new item is introduced to your catalog? Recall that collaborative filtering methods depend on user interactions. Because no one has ever interacted with the new item, *no personalization* happens. You can't recommend a new item based on behavioral patterns that don't exist; this is known as the *cold-start problem.*

This begs an important question, though. You do at least have *some* information for the item: its textual content. Can this be used to generate personalized recommendations? Yes! To do this, you incorporate aspects of concept search into your personalization strategy. With concept search, you augment documents with a broader, conceptual understanding of the text. When pulling concept search into personalization, you must instead augment your user profiles to track the *concepts* that they're interested in. And in this case, just as in the preceding section, *concepts* are the important words and phrases that a user has shown high affinity toward.

There are plenty of ways to determine content that holds high affinity to your users. One way is to turn back to machine learning and somehow infer user-to-term affinities based on the user's interactions with documents and the text of those documents. But there's no need to get overly sophisticated; users are constantly feeding us high-affinity terminology in the searches that they make. And if you're fortunate enough to have highly engaged users, you may even be able to directly ask what types of content they're interested in.

Now, reversing the perspective, consider how the behavioral information used with collaborative filtering can also be used to augment concept search. In section 11.2, you saw how collaborative filtering could establish a relationship among camera equipment and a different relationship among fashion items. These relationships were established based solely on user behavior; the items' textual content played no role.

Nevertheless, as this example demonstrates, behaviorally related items are often conceptually related as well. Therefore, when the textual content associated with an item is weak, behavioral information can be employed to help users find what they're looking for.

11.6   *Recommendation as a generalization of search*

Throughout this book, we've covered the ins and outs of search. We've pulled open the search engine, explained the inner workings, and built techniques for producing a highly relevant search application. We discussed business concerns, describing how to shape a culture that makes search relevance a central issue. In this chapter, we've pointed to ways to imbue search with an almost spooky ability to understand the user's intent.

But here, at the end of this last chapter, we expose a new challenge to everything we've written to this point:

> Maybe *search* is not the application you should be building. Maybe you
> should be building *recommendations*.

Consider what happens if there's no explicit search in a personalized, concept-based search application. What if the search box is left empty and filters left unchecked? Can the application still be put to use? Yes! Even without immediate input from the user, the application has a significant amount of context that can be used to make rich recommendations. For instance, if the user looks at an item detail page, then the application can use methods discussed in this chapter to recommend related items. If the user interacted with the application in the past, the recommendations can incorporate the user's behavioral and conceptual information so that the recommendations will be personalized. So you see, *recommendation* is something that can still exist without an explicit query from the user. As we'll show in the following paragraphs, it may even be useful to think of search as a subset of recommendation.

Let's dig farther. Think about the analogues to search and recommendation that exist in real life. When viewed in its worst possible light, a basic search application can be like a gum-chewing, disinterested, teenage store clerk. You say, "I need a shirt," and the clerk points to a wall of shirts. There are hundreds of shirts—a mixture of all styles, sizes, and prices imaginable. It's too much to process, so you attempt to filter the search: "Yeah, but do you have anything in size M?" The clerk (still smacking gum) glances up and points to the bottom rack. There are still a lot of shirts to choose from—a mixture of various styles and prices—but you need a new shirt, so you walk over and start looking through the shirts in your size.

Even though we've couched this story in terms of a search for a new shirt, the store clerk is effectively making recommendations to the customer. They're just not particularly good recommendations. The clerk ignores the other personalization and conceptual context clues that could help direct customers to just the item they're looking for.

Continuing with the analogy, let's replace the gum-chewing store clerk with your own personal fashion consultant. This time you walk into the store and say to the fashion consultant, "I need a shirt," and the fashion consultant takes you directly to the shelf with shirts that match your size. The fashion consultant is a well-studied expert, keenly aware of the types of clothing in style and how to pair clothing items to make a good outfit. She's also keenly aware of your personal style. The fashion consultant busies herself looking through the rack, pulling out the shirts that are a good match, and arranging them for you to look through yourself. Then she looks up and asks, "Oh, what price range are we looking in today?"—extra context. Upon hearing your response, she plucks out a couple of the overpriced shirts and hangs them back on the rack. Finally, she helps you look through the remaining items.

Now you're getting somewhere. The attentive and highly educated fashion consultant doesn't leave you wandering aimlessly to search for a shirt by yourself, but works with you to provide recommendations that take into account information about both you and the fashion domain. And you know what? After helping you pick out that shirt, the fashion consultant takes you over to the hat rack beside the register and says, "Check out this hat. This is a perfect match for you and would look great when you're wearing that new shirt." And she's right; it's a cool hat! This is the epitome of recommendation, because, even without making an explicit search, the fashion consultant is ready to provide feedback based on whatever information is at hand.

11.6.1 *Replacing search with recommendation*

As the preceding story illustrates, *recommendation* could be seen as an overarching and unifying concept—which happens to include the notion of search. Here's a formal definition:

> *Recommendation* is the ability to provide users with the best items available based on the best information at hand.

The most interesting part of this definition is the word *information*. Here, information comes in three flavors: information about the users, about the items in the catalog, and about the current context of recommendation:

- *User information*—As users interact with the application, you can identify patterns in their behavior and learn about their interests and tastes. Particularly engaged users might even be willing to directly tell us about their interests.
- *Item information*—To make good recommendations, it's important to be familiar with the items in the catalog. At a minimum, the items need to have useful textual content to match on. Items also need good metadata for boosting and filtering. In more advanced recommendation systems, you should also take advantage of the overall user behavior that gives you new information about how items in the catalog are interrelated.

- *Recommendation context*—To provide users with the best recommendations possible, you must consider their current context. Are they looking at an item details page? Then you should make recommendations for related items in case they aren't sold on this one. Is the user getting ready to check out? Then let's recommend popular, low-cost items. Are you sending out an email newsletter? Then let's show the users some highly personalized recommendations and see if you can bring them back on the site.

You might notice that search is barely mentioned in this discussion. What gives? Is it just … gone? Quite the opposite! Search is still present; it's just another one of the possible contexts for recommendation. And as a matter of fact, search is the most important context, because it represents users telling you exactly what they're looking for *right now.* When a user makes a search, you have access to the richest information possible and should therefore be able to make better-informed recommendations. To pick back up with the fashion consultant example, search is the point where you tell the consultant, "You know what? Today I'm looking for an Hawaiian shirt." And the consultant *recommends* a shirt that not only matches the current search context (it's Hawaiian), but also matches your established personal preferences.

11.7 *Best wishes on your search relevance journey*

We've finally come to the close of this book. Before you leave, consider how far you've come:

- *Chapter 1* helped familiarize you with the problem space and the challenges that you'll likely encounter as you work to improve your own search relevance issues.
- *Chapter 2* laid the foundation for technical discussions in the book by explaining how search technology works—inside and out.
- *Chapter 3* introduced debugging tools useful for isolating a wide range of relevance problems.
- *Chapter 4* described how text is processed in order to extract the features most useful in search.
- *Chapters 5 and 6* discussed how textual features are used to build higher-level relevance signals and the various ways that these signals can be combined.
- *Chapter 7* explained how functions and boosting are used to further tune relevance and to shape search results to achieve business goals.
- *Chapter 8* revealed that relevance is more than just tuning parameters; it's also about helping users understand and refine the information being made available to them.
- *Chapter 9* provided an end-to-end relevance case study that combines the lessons of the previous chapters and outlines a systematic approach to designing relevant search applications.

- *Chapter 10* described how to shift the organizational culture to focus on relevance.
- *Chapter 11*, this chapter, broadened the horizons of search to include personalized search, concept search, and recommendations.

After covering all these topics, we're sure that you'll find—and are probably already finding—that each search application has its own set of relevance challenges. But after reading through this book, you should find yourself much better equipped to meet and overcome these challenges.

11.8 Summary

- Personalized search provides a customized experience for individual users and allows high-affinity items to be boosted toward the top of search results.
- Build basic search personalization by creating user profiles that track preference and demographic information. Make sure that this information is represented in the search index.
- Use collaborative filtering to create personalized search based on the user behavior.
- Concept search provides users not only with documents that match their search terms but also with documents that match the *meaning* of their search.
- Concept search requires adding new content to the index or to the users' queries in order to improve recall. It's important to carefully balance the new concept signals in order to retain precision.
- Use personalized search and concept search together to complement and augment one another.
- Personalized and concept search without an explicit user query is effectively the same thing as a recommendation.
- Consider recommendation as a generalization of search.

appendix A
Indexing directly from TMDB

Starting in chapter 3, we used examples from TMDB, The Movie Database. We prepackaged a tmdb.json file for ease of use with the examples. But we're strong believers in showing your work. In this appendix, we show you how to use the examples with an up-to-date version of TMDB's data.

We warn you that we have no control over TMDB, so TMDB may make changes to its API or policies that over time make this appendix obsolete. That being said, we also want to add that we're grateful to TMDB for permission to use its data for this book. We encourage you to visit TMDB (http://themoviedb.org) and make a donation for all their hard work!

This appendix walks you through the following steps:

1 Obtaining an API key from TMDB
2 Setting up Python code to talk to TMDB
3 Pulling back a list of movies, by crawling TMDB's top-rated movies
4 Pulling back extended data on each movie

You're going to set up a process that crawls TMDB for movie IDs and then visits several API endpoints such as /movie/<id> and /movie/<id>/cast to extract extended details for each movie. The code for this can be found in the appendix A IPython notebook examples in the GitHub repo (http://github.com/o19s/relevant-search).

A.1   Setting the TMDB key and loading the IPython notebook

The first steps are to obtain an API key from TMDB. This key gives you authorization to use the API. You pass the key to TMDB to identify yourself when accessing the API. Follow the instructions at this website to get an API key: www.themoviedb.org/documentation/api.

Armed with your API key, open up whatever command prompt you plan to use for these Python examples. Before accessing TMDB using the Python examples in this appendix, you'll need to set the environment variable TMDB_API_KEY.

In a Mac/Linux system, set this with the following:

```
export TMDB_API_KEY=<API KEY from above>
```

In Windows, type this at the command prompt:

```
set TMDB_API_KEY=<API KEY from above>
```

A.2 *Setting up for the TMDB API*

Next, you'll perform the setup you need to interact with TMDB. You'll install a library, import a few system libraries into your Python code, and set up Python to talk over HTTP.

The only additional Python library used here is requests. Be sure to install the requests library using Python's package installer, pip. If you don't have Python's package installer, you should still have Python's built-in easy_install utility:

```
easy_install pip
pip install requests
```

With an API key and the right libraries, you're ready to begin pulling movies down from TMDB. But first, let's make sure you have all the setup code needed to support the functions that interact with the API. This code, shown in the following listing, imports the needed Python modules, fetches the TMDB_API_KEY environment variable, and creates a dedicated HTTP session for communicating with TMDB's API.

Listing A.1 How boilerplate is done

```
import requests          ←  Be sure you installed
import json                 the Python "requests"
import os                   library
import time
                                                    Reads the
tmdb_api_key = os.environ["TMDB_API_KEY"]    ←   TMDB_API_KEY
                                                    environment variable
tmdb_api = requests.Session()          ←  An HTTP session
tmdb_api.params={'api_key': tmdb_api_key}     you'll use to interact
                                              with TMDB
```

The most important part of this code is the last two lines. Here you ask the Python requests library to create a session. The returned session is configured with an api_key argument, using your tmdb_api_key. Now that you have boilerplate code out of the way, let's get cracking on using the TMDB API directly.

A.3   Crawling the TMDB API

Next, you'll get to the fun work of extracting movies from TMDB! As we stated, this requires two components:

- Code to pull back a list of movie IDs
- Code that, for each movie ID, fetches additional details

First, you'll construct the `movieList` function used to pull back a list of movie identifiers. The TMDB API is organized around a series of endpoints that list movies, such as `/movies/popular` (list of movies by popularity) or `/movies/top_rated/` (list of movies that are top-rated). As you access each endpoint, you'll have an outer loop for passing a page URL query parameter. Because each request returns 20 movies at a time, you'll need to continue to request additional pages to have enough movies to search.

To start, you'll pull down movies you'd like to place in the search engine in the `movieList` function. To do this, the function snags the IDs of popular movies by paging through `top_rated`, collecting each ID in a `movieIds` list. Then, after each ID is collected, `movieList` returns a list of TMDB movie IDs.

Listing A.2   Crawling movies from TMDB—`movieList`

```
def movieList(maxMovies=10000):
    url = 'https://api.themoviedb.org/3/movie/top_rated'
    movieIds = [];
    numPages = maxMovies / 20
    for page in range(1, numPages + 1):
        httpResp = tmdb_api.get(url, params={'page': page})
        try:
            if int(httpResp.headers['x-ratelimit-remaining']) < 10:
                time.sleep(3)
        except Exception as e:
            print e
        jsonResponse = json.loads(httpResp.text)
        movies = jsonResponse['results']
        for movie in movies:
            movieIds.append(movie['id'])
    return movieIds
```

Accesses the ❶ top_rated endpoint for this page

Parses ❷ the JSON response

For each page of top_rated movies …

… throttles the access to the API (TMDB API throttling rules subject to change) …

… iterates the page of movies, storing the movie's ID …

… returns the accumulated movie IDs.

In `movieList`, you issue a GET request to the TMDB API ❶. Next, you parse the HTTP text body, loading the JSON body into a Python dictionary ❷. The entry `results` contains the meat of the response, holding each movie for you to work with. You needn't concern yourself much about the structure of the response, as you simply extract the ID of each movie returned, append it to a list, and discard the rest. This process is repeated as you page through additional responses from TMDB.

Now to pull back extended information on each movie. In the book we used the `extract` function to pull movies out of the tmdb.json file. In this version of `extract`, in listing A.3, you pass in the list of movie IDs returned from `movieList`. The function `extract` pulls back even deeper information about movies, by accessing each movie's detailed information individually. This function also accesses additional details needed in chapter 5 and later regarding the cast and crew. Finally, `extract` returns the accumulated details in the form of a dictionary that maps a movie ID to movie details.

We show this code in reverse order for context. First, `extract` pulls back movies one at a time, calling a `getCastAndCrew` function. Farther down, you see `getCastAndCrew` implemented by accessing each movie's `/credits` endpoint.

Listing A.3   Extracting each movie from TMDB—`extract`

... accesses the movie/<id> endpoint for additional details

```
def extract(movieIds=[], numMovies=10000):
    movieDict = {}
    for idx, movieId in enumerate(movieIds):
        try:
            httpResp = tmdb_api.get("https://api.themoviedb.org/3/movie/%s"
                                    % movieId, verify=False)
            if int(httpResp.headers['x-ratelimit-remaining']) < 10:
                time.sleep(6)
            movie = json.loads(httpResp.text)
            getCastAndCrew(movieId, movie)
            movieDict[movieId] = movie
        except ConnectionError as e:
            print e
    return movieDict
```

For each movie ID in the movies ...

... throttles the access to the API (Note: TMDB API throttling rules subject to change)

... parses the JSON response, adds entry to movie dictionary

... enriches movie with additional cast & crew information

... returns a movie dictionary.

In the next listing, we show you how cast and crew information is accessed. This function accesses TMDB's `/movie/<movieId>/credits` endpoint and adds information about directors and cast details to the movie record.

Listing A.4   Get cast and crew

```
def getCastAndCrew(movieId, movie):
    httpResp = tmdb_api.get("https://api.themoviedb.org/3/movie/%s/credits"
                            % movieId)
    credits = json.loads(httpResp.text)
    crew = credits['crew']
    directors = []
    for crewMember in crew:
        if crewMember['job'] == 'Director':
            directors.append(crewMember)
    movie['cast'] = credits['cast']
    movie['directors'] = directors
```

Accesses the TMDB credits endpoint

Parses the credits JSON response

For each crew member, pulls out the directory and adds the record to the director list

Saves the cast and directors to the movie

A.4 Indexing TMDB movies to Elasticsearch

With all the pieces in place, you can use the `reindex` function from chapter 3 and index all the movies into Elasticsearch. Recall that `reindex` presumes you have Elasticsearch running at http://localhost:9200, the default install location of Elasticsearch. But you can also visit the book's GitHub repo (http://github.com/o19s/relevant-search-book) for other options for running Elasticsearch.

The following listing restates the `reindex` function for completeness. There's no need to get into too many details here. The big point to remember is that this function deletes and re-creates the index with the provided analyzer and mapping settings.

Listing A.5 `reindex` function

```
def reindex(analysisSettings={}, mappingSettings={}, movieDict={}):
    settings = {
        "settings": {                              ←┐ Default settings
            "number_of_shards": 1,
            "index": {
                "analysis" : analysisSettings,     ←┐
            }}}                                     │ Uses the provided
                                                    │ analysis and
    if mappingSettings:                             │ mapping settings
        settings['mappings'] = mappingSettings     ←┘

    resp = requests.delete("http://localhost:9200/tmdb")    ←┐ Deletes and
    resp = requests.put("http://localhost:9200/tmdb",         │ re-creates the
                        data=json.dumps(settings))            │ tmdb index

    bulkMovies = ""
    for id, movie in movieDict.iteritems():
        addCmd = {"index": {"_index": "tmdb",       ←┐ Bulk-indexes the
                            "_type": "movie",         │ provided movies
                            "_id": movie["id"]}}
        bulkMovies += json.dumps(addCmd) + "\n" + json.dumps(movie) + "\n"
    resp = requests.post("http://localhost:9200/_bulk", data=bulkMovies)
```

With that function in place, you can pass the `MovieDict` into `reindex`, as shown in the following listing.

Listing A.6 Index to Elasticsearch

```
movieIds = movieList()
movieDict = extract(movieIds)
reindex(movieDict=movieDict)
```

Further, should you want to overwrite the tmdb.json file, encode the `movieDict` as JSON and save it to a file, as shown in the next listing.

```
with open('tmdb.json', 'w') as f:
    f.write(json.dumps(movieDict))
    f.close()
```

That's it! `tmdb.json` is a direct reflection of the source data model from TMDB. It holds the contents of the `/movies/<id>` endpoint enriched with content taken directly from `/movies/<id>/credits`.

appendix B
Solr reader's companion

Welcome, Solr reader! The lessons of *Relevant Search* apply to your work as well. As we noted earlier, both Solr and Elasticsearch provide a friendly interface on top of the underlying core Lucene search library. In this appendix, we point out how your search engine's features fit into the discussion by highlighting, chapter by chapter, where you'll find comparable functionality in Solr. We also point out some of the pros and cons of both search engines when it comes to relevance.

To be clear: our goal is to provide scaffolding to your learning efforts. We don't reimplement the examples one for one. This book is too general for one search engine. Instead we want to provide, as much as possible, a *mapping* of Solr *features* into the book's larger relevance discussion. This discussion assumes that you have general knowledge of Solr and how it's configured. If you hit a topic in this appendix that you'd like to learn more about, we invite you to examine Solr's official reference guide (https://cwiki.apache.org/confluence/display/solr/Apache+Solr+Reference+Guide), the *Solr Start* online series (www.solr-start.com), or great books like Trey Grainger's *Solr in Action* (Manning, 2014).

To structure our discussion and help you follow along with the book, we roughly subdivide this appendix by chapter. Luckily, this tends to correspond to functional components of the search engine. We cover chapters 4–8, as these chapters focus on hands-on interaction with the search engine. We omit chapter 3, as we included some footnotes in that chapter to get you started. We also omit chapter 9, because it uses Elasticsearch features introduced in previous chapters. If you'd prefer to avoid the detailed discussion, you can also get a rough mapping from the table included in each section.

So let's get started turning your Solr search engine into a relevant search powerhouse!

B.1   *Chapter 4: taming Solr's terms*

Chapter 4 focuses on analyzers. Let's see how Solr allows you to configure the analyzers found in this chapter. Analyzers translate text like

```
"the doctor's brown fox"
```

into stemmed tokens without stop words:

```
[doctor] [brown] [fox]
```

The big takeaway from chapter 4 is that these tokens model features of your data. Controlling this process is fundamental for managing your relevance. The same lessons hold 100% for Solr; only the implementation nuts-and-bolts differ. In this section, first you'll see how to build a custom analyzer in Solr. Next, you'll see how to map an analyzer to a specific field in an incoming Solr document.

B.1.1   *Summary of Solr analysis and mapping features*

Table B.1 maps general analysis and mapping features to their Solr counterparts.

Table B.1   Solr analysis features

Chapter	Feature	Solr analogue
4	Custom analyzers	Implemented in schema via custom `fieldTypes`
4	Field mappings (mapping each field to an analyzer)	Done by creating a field of a custom `fieldType`

B.1.2   *Building custom analyzers in Solr*

In chapter 4, you saw how Elasticsearch creates analyzers by using JSON. These JSON settings are part of the configuration for a particular index. Typically, when creating an index, you specify the custom analyzers and mappings to be used in Elasticsearch:

```
{
  "settings": {
    "analysis": {
      "analyzer": {
        "standard_clone": {
          "tokenizer": "standard",
          "filter": [
            "standard",
            "lowercase",
            "stop"]}}}}}
```

Luckily for you, Solr reader, the code in this chapter can be easily translated from Elasticsearch to Solr. You need to understand just one key difference: instead of JSON over HTTP, Solr configures analyzers by using XML within Solr's schema.xml configuration file.

Solr allows you to define custom `fieldTypes` that control analysis—for example:

```
<fieldType name="text_standard_clone" class="solr.TextField">
    <analyzer>
        <tokenizer class="solr.StandardTokenizerFactory"/>
        <filter class="solr.StandardFilterFactory"/>
        <filter class="solr.LowerCaseFilterFactory"/>
        <filter class="solr.StopFilterFactory" words="stopwords.txt" />
    </analyzer>
</fieldType>
```

Beginning to look familiar? This analyzer block corresponds to the analyzer configured previously in Elasticsearch. Once you see the correspondence, you can easily implement chapter 4's examples in Solr. In the preceding snippet, a single `<tokenizer .../>` configures this analyzer with a standard tokenizer (`class="solr.Standard-TokenizerFactory"`). This corresponds to the `"tokenizer"`: JSON element for the previous Elasticsearch specification. Similarly the `<filter .../>` lines specify a sequence of token filters to run, just as Elasticsearch's analyzer has a `filter` element followed by a JSON list.

Unlike Elasticsearch, in which you'd configure the `stopwords` filter elsewhere with a stop-words list or file, Solr places the configuration options on the filter itself (notice `words="stopwords.txt"`).

Elasticsearch provides fine-grained control of analysis, allowing you to specify analyzers even at query time. Solr works a bit differently, giving you the capability to customize only at the `fieldType` level. The `fieldType` allows you to define whether the analyzer applies to index or query time. So to analyze differently when querying, you'd use the following structure:

```
<fieldType name="text_standard_clone" class="solr.TextField">
    <analyzer type="query">
        ...<!-- query-time analysis -->
    </analyzer>
    <analyzer type="index">
        ...<!-- index-time analysis -->

    </analyzer>

</fieldType>
```

Great! You have a custom field type with a custom analysis chain. Next you'll see how to associate it with a specific field.

B.1.3   *Using field mappings in Solr*

How does Solr associate a field such as `title` with a custom analyzer? In Elasticsearch, analyzers are assigned to fields via mappings. Field mappings are created using JSON syntax such as this:

```
"mappings": {
    "movie": {
        "properties": {
            "title": {
                "analyzer": "standard_clone"
            }
        }
    }
}
```

Solr differs slightly, not radically. In Solr, you declare a field in your schema, specifying the `fieldType` to be used with the `type` attribute. Here a field `title` is of type `text_standard_clone`:

```
<field name="title" type="text_standard_clone/>
```

The search engine will transform text for documents containing a `title` field by using the `text_standard_clone` index analyzer. A search against the `title` field will use `text_standard_clone`'s query analyzer to break apart the query terms.

As you see, with some differences, chapter 4's examples apply straight to Solr. The hands-on work differs, and you'll find the various knobs and dials that control settings in different places. Nevertheless, now you can get to work modeling text as terms with your tools!

B.2   *Chapters 5 and 6: multifield search in Solr*

Chapter 5 begins your journey into *signals*. Solr implementations need signals too. Signals map query-time relevance scores to factors meaningful to users. Is the query looking for a title? Is it mentioned prominently in text? Fields become a unit for measuring these factors. In chapter 5, you begin controlling precisely how each field is constructed to measure signals. Chapter 6 continues this discussion by introducing the idea of term-centric search, which considers documents more relevant when more query terms match.

B.2.1   Summary of query feature mappings

Table B.2 maps the Elasticsearch query strategies to those of Solr.

Table B.2   Solr query features

Chapter	Query strategy	Solr analogue
5	`best_fields`	edismax with `tie=0.0` close, but not identical
5	`most_fields`	edismax with `tie=1.0`
6	Elasticsearch `query_string`	edismax query parser
6	Custom all fields using `copy_to`	Using `copyField` in your schema to build a large all field
6	`cross_fields`	No analogue or close feature, but can be implemented in a custom query parser using Lucene's `BlendedTermQuery`

B.2.2   Understanding query differences between Solr and Elasticsearch

In this overview of query functionality, you'll notice we've combined chapters 5 and 6. This is because a Solr-centric discussion would be organized quite differently across these two chapters. Why?

- The Solr out-of-the-box experience doesn't start on field-centric search, but Elasticsearch does.
- Solr starts you out with term-centric search, using its edismax query parser. Query parsers are less central to Elasticsearch.
- Solr doesn't have cross-field search, but you could easily add it with a query parser.

What accounts for these differences? Solr is a thick server querying system; it does quite a bit for you. Elasticsearch, more of a thin server, layers on relatively little. Instead, Elasticsearch exposes an API closer to the raw Lucene query API. Figure B.1 illustrates this difference.

What do we mean by a thick versus thin query API? When querying, Solr adds a lot of capabilities in its extensive library of meaty query parsers. A query parser lets you interact with search by using its own custom query syntax. It then translates this into underlying Lucene queries such as Boolean queries, term queries, or dismax. These query parsers abstract many of the Lucene details from you. Elasticsearch's strategy is quite the opposite. Elasticsearch works to give you primitives closer to the underlying Lucene queries for you to construct larger, more complex queries outside the search engine. Elasticsearch's query API does relatively little for you. The exceptions to this don't add a lot of magic, and translate one or two basic settings to Lucene queries (for example, `multi_match`). Only `query_string` stands out as a true query parser as Solr would define it.

Solr vs Elasticsearch
query interface

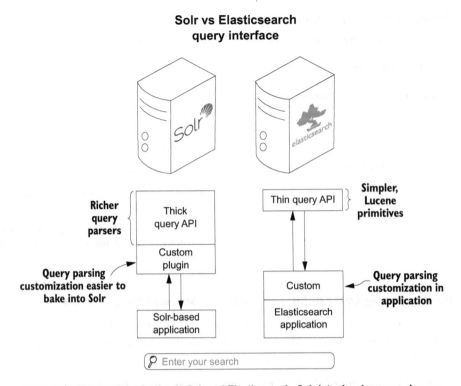

Figure B.1   Query customization in Solr and Elasticsearch. Solr lets developers push more customization into its thicker query API. Elasticsearch exposes simpler primitives to work with.

In many ways, this makes Elasticsearch a better choice for teaching you about Lucene search: its API is closer to the underlying Lucene queries. Solr, while often giving you some powerful query parsers, obscures the nuts and bolts. Solr, however, makes it easy to create *your own* query parsers by using underlying Lucene code. For a Solr developer, this would be one of the first plugins you'd implement. There's also a thriving ecosystem of query parsers implementing functionality such as graph search or complex phrase search. For Elasticsearch developers, however, a custom query parser would be one of the last things you'd try to do. The Elasticsearch developer would be more likely to attempt to implement comparable functionality outside the search engine itself by using the query API.

With that context in place, you can begin to see where Solr fits into our discussions in chapters 5 and 6.

B.2.3   *Querying Solr: the ergonomics*

As a Solr developer, you know that the ergonomics of querying Solr differ quite a bit from Elasticsearch. The most common way to interact with Solr is through URL parameters over HTTP. You saw this in chapter 3, when we pointed out how to search Solr. Solr queries come in this form:

```
http://solr.quepid.com/solr/tmdb/select?q=sea biscuit likes to fish!
```

By controlling parameters passed to the URL, many of which depend on knowing the current query parser, you control how the query string is translated into underlying Lucene queries. You control the query parser with the defType parameter. Here, enabling the edismax query parser also lets you pass in the fields to be searched via the qf parameter:

```
http://solr.quepid.com/solr/tmdb/select?q=sea biscuit likes to
fish!&defType=edismax&qf=title overview
```

Solr also has a fairly unique syntax called *local params*. This syntax lets you scope parameters to a part of the query string (hence the name *local*). The preceding edismax query could be rewritten in local params syntax as follows:

```
http://solr.quepid.com/solr/tmdb/select?q={!defType=edismax qf='title
overview'}sea biscuit likes to fish!
```

With these basic ergonomics out of the way, let's take a look at this edismax query parser—the starting point for most Solr query solutions. How does it fit into the discussion in chapters 5 and 6?

B.2.4 *Term-centric and field-centric search with the edismax query parser*

Solr often advocates that developers start with the edismax query parser, Solr's Swiss Army knife. As a Solr developer, edismax often sits at the root of your relevance work. The edismax query parser does the following:

1. It evaluates whether the query string (q = …) corresponds to a Lucene-style query string or a regular query string.
2. If the query string is a Lucene-style query (q=title:"taco nacho"), that query is evaluated.
3. If the query string is not a Lucene-style query (q=sea biscuit likes to fish), edismax runs a dismax-style term-centric search.
4. Then it layers on various boosts.

Here you'll focus on the precise behavior in step 3 to see how it maps into the discussion of chapters 5 and 6. It's worth noting that edismax comes with additional parameters for additive and multiplicative boosting; we'll get to these in section B.3.

In chapter 6, we discussed that query parsers, such as query_string, must choose a consistent method for tokenizing query text that doesn't involve an analyzer. What edismax does (and what Solr does on all query parsers) is break up the search query on whitespace prior to analysis. So edismax takes the following query

```
q=sea biscuit likes to fish!&defType=edismax&qf=title overview
```

and turns it into a term-by-term dismax query:

```
(title:sea | overview:sea) (title:biscuit | overview:biscuit)
(title:likes | overview:likes) (title:to | overview:to)
(title:fish! | overview:fish!)
```

Recall that | here corresponds to picking the dismax operation—taking the maximum query scores. Pure dismax corresponds to a best_fields, "winner takes all" strategy. The fields that score the highest will always win the competition. One way to adjust this equation is by adjusting boosts. The edismax query parser lets you adjust boosts by using the same syntax you saw with Elasticsearch:

```
qf=title^0.1 overview^10
```

Also recall that we discussed the tie_breaker parameter, which allows you to layer in scores from the other "losing" fields. Luckily, edismax comes with a tie parameter that performs the same functionality:

```
tie=1.0
```

In chapter 5, we discussed how setting tie_breaker to 1.0 results in the searched fields being summed. This moves the search from a best_fields "winner takes all" multifield search strategy to a most_fields "every field gets a vote" strategy in Elasticsearch parlance. You used this strategy to let every field's score have a say in the ranking function. To replicate this multifield most_fields search discussed in chapter 5, you would simply run an edismax query with tie set to 1.0.

B.2.5   All fields and cross_fields search

To round out our discussion from chapters 5 and 6 are two topics: cross_fields search and all fields. Remember, the goal of these two strategies is to resolve *field discordance*. By default, the scoring component IDF isn't counted across fields. We pointed out in chapter 6 that query parsers, like edismax or the query_string query parser, solve part of the term-centric search problem. But they don't solve field discordance. We presented two strategies commonly used to resolve field discordance:

- *All fields*—Combining fields into a single field. This combines the document frequency of the source fields.
- cross_fields *search*—Using Elasticsearch's cross_fields search to account for document frequency across fields at query time, albeit somewhat less accurately.

ALL FIELDS IN SOLR

For all fields, you're in luck. Just as Elasticsearch has `copy_to`, Solr's schema comes with `copyField`. Using what Solr calls *copy fields*, you can implement the same behavior. Copy fields sit alongside field declarations in the schema.xml file:

```
<copyField source="title" dest="text_all" />
```

Here Solr copies the `title` field into the `text_all` field at index time. Unlike Elasticsearch, there's no built-in _all field. But default Solr schemas often define a `text_all` field with several copy directives. This field often acts just like the default _all field.

CROSS_FIELDS SEARCH IN SOLR

For `cross-fields` search, there's no comparable functionality in Solr. But as we discussed, it's easy in Solr for you to implement your own query parsers. The underlying intelligence exists in Lucene, in the Java class `BlendedTermQuery`. This query performs the hard work of the `cross_fields` functionality in Elasticsearch. If you're interested in having this functionality in Solr, we recommend using Solr resources linked previously to implement your own query parser.

B.3 *Chapter 7: shaping Solr's ranking function*

Chapter 7 encourages you to see relevance as something you can tightly control. The good news is, Solr brings a ton of power to the table. Recall that chapter 7 focuses heavily on boosting, both additive and multiplicative. We also discuss two modes of boosting: using a function query or a Boolean query.

Solr, largely through the edismax query parser, supports all of these capabilities. Solr surpasses Elasticsearch in the power of its capabilities, even if ultimately Solr leaves something to be desired in its ease of use.

B.3.1 *Summary of boosting feature mappings*

Table B.3 maps general types of boosting to the equivalent Solr features.

Table B.3 Solr boost features

Chapter	Feature	Solr Analogue
7	Additive boosting, Boolean	edismax with bq parameter
7	Additive boosting, function	edismax with bf parameter
7	Multiplicative boosting, function	edismax with boost parameter

B.3.2   Solr's Boolean boosting

In chapter 7, we used additive boosting via Boolean queries. This syntax uses the `bool` query primitives that map straight to Lucene's Boolean query, as in this query snippet:

```
"query": {
    "bool": {
        "should": [
            {
                "match": {                         ◁── Additive boost
                    "title": "Rambo"                   Boolean clause
                }
                ...
            }
        ]}}
```

Solr's "Boolean" boosting acts similarly. As with Elasticsearch, you can boost using any query you like. The syntax, however, looks quite different. With Solr, you apply a query boost with the `bq` parameter. Recall that Solr has a local params query syntax that lets you specify the query parser used. An additive boost would leverage local params syntax with a `bq` additive boost like so:

```
bq={!defType=lucene}title:Rambo
```

Here, you tell Solr to boost additively by running the query string `title:Rambo` through the Lucene query parser. The result of that query parser is appended to the base edismax query as a Boolean SHOULD clause. For Solr, the addition of query parsers makes this a rich piece of functionality. Solr's richness here allows you to layer all kinds of custom functionality into the boosting process.

B.3.3   Solr's function queries

Just like Elasticsearch, Solr lets you run additive or multiplicative function queries. In Elasticsearch, this takes the form of a list of functions specified in JSON. Consider, for example, this simple boost on a TMDB movie's ratings (`vote_average`):

```
"query": {
    "function_score": {            ◁── Root search
        "query": {                     query
            ...
        },
        "functions": [
            {
                                                   Takes the square root
                "field_value_factor": {      ◁──   of vote_average
                    "field": "vote_average",
                    "modifier": "sqrt"
                }],
        "boost_mode": "sum"            Adds the results of
    }                            ◁──   these functions and
}                                      the root query score
```

In Solr, the syntax looks more like a formula from an Excel spreadsheet. Further, Solr comes with an extremely powerful addition that Elasticsearch sorely lacks: the `query` function. That's right, kids, you can add `query` functions to your function queries— say that three times fast! The `query` function lets you run an arbitrary query and inject its TF × IDF relevance score into the function query itself (as if specified in the list of `functions` in the preceding Elasticsearch snippet).

So what does a Solr function query look like? As we promised, it looks like something straight out of a spreadsheet. The edismax `bf` parameter performs an additive function boost. Here's an additive function query boost by a numeric `popularity` field:

```
bf=sqrt(popularity)
```

Or to multiply the `sqrt` of `popularity` by the TF × IDF score of `rambo` in the title, you might use the `query` function:

```
ramboScore={!defType=lucene}title:Rambo
&bf=product(sqrt(popularity),query($ramboScore))
```

Taken as a full Solr query, with all parameters included, this would be as follows:

```
http://solr.quepid.com/solr/tmdb/select?q=*:*&defType=edismax
       &qf=titleoverview&ramboScore={!defType=lucene}title:Rambo&
       bf=product(sqrt(vote_average),query($ramboScore))
```

Here we've broken up the boosts into two components: a query and a function. For the query, you can see that Solr lets you organize components into variables. You see that with the previous `ramboScore` variable.[1] This query runs a simple search for Rambo in the `title` field. The function, bf, takes the square root of the movie's popularity and multiplies it by the movie title's TF × IDF score for Rambo. This value is then added to the overall relevance score (an additive boost). The end result is popular Rambo movies are boosted to the top.

As you can see, Solr's function queries are far more concise than Elasticsearch's. But you may also see that given sufficient complexity, they become hard to work with! In this realm, Solr can be like Perl; loyalists have learned to do surprisingly amazing things with its power, but detractors see the result of such a function query and cringe at the poor readability.

Elasticsearch lets you go so far as to write custom scripts as a function in `function_score_query`. Scripts in Elasticsearch are implemented in several programming

---

[1]   To learn more about ways of organizing Solr boosts, we recommend this article, written by one of the authors: "Parameterizing and Organizing Solr Boosts" on the OpenSource Connections blog, http://opensourceconnections.com/blog/2013/11/22/parameterizing-and-organizing-solr-boosts/. For strategies like those discussed in chapter 7, but heavily targeted at Solr, we recommend "Improve search relevancy by telling Solr exactly what you want" on the OpenSource Connections blog, http://opensourceconnections.com/blog/2013/07/21/improve-search-relevancy-by-telling-solr-exactly-what-you-want/.

languages such as Groovy and JavaScript. A true programming environment has the advantage of being far more readable.

B.3.4 *Multiplicative boosting in Solr*

Elasticsearch multiplicative boosting occurs by changing the sum line in the preceding `function_score_query` to `product`. Similarly, applying multiplicative boosting in Solr requires a simple change to the additive boost.

Solr multiplicative boosting means using the `boost` parameter to multiply the base relevance score by the result of a Solr function query. For instance, to bias results toward popularity, you might implement the following multiplicative boost:

```
boost=sqrt(popularity)
```

B.4 *Chapter 8: relevance feedback*

Chapter 8 discusses the importance of user experience components such as faceting, autocomplete, highlighting, and field collapsing. The chapter implements these by using many relevance features discussed in earlier chapters. But it does discuss some features not introduced in previous chapters. So we'll round out our Solr discussion by mapping the grab bag of features to help you get through the content in chapter 8.

B.4.1 *Summary of relevance feedback feature mappings*

Table B.4 maps Elasticsearch feedback features to Solr equivalents.

Table B.4   Relevance feedback features in Solr

Chapter	Feature	Solr analogue
8	Facets (in Elasticsearch via terms aggregation)	Solr faceting
8	Phrase prefix querying	Solr's `complexphrase` query parser
8	Grouping (in Elasticsearch via top hits aggregation)	Solr's field-collapsing functionality
8	Suggestions and spell-checking	See documentation for Solr's suggestion and spell-checking features
8	Highlighting	See documentation for Solr's highlighter

B.4.2 *Solr autocomplete: match phrase prefix*

One strategy used in Elasticsearch to implement an autocomplete solution depends on the `match_phrase_prefix` query. This query runs a phrase query with a prefix on the last term, such as in this snippet:

```
{ "query": {
    "match_phrase_prefix" : {
      "title": "star tr"}}}
```

Solr delivers comparable functionality in its `complexphrase` query parser. This query parser interprets a string with a trailing * identically to the `match_phrase_prefix`. So the preceding query becomes `title:star tr*`, as shown here:

```
http://solr.quepid.com/solr/tmdb/select?q=title:star
      tr*&defType=complexphrase
```

This Solr query runs a phrase query identical to `match_phrase_prefix`, focusing on the phrase up until the last term. Then the trailing * tells the query parser to perform a prefix search on the last term.

B.4.3 *Faceted browsing in Solr*

Facets are a crucial component of most search and browsing applications! These are the components on the side of the search application that divide search results into filterable categories. Chapter 8 uses Elasticsearch's terms aggregation to implement faceted search and some autocomplete functionality. Consider the following snippet:

```
"aggregations": {
  "completion": {
    "terms": {
      "field": "title"}}}
```

You'll find comparable functionality with Solr's facets. The preceding aggregation can be implemented as a simple facet on the field `title`:

```
facet=true&facet.field=title
```

Similarly, Elasticsearch allows you to include/exclude aggregation results by using the `include` parameter, as in this snippet:

```
"terms": {
  "field": "title",
  "include": "rambo*",
}
```

Solr provides this capability via the `facet.prefix` option:

```
facet=true&facet.field=title&facet.prefix=rambo
```

Taken together, the entire facet query then becomes the following:

```
http://solr.quepid.com/solr/tmdb/select?q=*:*&facet=true&
      facet.field=title&facet.prefix=rambo
```

Now you can go forth and facet!

B.4.4 Field collapsing

Chapter 8 notes that you often want to group search results in a hierarchy. Elastic-search supports this with its `top_hits` aggregation. This groups search results by a common, shared property. For example, consider this query:

```
"aggs": {
    "original_versions": {
        "terms": {
            "field":"original_id",
            "order": {"top_score": "desc"}},
        "aggs": {
            "hits": {
                "top_hits": {"size":1}},
            "top_score": {
                "max": { "script": "_score"}}}}}}
```

Group by original_id

Top hits subaggregation per unique original_id term

This groups results by the `original_id`, and then shows scores bucketed by `original _id`. Solr can do this too! Solr has a field-collapsing feature for the same functionality via its `group` parameters:

```
&group=true&group.field=original_id&group.limit=3
```

Results for such a query come back grouped by `original_id`, with three results per unique ID in this case. You can explore additional grouping parameters in Solr's documentation.

B.4.5 Suggestion and highlighting components

Spell-checking, query suggestions, and highlighting go a long way to support any search application. Chapter 8 demonstrates Elasticsearch's suggestion and highlight-ing features. As these are topics in place to support the relevance discussion, we won't dive into a detailed comparison of the two search engines' spell-checking and high-lighting components.

Instead, we'll just point out that nearly identical functionality exists in Solr. Solr comes prepackaged with a suggestion component *and* a spell-checking component. Solr also comes with an extremely configurable (and pluggable) highlighting compo-nent. For the most part, with out-of-the-box settings, you can turn on these features with `suggest=true` and `hl=true`. For example, this result of this query contains a highlighted response:

```
http://solr.quepid.com/solr/tmdb/select?q=sea biscuit likes to fish!&hl=true
```

The number of features available on these components is extensive. We invite you to explore their capabilities in the official documentation.

index

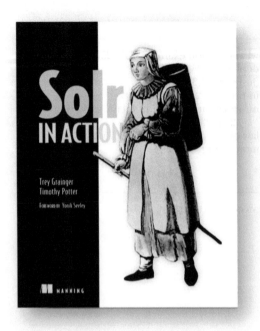
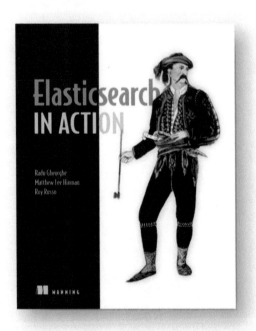

MORE TITLES FROM MANNING

Taming Text
How to Find, Organize, and Manipulate It
by Grant S. Ingersoll, Thomas S. Morton,
   and Andrew L. Farris

 ISBN: 9781933988382
 320 pages
 $44.99
 December 2012

Practical Data Science with R
by Nina Zumel and John Mount

 ISBN: 9781617291562
 416 pages
 $49.99
 March 2014

For ordering information go to www.manning.com

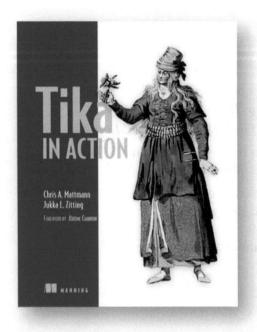